ALSO BY BILL BUFORD

Heat
Among the Thugs

DIRT

DIRT

ADVENTURES IN LYON AS A CHEF IN TRAINING,
FATHER, AND SLEUTH LOOKING FOR THE
SECRET OF FRENCH COOKING

Bill Buford

ALFRED A. KNOPF

NEW YORK

2020

LIBRARY OF CONGRESS CATALOGING-IN-PUBLICATION DATA
Names: Buford, Bill, author.
Title: Dirt : adventures in Lyon as a chef in training, father, and sleuth
looking for the secret of French cooking / Bill Buford.
Description: First edition. | New York : Alfred A. Knopf, 2020. |
Identifiers: LCCN 2019039927 (print) | LCCN 2019039928 (ebook) |
ISBN 9780307271013 (hardcover) | ISBN 9780385353199 (ebook)
Subjects: LCSH: Buford, Bill—Travel—France—Lyon. | Cooks—United
States. | Cooking—France—History. | Food habits—France. | Lyon (France).
Classification: LCC TX649.B84 A3 2020 (print) | LCC TX649.B84 (ebook) |
DDC 641.5092 [B]—dc23
LC record available at https://lccn.loc.gov/2019039927
LC ebook record available at https://lccn.loc.gov/2019039928

Jacket photograph by R.Tsubin / Moment / Getty Images
Jacket design by Abby Weintraub

Manufactured in the United States of America
First Edition

For Jessica,

sans qui rien ne serait possible

Contents

———

No French

Dans la vie, on fait ce qu'on peut. À table, on se force.

In life, we do what we can. At the table, whoa, we eat
everything!

ANONYMOUS LYONNAIS SAYING,
TRANSLATED (LOOSELY) BY THE AUTHOR

On a bright, chilly, autumnal afternoon in 2007, I met Michel Richard, a chef and the man who would radically change my life—*and* the lives of my wife, Jessica Green, and our two-year-old twins—without my quite knowing who he was, and in the confidence that, whoever he might be, he was someone I would never see again.

My wife and I had just celebrated our five-year wedding anniversary, and were at the head of a line in Washington, D.C.'s Union Station, waiting to board a train back to New York. At the last minute, the man I didn't yet know to be Michel Richard appeared off to the side. He was out of breath and sizable, not tall but round, and impossible to miss. He had a modest white beard, a voluminous black shirt, tails untucked, and baggy black trousers. (Baggy *chef* pants, I realize now.) I studied him, wondering: I don't know him, do I?

Of course I knew him! By what algorithm of memory and intelligence could I *not* have recognized him? He had written a book, *Happy in the Kitchen,* that, by a fluke of gift-giving friends, I owned *two* copies of, and, six months before, had won the "double" at the James Beard Foundation Awards in New York City, for Outstanding Wine Service *and* for being the Outstanding Chef of the United States—*and* I had been in the audience. In fact, at that moment, I had French chefs on my mind (for reasons that I was about to spell out to my wife), and here was one of them, regarded by many as the most delightfully inventive cooking mind in the Northern Hemisphere. He was, to be fair, looking neither delightful nor inventive and was smelling unmistakably of red wine, and of sweat, too, and I suspected that the black show-no-stains shirt, if you got close to it, would have yielded up an impressively compressed bacterial history. And so, for these and other reasons, I concluded that, no, this man couldn't be the person I couldn't remember and that, whoever he might be, he was definitively a queue jumper, who, casting about for a point of entry, had fixed on a spot in front of my wife. Any moment the gate would open. I waited, wondering if I should be offended. The longer I waited, the more offended I could feel myself becoming, until, finally, the gate did open and I did a mean thing.

As the man made his dash, I stepped into his path and, *smack,* we collided. We collided so powerfully that I lost my balance and flopped awkwardly across his stomach, which somehow kept me from falling, when, without knowing how, I was in his arms. We stared at each other. We were close enough to kiss. His eyes darted between my nose and my lips. Then he laughed. It was an easy, uninhibited laugh. It was more giggle than laugh. It could have been the sound a boy makes on being tickled. I would learn to recognize that laugh—high-pitched and sometimes beyond controlling—and love it. The line surged. He was gone. I spotted him in the distance, padding down a platform.

We proceeded slowly, my wife and I, and I was, for my part, a little stunned. In the last car, we found facing seats, with a table between. I put our suitcases up on the rack and paused. The window, the light, the October slant of it. I had been here before, on this very same day of the calendar.

Five years ago, having celebrated our just-marriedness with an impromptu two-night honeymoon in Little Washington, a village in the Virginia countryside, we were making our way back to New York and boarded this very train. At the time, I was about to suggest to my wife of forty-eight hours that we celebrate our marriage by quitting our jobs. We were both magazine editors. I was at *The New Yorker.* She was at *Harper's Bazaar.* I'd prepared a speech about moving to Italy, the first step in the direction of the rest of our lives. I wanted to be taught by Italians how to make their food and write about it. Couldn't we go together? It wasn't really a question. Jessica lived for the next chance to pack her bag, and had a mimic's gift for languages which included, conveniently, the one they speak in Italy, which, as it happens, I couldn't speak at all.

We never went back to being editors.

We lived in Tuscany for a year, and, somehow, I went reasonably native and, to my continuing astonishment, when I opened my mouth and uttered a thought, it came out (more or less) in Italian. In the aftermath, I wanted to "do" France. It wasn't next on the list (as in "Then we'll 'do' Japan!"). It was secretly where I had wanted to find myself for most of my adult life: in a French kitchen, somehow holding my own, having been actually "French-trained" (the enduring magic of that phrase). But I could never imagine how that might happen. Our time in Italy showed me that it didn't take much imagining—just get yourself there, and you'll figure it out. Besides, Jessica's gifts for languages included, conveniently, the one they speak in France, which, by another coincidence, I also couldn't speak.

Jessica, no longer in an office job, had also owned up to a lifelong longing involving wine, its history as ancient as food, and she seemed to have a skill, comparable to knowing a foreign language, of being able to translate what she found in her glass. I bought her a gift, a blind tasting session hosted by Jean-Luc Le Dû, a celebrated New York sommelier and wine merchant, which consisted of twelve great wines from his personal cellar, attended by fifteen people, including Jean-Luc's own manager, who had won international awards at blind-tasting competitions. Jessica was the only one who identified all twelve wines. Jean-Luc was baffled, and they were *his* wines. ("Where do you work?" he asked her.) She started a tasting club at home, ten women picked by her, educated New York City professionals who all said that they "love wine but don't know anything about it." She signed up for a course run by the British Wine & Spirit Education Trust, the so-called WSET, with several levels of advancement culminating in a famously challenging "Diploma." By her second class, she discovered that she was pregnant.

It was a wonderful moment. We promised ourselves that our lives would not change.

We will be gypsies, she said. We imagined a worldly infant suspended in a sling contraption.

Four weeks later, she discovered that she was pregnant with twins, boys, the future George and Frederick. This, too, was a wonderful moment, doubly so, but we gave up on the idea of our lives' not changing. In fact, we panicked (a little).

The train pulled out. Baltimore, the first stop, was half an hour away. What we'd planned to discuss, what *Jessica* wanted to discuss, was why, after three years, my French plan hadn't been realized.

It wasn't a mystery, was it? Weren't their names George and Frederick?

It also wasn't so complicated—I needed a kitchen—and I hadn't found one yet. Once in a kitchen, I would pick up the skills.

I had met Dorothy Hamilton at another James Beard event, a charity gala and auction. Hamilton ran what was then called the French Culinary Institute. She was blonde, slim, a youthful sixtyish, indefatigably positive, the corporate executive whom American chefs trusted. When the James Beard Foundation ran into an embarrassing accounting issue (i.e., when its chief executive was systemically skimming the scholarships awarded to young cooks and went to jail), she stepped in to re-establish the institution's integrity. She wasn't paid for it. She implemented the fix in her spare time.

I ran my idea by her: the learning-on-the-job shtick, etc.

"France is not Italy," she said. "You may," she added diplomatically, "want to attend a cooking school." She was so diplomatic that she didn't make the obvious proposal—namely, *her* cooking school, even though it was both the only one in the United States dedicated to *la cuisine française* and walking distance from our home.

I described what I'd done in Italy: i.e., arriving and figuring it out. Then, for intellectual emphasis, I added: "Cooking schools are a modern confection, don't you think? Historically, chefs have always learned on the job."

My approach, I explained to the chief executive of the French Culinary Institute, was to find a venue, make mistakes, be laughed at and debased, and then either surmount or fail. My plan, I elaborated, was to start out in a good French kitchen here in the United States ("But which one?" I mused), and follow that with three months in Paris.

"Three months?" she asked.

"Three months."

She said nothing, as if pretending to reflect on my plan. She asked, "Do you know Daniel Boulud?"

"Yes." Boulud is America's most successful serious French chef. He runs fourteen restaurants, most of them called Daniel, or Boulud, or a variation involving his initials.

"He grew up near Lyon," Hamilton said.

"Yes, I'd heard that." I had been to Lyon once, to get a bus at six in the morning. I had no sense of it except that it seemed far away.

"Some say that it is the 'gastronomical capital of the world.'"

"Yes, I had heard that, too." She could have been talking to my toddlers.

"The training, the discipline, the *rigor*." Hamilton drew the word out, slowly, like a nail. "For two years, Daniel cut carrots."

I nodded. "Carrots," I said, "are very important."

Hamilton sighed. "You say you want to work in France for *three months*." She illustrated the number with her fingers. "And what do you think you will learn?"

I wasn't about to answer.

"I will tell you what you will learn. Nothing."

The auction opened and bidding commenced. The lots included a massive white truffle (that is, a massive *Italian* white truffle), which was only marginally smaller than young Frederick's extraordinarily large head, and which Hamilton secured with a flamboyant oh-let's-put-an-end-to-this-nonsense bid of $10,000, whereupon everyone at our table, plus a few friends met en route to the exit, were invited to her apartment on Sunday for lunch.

"I have been thinking about your plan," Hamilton told me when I showed up, "and I have a gift for you." She gave me a copy of her school's textbook, *The Fundamental Techniques of Classic Cuisine*.

I found a chair in the corner. The book was impressively ponderous, 496 big landscape pages of double columns and how-to pictures. I opened it and landed on "Theory: General Information About Fish Mousseline." I flipped. Ten pages were dedicated to making a sauce from an egg. The philosophy of a fricassee got three. My life had been a happy one, not quite knowing what a fricassee was. What person would I have to become to master half of this?

Hamilton sent one of the guests, Dan Barber, over to me. Barber ran two restaurants, both called Blue Hill, one in Manhattan and the other on a farm. I knew him and liked his cooking. It was ferociously local and uncompromisingly flavor-dedicated. I once ate a carrot at a Barber restaurant: by itself, pulled from the earth thirty minutes before, rinsed gently but not skinned, suspended on a carved wood pedestal, and served with several grains of good salt and a drop of perfect Italian olive oil. Barber is thin, with the nervous chest of a long-distance runner, and is wiry, like his hair, and is bookish and articulate. He asked about "my French project," but before I could answer he interrupted me.

"French training," he declared. "Nothing more important."

The statement was unequivocal. It was also refreshing. At the time, the charisma of France was at a low point. People weren't going there to learn how to cook. They went to extreme outposts of the Iberian peninsula, or isolated valleys in Sweden during the winter.

"Americans think they can do without French training," Barber said, "but they don't know what they are missing. I quickly spot cooks who haven't been to France. Their food is always"—he hesitated, looking for the right word—"well, compromised." He paused so that I would appreciate the implications.

"You should work for Rostang. Michel Rostang," he said. The tone was imperious. It was an instruction.

"Rostang?" I knew the name. Paris, one of the fancy guys—linen tablecloths, art on the walls.

"Learn the classics. Rostang."

I nodded, took out a notebook, and wrote: *Rostang.* "But why Rostang?"

"Because"—Barber leaned in close—"he is the one I trained with."

"You worked in Paris!" This came out as a loud blurt. Barber looked over his shoulder, as if embarrassed. I hadn't meant to blurt. I was just surprised.

"Yes, I worked in Paris. And in Provence. And..." The tone was: Duh? "I am French-trained."

Barber was remarkably tall, which I hadn't noticed until now, maybe because he is so thin and uses less space than a normal tall person. I also hadn't noticed that he was wearing a beret.

"You speak French?" I asked. Blue Hill had been the name of Barber's grandmother's farm and was important to how he presented himself: Grandma's kitchen on Saturdays, the down-to-earth Americana of it all. Barber sits on panels in Washington and knew about the chromosome constitution of Hudson Valley garlic root. The Frenchness was confusing. "Do people know this about you?"

He stepped closer. "You can't get the skills anywhere else."

We reached the Chesapeake, its vast brackish sea, America's largest estuary.

France would be six hours ahead, a Saturday evening, the dinner service about to start. I tried to imagine a bistro in Paris, a bar with stools, a low-ceilinged room with a hearth, a city, a village, and couldn't. I'd lived in England for twenty years. There it had been easy to imagine France. It was a ferry away. You could drive there. A flight was an hour.

Our train was scattering ducks, their colors blue and orange, when I spotted, on the glass of my window, the reflection of a computer screen, a bright movement. It appeared to be a slide show of French food.

Why did I think it was French? Because the plates looked like paintings? Because they had a sauce? They appeared, one after another, a fade, a new image, very Ken Burns.

I turned to get a closer look and spotted a guy, about thirty. I studied him: short hair, military buzz, skinny, tiny shoulders. French? I couldn't tell. He didn't speak. He snarled. He looked European. He looked like a football thug. It was his meanness.

I addressed my wife. "Favor?" I nodded in the direction of the computer.

She twisted in her seat, looked, and sat back down. "God is talking to you."

"God doesn't talk to me."

She had another look, a long one, recomposed herself, folded her hands, and took a breath. "Trust me."

I peered over her shoulder. Another guy was looking at the screen, his back to me. It was the queue jumper.

I asked my wife, "Should I talk to him?"

"You have to."

"I think I know him."

"Talk to him."

"Unless I am wrong."

"Talk to him."

I rose and walked to his table.

"Hello. I am sorry to interrupt." The queue jumper had two carafes of red wine and was reading a French cookbook (*La Cuisine du soleil,* a worn, out-of-date-looking cover). He looked up. Oh. I *do* know this man. This face: It had *seemed* familiar before because it *was* familiar, the James Beard award ceremony, the photo on the book jacket that I had two copies of.

But the name? It started with "M."

Michelin?

Mirepoix?

They stared up at me, this now famous-seeming James Beard guy and his hooligan.

I thought: Wow. This is the man I just assaulted.

I said, "Are you a chef?"

I couldn't bring myself to say: Are you a French chef whose name begins with "M," which I can't remember because I can't remember French names?

I added, "Are you, in fact, a very famous chef . . . by chance?"

The man didn't move. Maybe he didn't speak English.

He took a breath. "Yes," he said, "I am a famous chef. Yes! I am *very* famous." He was grand—a little ridiculous, but grand people often are. "Allow me to introduce myself." He extended his hand as though I should kiss it (Panic! Should I?) and declared, "I am Paul Bocuse."

Paul Bocuse! I'd got it wrong! I'd assaulted Paul Bocuse? Bocuse is *the* most celebrated French chef in the world! Am I meeting Bocuse? Now I was confused. Also, wasn't Bocuse 115 years old? And didn't he live in Lyon?

"No, no, no, no," the man said. "I am only joking."

(Oh, joke, right, funny.)

"I am not Paul Bocuse."

(Whew!)

"Paul Bocuse is dead."

(What?! I *am* being made fun of, *and* Paul Bocuse is dead!)

"Or maybe he's not dead."

(He wasn't.)

"I don't actually know. I am Michel Richard. The chef and *patron* of Citronelle, Washington, D.C.'s finest restaurant. I repeat. Michel"—he paused in order to give the surname the full operatic treatment— *"Reeeeeeeeeeeeeeeee-CHARD!"*

I would spend most of the next eight months in Richard's company, off and on, not too much at first, and then, by the spring, pretty much full time, when I found a place on the line, cooking at the fish station. Our next meeting was a dinner at Citronelle, at the chef's table, in the kitchen and with a view of its workings, and involved Jessica and me, Richard and his wife, Laurence, an American born of French parents whom Richard met when he lived in California. ("She never eats in the restaurant, she doesn't like my food," he said with a curiously upbeat irony, "but she will want to meet Jessica, and they will speak French." And they did.)

The first course was scrambled eggs with salmon, which it obviously wasn't going to be and wasn't (it was raw scallops that had been lique-fied in a blender with cream and saffron, and *cooked* like scrambled eggs, French style, admittedly, which is to say slowly, but they were still what they were: shellfish). The next was a cappuccino. (Ditto.) It was actually mushroom soup, except that it wasn't, not actually, because it had been made without water, or stock, or any other liquid. It also had no mush-rooms. (Mushrooms sweat when heated; the "soup"—which calls for fifty kilos of various fungi—was, in effect, nothing but the sweat. It was brilliant, and unheard of, and very concentrated—I would eventually try it at home and spend hours trying to put monstrous dark gobs of leftover mushroom goo to some kind of second use only to give up—it started to harden into a black crust—and, with a thud, threw it into the trash.)

Richard made a salad inspired by Claude Monet's water lilies.

I thought: really? There are centuries of paintings inspired by food. How many foods inspired by painting?

I wandered into the kitchen to watch its being assembled. Around a white platter, floppy circles of "tube food" were being arranged—they had been sliced thin on a meat slicer—and included (I was told) tuna, swordfish, red and yellow peppers, beef, venison, and eel. The platter was dressed—frondy-looking herbs, a basil-infused, exaggeratedly green olive oil—and transformed into a swampy, mossy masterpiece. It was very Zen-making to look at, even if such a challenge to think about—I promise, the first thought that occurred to me when eating a thin round white disk was not "Oh, it's eel!"—that it made you realize how recognizing your food, which we do all the time, was a precondition to our being able to taste it. (And I'm still trying to figure out what I'm meant to learn from *that*.)

Before bed that night, I found myself recalling, with unexpected fondness, Dorothy Hamilton's *Techniques of Classic Cuisine*.

In January, I began learning Richard's preparations in earnest, beginning suitably enough with one of the tubes that he had used in the Monet salad—the red pepper one, as it happens.

"Tubes are very important in Michel's cooking," David Deshaies said. David was the hooligan on the train. He was the executive chef.

By now, I knew enough to know that "tubes" probably didn't figure among the classic techniques.

We roasted five dozen red peppers, peeled them, and laid them out, still warm, on long sheets of plastic film, which David then bombed with aggressive clouds of Knox gelatin—quickly before the peppers cooled. Arranged thus, they looked like a thick, undulating red carpet, which he then tried to roll up, peppers squeezing out the sides of the film, and looking like three-foot-long, squishy burritos. There was obviously no tidy way. He kept having to push the red-pepper slop back inside until, finally, he succeeded enough to be able to tie up one end with string. After tying up the other end, he picked up his massive tubular confection and whipped it around his head like a lasso—the image, which was actually rather alarming, was of a cowboy twirling a very long pastrami. But it was beautiful when done: very red, very symmetrical, very shiny, like a primary-colored sausage stuffed to a degree less than bursting.

"Okay," he said. "Your turn."

"We" made ten—David made nine, and I made one (it takes a while to lasso with confidence)—whereupon I was told to hang them in the "tube walk-in."

It was a freezer. Tubes hung from ceiling hooks as though in a butcher shop, except that they were pastel green, Easter yellow, white, pink, a few robust reds, and purples. They could have been frozen party balloons. The longest was five feet. The white one, a three-footer, was the eel.

You have never seen anything like them. No one has seen anything like them, because outside of Richard's kitchens you will find them nowhere. There were tubes for blini batter, uncooked bacon, coconut, beet, various fish, and a dough for club sandwiches. There were really a lot of tubes.

Strangely, it never occurred to me that Richard didn't make sense, that I should do something else. He was in Washington, D.C. I was in New York, an inexperienced father of twin toddlers. What do I do? Leave my family? Also I wanted basics. Richard was obviously "anti-basic." He was also anti-obvious and subversive at every chance. His approach (more accurately described as his "anti-approach") was to surprise the diner at every chance. He was an entertainer. His promise: to leave you delighted and pleasured. No, this wasn't what I had in mind, but I couldn't resist him.

He was educated in the classics, and many mornings I would find him at the chef's table reading one, especially Ali Bab's *Gastronomique Pratique,* a work largely unknown in the English-speaking world but a bible for many French chefs in the early twentieth century, published in 1907, 637 pages of detailed, practical explanations of the dishes of the French repertoire. But Richard never made a thing from it. Nothing.

Why do you read it? I asked.

"To be provoked. People think I have such original ideas, but I don't, not really, they start with something I've read."

No, Richard was not the obvious chef to teach a novice French cuisine. But pass this up? Not a chance.

Besides, he knew everyone: He would find a place for me in France.

Citronelle was in the basement of an old hotel, the Latham, a 140-room, not-too-pricey Georgetown property that, despite its condition (it showed an alarming tendency to tilt), had actually seen worse days. (Movie buffs might recognize it as the seedy hideout that shelters young Julia Roberts in *The Pelican Brief.*) Once Mel Davis, Richard's PR person and deputy, negotiated a weekly friends-of-the-family rate for a room, I was resolved: I would come down to Washington, domestic urgencies permitting, on Sunday evening and return on Friday. (Those domestic urgencies weren't always permitting, because any arrangement that resulted in Jessica's being the unprotected parent of twin toddlers would turn out not to be such a happy one.)

RATATOUILLE. It was the next preparation that I learned, and I loved making it. It was served cold, with just-fried, hot-to-the-touch soft-shell crab. It seemed so radically basic—and, well, not.

According to David, my instructor, it is the taste of a French summer, because it is made with ingredients that every French household grows in its garden plot: eggplant, peppers, zucchini, onions, and tomatoes (plus garlic), in roughly equal quantities (except the garlic). Each ingredient is cut up chunky. "We once made a nouvelle-cuisine version, with small and perfect cubes," Richard said, watching us from the chef's table, "but it was too fancy. It's a rustic dish and should always be one."

The most important lesson: that each ingredient should be cooked separately. The onions are sautéed in olive oil. Then the zucchini (lightly); and finally the eggplants, but quickly and in a nonstick pan (no oil, because eggplant is an olive-oil sponge). The peppers are oven-roasted; then the tomatoes, but, according to the particularly French insistence of needing to remove the skin first. ("The French never eat it, because the skin comes out in your poop," Richard told me confidently. "Really?" I asked, skeptical. "Really," he said.)

You remove it by dropping each tomato into a bowl of just-boiled water, transferring it quickly to icy water, and peeling while it is in a state of shock. You then cut the naked tomatoes into quarters, scoop out the liquid and the wet, jellylike seeds, and drop them into a sieve atop a bowl. (This will be for later—for tomato water. By the end of your session, there ought to be a formidably goopy pile drip-dripping into a bright-red pond.) You then arrange the quarters—they look like red flower petals—on a baking sheet, paint with olive oil, sprinkle salt and sugar atop, and cook at a low heat for ninety minutes, until they're plump and swollen. They are the jammiest of the jammy ingredients.

Only then does Richard mix the ingredients together—in a pot, with shots of red-wine vinegar (an unusual addition, a bright, slightly racy acidity to balance the dish's summer sweetness)—and heats them gently for a short time. The practice—each vegetable cooked separately—is said to produce a more animated jumble of flavors than if everything had been plopped in at the same time. I didn't think further on it, except to recognize that it had been a long time since I had prepared a ratatouille and that I liked this one so much that I would make it every summer, without fail, thereafter. ("Vegetable jam" is how David describes ratatouille: "My mother made it on Sundays and served it with roast chicken, and we ate it cold for the rest of the week.") It was only on serving the dish to friends (who were excited by the result) that I learned that most people don't bother cooking the ingredients separately, and many didn't know it was a possibility. Even the most recent and generally pretty impressive edition of *Joy of Cooking* tells you to heap all your vegetables into a pot, give it a stir, cover, and cook, which put me in mind of that last ratatouille I'd made ten years before, inspired by the languidly lazy, self-consciously I-am-literary prose of M.F.K. Fisher, who had learned her preparation, in France, from "a large strong woman" who came from "an island off Spain." This, too, was a dump-and-stir preparation that was then stewed for five to six hours. It tasted of mush. (Julia Child's ratatouille is about half onboard and honors the basic practice—"each element is cooked separately"—but then, curiously, does some of the ingredients together.)

The cook-it-separate approach was my first genuinely French cooking lesson. Vignerons, bottling a wine made of different grape varieties, do something similar and either toss everything in a vat together and ferment the lot (like a "field blend"), or vinify each one separately and blend at the end: a more controlled effort in which you can often taste each grape. And many famous French stews turn out, at least in their traditional recipes, to be minimally stewed. Like a *Navarin d'agneau*, the spring-lamb-and-vegetable dish named after the *navet*, turnip, the traditional accompaniment until the advent and acceptance of the potato (circa 1789): The vegetables are cooked while the meat roasts— turnips (if you're a traditionalist), potatoes (if not), or turnips *and* potatoes (if you're both), baby carrots, small onions, and spring peas—and only then combined at the end.

The practice doesn't seem to have a name, which is a curiosity in a culture that I was about to discover has a name for every tiny ridiculous preparation or tool, or if there is one I haven't found it yet, although I may have come across the first instance of its being described: in Menon's *La Cuisinière bourgeoise* (*The Household Cook*—the *bourgeoise* in the title has its eighteenth-century sense, "of the home"). There are many *"cuisine bourgeoise"* books in France—almost every accomplished chef has written for the layman—but Menon's was the first. (Menon, probably a pseudonym, also wrote the first "nouvelle cuisine." There are many nouvelle cuisines as well.) Menon's *Cuisinière bourgeoise* describes two ways of making duck and turnips: the cheffy approach, with turnips and other ingredients cooked separately while the duck roasts, and the other, more informal one that involves, once again, the plop, the pot, the lid, and leaving until done. *"Voilà la façon de faire le canard aux navets à la Bourgeoise."* (The recipe is not in the book's first edition, published in 1746, but in the second, in 1759.)

Spoiler alert: Astonishingly, albeit painfully, I would indeed learn to read French and even speak it.

I made breadcrumbs the Richard way, which were not uniform or powdery (he shook out the dust in a sieve) but jagged and uneven and rough to look at, and then toasted in the oven until deliciously noisy. With a dab of mousse, they adhered to Richard's "chicken nuggets," and then, when fried at maximum heat, emerged highly textured on the outside (they snapped when you bit into them), soft in the middle, with a hint of chicken cream in between, and very surprising in the mouth. (I tried the nuggets on my children. They liked them. They also liked the frozen ones from the supermarket. They were not discriminating. What they really liked was ketchup.)

I made tuna burgers the Richard way (tuna burgers at a high-end restaurant? Why not? They were scrumptious). You start with a thick red slab of the fish, dice it, and then mash the cubes vigorously with the back of a wooden spoon against the sides of a bowl. As the cubes break down, you're effectively whipping them. You add a splash of olive oil. You continue mashing. By now, you're probably starting to sweat (unless you're me, and you're streaming off the tip of your nose). Midway through, you spoon in a vaguely Japanese-y sauce that you've made in advance (ginger, shallots, and chives emulsified in a blender with soy sauce) and mash some more. The goal is to break down the tissue so effectively, smooshing it, as to render the fish's natural fats. They are the binder, what will hold the shape of the burger. It is then cooked rare, and has zingy freshness, with an unapologetic almost-sushilike gingery rawness, and is served in a bun made with olive oil and wild yeast, something like a Mediterranean version of a brioche.

I enjoyed the burgers so much that I always made an extra one just before we broke down the kitchen and kept it warm on the flattop to eat at the bar upstairs along with my customary glass of Pinot Noir.

I was taught how to make a Richard soufflé that never fails (it uses three different meringues, Italian, Swiss, and French). I prepared savory potato tuiles that have as much snap and texture as a Pringles chip but no fat (they were inserted into Richard's burgers to give them crunch). Both were among the house secrets, kept in a much-guarded recipe bible, and the fact that Richard was prepared to share them with me was proof that, in his eyes, I was utterly harmless. During my tenure, the kitchen wasn't making the "mosaic salmon," regarded by many as Richard's most accomplished dish, a gravity-defying masterpiece covertly held together by transglutaminase (i.e., meat glue) and known to me from how it figured in the story of a former sous-chef, Arnaud Vantourout, a Belgian who confessed to me that, after he left Citronelle for a grand-sounding position at a famous Brussels restaurant that he asked me not to name, he realized that he had been hired only for Richard's recipes. "They made me tell them everything"—the Tube Technology, the soufflé, the tuna burger, Richard's perfectly peeled apples, and the "mosaic salmon." ("They really wanted the mosaic salmon.") Then, after the famous Brussels restaurant that Arnaud asked me not to name had exhausted all the good ideas that he'd learned from Michel, they had no use for him. "They threw me away." (Frankly, I don't understand why the good-hearted Arnaud was so careful to protect an asshole establishment, and even though the late great *New York Times* food critic R. W. Apple, Jr., named it among the top ten dining experiences in the world, I, for one, have vowed never to go there.)

On a Thursday afternoon, just before the dinner service, I learned that none other than Michel Rostang and his *brigade* had arrived from France and would be showing up in the kitchen in the morning. They would be taking over Citronelle for a weekend of elaborate meals, an annual event, something like a "Paris in D.C." festival. There was no reason why I should have known about it in advance—I was still finding my way. But the news astonished me: Michel Rostang—*the* Michel Rostang, the very person that Dan Barber had worked for and urged me to train with as well—would be here, with his executive chef, his sous-chef, his line cooks, everyone. It was my chance. I was excited. I was frightened.

I needed to call Jessica.

In one respect, the timing was positively apposite. I had only recently taken on board that our children needed to attend some kind of preschool in the fall. To be honest, until then, I hadn't considered, in any kind of specific way, that they needed to be educated. Obviously, I knew that they had to be, eventually, but I hadn't thought through the logistics. It was the first week of March. I had only just begun trailing at the fish station (following a cook who knows the station so that you can learn the routine). Also I was only now starting to realize how little time I had to find a restaurant in France. Between March and September, I was committed to acquiring whatever basics there were to learn in Richard's kitchen (if any), *and* doing a stint somewhere, venue unknown, in Paris: six months. And then, like that, here was Rostang: my opportunity, my passage, my future, my venue.

In another respect, however, the timing was not so positive. In the arrangement that Jessica and I had established, I needed to be home by Friday evening to take over the care of the children: no matter what. By Friday evening, she would be at one of those I-can't-do-this-a-second-longer moments. Do I phone and say, well, actually, would you mind doing a few more days—say the weekend and, well, the rest of next week—on your own?

Richard was at the chef's table, working on a recipe. I hesitated to interrupt him. Besides, I hadn't explicitly asked him, not yet, if I could count on his help to find me a kitchen in Paris. He then disappeared before I had a chance to speak to him and didn't return in the evening. (Probably having dinner with his dear friend Michel—the two Michels at a table somewhere.)

On Friday morning, David got a text. "They're coming!"

Besides, how was I even remotely qualified? I knew how to lasso red-pepper sausages. I could make breadcrumbs and a tuna sandwich. I couldn't speak French.

"They're here!"

I heard them before they appeared: Had they been chanting? They burst through the door in a sprint—I had to jump out of the way—and went straight to their positions. They looked like an occupying army. It was the first time I witnessed what I would learn to describe as "kitchen focus." Each team member looked straight ahead—no small chat, a perfunctory firm-handshake hello—and then they set up their stations. It was exhilarating to witness. It was intimidating. They were so different from the Americans at Citronelle. We seemed pampered, unserious, soft. They seemed like street brawlers. They were—there is no other word—terrifying.

Rostang has two Michelin stars. I had never seen a Michelin kitchen *brigade* before.

They spoke no English, or if they did, they kept it to themselves. It didn't matter because they weren't about to speak to an American anyway. During a break, they fell in with Citronelle's French staff members, the "executives"—David, Mark Courseille (the pastry chef), Cedric Maupillier (a former sous-chef who was now at Richard's Central, his "American" bistro), plus a chef from the French embassy, a former Richard employee.

The Americans retreated, got on with their tasks, rarely looked up, and conveyed, unmistakably, that they were weak, frail, and catastrophically inadequate.

I reflected: What did I have over the American cooks, all of them trained and experienced, who now looked out-skilled and intimidated? I couldn't imagine being a member of the Michelin team. Two stars? Not a chance.

Where was Richard? Were the two Michels now having lunch as well? By the afternoon, I had a train to catch. Jessica and I had our agreement. And I wasn't too unhappy about it. But I did wonder: Had I just missed my chance to work in Paris?

Three weeks later, there was another opportunity. I was on the line one night, at fish, finally learning the station, when David called out from the pass: "Michel wants you upstairs. There are people he wants you to meet."

I didn't move.

"Michel is my boss. You must leave the line."

Richard didn't give a flying fig if I cooked or not—I wanted to be cooking, so he indulged me—and since I was basically there at his pleasure, he was fully entitled to summon me at will to be at his side. This was, in itself, a great pleasure, except that the interruptions were often longer than the time I was spending on the line, and I still believed that I would learn to be a French cook there. (Spoiler alert number two: I wouldn't, although I would learn how to be a cook in Richard's kitchen, which was not nothing.)

The friends were Antoine Westermann, an acclaimed Alsatian chef, and his wife, Patricia. They were outside on a warm evening—wooden tables and benches, like a pop-up sidewalk café. I joined them. A platter of oysters was produced, a bottle of Chablis. Richard was telling stories of his childhood, his "mom" and her terrible cooking. More food appeared, charcuterie on a tree-bark platter; my glass refilled, another bottle put on ice. I relaxed. Why not? It wasn't such a hardship not to be in the kitchen.

(Meanwhile, I did, I admit, think about my wife, decisively even if briefly, and wondered what version of hell, at this particular moment, she was going through with the twins.)

Westermann's first restaurant, when he was twenty-three, had been a converted barn, in the heart of Strasbourg, that combined high technique with his grandmother's recipes, and, over a twenty-five-year period, earned him three Michelin stars. Then he gave them up for love ("for the beautiful Patricia," Richard clarified), left his former wife, and signed over his restaurant to his thirty-two-year-old son; Westermann and Patricia moved to Paris, where he bought Drouant, founded in 1880, one of the city's venerable establishments.

Westermann came to Washington regularly—he had a consulting arrangement with the Sofitel Hotel—and always saw Richard. For many French chefs (like Westermann or Alain Ducasse or Joël Robuchon—i.e., some of the greatest talents of their generation), coming upon Richard in the United States was akin to discovering an unrecognized national treasure—how could someone so accomplished be so unknown in France? They instantly "got" him, came to adore him, and were then lifelong members of the Michel Richard fan club.

Westermann was demonstrative in his affection for Richard. The two chefs were about the same age. Westermann was tall and fit—he did mountain cycling—with perfect posture and round bookish glasses and a manner of vigilant rectitude. In a chef's coat, and he seemed always to be in a chef's coat, he had the manner of a scientist, a stiff, slightly formal manner that disappeared when he smiled, and in Richard's company he smiled easily. Until that evening, the only people I'd met with Richard were employed by him.

"You know, Michel, you really need to exercise."

"Yes, I will, Antoine, I promise."

"It doesn't take much—a little, but every day." He was concerned about Richard's health, and there was tenderness in the concern.

Richard had once been a broad-shouldered man. In photos from his Los Angeles days, he conveys power. But now those hefty broad shoulders had lost their heft, and the mass of what remained seemed to have slid down to his middle. He was still a beautiful man—it was in the joy he exuded whenever you were lucky enough to be in his company—but his body was in distress. Three years earlier, he'd had a stroke. "It was here at the restaurant," he told me. "I wasn't making sense. I was saying random words."

"It's your weight, Michel. You just need to lose it." Westermann wanted to help.

"Yes, Antoine, *ma petite* Laurence tells me the same. I will start tomorrow."

Richard loved his pleasures immoderately and was only able to moderate them by avoiding them. His Sunday lunches in Los Angeles were raucously drunken and taught him not to keep wine in the house. Food was more difficult. You can't live without food. ("Once, Laurence gave me cottage cheese. Have you ever eaten it? I tried it for lunch. I wanted to make Laurence happy. But I couldn't. It's terrible.")

"Look at those cheeses," he said one night when we were sitting at the chef's table. "So creamy and fat and luxurious." The cheeses were for the dinner service. "Laurence told me, No more cheese, please Michel, promise me, no more. I promised. *Mais regarde!*" He drank a glass of water. He had another glass. Then he succumbed, a large plate prepared for him, no bread, just cheese, and his eyes rolled up into his head in a long protracted *"mmmmmmmmm"* of ecstasy. "It is butter's greatest expression."

At the end of my evening, I returned to the kitchen to help clean up. I asked David: "What about Westermann? He has a good heart, and knowledge and famous skills."

David frowned. "An Alsatian in Paris? It is a kitchen unconnected to a place. Paris could be anywhere. Paris could be New York. I'll speak to Michel. We will find you something."

Michel Richard was born in Pabu, a farming village in Brittany, the forlorn, far-northwesterly part of France, half an hour from the sea. His parents—André, a member of the Resistance, and Muguette, a young live-in chambermaid at a castle—had met fleetingly toward the end of World War II, as the Nazi army was in retreat. Months later, the war just over, the country a muddy crisscrossing of carts and two-cylinder vehicles, Muguette, now very pregnant, struck out for the village where she remembered that the parents of her Resistance lover came from. She got as far as Rennes, the capital of Brittany, where Richard's older brother, Alain, was born in May 1945. She resumed her trek, and in Pabu, knocking on doors, found the infant's father. Richard was born three years later.

The young family lived with André's parents. Richard's memories are in images, mainly indoors, mainly wintry, a flickering fireplace darkness. Electricity was conserved like water drawn from the well—no lights after 8:00 p.m. The grandparents didn't speak French. They spoke Breton, burned peat, had a dirt floor, and didn't use plates but spooned dinner into rounded indentations, like bowls, carved into a thick wood table. Richard's father was the village baker. Richard, who would eventually teach me how to create those perfectly spherical bread rolls for the tuna burgers (you knead them with your thumb as you roll them), remembered how his father made them fast, two at a time, against an unwashed apron that he crushed the boy's face into in sloppy predawn hugs. He smelled of unfiltered cigarettes and wine—the father was an alcoholic—and was bristly and sweaty in the light of a wood-burning oven.

There were jobs in the Ardennes—in the east, near Belgium, where factories were being revived. When Richard was six, and his mother pregnant with her fourth, the family moved, exchanging one of the most backward places in France for one of the most undeveloped. The marriage ended a year later, after an act of drunken brutality perpetrated by the father on Muguette, pregnant again, with her fifth. The next morning, she and her children boarded a bus and left.

The mother is the most important and least likely first influence on Richard's culinary calling because she provoked him to cook. She was too busy to make dinner without stress—she worked in a factory—and Richard, aged nine, stepped in to do it. He also stepped in because what she did cook, when she cooked, was inedible. He recalls many dishes, but my favorite is the rabbit cooked in a pot for so long and inattentively that, when it was brought to the table, and the lid lifted, he and his siblings had to stand up and peer over the rim to see if there was anything inside: The rabbit had shriveled to a hard black thing the size of a sparrow. Those same siblings were joyful when Richard took over—an early lesson in the happy love of happy diners.

The mother also introduced Richard to pastry, again indirectly but unequivocally. When he was thirteen, the age when she either kicked her children out or made them go to work (she had already dispatched the elder brother to learn bookkeeping at a trade school while being given room and board), his mother got a job for Richard at a local bronze foundry. He was burned and his hands swelled and he was unable to continue. She talked to friends—he had to do something—and came up with his being an apprentice at a pâtisserie, room and board, plus 50 francs a month (around $10.00), in Carignan, a hundred kilometers away, no trains or buses in between. A flour supplier picked up the boy early on a summer morning—a blue Renault van, a pink sky, the smell of August flowers. Richard didn't return for three years, not once.

"Recently," Richard told me, "I realized that I have no memory of my mother kissing me."

I asked him about his father: Was he an influence? A pastry chef is not a baker, but they are not so different.

"Absolutely not," he said. "Pâtisserie is a grand profession." He was quiet and seemed to be musing. "Well, maybe."

The father he never had, he said, was Gaston Lenôtre, the twentieth century's most famous French pastry chef. Richard was hired shortly after his twenty-third birthday, in 1971, and shortly before the restaurant review *Gault & Millau* published its famous October 1973 issue proclaiming the arrival of nouvelle cuisine and naming Lenôtre among the movement's swashbuckling practitioners.

Lenôtre, the famous Lenôtre, regarded Richard as the artist—for Richard that regard was emboldening and liberating—and would come to depend on him as his secret weapon. (Much later, David Bouley, the New York chef, trained with Lenôtre. "People were still saying how Michel had created this, and created that, how he created all these other things as well." This was years *after* Richard had left. "He was very big in Lenôtre's world to have that kind of influence still.") Because of Lenôtre, Richard discovered his own genius. Because of Lenôtre, he ended up in America: He accompanied him to open the first Lenôtre French pastry shop in New York. Because of Lenôtre (even if only indirectly), he discovered California, because Richard went there after Lenôtre's New York operation failed. In Los Angeles, Richard opened an almost incomprehensively successful pastry shop in 1976 (chef Wolfgang Puck recalls being astonished by the lines outside the door—"Longer than I have ever seen") and, later, Citrus, his first restaurant.

What was Lenôtre's achievement? I had purchased Lenôtre's first book, *Faites votre pâtisserie comme Lenôtre* (*Make Your Desserts like Lenôtre*), a three-hundred-page classic, now out of print. It includes recipes for tarts and éclairs and baba au rhum. How was this meant to be nouvelle cuisine?

"Lenôtre didn't invent new dishes," Richard said. "He invented new ways of making the old ones. He had a simple rule. You can change anything as long as the result is better than the original."

The rule, which is among the most succinct descriptions of nouvelle cuisine that I've come upon, governed everything Richard did, even if his applications were more anarchic than any of Lenôtre's. There was a fake caviar that Richard invented. We made it at the fish station. It looked and smelled like caviar, and was served in a fake caviar tin with a "Begula" label [*sic*] printed on the lid. It was pearl pasta soaked in a rich fish stock and dyed with squid ink. It is obviously not strictly a substitute for caviar, but, owing to the precision of its preparation and the little treasures found inside (a perfect sous-vide poached runny egg, a lobster knuckle simmered in butter), it *is* "better" than the original if "better," in this case, means a "more enjoyable eating experience." (Ever mischievous, Richard serves real caviar on a bowl of atmosphere, as though it were airborne, a trick of presentation made possible in a darkened, candlelit room, where the caviar sits atop a piece of plastic film stretched across a bowl floatingly.)

One night, Jessica was wakened by the sound of boys' giggling. She had put them into their cribs two hours before. She peeked past the bedroom door and saw them in the living room, pulling books off the shelves. They had learned how to climb out of their cribs, an unnerving milestone. She called me in Washington. I didn't hear the ring.

Showing no affect (it is what the experts say to do), she duly picked up each boy as though a kitten—no eye contact, no verbal acknowledgment—and returned them to their cribs, ho hum, and went back to bed. They climbed out. She put them back. They climbed out. After the routine had been repeated fifty times, she phoned me.

No answer.

After another fifty episodes (which seems improbable, but she assures me that she returned them to their cribs more than a hundred times), she tried my phone one more time, gave up, and went to sleep. She later found the boys sitting cross-legged with the fridge and freezer doors opened, white handprints everywhere. On the floor were butter, milk, orange juice, broken eggs, and ice cream, which they were eating from the carton with their hands. Frederick had chocolate syrup in his hair.

I showed up on the Friday evening. Jessica and I spoke in the morning. "This is not working," she said.

"I understand," I said, but I was back in Washington on the Monday.

AT THE FISH STATION, I DID PROTEINS. No one on the line—and we were all Americans—ever thought, Hey, I am a French cook. The skate took more or less the same savvy skill set that you would use to make a cup of tea: i.e., add hot water.

Skate is like mini-stingray with maxi-big bones that, in France, is served with a brown-butter-and-caper sauce: not complicated to make, but not one that David trusted any of his cooks either to know or recognize the taste of. "Their mouths have been ruined by sugar." So David made the sauce—always. He also boned the fish, then slipped it into a sack, poured in his sauce, vacuum-sealed it, and froze it. When the order came through, the fish went into a water bath for twenty minutes (controlled temperature, nothing to think about) and, when "fired" was removed from its sack. You didn't have to know what you were doing. You didn't have to know it was fish.

The striped bass: grilled skin-down until crispy, five minutes, and then finished by a minute on the fleshy side. The exotically oily sablefish: four minutes in a 500-degree oven, boned with a pair of fish pliers, painted with a soy-and-sake glaze, and then (when fired) sizzled in the salamander until it bubbled blackly.

Soft-shell crabs were the exception, arriving daily in a box, alive, with eyes, lined up in rows on a straw bed, each no bigger than a child's fist, ocean-wet, stirring slightly, and smelling of barnacles and anchors. They were also fun to eat, crustaceans that you could pop into your mouth and munch on in their entirety, claws, shell, everything.

They are a specialty of the Chesapeake Bay, but not a unique breed. What is unique is the breeding. Crabs shed shells and regrow them. They molt. Chesapeake Native Americans discovered that if you pull a mid-molting crab out into the air, the shell never hardens. It is, therefore, delightfully crispy when sautéed. Richard's were especially crispy, because they were deep-fried, after being filled with a mix of mayonnaise and crabmeat, an unconventional touch, stuffing a baby with the meat of the adult—basically, with what the little soft-shells would have grown up to be had their adolescence not been abbreviated.

"The mayonnaise is for the acidity," David told me during a lesson on crab prep. He searched for an example I might understand. "Think fish and chips. The English splash them with vinegar. Fat loves acidity." (David, I have to observe affectionately, had an inexpressibly charming, sweet way of conveying the utter awe he felt in the face of my culinary stupidity.)

To do crabs, you need only a pair of heavy-duty clippers and a metal bowl. With your left hand, you pick up the critter from just behind the claws; with your right, you snip off its head from just behind the eyes, which makes a light plonk when it hits the bowl. The now wide-open carcass is impressively roomy, especially after a little squeeze, which, when you think about it, makes perfect sense. A crab's new shell is like buying a coat for a fast-growing child—you want something the little guy will grow into. Of course Richard would make use of this space! It was as much a feature of a soft-shell's uniqueness as its paper-thin housing. A crab filled with mayonnaise? It was like a fried seafood sandwich. Why hadn't more restaurants stolen the idea?

To fry, you dip the crabs in a batter made of two parts pastry flour (low-protein, fluffy), one part corn flour (for mouth feel), a bottle of sparkling water (the effervescence of which mysteriously survives the frying), and an elusive ingredient called "curry love." The term was used by a line cook, Gervais Achstetter, who shouted, "Chef, the crabs need a little more curry love."

"Gervais, be careful, please," David said. "There is a journalist in the house."

Curry love, once it was finally accepted that the journalist wasn't going away anytime soon, turned out to be food coloring. Its use in savory dishes is universally forbidden, although for no reason that entirely makes sense, since it is tolerated in the pastry kitchen, which, in essential philosophic ways, Richard never left. A lot of Richard's dishes had a little extra love. The bright green of the "basil oil"? Or the ratatouille, its vibrant saffron-red? Or the deep, deep purple-red of the "wine sauce" that went with a steak?

I later asked Richard straight-out—"Do you use food coloring?" We were having lunch. It was mischievous of me. He didn't know that I knew. He paused, trying to read me.

"No," he said. "Never. Beet juice, of course. But not food coloring."

I repeated the exchange years later to Daniel Boulud—the brazen audacity of it—and he said, "Huh."

When I later found myself in Boulud's kitchen, and was on my own, downstairs, among the prep cooks, I fell into admiring the deep, egg-yolky tortellini that the pasta guy was making, and after asking if I could see the recipe discovered that, oh my, it included yellow food coloring.

Spoiler alert number three: I would end up cooking with Daniel Boulud.

One weekend, flipping through a magazine, Richard had come upon a picture of a flowering plant in a glass vase. The vase made him stop. He closed his eyes and visualized the possibility of a salad that looked like a gift from the florist, with "soil layers" below and leaves and edible flowers on top. By the time he got to the restaurant on Monday morning, he couldn't wait to get started. He had already grabbed a sheet of paper and was drawing what it might look like: on the bottom, the "dirt" (eggplant, sautéed with shallots in olive oil and finished in the oven to a sweet paste); on top, jellied tomato water; and in between a fluffy yogurt—"Not sweet, Americans always want sweet, but savory, seasoned with cumin" (a low-note heat, North African, earthy)—whipped by a technique that he had learned from Lenôtre.

"Which was?"

Basically yogurt plus gelatin, Richard said.

I was perplexed. Even I knew that you can't add gelatin to a refrigerated yogurt and expect it to set. Jell-O 101 teaches you that you have to dissolve it in a hot liquid and chill it.

"Ah, *mon ami,* we don't dissolve the gelatin in the yogurt. We dissolve it in a cup of hot cream and *then* fold it in."

And for the whipping?

You put your mixing bowl inside a larger bowl of ice. The effect is to heat and chill at once, but more chill than heat. The result is richer than the normal yogurt, owing to the cream, and disjunctively savory, owing to the cumin, and wonderfully textured, pillowy and expansive, like the soft-serve that you get from an ice-cream van. It is also stiff. You can poke salad leaves into it.

But there was a problem with the dirt. *"Merde!"* Richard said. The eggplant looked like shit. Food must never look like *merde.*

He came up with a fix the next morning. He would roast the eggplant as before, but substitute onion (red) for the shallot, and add beets (red), tomato (red), and vinegar (red)—plus garlic, this time, for intensity. He put everything in a blender and strained it through a sieve, which yielded a bulky, almost dry texture like baby food. It also had an appealingly deep red-brown hue. (I couldn't help myself: Had Richard added food coloring when I wasn't looking?) It looked like a desert at sunset. It was too beautiful to be buried. It would be the topsoil. The weird, wobbly tomato would go to the bottom and be a summery surprise when your spoon reached it.

The weird, wobbly tomato, incidentally, was basically tomato water intensified, what is left over after skinning your tomatoes, having plopped the seeds and skins in a sieve. Richard loved tomato water. I wasn't unfamiliar with it, but found it pretty fussy. Now, transported by Richard's enthusiasm, I regard it as such a rare and essential feature of summer that it deserves its own molecular describer: H_2OT_4, say. If you put the H_2OT_4 into a pot, reduce it slowly, and poke your finger in to taste, you will discover a liquid so intense that, for no reason you understand, you find yourself thinking of hot, listless afternoons in August. Cool it with gelatin and you have some very weird wobbly. Richard loves the really weird wobbly.

The salad was a miracle to look at, with the come-hither appeal of a dessert, but wholly savory. It was like a ratatouille that had been rendered into a flower. It was sprayed with a vinaigrette.

We were about to taste-test it, Richard and I at the chef's table, when Tyler Florence showed up, in town, no reservation, hoping for a bite to eat. Florence is a restaurateur and Food Network host. We ate the salad together. Florence ate his with a spoon.

"Whoa, Michel. What is the white custard thing? It is unbelievable."

"Yogurt," Richard said.

Florence tasted it again. "This is not yogurt."

"It is. Taste it again."

"Michel. I know what yogurt tastes like."

"No, you just don't know good yogurt." Richard stretched out the word "good." "This is gooooooood whole-fat yogurt."

Florence had another bite, and conveyed, unmistakably, that he knew he was being bullshitted and that Richard was an asshole.

I later asked Richard why he didn't tell him.

"And then watch him getting credit for it on his television show, and on his Web site, and his next book? No."

Chefs do not invent dishes daily. Jean Anthelme Brillat-Savarin, the author of *The Physiology of Taste* (1825), the *famous* meditation on eating, compares a new recipe to discovering a star. But here, in Richard's kitchen, just about every item on the menu was new. And new ones appeared routinely, a bright idea on a Monday morning, a long-term experiment (like his effort to reinvent *pâté-en-croûte*—"Don't you find the crusts are always soggy?"), or some impromptu innovation done in the spirit of "Why not?"

One afternoon, I overheard Courseille, the pastry chef, mention Marc Veyrat. I knew about Veyrat, the "mountain chef" in the Alps. I had never eaten at his restaurant, though I had tried once when visiting a friend in Geneva, and it was closed.

In Courseille's description, Veyrat had ghostly transparent skin, wore a black, rimmed Savoyard peasant's hat even when indoors, a black cape-like shirt, Sgt. Pepper round tinted glasses, had the manner of a seer, and was just awful, utterly terrible to work for. "Rude. Condescending. Treated his cooks like slaves," Courseille said. "The staff starts at dawn, are given straw baskets and clippers, and told what trails to climb, and what to look for, and then they all go into the mountains—as in the Alps, as in Mont Blanc—and don't return until their baskets are full. They clean what they gathered. They prep it. *Then* they get ready for the dinner service."

I thought: He sounds mad. I thought: He sounds perfect.

I also thought: This was the virtue of being in Richard's kitchen. For the gossip, and the talk, and the visitors. This was how I was going to find where to work in France. In fact, maybe I had just found it.

"Almost no one in the United States knows him," Courseille continued, "except Jean-Georges"—Jean-Georges Vongerichten, in New York City. "Veyrat came to see him once in New York. They went foraging in Central Park."

I called Jean-Georges.

"I love Marc," he said. "He is my spiritual cousin."

Could he help me reach him?

He wrote an introduction and gave me an e-mail address and a phone number. I was surprised how easy it now seemed: You learn about a figure, you get an introduction. Jessica, my French ventriloquist, wrote a masterpiece letter (I would never again sound so good), respectfully expressing the hope that I might work with him, and off it went.

No reply.

She sent it three times. We phoned. Nothing. I asked Jean-Georges for advice.

"Marc is an unusual man."

The next day we got an e-mail from an assistant. (Had Jean-Georges intervened?) Marc Veyrat and his *brigade* were looking forward to welcoming me. *Nous vous accueillerons.* The verb, Jessica said, *accueillir,* is important. It is not used casually. It means to welcome you in one's home. I stared at it. I didn't try to pronounce it. Did this amount to my having a plan?

I mentioned it to David.

"What a terrible idea." David once applied for a job there and spent a weekend trailing in the kitchen. "His executive chef cheats at soccer." Here David paused, giving me the chance to take in the enormity of the claim.

"Wow," I said.

"Exactly."

"We'll think of something," David said. "I'll speak to Michel."

I didn't dismiss the prospect.

A proposal came soon enough.

Cedric, the chef at Richard's Central, and David were an unlikely pair. They regularly finished their evenings together in the Citronelle kitchen, drinking a bottle of wine, sometimes until two in the morning (by which time I was the guy drooling with his head on the chef's table). Cedric was forceful, strong, a large neck, a big chest, a rugby player to David's quick-twitch soccer hooligan. Also in their relations with Richard: David worked to realize Richard's will; Cedric fought it. ("Doesn't Cedric understand I own the restaurant?" Richard asked me once. "Doesn't Michel understand that these are my *grandmother's* recipes?" Cedric asked) One night, Cedric and David were telling me how they met. They had both worked together in northern Bur-gundy—at La Côte Saint-Jacques, a two-Michelin-star restaurant in the Yonne. It was, in their description, family-run, second-generation, situ-ated on a famous river, with plenty of fish, and on the edge of a forest, with plenty of game, and near legendary vineyards.

I couldn't quite picture where it was, and they tried to locate it for me, in the north of France, and not far from Lyon—

"An hour," Cedric said.

"No, not an hour. More like three hours," David said. They stopped. They had the same thought.

"Lyon," David said.

"Lyon," Cedric said. "Americans don't get it."

"It's the gastronomic capital. I'm going to talk to Michel. I am sure he has a friend there, someone."

Lyon. I hadn't been, except for that one-off bus transfer at dawn, but for the longest time I had wanted to learn about it. In Chianti, when I was at the butcher shop, it was mentioned regularly. It had been a city that Tuscans, at the height of the Italian Renaissance, had virtually appropriated: settling there, selling Italian goods at the city's famous fairs (*les foires*), building themselves mansions. It was also the city where Italians, at least according to Italians, first taught the French how to cook.

The first time I heard this—that French cuisine originated in Italian Renaissance kitchens—I had been in the butcher shop, and it wasn't someone's throwaway provocation, but a chorus of Tuscans, loud, declamatory, and theatrical. I made the mistake of asking them to repeat it—it was too ridiculous. They repeated it, even more loudly, with even more gesticulation.

In practice, the idea wasn't without merit: Namely, in Italy (or the peninsula we now call Italy), from the late 1300s to the early 1600s, grand meals were treated like works of art, orchestrated productions, with many plates and much showing off of the kitchen, a *festa*. At the time, the French did not eat this way. But in its telling, the idea could seem pretty cartoonish: that the changes in what we now think of as French cuisine were the doing of the princesslike daughter of the famous Florentine Medici family, Caterina, who, in 1533, at the age of fourteen, traveled from Tuscany to marry a prince who would become the king of France, whereupon she introduced Italian ingredients and culinary secrets to her subjects. Today people refer to this as the "Catherine de' Medici myth," which they cite with much hilarity.

I researched the idea. Not much was written in support of the thesis. Considerably more, however, was written against it. But it wasn't always persuasive. Some critics didn't appear to read Italian. Some rarely (or never) alluded to the Italian Renaissance. Many, in my humble opinion, sound more Franco-chauvinistic than scholarly. In any case, the implications were intriguing to consider: that at one point French cuisine did *not* exist, or at least not in a form that we would recognize today; and that then, at another point, it *did,* and that the Italians may have had something to do with its coming into being.

And then, I don't know, maybe it was farfetched after all, and, besides, I wasn't sure I had the scholarly equipment—I certainly didn't have the French—and I abandoned my research. And then, now, here I was: contemplating Lyon.

I called Jean-Georges.

"Lyon is a wonderful city. I cooked there." He had been a saucier—the person who made the sauces—for Paul Bocuse.

"Lyon is the Ville des Mères, the city of the mothers, the *mère* chefs," he said. "You don't know? Since I don't know how long, a long time, they've done the cooking. It is where it all started," he said. "You really should go to Lyon."

When I next saw Richard, he was waiting for me at the chef's table.

"Lyon is perfect," he said.

Richard went to Lyon often and had a close friend, Jean-Paul Lacombe, another chef who had made the trek to the United States and regarded Richard as an unrecognized deity. "Jean-Paul runs Léon de Lyon. It is a Lyonnais institution. I will get Mel to write him a letter. You have found your restaurant."

Amid all this, Jessica, a sympathetic soul, who believed what her husband told her, had been planning her family's future based on two assumptions—that we would be spending the summer in Paris and that our children would be back by the fall enrolled in some kind of educational institution: i.e., preschool.

Getting your New York offspring into one turned out to be a competitive urban sport, and my wife was a proven competitor. She attended twelve admissions meetings. One was held in a gym with bleachers not large enough to accommodate the applicants, who sat on the floor of a basketball court: The crowd, estimated to be eight hundred, was told that there were fifty-two places. She got our boys not only into that school, but into every other one she applied to (it was very throw-down stuff), and finally settled on an establishment called Jack & Jill, her first choice. She texted me: Could she go ahead and pay the tuition?

Yes, I said. I understood the implications. I was committed to finishing my French training by the fall.

The next morning, Jessica phoned. "Jack & Jill starts on September 16. But the teachers want to meet the boys first, at *our* home, at nine a.m. on the tenth. Will we be back by then?"

"Yes," I said.

Jessica had been monitoring flights. It was already June. Fares, which had once been reasonable, were now very high. "May I buy us tickets?"

I told her to wait. I had a new plan.

That weekend, we sat on a bench against a wall.

My plan, I said, involves our going to France "as a family" until September and my then staying on afterward "on my own."

There was a long silence: that is, a really, really long silence.

"You stay on in Paris on your own?" she confirmed finally.

"No."

"No?"

"I didn't say Paris."

"Or wherever, you go to France . . ."

"Lyon. I was thinking that I should go to Lyon. . . ."

"I don't care where you want to go. You are not going off on your own while I stay behind and put the boys through their first semester of school by myself."

"I'm not?" I braced myself. She'd had a brutal time with the toddlers.

"No." She paused. "We're going together."

"Really?"

"We're moving to France."

"We are?"

"As a family."

"But how?"

"I don't know yet. Go back to work. I'll figure it out."

The exchange was among the most profound and consequential conversations of our marriage.

One immediate problem was the duration. Americans can "visit" France as tourists for up to three months. A longer stay requires a visa, which concerned Jessica.

I knew this but hadn't taken it seriously. We'd been in Italy for more than three months and were never told we needed a visa. Dan Barber didn't have one when he did his internship in France. ("I didn't even know I needed one.") Nor did Thomas Keller. ("It was a different time.") Americans got their French training very quietly.

"They didn't have children."

True, I said. It was also true that two people in the Citronelle kitchen had gone to France to work, been found out by the police, and given twenty-four hours to leave.

Our children, she said, should go to bed at night without fearing that they are about to be exiled. "We can't be in France without a proper visa. Go back to work. I'll figure it out."

She then contacted the French Embassy, which gave me a fright, that she had gone ahead and contacted an *official* at an *institution*. It seemed so public and irreversible.

The next morning, she e-mailed me the forms.

She phoned. "Are you sitting down?"

"Too late."

"Stay calm. Call me tomorrow."

It was a staggeringly fastidious document, confirming every fear and caricature of the bureaucratic French. I looked at the requirements: tax returns, proof of income, net worth, your French bank account (our *French* bank account?), proof of your French residence, and a declaration of purpose, explaining (in French) why you needed to be in France.

Three nights later, the French ambassador happened to be in the dining room and ordered a soft-shell crab. The whole kitchen knew about my plans.

"Don't fuck this one up," David said. "This is your future."

The next day, I wrote: "Dear Ambassador, I am a writer and a student of the French kitchen. The soft-shell crab that you ate last night at Citronelle was cooked for you by me. I am wondering if you might be able to help me. . . ."

To ensure that the letter reached the addressee, I called upon Victor Obadia. Monsieur Obadia, a sales rep for Silver Spoon, a gastronomic-restaurant supplier (bark, bowls that look like Gaudí apartments, and impenetrable postmodern designs that thrusting molecular-gastronomy types covet), was a member of an informal group of foodies who could be found on weeknights having a drink at Citronelle's pop-up sidewalk café. The ambassador of France was an Obadia client. The dining room at the embassy was famously one of the best, and the least accessible, tables in Washington, D.C.

The French ambassador never replied.

But I did get a call from a senior official, a grand-sounding figure with flawless Oxbridge public-school-educated English. He was perplexed, he confessed, by what exactly I wanted the ambassador to do.

Give my family and me a visa to live in France, I said.

"I see," the accent replied. The ambassador does not give visas, the accent said, but it did give me a name, Marc Selosse, and a Manhattan telephone number, for the French Consulate in New York, on Fifth Avenue.

Selosse was sympathetic and educated and spoke many languages, and wanted to help but only if I understood that he wouldn't be able to do anything.

"D'accord?"

"D'accord."

He had lived in New York, he explained, long enough to see that most New Yorkers have no idea that in France people really believed in rules, genuinely, and that everyone has to suffer them equally, and there wasn't a lot to be done, because there were no exceptions: ever.

But Selosse was prepared to be my coach and put through our application on an expedited basis.

This was wonderful news. I thanked him and asked how long it might then take.

"If you're very lucky, three months."

June. So—visas, if we were lucky, by September.

"But only if," Monsieur Selosse added, "and it is a very big *if*, your applications are perfect."

Selosse gave us an appointment, ten days hence, to present our applications and supporting documents for the consulate's approval. I protested the wait—we were in a hurry—but he assured me that I would need the time. "And don't forget that the financial statements are to be done in quadruplicate, with one for each child."

"Of course," I said. Financial statements for our children, who are not yet three?

"And your children," he added, "you have to bring them in, too."

"Because they will be interviewed?"

"No, no, not them. We just need to fingerprint them. It is you who will be interviewed. In French."

"I don't speak French."

"It will be a short interview."

I got to work. Everything was perfectly, even if excessively, straightforward, except one requirement: We had to prove our residence in France. I had read this requirement in the application and ignored it: How can we, who are applying to be residents, establish that we are already residents? I had friends in Paris. Maybe I could get one to "lend" us an address?

I phoned Monsieur Selosse.

"The proof of residence is very important. And you must establish it in the city where you will actually reside." He mentioned a recent case, a woman who had proved residence in Paris but intended to live in Toulouse. "When she showed up at the prefecture in Toulouse"—a requirement is that you register with the local authority within two months of arriving—"we were immediately notified. 'This is not correct,' we said, and we ordered her out of the country."

I went back to the instructions. You had to produce a lease or property deed, supported by utility bills with both your name and address. There wasn't a lot of room for improvisation.

It was Friday. A week had elapsed. Our appointment was on Monday. I called Selosse, but he didn't pick up. I left a voice-mail message, and paced. It was five o'clock before he phoned back.

What had I got myself into? "Do I really have to produce these documents? We don't *live* in France."

"Yes, you just need to give us a copy of the property deed," he said, very cheerful. "But make sure that you bring the original."

Had he not heard me? "But I don't have a deed. I don't own property in France."

"Oh. Well, then, you'll need your lease. But make sure that you bring the original."

"But I don't have a lease."

"Oh."

"We are not residents."

"Oh."

There was a long pause. I wondered: Does this mean we give up?

"If a Lyonnais family is prepared to accommodate your family," Selosse said, "make sure that they produce all the normal documentation. They also need to cite, in writing, the name of every member of your family, including your children."

I hadn't mentioned a Lyonnais family. "Every name?" I asked, playing along.

"Every name."

Was Monsieur Selosse, a professional diplomat, diplomatically suggesting a fix?

But who to call? It was a summer Friday, late. Should I rearrange our Monday meeting? Selosse had warned me that there wouldn't be another appointment until August, which was useless, because all of France would then be on vacation, so that effectively there wasn't anything until September.

I concentrated: Do I know anyone *in* Lyon?

No. I had never been to Lyon.

Do I know anyone *from* Lyon?

I *might* know someone, even though I scarcely knew him. The French chef Daniel Boulud. He is famously from Lyon.

I had met him. Would he remember me? I called the restaurant.

No, he wasn't there.

I pressed.

He was out of the country.

I pressed.

He was in Shanghai.

(Shanghai? Shit.)

I recalled an e-mail press release from Daniel's publicist, Georgette Farkas. She was worth a try. I called, no reply (was she in Shanghai, too?), left a message, then wrote a desperate e-mail, telling her what I needed, the various "proofs"—residency, ownership, the names of our children ("and Frederi*ck* is with a '*ck*,' not the French way with only the '*c*,' because there can't be a misspelling")—and asked: Could she possibly reach Daniel in Shanghai?

In the morning, a three-page fax was sitting on the rack of my machine, not from Shanghai, but from Lyon.

I called out to Jessica. "Hey, read this."

It described an ancient residence, with many rooms, large enough to accommodate George, Frederick, Jessica, and me, in the grandest, most ancient arrondissement in Lyon. Unfortunately, the property had been in the family so long that no one had been able to locate the original property deeds. Would this testimony suffice? It was signed Julien Boulud.

"Who is Julien?" Jessica asked.

"I have no idea. Daniel's father? But look at the description. Do you think we could live there?"

"Of course not. It doesn't exist. It's made up." She gave me a puzzled, "How have you managed to survive on the planet so far?" look. "Daniel's father didn't write this. You believe that's his signature?" (Boulud later confirmed that he and his sister drafted the document, but I continue to believe that the house is where we ought to be living today.)

We showed up for our appointment, our piles of supporting documents, in quadruplicate, pulled behind me in a Radio Flyer red wagon, last year's Christmas gift, and turned them in.

Passportlike portrait shots were taken, a payment made (99 euros times four—then about $575), and the documents examined by Monsieur Selosse. He raised his head. "Congratulations," he said, "it is perfect."

It had worked. We would be in France in September. Probably. Maybe.

Three weeks later, Selosse phoned. An administrator had spotted a mistake, committed by a cashier (who had written "Frédéric," not "Frederick"). The applications were being returned to New York. Could we come back to the consulate on Thursday? "And please bring your children. They will need to be photographed." Again? Really? "They're children. They may have changed. And the recent financial statements."

We completed our second set of applications. We obviously would not be in France by September.

But then—with unexpected efficiency (midway through the August *vacances*)—our visas came through. We jumped in the air with grateful glee, took the subway uptown, bounded up the stairs, collected our passports, and stared wondrously at the ornate full-page French visa stamped inside. We'd done it!

And then, like that, I was going to throw up.

I had been so caught up in the applications frenzy that I hadn't considered what we might do if they succeeded. Frankly, I had become so convinced that we would have to slink into the country, bluffing our way past immigration officials, that I was now intimidated by the utter orthodoxy of our plan, that we were legitimately moving to Lyon.

And what a thought: Lyon! Because I still hadn't seen it. I didn't have any better sense of it than I had when David first proposed it, except that (now) I had heard it maligned by English friends ("ugly city") or read dismissals of it by postwar food writers (like Waverley Root, who hated it, or Roy Andries de Groot, who hated it even more). Jessica, ever upbeat, showed me an aerial photo illustrating how the city had been created by two great rivers' coming together, the Saône (flowing south from Beaujolais) and the Rhône (flowing west from the Alps), and how the heart of the city was almost like an island, "which is why it is called

Presqu'île, which means 'almost an island,' and looks a little bit like a mini-Manhattan, no?"

I stared. No. It doesn't look like Manhattan. It looks far away.

Jessica, undeterred, planned a reconnaissance long weekend in what she was confident would be our new residence, telling the boys only at the last minute, three weeks short of their third birthday and one week before they started school, that their parents were going to France, but not why (such is the innocent bewilderment of toddlers that they had never once asked about the many visits we made to a place called "the Consulate"). On the Thursday afternoon before our nighttime departure, I took them both to a park, allowing Jessica to pack without interruptions, and young George fled to a playground and Frederick sat by himself on a bench, and could sense the agitation and wouldn't be budged from his seat, and searched my face for clues, and was uneasy and needy and tender, and I was moved by his unexpressed pathos, and felt, unexpectedly, the responsibility, like walking always with a heavy backpack, of having a family, and the misfortune that its fate was so often in the out-of-control control of my erratic self. (Young George, meanwhile, was flying facedown on a slide, screaming with hysteric oblivion.)

Jessica booked us a room at Le Royale, a hotel that seemed to be patronized by businesspeople, and she liked that: We were there to work, we weren't vacationing, and she wanted people we met to know we were. We had appointments: a broker (for an apartment), a bank, an agency, "Only Lyon," recommended by Georgette Farkas that helps foreign businesses get settled; and Marc Veyrat, which involved our spending a night away, at the foot of the Alps, on Lake Annecy, in the rooms above his restaurant.

We arrived on a Friday morning, at the Aéroport de Lyon–Saint-Exupéry, named after *the* Antoine de Saint-Exupéry of *Little Prince* fame (which is a children's book, or an adults' book that children like, or an adults' book about childhood, and, in any event, a very good book). I found myself musing about other airports that had been named after writers, and couldn't think of one (even Chile would reject an effort to name theirs after the poet Pablo Neruda), and I liked the fact that the airport of our new home was literary.

Waiting for our bags, and in a condition of heightened watchfulness, I studied faces with the exacting eye of an anthropologist who had just landed at a potentially hostile outpost. The women were beautiful, as you would expect—it was France. It was the men who were unexpected. Their look was almost uniform: blunt, short-cropped hair, unshaven, sometimes a cheek scar, thuggish—ugly: forthrightly so. These were not New York faces. They were not Parisian. They were more English than French, an aging-lad look. I thought: I know these people. They are not fancy or fussy, and they unexpectedly put me at ease. Maybe I can make this place my home.

At a taxi stand, we spotted the Alps, distantly, a rugged eastern horizon. In the other direction was the city; and, in between, farms, including the one where Daniel Boulud grew up and from where, on a visit to see his parents, he wrote his fraudulent testimony. I felt grateful to him all over again.

The hotel was on the unnervingly vast Place Bellecour. We ventured out to the middle of it, trying to take in the expanse of the *place,* the largest open-air square in Europe: unadorned red clay, a distant perimeter of green trees, an immense blue sky. It looked as though a desert had been plopped down where people would normally build homes. Napoleon paraded troops on it. And lo and behold: a plaque commemorating the birthplace of the author of *The Little Prince,* only a few doors down from where we were staying.

We phoned our children (and Frederick said uncannily, "I dreamed you were somewhere red and green"). I looked east and spotted the wide river Rhône. I looked west and, *voilà,* there was the Saône, and on the other side a steep, mountainlike ascent of pastel-colored sixteenth-century buildings, reminiscent of the Arno in Florence. I would learn later that the buildings were in "Vieux Lyon"—Old Lyon—and date from the Italian Renaissance (a century before the French version), and remind you of Florence because they had been built by Florentines. Near the top of the mountain was a diminutive replica of the Eiffel Tower—built in a late-nineteenth-century moment of civic self-doubt, an explicit imitation of the real Eiffel Tower, in the hope that Lyon's, too, might attract tourists. (The tension between Paris and Lyon is historic, at some times deadly.) Lyon's tower, alas, is dinky in comparison to the Eiffel, and no one came, and now it houses a radio and cell-phone antenna.

For lunch, we ate at L'Espace Brasserie for no reason except that it was there, and had tables outside. I asked for an *andouillette,* winning clicks of approval from the waitress. I mistakenly believed it was related to an "andouille," the spicy sausage found in New Orleans gumbo. An *andouillette* is not an andouille. It is also not really a sausage. It *looks* like a sausage because it is dressed up like one, a large casing tied tight by strings on each end, but into which is crammed so many crushed wirelike intestinal tubes that you have to pick them apart to confirm that you are looking at what you thought you were looking at: basically, the insides of a skinny tummy. It was tripe. I was not unfamiliar with tripe. At the butcher shop in Tuscany, I had even made a preparation of it, and knew that there were two kinds: the subtle variety, in which the basic digestive aromatics of the animal are dispersed into a slightly gamy flavoring; and the not-so-subtle, in which you are made to feel that you have been asked to inhabit an animal's stomach. This one was the not-so-subtle. It was an introduction.

In the evening, we went to La Machonnerie, a *bouchon* in Vieux Lyon. Jessica addressed the owner (Lucas, midseventies, wide girth, scraggly beard, and a practiced jollity) in a French so assured that he directed us through the front bar (airy, with windows, and clusters of nervous British tourists) to a low-ceilinged room in the back, no windows, red-and-white-checkered tables, noisy, raucous, exclusively populated by French, except that they didn't seem French, or not like the restrained versions that I'd seen in my life until now. They were in a sweat. It beaded up on their foreheads and showed darkly through their shirts. They were talking, talking, talking—to anyone, to everyone, poking their heads into each other's plates, laughing hard, and drinking bountifully by the *pot* (a vessel without a label, pronounced to rhyme with "dough," slightly smaller than a bottle, making it acceptable for two people to drink two during a meal—and, on festive occasions, ordering a third or a fifth).

Our appetizers were *grattons,* curly brown scratchings of deep-fried pork fat (fat with fat). We ate a local *pâté-en-croûte,* pork with foie gras in a buttery casing (fat with fat with fat). My heart racing, and in a health panic, I ordered fish: a lake fish, a *brochet* (pike), famously bony, and prepared (bonelessly) as a dumplinglike soufflé floating in a sauce made from local crayfish and cream. It was my first Lyonnais quenelle. It was served, confusingly, with the Lyonnais version of mac-and-cheese—macaroni with heavy cream. (Fat with fat with fat with fat . . .) *Bouchon,* the word, has many meanings (traffic jam, plug, cork) but its sense as "a place you enter to drink and eat, get sweaty, and stand on the table and sing midway through your meal" appears to date from the sixteenth century, and described "the grapevines placed over the door of an eating-and-drinking establishment." The message then, and now, was from Bacchus: "Come on in and get blotto."

Our host, making the rounds of the rowdy room, reached our table and realized that we were Americans. He instantly changed his affect and, seeming not to trust us, started performing tourist shticks, including the three-rivers-that-flow-into-Lyon joke (the Rhône, the Saône, and the Beaujolais) and apologized for serving us San Pellegrino. ("It was bottled in Italy as a still water but became so excited crossing into France that it began bubbling.")

Afterward, we walked back to our hotel, pausing on the Pont Bonaparte, the bridge crossing the Saône (Lyon and Napoleon always liked each other)—a cold wind, a storm coming—and regarded the city: Roman steps, a medieval wall, an abandoned convent, stone churches, lights everywhere, ripplingly reflected on the river.

The next day, we explored the arrondissements that various advisers had recommended to us for a place to live. We began with the sixth ("Good for children," a home-fixer from Only Lyon had told us), on the other side of the Rhône River, near the Parc de la Tête d'Or (vast pond, a zoo, forests), Haussmannian architecture, boulevards evocative of Paris, and expensive cars of families returning from their summer holidays. It was the weekend of *la rentrée,* when all of France comes home from their vacations, and the mood is never exactly jubilant. Even so, the people of the sixth had a closed-in quality, an insularity verging on unfriendly. An impression, in any case.

We tried the fourth ("You'll adore it, it's just like the East Village," the home-fixer had said), known as the Croix-Rousse, named after a cross planted there in the sixteenth century, a high point of the city, with panoramic views and a steep escarpment. During the eighteenth and nineteenth centuries, silk workers wove their fabrics here (because of the light). But if it was like the East Village, that wasn't for its vitality, but its grittiness, shop fronts closed up, shutters padlocked shut, jumbly and scrappy and conveying a strong imperative to bathe after visiting it.

The fifth, Vieux Lyon, the Renaissance part of the city, had historical appeal. But it was also busy with tourists, "Irish pubs," "English pubs," Saturday-night binge-drinking bars, and a perimeter of strip joints.

This wasn't going to be easy. What we were finding was a city that knew what it was, whether you liked it or not. It had a personality, a strong one. It wasn't a boutique destination. It wasn't naturally friendly. It was a little rough. (I would turn out to be wrong: It was actually very rough and entirely unwelcoming.)

The prospect of dinner was a relief. I proposed Léon de Lyon, Richard's recommendation for my future employment. I hadn't contacted the proprietor-chef yet, Jean-Paul Lacombe, hoping to try out the place before signing on. In the event, he wasn't there, since it was, technically, the last weekend of the *vacances*.

The entrance was on a corner. There were red velvet banquettes and stained-glass windows. The aesthetic was fin-de-siècle, exuberantly ornate, and evoked an era when Lyonnais meals were eaten by gaslight or candle. It seemed unchanged since the original café that had opened its doors in 1904. We were wowed. Lacombe's father, Paul Lacombe, bought it just after World War II, and then, in 1972, and after his first Michelin star, he died of a heart attack. At the age of twenty-three, his son, who had been working in Paris, was summoned home. Six years later, Léon de Lyon earned its second Michelin star. A 1980s guide to the city's restaurants declared that everyone should eat there at least once in his or her lifetime.

A maître d' briskly ushered us to a *"salle."* Jessica protested nervously, fearing that we were about to be quarantined. The maître d' insisted in English. She objected again in French, but we were feeling less than confident, and followed him into a *salle* that was boxy and out-of-the-way with a low ceiling, too much light, and a feeling of mumbled self-consciousness. The other diners were British. The exception was a

Frenchman, eating by himself. He knew the restaurant and had asked to be seated here. He wanted to practice his English.

"You should order the *pâté-en-croûte*," he told us. He was well into his second bottle of wine. "It's the only good thing on the menu." He whispered, "The restaurant is having a difficult time."

Unknown to Richard, Lacombe had just renounced his stars. He was abandoning the pomp and the competitiveness, and was concentrating on several bistros that he had opened around the city. Downstairs, on my way to the restroom, I saw mementos of Lacombe's earlier life hanging from the walls: photos of Bill Clinton, Charles de Gaulle, the Rolling Stones. In the one picture of *père* and *fils,* circa 1950s, the father—towering, erect, formidable, and probably a dickhead—teaches his child, aged twelve, how to make a sauce. Shelves held three centuries of French cookbooks: They were about to be sold off. A deep cellar of Rhône wines had been discounted heavily. We chose an old bottle for our meal, a historic Côte-Rôtie made from Syrah grapes that would have grown twenty miles away, but the service was so slow that we finished it before our food arrived. We ordered a second. The maître d' said, "*Non.* You want something else."

"We do?" Jessica asked, but he didn't hear. He returned with an already opened bottle and disappeared.

"The treasures of the cellar," the Frenchman next to us explained, "are not for tourists."

The wine, as the maître d' would have known, was undrinkable.

We didn't order the *pâté-en-croûte,* which was a mistake. We also didn't order any of the other Lyonnais dishes, which was a bigger mistake. What we got was inedible. A plate of quail was vibrantly raw. At one point, in the long intermission between courses, I strolled back to the kitchen and saw a so-called team of young men, angry, slamming into each other. They may have been in a *rentrée* bad temper, or disgruntled because they were having to work on a *rentrée* weekend, or just unhappy. This wasn't cooking with love. It was cooking to injure.

As I asked for the check, Jessica picked up a feeling that she wasn't liking and said she would wait for me at the end of the street. I stood and congratulated the maître d', his deputy, and a sous-chef who had just then wandered out for having produced one of the rudest, ugliest, most unpleasant meal experiences that I could remember having suffered in a long time. "Congratulations!" I said. I seized the maître d's head between my hands and kissed him robustly on both cheeks. He was so stunned that I felt encouraged, and kissed his deputy and the sous-chef. Then I gave them each my card.

"You did what?" Jessica asked when I found her hiding behind a bus. "Why did you give them our card?"

I reflected. It was not an unreasonable question. "Actually, I don't know."

Jessica seemed to ponder the situation. "Not such a good day."

The Lyonnais, I had been told, really don't like outsiders. At the end of our first full day, I agreed: They really didn't.

The next morning, we set out to meet Marc Veyrat, the man our hotel concierge confirmed was "the craziest chef in France."

He was a long shot. In the unlikely event that Veyrat took me on, how would we reside in Lyon, where, as the French Consulate had made clear, we were constrained to be, while I commuted to the crazy man's restaurant, one hundred miles to the east, on the Lac d'Annecy?

We arrived amid sleeting rain, high winds, and cresting whitecaps on the lake, and, at the base of a steep mountain that disappeared into stormy clouds, discovered an address that looked like a Victorian candy box, a four-story mansion, painted an elegant gray-blue, with bright white balconies. We checked in, removed wet clothes, asked for a towel, and confirmed that the chef was around.

"If the dining room is open, he is here," a receptionist said. "It's a rule. If he goes away—to see a doctor in Paris—he closes the restaurant, booked up or not."

I said that we were lucky.

"He is expecting you."

Veyrat grew up in the village of Manigod, not far from the lake, but several thousand feet higher, facing Mont Blanc. His parents had a small farm, raised animals, and ran a simple table d'hôte—a table with food—for villagers and walkers. ("I grew up," he would tell me later, "with my face in the ass of a cow.") His father taught him how to forage ("he made me recite every herb, fern, and berry that I saw on my way to school"). The mountains, he said, were too extreme for conventional agriculture.

There were evocative props: a wooden wheelbarrow, a pair of wooden clogs, a thresher, a hoe, a walking stick, wooden baskets. The walls were white, roughly plastered, and videos were being projected on them, depicting Veyrat engaged in country activities: picking wild celery, or showing children how to make a *galette des rois,* the Epiphany cake, or deep in conversation with a goat, always in the black shepherd's hat and capelike shirt.

The dining room furniture was made from recently woodsman-chopped pines—and held in place with wooden pegs. It was a coherently contrived natural message: Among our sixteen courses, we ate a lake fish served on bark, small eggs retrieved from mountain nests, and soup made from ferns.

And yet, for all the rusticity, it was also a high-tech performance. A large flat-screen in the kitchen, like a flight display at an airport, depicted which course each table was eating. The staff was equipped with Bluetooth headsets. Our table was bugged.

Jessica has an allergy. She whispered, "There are nuts in the bread."

A server appeared. "Madame, may I give you a different bread?"

And, later, I said softly, "The cheese is a little rich."

A different server appeared. "Sir, may I propose an Alpine cooked cheese?"

I have since come to regard the bugging as a piece of flattery. Ever since I heard about Veyrat, I had been petitioning for his attention, but the man, philosophically unreachable, never really responded. I sent him a French translation of my book about Italy. Again, no response. But a waiter then told us, sotto voce, that many people in the restaurant had read it. I became excited: I seemed to be breaking through.

Veyrat showed up, moving from table to table, in costume, the hat, shirt, the spectacles. His face really was white—not like milk, but like a dead person. It was a too-long-indoors white, with a spooky pale transparency. Also, he had two canes.

He'd had an accident, he explained, describing it in French, which I struggled to follow; when I gave up, Jessica translated. He had been skiing and went over a cliff. "I broke my neck, both shoulders, a collarbone, and the tibiae and the fibulae in my leg." He'd had several operations. Another was scheduled the following week.

He returned to our table later to administer our fourteenth dish, which involved a cauldron of liquid nitrogen and two doughy green-brown balls on a tray. He picked them up with tweezers and dropped them into the cauldron, where they boiled with instant bubbling fury.

He told us to close our eyes.

"You have embarked on a walk on a summer morning," Veyrat intoned. "You have entered the forest. Leaves brush across your face, when—"

He stopped. I had opened my eyes. He stared at me. I closed them.

He inhaled deeply. "When a root trips you. You try to catch your balance. But you fall, face-first, into the dirt."

He pulled out the clods with a spoon, trailing vapors of nitrogen.

"Now, with your eyes closed," he whispered, "open your mouth." He waited. *"Très bien,"* he said, approvingly, and inserted the balls, whereupon, if you are Jessica, and have obeyed the instructions, a nitrogen-boiled earth-grenade has arrived on your tongue without your seeing it coming, and your palate explodes with every forest experience of your life. If you are me, and peeking through your eyelashes, watching out for the trick, and are on the verge of dismissing the whole exercise as a silly piece of vaudeville shtick, the dirt clod nevertheless manages to be an impressive object to find disintegrating in your mouth.

In France, Veyrat is loved and loathed, but mainly loved, because few people are so eccentrically themselves.

I looked back into the kitchen and tried to imagine myself wearing headphones (and, astonishingly, I could).

Veyrat and I met in the morning, and tried to make plans. There was also the question of his surgery.

"If it fails," he said, "I close the restaurant."

Besides, he said to Jessica, quietly, "Your husband has to learn French. I'm happy to have him in my kitchen, but he has to know what I'm saying."

He was right, of course. I wondered: Could I learn French in two weeks? The question then became urgent: On the eve of our return to New York, we found a place to live.

In our brief absence, a new friend, an American, Victor Vitelli, had found an apartment listing we might like. It was by the Saône river, situated auspiciously on the Quai Saint-Vincent—Vincent was the patron saint of winemakers—and opposite *La Fresque des Lyonnais,* a mural of two millennia of the city's famous citizens, painted onto the side of a six-story windowless wall. "There's also a famous boulangerie," Victor told us, the bakery where all of Lyon knows to buy its bread. The rent was 1,900 euros a month, which was high for the city, but to us, accustomed to Manhattan, seemed exceptionally good value. Jessica made an appointment.

On our walk over, I peeked through windows—few had curtains— and saw high wood-beamed ceilings. I poked into entryways and found stone stairs rendered concave by boot traffic. Some buildings dated from the fifteenth and sixteenth centuries. A gnarly first-century aqueduct column by a post office reminded us that the Romans had been here. So did the street called the "Rhine road," the route their troops followed to do battle with the "Franks" (i.e., the Germans) to the north. There was an anachronistically graceful former-monastery courtyard, overgrown, but with a sweeping outdoor staircase. In the neighborhood—what I would learn to call the "quartier"—there were workshops, not shops: a bookbinder, a violin maker, two botanists producing "snail dirt," a guitar maker, a one-room pastry "factory," a radio station, and a puzzle club. One street over, Arabic was the principal language, and three women, their heads covered, were fetching water from an archaic faucet, bearing large buckets.

There was also—on the square, the Place Sathonay—a porn shop, park benches occupied by drunks, drug deals (I saw one, Jessica two), a prostitute, graffiti on most surfaces, dog shit everywhere. At a playground, sparkly with bits of broken glass, we watched small children hitting each other. I had a picture, tingling in my brain like an unpleasant laceration, of our progeny, not quite three years old, here, in a foreign country, struggling to express themselves, and learning how to fight with their fists—a bleeding lip, a broken nose.

Our building had a plaque over the door: It was where the end of World War II was announced and celebrated. It had been built in the nineteenth century and had extravagantly high ceilings. You could see the midget Eiffel Tower from several windows. You could study *La Fresque des Lyonnais* from a balcony. You could watch the flow of the river Saône.

It was everything a future resident of the city could hope for. It seemed to play out what our future life in Lyon might be. It also made me very uncomfortable.

The apartment echoed. It had a kitchen but nothing in it: no oven, no stove top, no dishwasher. There was no washing machine or dryer. There were no light fixtures, or curtains, or doormat. In France, renters carry their stuff, all their stuff, piggyback to their new residence. We were going to have to buy everything. Finally, it seemed like too much.

I had just wanted a stint somewhere in a restaurant to learn how to cook French. Moving to Lyon: It was a bigger choice. Should we be selling our apartment in New York? The lease called for a six-month security deposit (because we were foreigners) and a six-month notice to terminate (because we were foreigners).

Jessica, meanwhile, was admiring the apartment's marble fireplaces (six of them), the view of the river, the bedrooms (four), the bathrooms (three), the vast living room, the antique wooden shutters, and the breezes that blew crosswise when you opened them.

I was mentally compiling a list of what we needed (including a new computer—since the voltage was different in France, no?—and a printer), plus beds and cribs and toys and rugs and a table for breakfast, and a television, and had just reached the conclusion that, no, this whole moving-to-France thing was, alas, mathematically impossible, when I overheard Jessica tell the agent, in French, "Thank you, it's perfect, we'll take it. *N'est-ce pas,* Bill?"

"We will?" I blurted.

She ignored me. She was looking through the window and asking if what she saw was a school.

Once Jessica reconfirmed our commitment ("Don't worry about my husband"), and was promised a lease before the end of the week, she then led me outside to investigate "that school."

It had been built in 1908, and was called L'École Robert Doisneau, after the legendary photographer, famous for the smoochy kiss shots in the Paris streets. He was also accomplished at capturing the poetry of children's faces, and many of *those* photos adorned the classroom walls.

The semester was about to start, and the principal happened to be in her office, the only one there besides a custodian. She introduced herself as "Brigitte" (no "Madame," no *vous,* no last name), and when Jessica, not wasting the chance, asked if places could be found for our twin boys, aged almost three, she said, "Absolutely," and put them in the class roster, just like that. There was no question of tuition because we now had residency visas. It was free, although we would have to register at *la mairie,* the quartier's mayor's office, when we returned. She then assigned them cubbyholes to put their things in and invited us in so that we could help the boys find them on their first day, in two weeks.

I thought: Two weeks?

In the morning, we checked out of the hotel and caught an early flight, feeling outright pleased with ourselves, having completed a remarkably productive visit. We had an apartment. We had enrolled our boys in a school. And I probably had a kitchen.

The next day, September 10, we had nothing.

Another party had seen the apartment before us—the broker was sorry, a colleague had handled the visit—and they had taken it. Like that: We'd had it. Like that: It was gone.

And Marc Veyrat's surgery failed. He would close the restaurant.

At nine o'clock, by which time I had fled and disappeared into an office at *The New Yorker,* my wife, jetlagged and unshowered, was surprised by the arrival of two Jack & Jill teachers at our door.

At midday we conferred: Now what? Lyon now seemed very far away.

Jessica bought the boys urgent school supplies.

Undeterred, I embarked on a long-overdue urgent French-language education and engaged a native speaker for private lessons—Arlette, a wiry bohemian figure with a cigarette-raspy voice and a blunt manner.

Midway through our second week, only my fifth lesson, I had a precocious breakthrough. I'd thrown myself into telling a story with a punch line.

Arlette listened intently, chin on her palm, nodding. "That was interesting," she said.

"Thank you."

"I think I understood most of it."

"Rough?" I had issues with pronunciation, but in the telling, I'd experienced a metaphysical grammatical clarity of some kind.

"The difficulty, for me, is that I don't speak Italian." I must have looked confused. "You didn't know that you were speaking Italian?"

On September 24, the day our boys turned three, students at the Jack & Jill preschool, our new normalcy, Jessica received an e-mail from the rental agency in Lyon. The deal for the apartment had fallen through. The property was available. It was ours, *if* Jessica returned to Lyon by September 30, signed the lease, made the deposit, and concluded an inventory of the apartment before midnight.

Were we interested?

Well, yes! No! Yes, of course!

On September 29, Jessica left me and the boys behind, took an all-night flight, arrived in Lyon at 7:00 a.m., met with a banker at 9:30 to arrange the deposit, appeared at the Realtor's office at 11:00 to sign deeds in multiples, ate lunch at 12:00, conducted an exhaustive inventory of the apartment (e.g., "one cracked electrical socket plate under the second window of the first bedroom"), and by the end of the French workday phoned me to say that she'd done it. Her voice betrayed spent adrenaline. It echoed against the walls of the apartment. She had the keys. The apartment was empty, but ours.

We were moving to Lyon. We hadn't told our families, or our children, or their teachers, or the magazine where I worked. We hadn't told anyone. But it was a fact: We were moving to France.

Jessica returned to Lyon a month later, the beginning of November, to get our apartment ready for dwelling in. Jessica, who loathes shopping, was self-dispatched to acquire, well, everything: appliances, computers, IKEA furniture, light fixtures. . . .

I went to a dark office, my windowless cubicle at *The New Yorker*, wrote out verb conjugations, and read Brillat-Savarin.

Brillat-Savarin is the author of three books, but only one matters. *The book is (probably) the first book about food that isn't about how to* make it but how to *think* about it. It is referred to as *The Physiology of Taste,* but this excludes the subtitle. To wit: *Meditations on a Transcendental Gastronomy, a work of theory, history and topicality dedicated to the Parisian gastronomes by a professor and member of several literary and scholarly societies.*

The "professor" referred to, incidentally, is the author. He wasn't a professor. He was called "the professor" by people who suffered his pontifications. He was a lawyer in a small town (Belley, population two thousand at the time, sixty-five miles east of Lyon, on the river Rhône, at the foot of the Alps, once the idyllic home of Gertrude Stein and Alice B. Toklas). He was also a member of an amateur orchestra, a deputy to the National Assembly during the French Revolution, subsequently an exile in flight fearing execution, a violin teacher on New York's Lower East Side, and an inventor of culinary aphorisms.

Like: "Tell me what you eat and I will tell you what you are."

Or: "A dessert without cheese is like a beautiful woman with only one eye."

The difficulty of the book, which Brillat-Savarin worked on for three decades (and died just before it was published in 1826), was that it is pretty tough going. Every time I tried to read it, I gave up. (Why is no one else saying this? In the two-hundred-year history of this book, am I really the only one who finds it to be a slog?)

But this time, on the eve of my French future, I pressed on, and the second part was simpler and clearer and a revelation. There are many passages worth thinking about, but, studying the book in my Manhattan corporate-office space, I was struck by an appealingly pastoral account. It describes a meal that Brilliat-Savarin ate at a monastery on an isolated plateau high in the mountains, after a hearty all-night walk from his home, in the summer of 1782, when he was twenty-seven years old. It is a poignant recollection, written long after the event. I now refer to it as "The Walk" and have read and reread it as though it were a poem.

I located the monastery. It is not far from Lyon. It is now a ruin.

The monastery was among the first items on a to-do list that I would then begin compiling. Brillat-Savarin had walked there from Belley. I wanted to see what he saw. It was a small thing, but a first thing. I was imagining a life in France.

Meanwhile, Jessica, dealing with our prospective life there on a more practical level, had bought toilet seats, studied up on gas BTUs of stove-top burners, nailed the measurements of the space we had for a refrigerator, and become an expert on flat-screen televisions. I had never owned a flat-screen TV. I coveted one, even if we would mainly be watching *Scooby-Doo*. The boys would like the television for how it connected them to the United States, and they eventually watched only the English-language stations, studying them for phrasings that American children used and then trying them out on their parents.

In the evenings, Jessica began investigating the eateries. One night, she joined an American friend of a friend, Jenny Gilbert, who introduced her to a brasserie run by Paul Bocuse. "It is where the musicians eat because it's open late." Jenny is the first violinist in the National Orchestra of Lyon. The city, Jessica had discovered, hummed in the key of Fauré and had more violin makers (artisanal shops, one person, rarely two, instruments hanging from a rafter) than she had seen in her life. Jenny would be one of three English-language speakers, two Americans and one Liverpudlian, who became how-to-live-in-Lyon coaches. (And the food at the Bocuse brasserie? I asked. "I had sole *meunière*," Jessica said—the famous flat fish served with brown butter and a squeeze of lemon, famously simple provided that the timing is flawless—"and it was exquisite.")

I visited Daniel Boulud at his New York restaurant, an overdue expression of gratitude.

That first time I had met Boulud was in 1995, not long after he opened Daniel, his first restaurant. It is now called Café Boulud, a name inspired by the village "café" that his family had once run out of its home. Boulud's parents are peasant farmers. In 1995, Daniel didn't seem like much of a peasant. He was a Frenchman at ease among New York City's power players—effortlessly charming, always on, meticulously presented—and the food he made could be counted on to satisfy an expectation of what a French meal should be, a special occasion, a performance piece, perfect.

The Boulud I met now was a citizen of Lyon. He seemed so different I wondered if he deliberately kept his Lyonnais side hidden. I felt a new comradeship.

"Mathieu Viannay," he was saying. "You must meet Mathieu. Write that down. Younger chef, very Lyonnais, the future. He just reopened La Mère Brazier—last week, in fact." He shouted to an assistant to produce a phone number. "You know about La Mère Brazier, no?"

I nodded. Its reopening had been talked about when we were there.

"You went to Vienne?"

"Vienne?"

"South of Lyon? You were in a hurry. For La Pyramide."

"Of course, the famous." It was said to be the birthplace of modern French cooking.

"When you return, you will go to Vienne. *D'accord?*" He called out to his assistant to add La Pyramide to a list.

"Mionnay," Boulud said, accelerating. "For Alain Chapel. I used to stop there on my way home. When I worked for Georges Blanc. Oh. Bill should know Georges, *non?*" he shouted to his assistant.

"Orsi," he said next.

"Orsi?"

"Pierre Orsi. And Nandron, of course."

"Nandron?"

"Nandron."

I asked him to spell it.

"You don't know Nandron?" He stared at me to see if I was joking. "*C'est vrai?* I don't believe you."

No, I confessed, and made a note to investigate.

"Nandron is very important. Two stars. Two-star restaurants belong to the town. It's where the locals go. Three stars belong to the rest of the world." (Nandron died in 2000, and was in fact very important to Boulud: His restaurant was the first place Boulud worked, at age fourteen.)

"You know about the Bocuse d'Or?"

I didn't know about the Bocuse d'Or.

"You will. I'll be over for it. In January. With the American team."

He mentioned societies, journalists, a member of the city council, a money guy. . . . "Write down the money guy for Bill."

"A money guy? You mean an investor type?"

"You never know."

The list was three pages. Who had I heard of? Almost no one. I wondered: Will there be a time when I will know everyone?

Jessica returned the following evening. We had designated it as the night when we would break the news.

We summoned our children for a family meeting and gathered on our bed. We had never had a family meeting. We had never gathered on the bed.

I set a globe in the middle. We sat around it cross-legged.

"We have an announcement," I said.

I showed them where we lived, a spot on the East Coast of North America. I introduced the idea of hemispheres and continents, and invited them to imagine that my finger was an airplane flying over a large blue-green expanse. "This is the Atlantic Ocean," I said. "This is Europe. This is England, where I once lived. This is Italy, where we once spent a summer vacation with your cousins. And this is France. Do you see it?" The boys leaned in close. "*And* near the bottom of France, between the mountains and the sea, is the city of Lyon. Do you see it? This is where we are going to move to."

George leapt off the bed, tipping over the globe, and dashed out of the room. We could hear him in his closet. He returned, dragging behind him a small yellow plastic carry-on SpongeBob suitcase.

"I am ready to start packing!"

We were leaving soon, I explained, in about two weeks, and he didn't need to pack this very minute.

"We can't leave now? Oh, please, can we? Can we?"

No, I said.

He fell to the floor, as if the bones in his little body had been made of string, and wailed.

I don't know the best age for moving to another country with your children. Maybe any age is a good age. But age three might be perfect. Or maybe it was that, at age three, the child has no idea what he or she is about to get into: And that ignorance is what's perfect.

By a happy coincidence, I won an Italian literary prize and was invited to Rome to receive it on December 17. We now had a plan. Jessica would fly once more to Lyon without us, on Monday, December 8, to prepare our new home. The boys and I would follow, leaving on Friday, December 12, the day they finished their semester at Jack & Jill, and the family would spend its first French weekend together. On Monday, we would confirm that the boys still had a place at l'École Robert Doisneau, even though they hadn't been seen, register them at *la mairie,* and fly off the next morning for a three-day, expenses-paid sojourn in Rome, the beginning of our European life. We would have Christmas in our new home.

The eve of Jessica's departure, we held a party for friends. We drank an imperial of Le Pergole Torte, a festive but not exactly apposite wine from Tuscany, and said goodbye. We would be back by Labor Day, I said, for the new school year. In the event, we *did* return on Labor Day—not nine months later, but four years and nine months later. Jessica was animated, she was buzzy—the radicalness of it all, our next life, this life, whatever it was going to be, our nextness.

Once she was gone, I started packing. On Thursday morning, I had a mischievous thought. I could get a babysitter. And then, with the boys looked after, I could slip off to Washington, D.C., to say goodbye to Richard.

I got there in the afternoon. We ate, we drank, we talked food. Actually, I have no idea what we talked about. We were two friends hanging out.

In Lyon, he reminded me, I would learn French with a Lyonnais accent. He pronounced *"beurre,"* butter, with an extended guttural quadruple *"rrrr."*

In Lyon, I would meet Paul Bocuse.

"You will meet Bobosse—a friend of Monsieur Paul. Oh, and that's the other thing, in Lyon everyone calls him Monsieur Paul."

He pondered.

"You will meet Jean-Paul Lacombe, of course. What's his restaurant?"

I said nothing.

"Lyon de Lyon? No, Léon de Lyon. I met his father, too. Jean Lacombe. All the chefs in Lyon are the children of chefs. You will discover that, too."

He said: "In Lyon, you will be introduced to the community of Lyonnais chefs. It is like nowhere else in the world."

I felt close. I was grateful. I now thought: I couldn't have had a better first teacher.

"Oh, Michel, please excuse me, I've got to get to the station." Without my realizing, the hour had got late. It was nearly nine o'clock. The last train was at nine-thirty. The babysitter had her own children to go home to.

I made to leave, shoving everything into my bag, making haste.

"I will drive you," Richard said.

"No, no, no, really. I'll get a taxi."

"I insist."

This was a bad idea.

"It is our last evening together."

"You are right," I said.

Richard's car was in a garage basement. I waited outside. (I really should have taken a taxi.) His vehicle emerged, a long black thing. I got in. There was a pinging sound. Richard carried on with his Lyonnais riff. "How in Lyon everyone makes a *pâté-en-croûte.* And their charcuterie. There was a woman famous for it. What was her name? Sybil? And the other one, known for her cheese? Mère Richard. That's it. Like me!" Other names came to him, or didn't, and the more people he mentioned, the more his sense of urgency seemed to drain away. He stopped early for a red light.

David had told me about such moments. When Richard tells stories, he forgets that he is driving. He is the only person I know who has been ticketed, *often,* for going too slow. Once, he and David drove to New York from Washington. As they talked, Richard drove more and more slowly, until they both became worried about the time. "We should have arrived by now," Richard said. At last, the city came into view, but when they reached it they discovered it wasn't New York. It was Philadelphia. "Oh là là!" Richard said, laughing at himself. They carried on. Talking, talking. After another two hours, they finally reached New York. Except it wasn't New York. It was again Philadelphia. "For two hours," David said, "we had been driving in circles."

It was now nine-fifteen. What was that pinging?

"Michel," I said, "what is that noise?"

"What is *that* noise? Oh, it's my gas. That's the noise the car makes when my gas is low. Oh. I didn't know it was that low. What time is your train?"

I told him again.

We stopped for gas.

It was nine-twenty-one.

"You know, I really have to pee-pee," he said.

He went off to pee-pee.

I rehearsed the two scenarios. In one, I exit Richard's car—bag ready, ticket in hand, fly—and I make the train. In the other, I don't.

I contemplated the consequences. What does a babysitter do when the derelict father doesn't come home?

Richard returned to the car. It was nine-twenty-three.

We pulled up to the station. I kissed Michel, I said goodbye. I had sixty seconds. I made it.

It was after midnight when I got home.

The next day, Friday, was our last day in New York.

I woke early, wondering: How do you pack for forever? How many socks?

I used every container with a handle or a strap—every Rollaboard, carry-on rucksack, duffel, even a nylon sleeping-bag storage bag—and thought: I'm going to get killed on the extra-baggage charges. In the event, the high cost wasn't the luggage. It was that, by the time we reached the airport, our plane had taken off, and the three seats that we had purchased on it had left New York City unoccupied.

I leaned heavily atop the check-in desk, having confirmed that our airplane was somewhere in the vicinity of Newfoundland and that, no, its being the Christmas season, there were no other flights tonight or tomorrow. The first available one was Sunday. My two children hung limply onto my knees; Frederick had just been horribly carsick. I had to accept that we were returning to our New York City apartment. I summoned the courage to phone Jessica, waiting for us in Lyon, to inform her that, well, there had been a delay. "Actually, not a delay. We missed the flight."

Once again, the empty sounds of an empty apartment, except that this time it seemed especially empty, a loud echo chamber of emptinesses, the hollowness of a heart in pain. My wife's voice was different. Something in it I hadn't heard before. Fear. The fear was basic. It was her husband. She was in Lyon, alone, because of him. She was there, with-out her children, because of him. She was in this—how to describe?—unplanned, dysfunctional, erratically impulsive, obstacle course of a life: because of him. What I was hearing, there amid higher ethereal notes of mounting panic, was that the real mistake, the very basic mistake, was her marriage.

The phone call was, for both of us, a big moment.

We had, only six months before, experienced another big moment, a very *positive* one, the aforementioned most profound and consequential exchange in our married life. This one was not positive, and would never be positive, and could not retrospectively be reconfigured in our nostal-gic imaginations as positive "in its way" or "not so bad, really," or even "funny." This was the nadir of our married life.

Nadir: I'd never used the word before. But here I was. At the nadir.

In fact, we weren't.

Lyon with Twin Toddlers

"How can you love Lyon?"

Ungracious question!

It is true that our town is not easy to love. It is an acquired taste. Almost a vice. No place in the world is less accommodating to tourists. The visitor finds nothing to look at and nothing to do. Like others, we have admirable and worthy monuments. But it must be conceded that the Lyonnais soul feels only a weak attachment to them. And the "views" themselves—the dome of the Hôtel-Dieu, reigning in all its dreary grandeur over the eternal Rhône; the Saône near Bellecour, its footbridges drawn in ink over the green-gold water; the whole pale silver city that peeks through the smoke—leave us indifferent, a banal daily décor, and we pay no more attention to them than to the immense industrial noise.

HENRI BÉRAUD, *VOUS NE CONNAISSEZ PAS MON PAYS (YOU DON'T KNOW MY COUNTRY)*, 1944, TRANSLATED BY JESSICA GREEN

We arrived on Monday. Frederick had a stomach virus, George had a fever, and their father wasn't in particularly top form. Jessica's plans—a family lunch out, Saturday and Sunday at the market on the *quai,* shopping for a Christmas tree (she had even arranged an English-speaking babysitter, a robust, strapping Lyonnais named Stephen, so that we might slip out for a romantic evening)—were for naught, because, she informed us, most of Lyon closes on Mondays. We ate a sandwich bought at a Casino, a chain food store, and napped, and woke too late to check in with the school. There was never a chance of getting to *la mairie* with the boys' passports. Besides, we had an early morning flight to Rome. We didn't miss it. We arrived five minutes before the gate closed. We sprinted.

Our return flight, the Friday before Christmas, left in the morning so we had a chance of getting back while the school was still open. There was a snowstorm. We arrived, late, just before the airport closed, and Lyon, a historically Catholic metropolis, observed the holidays by a nearly three-week-long, universally observed celebration, in which it did nothing. It was already locked up: restaurants (where I might have introduced myself to chefs), government offices (like *la mairie,* the mayor's office), and of course the schools.

The apartment was cold, at least to us, New Yorkers obviously too long acclimated to being overheated.

Frederick, who looked frail and pale, was in remarkably good cheer, sitting on our new IKEA sofa in front of the black unconnected television (the cable company was also closed). He took in the dimensions of our new IKEA living room and, sensing our new isolation, innocently asked, "Where are all the friends?"

"I don't know," I said.

The next morning, I took the boys to a café for a Lyonnais version of what had been our custom in New York City, a Saturday breakfast. The boys ordered hot chocolate, their habit, and asked for extra sugar, also their habit. The waiter snorted and returned with a pair of cubes that looked distinctly secondhand. They had been gathered up from the ones left behind on coffee saucers and reassembled into a used wrapper to form a pair.

Afterward, I proposed that we visit the indoor market, Les Halles de Lyon Paul Bocuse, on the other side of the Rhône River.

We took a taxi. The boys and I climbed into the back seat. The drive was five minutes. The fare was seven euros. I had a ten-euro note. The driver took it and made change, and just as I was about to tell him to keep it, he hit Frederick.

Frederick had put his dinky Velcro-secured footwear on the seat—short, pudgy three-year-old legs, tiny feet, little rolled-up white socks.

"Don't put your feet on my seat," the driver said, and thwacked the boy, twice: once on each shin, with the back of his hand (the one bearing a wedding ring).

I stepped out and took in what I'd just seen: a man, this stranger, pausing before completing a financial transaction in order to hit my child.

I searched for words, while securing my children on the sidewalk, and put my head back into the car to tell the driver, in my best possible French, that he must never (*jamais!*), ever touch (*toucher*) my child (*mon fils*) or I would rip the eyeballs out of his fat sockets and eat them.

Actually, I have no idea what I said.

"Merci, monsieur. Merci beaucoup!" He smiled and drove off.

I got a Christmas tree, a straggler (a brittle-needled, crisply dehydrated, abandoned loser-stump), Jessica bought candles, and I set out to procure a festive bird. I found nothing. No goose or turkey or duck. Every fowl had been bought. I settled on what I concluded was the city's last capon, a massive twenty-plus-pound neutered rooster, my first food transaction, a brutal piece of business with a butcher, in which he kept saying *"Quand?"*—"When?"—an utterly basic word that, in the urgency of the exchange, I kept failing to understand. (*"Quand?" "Quoi?" "Quand?" "Pardon?" "Quand, pour quand?"* "Oh, I get it. *Pour quand!* Now?")

On Christmas Eve, the four of us gathered around a small table in the kitchen, the only warm room in the apartment—a gusty black night, with candles that wouldn't stay lit—and I carved a bird that could have fed twenty-five people.

George, having become fascinated by the head—the first time that he had seen a bird with one attached—ate it and nothing else. I have an image, of his working his teeth around the beak and chewing on the wattle, his eyes dark with sleepless circles.

It got colder. We turned up the thermostat.

It was broken, we realized, which was immaterial, since the plumbers weren't working.

We isolated a hissing gale sound—not through the beautiful fireplaces (where we were forbidden by law from lighting fires), but via a crack between two large doorlike windows—easy enough to repair if we had a repairman to call.

Christmas morning happened. (No memory.) New Year's Eve happened. (No memory.) New Year's Day happened. (No memory.)

I got ill. Lungs. Phlegm. An infection.

Jessica got ill. Lungs. Worse. Pneumonia.

We summoned SOS Médecins, a house-call doctor service. It cost 120 euros, because we had no health coverage in France. Until we registered with the prefecture, we didn't exist in the eyes of the government. (The prefecture was also closed.) It was a long Christmas vacation. We fought. We were waiting for Thursday, January 8, the day when the schools reopened. We were waiting to learn if it was *their* school.

And if it was no longer their school? I asked. They were three months late.

Jessica was unusually confident. She'd had a bonding moment with the principal. Could you really enroll children on a feeling? Their places were being held (*if* they were being held) on nothing more than their

first names. (First names and a feeling?) At a playground on the *quai,*
I met parents, also newcomers to Lyon, who had tried to enroll their
child in the same school and been rejected because there was no more
room. Had a child been turned away owing to our no-show toddlers?

On the day of the school's reopening, we set out nervously. The principal, Brigitte, was at the top of the steps. She recognized Jessica instantly.
"Voilà les garçons!" she declared.

The mutual relief—hers, ours, but especially ours—felt like an enormous exhale. We felt airborne. We could have been balloons. Brigitte
led the boys to their cubbyholes. She was very excited. No one in the
school had met a New Yorker before. (The effect would eventually make
the boys celebrities. They were *les New-Yorkais.*)

Brigitte mentioned the canteen.

(Yes!)

But not yet, she said.

(What?)

It is raucous. It is noisy. Too much for now. "It would be better if *les
garçons* ate at home."

(Me: I love the idea of a raucous canteen. Why would we want to
interrupt our day to feed our children?)

This was terrible news.

The weekday home lunch is an honorable practice, a testament to the
importance that France attaches to mealtime, and in our building, all
families with children prepared lunch: The mother (usually) picked up
the children, and the father (often) came home from work, stopping
first at the local boulangerie for baguettes. At one-forty-five, the children returned. Ours refused. Every day, they refused. Demonstrably,
tearfully, implacably.

They liked home. They liked speaking English. They didn't understand French. (Agnès, their teacher, asked Jessica: *"Qu'est-ce que c'est le
mot 'potty'?* Every day your boys say, 'Excuse me, I need to potty.' What
is potty?")

It became my task, the indifferent patriarch, to take both boys under
my arms, and march them back.

"The lunches," Jessica said, "aren't working."

"They suck."

"But it's what good French mothers do."

"You're not French."

"I've got to get them into the canteen."

Jessica met with Brigitte and, like that, the boys were enrolled. And, like that, our lives began.

We had been in Lyon for a month. Finally, I could address why I'd come: to find a kitchen to work in.

WORK

One might ask how to reconcile the Lyonnais cult of good eating with their aversion to spending? Because finally nothing is more onerous than being a gourmand, if one is constant in the pursuit.

The answer lies in the common Lyonnais sayings: "skimping on the roast is a fool's savings," "the mouth comes before all else," or "the bottom of the bottle is for quitters."

HENRI BÉRAUD, *VOUS NE CONNAISSEZ PAS MON PAYS*

(*YOU DON'T KNOW MY COUNTRY*), 1944,

TRANSLATED BY JESSICA GREEN

La Mère Brazier was *the* place. I knew it ever since Boulud had mentioned it, in the very tradition of nineteenth-century *mère* chefs that Jean-Georges had referred to—*nos saintes mères*. They had all started as cooks in the grand homes of local industrialists, preparing *cuisine bourgeoise*—in effect, home cooking for a family with pretensions—become famous in their own right, and then struck out on their own.

Eugénie Brazier was, in many respects, a prototype *mère*. She was one of nine children, born in 1895 in the Dombes, the flat wetlands between Lyon and the Alps, and on a swampy peasant farm not far from Bourg-en-Bresse (where the famous chickens come from). At the age of five, Brazier looked after the animals—pigs first, then graduated to cows. When she was ten, her mother died (childbirth). At nineteen, Brazier was pregnant by a married man in the village; bore a son, Gaston; was banished by her father; and found employment in Lyon as a *nourrice* (wet nurse) in a bourgeois family called the Milliats and, in time,

as their cook. The Milliats were wealthy—they ran a pasta factory—
and their wealth made them gastronomes (because an appreciation of
food was how wealthy Lyonnais expressed high culture) and regulars of
the greatest of all the *mères,* Mère Fillioux. When Fillioux later asked
the Milliats if they could recommend a cook to help in her increasingly
busy restaurant, they proposed their own Eugénie.

There is no record of Brazier's contribution to the restaurant (she
was too embarrassed by her spelling ever to write), except that it is said
Fillioux grew jealous of her talent (when Brazier made the traditional
Sunday lunch for the staff, *"un civet de lapin,"* a rich rabbit stew, Fillioux made the mistake of asking whose was better—hers or Brazier's),
and they parted company. Brazier never married but had a companion,
Le Père, a chauffeur for one of the bourgeois families, and with his help
secured a ground-floor corner space of what had originally been an
eighteenth-century town house on the rue Royale. She opened for business on April 19, 1921. In 1928, she opened a second restaurant, without
water, electricity, or gas, in Luère, in the woods west of Lyon.

Brazier—in her prime, a hefty woman with exceptionally strong shoulders and powerful forearms, famously photographed in front of a steaming pot—had a reputation for being formidable and fearsome. There are
stories, which everyone enjoys repeating, of her intolerance of mistakes
and how she humiliated those who made them, especially Gaston, her
illegitimate son, who had the misfortune of always having to be by her
side in a kitchen from before he could walk. In 1933, she became not
only the first female chef to be awarded three Michelin stars but also the
first chef, male or female, to get three Michelin stars for two restaurants
at the same time, a feat that wouldn't be repeated for decades. La Mère
Brazier was the city's greatest restaurant—it said "Lyon" like no other
eating establishment—and then it closed, in 2007, and the city went
into culinary mourning.

Mathieu Viannay's reopening it was a big deal. Viannay himself was
probably a big deal—I didn't know (Boulud called him "the future of
Lyon")—and it was an urgent first piece of business for me to get over
there (the restaurant was on the other side of the Presqu'île from our
apartment, the Rhône side, a ten-minute walk). I wasn't the only one:
By then, everyone wanted to eat his food, because, one month after we

arrived in Lyon, the Michelin Guide had (exceptionally, flamboyantly) awarded him *two* stars. The normal practice was to make chefs climb the Michelin ladder. Even Paul Bocuse began with one star. It wasn't unprecedented, to start with two, but it was rare and, in the institutional parlance of the guide, an expression of high flattery.

I brought along a French edition of the book I had written about the Italian kitchen. We met him at the door. He asked if he could give us a tour.

The downstairs was divided into dining rooms. One had a chandelier. The message was "cozy." The bar had tables, too, and was brightly lit, with a white tile floor and leaded windows, stylishly 1930s—evocative of a heyday in Lyonnais cooking, when France had discovered the automobile and the meals that you could eat only by driving to the outposts where they were served. The kitchen—with noisy wooden stairs that led to the next floor—was anachronistic and unmodern, cooks standing at attention, the *brigade,* packed tightly together, staring at us. There was no microwave or vacuum sealer or sous-vide water bath or dehydrator. There were pots.

"*Les mères,*" Viannay explained, "were *the* experts at the local dishes." They were their own subculture, sharing among themselves a literature of tattered *mère* cookbooks. In 2002, Stéphane Gaborieau, then the chef at the Villa Florentine (originally a seventeenth-century convent, at the top of a hill in Vieux Lyon), bought a handwritten example from the 1850s at a book stall on the *quai* and produced a facsimile local best seller: ninety-seven pages, written out in an ancient, flourishingly beautiful script describing how to make dishes (quenelles, tripe, kidney, the chickens from Bresse) that you find in Lyon today.

Viannay was fortyish, trim (in the way that many Frenchmen are and Americans are normally not), and wore well-made English brogues, blue jeans, and a chef's jacket with sleeves that opened capaciously around the wrists, like bell-bottoms for the arms. He had heavy eyebrows, a flop of dark-going-slightly-silver hair (it fell into his face and was long in the back, French rocker style), and a five-day beard. His manner was grace and courtesy. He had nothing but time for us.

He led us upstairs and directed us to "the private dining rooms"—originally small low-ceilinged bedrooms overlooking the street—that were meant for family meals, especially on Sundays, another *mère* tradition, in which you were fed as though at your home—at least the fantasy high bourgeois version.

"You have children?" he asked us. "This is where you will bring them. You will eat *poulet de Bresse.*"

I pictured George and Frederick, pushing open the window and throwing drumsticks on pedestrians below, and thought: Nah, not anytime soon.

Our meal included two items that had been served in this very building for nearly a hundred years: an artichoke with foie gras (the artichoke, a famously Italian vegetable, was a local food in Lyon) and the breast of the Bresse chicken. I know they were delicious, I have eaten both many times since, but I wasn't tasting them. I was anxious. This, clearly, was where I should work.

Afterward, Viannay stood by the door, thanking diners. In manner, he seemed unconventional, anti-form, un-French, but there was a guardedness in his person. The restaurant had been open only three months when it got its stars. The feeling there wasn't celebratory; it was astonishment that Viannay was getting away with it.

I told him my story, what I wanted to do (to train to be a French chef), and gave him my book.

"I would like to do a *stage* in your kitchen," I said.

He looked at me.

"I would like to be a *stagiaire,*" I said, clarifying the expression.

Viannay looked at the book in his hand. It puzzled him.

"Italian cooking," he said. It wasn't a question. It was more like a discovery.

"Yes, Italian cooking." I mentioned *The New Yorker*.

He smiled, an odd half-smile, somewhere between amusement and sneer.

"I should sign it," I said, grabbed and autographed it with the exaggeratedly flamboyant flourish of someone who had nervously drunk too much Côtes du Rhône. I handed it back.

He stared at my dedication.

I waited.

He smiled that smile.

I thanked him. I shook his hand. I thanked him again. I bowed, and shuffled, and said goodbye.

Later, walking home, I asked Jessica, "'Mathieu' is not spelled with two 't's, is it?"

"No. In French, there is only one 't.'"

"Of course. I knew that."

The following night, following Boulud's advice, we went to Vienne, twenty miles south of Lyon. La Pyramide, once the home of the legendary Fernand Point, was Plan B.

————

The Financial Operations of the House of Point always mystified his friends, since he uses only the finest ingredients, yet charges prices lower than those of most high-class restaurants in Paris. His friends agree that Point might have gone bankrupt long ago but for his wife. "Mado" Point acts as a maître d'hôtel, purchasing agent, wine taster, cashier, house physician, confidential secretary, and chronicler. Someday, she hopes, she will collect her husband's recipes and put them in a book for posterity's sake. This won't be easy. M. Point takes a dim view of the printed word.

JOSEPH WECHSBERG, "THE FINEST BUTTER AND LOTS OF TIME,"
THE NEW YORKER, SEPTEMBER 3, 1949

VIENNE. I knew enough to know that, to any student of the French kitchen, La Pyramide was not Plan B material. For chefs, it has a house-of-worship status. It is the "Temple." The name, *la pyramide,* came from a Roman statue at the end of the street—it marks the place where chariot races were held (Vienne is said to have more Roman ruins per square meter than any town in France)—and the ancient, vaguely pagan iconography seems to have enhanced the restaurant's metaphysical pull. You would be hard-pressed to find a serious French chef who hasn't been there.

Its fame was the achievement of Fernand Point, and his restaurant was, in Curnonsky's day, the greatest restaurant in the whole Rhône Valley ("which every Lyonnais knows") *and* in all of France *and* among the very best in the world. Curnonsky, whose actual name was Maurice Edmond Sailland (he arrived at "Curnonsky" by combining a school nickname, *Cur Non?*—Latin slang for "Why not?"—with an aristocratic-sounding Slavic suffix), was a critic and historian. Until the 1950s, no one, in matters of French food, had more authority. It was Curnonsky who described Lyon as the "gastronomic capital of the world."

In 1949, the Czech-American journalist Joseph Wechsberg—who had been told by Parisian friends, "If I wanted to have the epicurean experience of my life . . . I would have to go to Vienne"—spent a day with the great chef. Point, in Wechsberg's description, was massive—six foot three, and three hundred pounds (others say he was closer to four hundred)—impressively at ease with his size, appearing in a capacious black suit and big silk bow tie with a flowery design, began each day with a magnum of champagne, and regarded butter, *lots* of butter, as an essential ingredient in a well-prepared dish ("Butter! Give me butter! Always butter!"). He also harbored a lifelong prejudice against skinny chefs, and was, in both bearing and sway, a fleshy illustration of the expression "larger than life." He was not, alas, stronger than it, and, six years after Wechsberg's visit, Point was felled, like many other chefs of his generation, in his fifties (at fifty-eight in Point's case).

His "art"—Curnonsky's word—continued in the hands of others, principally those of "Mado," the nickname of Point's widow, Marie-Louise Point. Indirectly, his art was continued by the cooks in his kitchen. Many came to be associated with nouvelle cuisine in the 1970s. Point is credited with being the movement's "godfather."

Patrick Henriroux is now the Pyramide chef. His name had also been on Boulud's contact list, just below Mathieu Viannay's. He joined us at the beginning of our dinner. Fernand and Mado had a daughter, Marie-José, he said, who had been prepared to sell the restaurant to a chef who understood her parents' legacy and had the wherewithal to continue it.

She asked Paul Bocuse. (Bocuse had worked for Point.) He said no.

She asked Alain Chapel, another former member of La Pyramide's *brigade*. He said no.

She asked Michel Guérard, the unequivocal genius of nouvelle cuisine. He said no.

She asked Alain Ducasse: No. Marc Veyrat: No. She asked every three-star chef in France.

"It was Point's reputation," Henriroux said. "No one wanted to be measured against it."

She approached the two-star chefs. Finally she asked Henriroux, then running the one-star kitchen of La Ferme de Mougins, in the south of France. Henriroux accepted the challenge, because, well, *"Cur non?"*

He began in 1989. He got his first star seven months later. He tried to buy the restaurant but was turned down. Two years later, he got his second star. By then he had the support of the locals (supporting Boulud's belief that two-star restaurants belong to the town), and, when the restaurant was in financial trouble, they supported him in his purchase. Now, fifteen years later, he has paid off the loan.

He asked us what we would like for dinner.

I wanted to try the *poularde en vessie.* I'd read about it in Point's *Ma Gastronomie,* which includes letters, details of the guests (Colette, Charles de Gaulle, Pablo Picasso, Édith Piaf), aphorisms (e.g., "In the orchestra of a grand kitchen, the saucier is the soloist"), and what is sometimes referred to as a "kitchen bible," a collection of all its recipes. Point's is understated in the extreme. Any instruction so specific as to mention, say, a measurement or a cooking temperature seems so arbitrary as to read like a mistake ("Take five liters of blood from Menon's animals, after they have spent the last month eating his pears").

I gave Henriroux my order. A *vessie* is a bladder. I had never eaten food cooked in a bladder.

Henriroux grimaced. "You have to be very hungry."

I assured him of my appetite.

"It is the whole chicken. It's a *poularde.*"

"I love *poularde,*" I said. I had no idea what a *poularde* might be.

(A *poularde* is a bird more than a year old; a *poussin,* less than six months; a *poulet,* more than six months. It's the Eskimo rule: In Lyon, there are many words for birds, including the generic one, *volailles,* which means "flying things.")

Henriroux persisted—"It takes a long time to cook"—and, as I was about to play along ("We're in no hurry"), he interrupted me and confessed: "Frankly, it needs to be ordered in advance."

I settled on a squab.

And to begin?

Perhaps a *sandre*.

I knew nothing about *sandre* except that it was a local freshwater fish. Lyon was said to be famous for its freshwater fish, all of it caught in the nearby rivers or the big lakes that surround the Alps.

The meal was well executed, and though it never reached the higher expressions of epicurean hyperbole, it illustrated why so many chefs had refused to step into Point's kitchen. Henriroux was born in 1958. Why should he be judged by a man who had died three years before his birth?

I wondered: Could *this* be my place? The history, the intimacy with what comes from here and nowhere else (the flying things, the swimming things), the Roman ghosts. Plus Boulud's rule: It had two stars!

Henriroux rejoined our table. He was comfortable with journalists, accustomed to their making the trek from Paris, a health checkup on the legend. His message wasn't complicated: "I am not Fernand Point. If you come here to eat, I will give you my food, not his. But I live in what had been his house, and am happy to share my impressions of what he did." In his person, Henriroux conveyed more stamina than flair. He had started in adversity and overcome it. He had muscular shoulders, a wispily receding hairline, soft blue eyes, furry brows, and a square face creased by deep lines that betrayed decades of slog. But he also had an easy smile, and wore the slog lightly. Now the restaurant was fully his. He had begun making changes, *his* changes. Outside: Henriroux had just landscaped the property (now more Versailles than Point's country house), built a patio, and considerably enlarged the number of tables in the garden. (Point abhorred outside dining.)

I told Henriroux about my project. "I would like to be a *stagiaire* at La Pyramide."

His smile vanished so quickly that it could have been wiped off by a sponge. He looked confused. "A *stage*? No, no, no. A *stage* is complicated. There is a protocol. You? No, it is out of the question."

He sounded so definitive.

"Really?" I asked, weakly. (I felt myself physically deflating.)

"No, I can't do that." His manner seemed to say: "An American? A journalist? In my kitchen?" I appeared to have offended him.

He thanked us for coming. He stood up.

"The *poularde en vessie*!"

He stopped.

"What if I came here one day, only a day, to learn how you cook a chicken in a bladder."

His diner was negotiating with him.

I pressed on. "No one in America eats food out of a pig's bladder."

He seemed to consider the possibility.

"One day. One dish," I said.

He sighed. "Okay."

We took a taxi back to Lyon, a long ride in wintry weather, freezing rain, the road slippery. We didn't talk much. I didn't have a backup plan for my backup plan.

What I did have was a home in the quartier that, for all its in-your-face grittiness, had energy, integrity, and an abundance of small eateries: twenty-two by my last count, nothing more than five minutes away. The food wasn't grand, but always good, and characterized by what is referred to as a *rapport qualité-prix*—an essential feature of the Lyonnais meal (i.e., good quality for the price).

Our favorites were already known to us by the people running them—such as Laura Vildi and Isabelle Comerro, two former waitresses who, the year before we arrived, opened the Bouchon des Filles, *not* with a woman at the stove but with a man, whom they robustly (and ironically?) treated like shit. It had checkered tablecloths, a wood ceiling, cheeky service, great Beaujolais, and established Lyonnais dishes lightly tweaked: like their *boudin noir,* the sausage made from fresh pig's blood (a staple in the city—you bought it by the meter), but served, in their version, inside a crunchy pastry and topped with an herb salad. From the Filles' door, you could see both the boys' school and a window of our apartment.

Or Mai and Franck Delhoum's Bistrot du Potager des Halles.

"Halles" refers to a nearby small historic food market. A *potager* is a kitchen garden. The eatery had also opened just before we arrived and became, in practice, the neighborhood bistro, open from breakfast to a late-night drink.

Or Roberto Bonomo's surprisingly authentic Sapori e Colori, which, despite our commitment to Lyonnais cuisine, we found ourselves routinely craving. Jessica, during her early IKEA forays, had found Roberto's in a state of desperation and declared that she had been in Lyon only three days and was already desperate for a plate of proper Italian pasta. ("Oh, Jessica," he said, very sympathetic, "this is not a good sign.") Later, I gave him an Italian translation of the book I wrote about the Italian kitchen. He read it and asked me to come cook with him. I briefly considered the possibility. "No, Roberto, thank you. I can't do that. I didn't come to Lyon to cook Italian."

And then there was the famous local baker, "Bob." His boulangerie was obviously where we bought our bread. I didn't know if it was actually the best in the city because we hadn't eaten anyone else's, but I did know that we were lucky when we got a loaf hot from the oven (a line began forming just outside the door—we could see it from our living-room window), carried it home jugglingly, and ate it with salty butter.

The boulangerie was where the boys discovered the word *goûter* (from *goût*, meaning "taste" or "flavor," and probably the single most important word in the entire language). A *goûter* was an afternoon snack—eaten universally at 4:00 p.m., when children got out of school—and an exception to two of the established rules about French food: that you do not eat while walking or standing *and* never between meals. A *goûter* was devoured instantly. Most parents brought it from home; we extravagantly bought ours at Bob's. The boys had discovered Bob's *pain au chocolat*—they had eaten nothing like it before—and didn't understand why they should eat anything else.

After being turned down by La Pyramide, I wondered if I should do a *stage* at Bob's—bread is a fundamental of the French plate, why not? I asked one of Bob's English friends, Martin Porter, a Liverpudlian in Lyon: Could he make inquiries on my behalf?

"I don't know," Martin reported Bob's saying. "Tell him to come see me one night."

We met our next-door neighbors, Christophe and Marie-Laure Reymond, and their four children—all boys, in robust, gorgeous health—over a welcome-to-the-building glass of wine and a plate of wintry *bugnes*. *Bugnes* are a Lyonnais fried-batter treat, coated in powdered sugar, made just before Lent to use up all the fat before fasting. (I have an image of young George, dressed up warmly for the market on the Saône that I insisted on taking him and his brother to every Sunday, eating a *bugne* that has just exploded in his hands, covering his face and dark-blue coat with sticky, powdery whiteness.)

During our getting-to-know-you chat, I described my project, including my suspicion that the Italians played a part in forming French cuisine. I may have spoken more bluntly than I'd intended. What I'd probably said was that Italians "invented" it. Marie-Laure and Christophe are not in the restaurant business. They are not historians. But they were born in Lyon, their families are Lyonnais, and they see themselves as of the city. What happened next was a veritable matrimonial dispute.

Marie-Laure: "Yes, I can see that. The Italian influence."

Christophe: "What are you talking about?"

Marie-Laure: "Oh, you know. Ravioli. Or rosette" (a Lyonnais dried sausage made from pork meat and studded with white pork fat, said to be a local interpretation of mortadella).

Christophe: "I don't understand."

Marie-Laure: "That it all started with the Italians. Of course it did."

Christophe: "Marie-Laure, are you out of your mind? The people who invented pizza?"

Marie-Laure: "Oh là là, Christophe. It is obvious. Think of Névache."

Christophe: "Névache? In the *French* Alps?"

Like many Lyonnais, the Reymonds had a simple second home in the mountains. Theirs was near the Italian border.

Marie-Laure: "Christophe, it is a mountain pass. The Italians have always been passing through. It is not hard to understand."

Christophe: "It *is* hard to understand, because it is not true."

When we got home, there was a voice message. I recognized the speaker—English, but with a strong French accent. It was Daniel Boulud. He was in Lyon for the Bocuse d'Or—"You do know about the Bocuse d'Or, don't you?" he asked, and this time I could certainly confirm that I did. It was a cooking competition held every two years. I'd been told by many people not to miss it, gastronomy in the gastronomical capital, and had already arranged to attend. Boulud was taking members of the American delegation to lunch in Ain.

"Could you and Jessica and the boys join us?"

Ain was in what I now know to be the beautiful and mysterious Dombes (that place of birds, rivers, swamps, and wild game that Mère Brazier came from), but I noticed none of it except that the roads were windy, the restaurant was sixty miles away, and George got carsick. Then Frederick did.

When we reached our destination, where a chef was preparing a monstrously overambitious meal (since the great Daniel Boulud and his team were guests), there was no food. There was also no immediate prospect of any. The boys, now hungry, were in a bad way. When the boys are in a bad way, their mother is in a bad way. When their mother is in a bad way, their father isn't doing so well, either.

We were positioned at the end of a long table, Jessica opposite me, both boys clinging to her. We were more self-ostracizing than ostracized. We did not deserve adult company. We had launched ourselves, with needy toddlers, into a strange city that no one visits on a prayer that I would become a French chef. Hah! We were in the wrong place.

Jessica hissed. I hissed.

George climbed onto his mother's lap, bearing a dessert that he had discovered in another room, something dark and sticky, which dribbled slowly and copiously down his crisply pressed button-down shirt. It dripped onto Jessica's dress.

She hissed again. I hissed back. Mid-hiss, Daniel appeared.

He had abandoned his role as host and crossed the room to sit with me. He was solicitous.

He wanted to know how it was going. (I looked over his shoulder at Jessica. She mimed Boulud's concern.)

"Oh, you know, maybe a little rough," I said, upbeat(ish).

(Jessica flipped me the bird.)

Boulud wondered: Had I found a place to work?

"Well, no, not exactly, not quite yet."

And what about my French? How was that coming along?

"Well, you know, slowly."

(Jessica chortled.)

Here I was in Daniel's territory, in the Dombes, in the heartland of the heartland, with an unruly family, manifestly struggling. He seemed to marvel at the audacity of our venture. He seemed to feel partly responsible. He wasn't, of course—the responsibility (or the irresponsibility) was all my own.

(Why didn't I drop down on my knees and plead: "Daniel, you know people! Help me"?)

It was dark when we started back. We went via taxi, the four of us, overlapping limbs, asleep.

The Bocuse d'Or began the next day.

UNTIL 1985 OR THEREABOUTS, BOCUSE WAS A VERY FAMOUS CHEF. He was a household name, with an image so widely disseminated that just about everyone could tell you what he looked like—big nose, big ears, the big lips, the toque, and holding a live *poulet de Bresse* in his arms, say, and petting its head—even if few people knew what his food was like. Then, around 1985, Bocuse turned into an icon. One moment: famous guy at stove. Then: pope of restaurant people. He became the undisputed emissary of the kitchen mission. He became Frenchness. He became, in every metaphoric sense of the word,

GIGANTIC.

It is not entirely clear how this happened, because (and Bocuse agreed) there were more talented chefs around. He never hosted a food show. Although a master of the photo op (hamming it up in drag, stripping down to show off his tattoo of a Bresse chicken, straddling his Harley-Davidson), he rarely appeared on television. He published cookbooks. None was a game changer. Apart from two forays abroad—one in Japan and another at Walt Disney World in Florida (Monsieur Paul, which thrives, run by his son, Jérôme)—he never franchised his name beyond Lyon. And yet, in the mysterious way of these things, Bocuse had something that no other chef has had in the same abundance: an undeniably infectious culinary charisma. Bocuse was what people want a grand French chef to be.

In Lyon, it was different. In Lyon, he was an even bigger deal. In Lyon, Bocuse was, extravagantly, undeniably, the biggest deal there was.

His main restaurant, L'Auberge, on the Saône, a couple miles north of the city, has been awarded three Michelin stars every year since 1965, making it the longest-running three-star establishment in the Michelin Guide's history. It was also Bocuse's home. He lived upstairs. In addition, he had (at last count) eight other, more informal Bocuse "brasseries," including four named after the compass points (*Nord, Est, Ouest,* and *Sud*). In Lyon, Paul Bocuse was, somehow, always nearby.

He created a school. In the 1980s, Jack Lang, the minister of culture, lamenting that France had no educational institution dedicated to preserving the patrimony of French cuisine, appealed to Bocuse. *Voilà:* Money, teachers, and in 1990, L'Institut Paul Bocuse opened for business. It is now regarded as the nation's pre-eminent cooking school, the place where serious culinary students go to learn how to cook serious French food.

He rejuvenated the *"foires."* In Lyon, the word, which conventionally translates as "trade fair," is loaded with history. Since 1419 the *foires* were a two-week-long tax-exempt international event, four times a year, around the religious holidays; vendors of everything—spices, wine, cheese, silks, musical instruments, cured pork legs—came from everywhere, by foot or by animal over the mountains or up the Rhône by barge. People composed poems for the *foires,* produced theatre, wrote ribald stories, performed music, sang songs, and played very, very hard.

But the modern *foires*? Not so much fun. Since 1916, when the modern *foires* were introduced (with symptomatic bad timing—in the middle of World War I), it had been a place where someone tried to sell you a tractor.

The modern *foire* had nothing like the history or the magic of the Renaissance *foires*. Even a biennial foodie spin-off (called Le Sirha, an international salon of restauration, hotels, and alimentation) was, well, just business. But once Bocuse became involved—with the advent of the Bocuse d'Or—it regained its wild glamour.

The event is organized like a World Cup (twenty-four nations competing, each represented by a team of two, a chef and a deputy) and run like a dog show, with dishes paraded through a stadium in front of forty-eight judges. It culminates in an award ceremony that manages to use the iconography of the Olympics (a podium for gold, silver, and bronze), the Oscars (the statuette), and a New York City bar mitzvah (strobe lights, loud oom-pah-pah music, and a ceiling drop of gold confetti). It is "Tacky" meets "Technique," but the "Technique" is real: On display is the flashiest, most accomplished food on the planet.

I showed up at 9:00 a.m. Chefs had been there since five. Each two-member team was crushed bumpingly into a mini-kitchen cubicle the size of a changing room at a bad beach resort. The mood was of adrenaline and stress and sweat. Every cook, intensely aware of the clock ticking, was focused and very quiet. The bleachers—installed to accommodate supporters of the national teams—were already filled. They held five thousand people. The Japanese spectators were dressed as samurais, the Mexicans, sombreros. The Swedes, the Danish, and the Americans, draped in national flags. There were a mariachi band, a drum-and-bugle corps, a pit-percussion team, some guys banging cymbals, and many morons with stadium air horns. There wasn't anything obvious to be thundering about: no eviscerating of live goats, no fist pumping, no chef standing up and saying, "Bam!" But the cheering, which was thunderous, never stopped.

I felt uninformed and naïve—how could I not have known that this kind of cooking (hunched-over, tortured people manipulating little things in little ways) was a nationalist sport?—when, lo and behold, Paul Bocuse appeared.

He had turned up backstage and taken it upon himself—the toque, the whites, in a collar that looked like a French flag—to walk across the floor. He padded by me, softly and stiffly, imposingly tall in his chef posture, doing small papal waves, and seemed not to notice that a queue of competitors was forming behind him. Only a moment before, they were locked down in their panicky prep when one of them noticed that Bocuse was in the house, abandoned his station, and began following the great man around. He called to the others in their mini-cubicle kitchens, urging them to join in. The line quickly became much longer, conga-style.

No one really knew what to do next—you can get away with doing the conga behind Paul Bocuse for only so long—when someone touched the great man and dropped out of the queue, satisfied by the contact. The next person in the queue touched a sleeve. Then it was a shoulder, the back of Bocuse's hand. An Asian chef was next up, and he seized Bocuse's apron by the hem, released it, and held the hand that had done the seizing by its wrist, staring at it and screaming as though his skin were burning. A cook fell to his knees and kissed the ground where the chef had trodden (which—I don't know, call me prudish—seemed a little excessive).

It got grabby, and just as it was seeming outright dangerous, Bocuse was gone. Handlers appeared and ushered him through a backstage door.

I got a lift back to Lyon, and reflected on the theatre of the day and how stubbornly inaccessible the kitchens of Lyon persisted on being for me. Maybe I should try Bob after all. By the time I reached the apartment, I was resolved. I know where to start my culinary training, I told Jessica, by learning the fundamentals. I'm going to work for Bob. I'm going to become a baker. In fact, I said, I'm going to walk over there now and present myself.

It was eight in the evening, but I was pretty sure he'd be there. Bob was known for his hours, his light on in the back when the rest of the quartier was dark. And he *was* there, but only just. He had his coat on and was heading home for a nap.

Bob knew why I was here. He also knew that I hadn't found a kitchen to work in. So, when I made my proposal, straight-out, no introduction—"Bob, I've decided, on reflection, that my book should start with you, that I want to do a *stage* here, in your boulangerie"—he knew I was lying.

I hadn't moved to Lyon to work with Bob. I wanted Marc Veyrat, or Mathieu Viannay, or Patrick Henriroux.

"No," he said.

"No?" The backup to my backup of my backup was rejecting me?

He stared. Was he trying to read me?

I come to you, I said, not only to learn how to make bread, but *your* bread. "It is famously good. What interests me is why."

His gaze drifted above my head. He seemed to be calibrating, imagining (I imagined) what the consequences of my being in his company might be.

Bob was forty-four. He was jowly and wide of girth and, when unshaven, looked something like a genetic intermarriage of Fred Flintstone and Jackie Gleason. His hair was brownish and shaggy and usually matted with flour. There was flour on his clogs, his sweater (he never wore an apron), his trousers, and adhering powerfully to his beard. Bathing was not a priority. He slept when he could, and didn't sleep often, and seemed to live by an internal clock set to an alarm that was always going off—yeast, dough making, the unforgiving speed of a hot oven, delivery urgencies. He was always on his feet. He seemed never to tire. He knew that his bread was exceptionally good. He also knew that no one knew how really good it was.

He was not, in his view, a genius. In a city of food fanatics, he was just a baker, even if a good one. He was in fact just Bob. And, of course, he wasn't even that. His real name was Yves. (No one knew why he went by "Bob." I once asked him, and he was vague: "Somebody, a long time ago...")

"Yes," he said slowly: *Ouiiiiii*. He actually seemed to be getting excited. I could see his excitement in his fingers. They were drumming a counter. "Come. Work here. You will be welcome."

"I will see you tomorrow."

We shook hands. I made to leave.

"You live across the street, right? You can stop by anytime."

I thanked him.

"If you can't sleep, come over. At three in the morning, I'll be here. On Friday and Saturday, I'm here all night."

I thought: If I can't sleep at three in the morning, I don't go for walks. But I understood the message. Bob was making himself available. I'll be your friend, he was saying.

The picture I had of Bob's operations was during the weekends, especially Sundays, which were outright wild, owing to a law, still observed, forbidding trade: except for bakers. In Lyon, many boulangeries opened on Sunday. But it was Bob's where people went.

On Sundays, the boulangerie belonged to Lyon, and Bob worked without sleep to feed it. Late-night carousers appeared at two in the morning to ask for a hot baguette, swaying on tiptoe at a high window by *le fournil,* the oven room, an arm outstretched, holding out a euro coin. By nine, there were so many people going in and out the door that it never closed, the line extended down the street, and the shop, when you finally got inside, was loud from people, and from music (usually salsa) being played at high volume. (Bob fell in love with salsa, and then with Cuba, and then with a Cuban, his wife, Jacqueline.) Everyone shouted to be heard—the cacophonous hustle, oven doors banging, people waving and trying to get noticed, too-hot-to-touch baguettes arriving in baskets, money changing hands, all cash.

The crowd fascinated me, all strangers, everyone leaving with an armful and with the same look—suspended between appetite and the prospect of an appetite satisfied. I learned something, I got it, the appeal of a good bread—as I was able to find it here, just across the street from our apartment: handmade, aromatically yeasty, with a just-out-of-the-oven texture of crunchy air. No one lingered. This was their breakfast. It completed the week. This was Sunday.

At three on a weekday morning, the boulangerie was different and lonely. The river was different, at least on the night I ventured out, very cold, and looked like motor oil when, eerily, a river barge appeared a few feet away, a massive entity (you never hear its coming), a heavy bow like a plow, sluicing thickly. Lyon, too, couldn't be more different, or more lonely: no vehicles, no people, not a light on in any of the apartments. (The city, from Thursday to Sunday—all-night drinking, loud open-windowed music, fights, car burnings, vandalism, vomiting—would never be described as of the "early-to-bed" variety. Maybe on other nights everyone rested.)

Bob ripped open a sack of flour—he was clearly waiting for me—lifted it without a sign of strain (it weighed fifty kilos), and emptied it into a large steel basin. (Bob was strong, but his strength seemed more an act of will than the contraction of anything muscular.) He grabbed a milk carton with the top cut off, and told me to follow him to a sink—a startling sight, filled with coffee paraphernalia, grounds everywhere, a sandwich floating in something black, a roll of toilet paper. He negotiated the carton to a position under the faucet and ran it hot.

"You arrive at the correct temperature by a formula involving two other factors," Bob explained. "One is the temperature of the air. This morning it is cold—it is probably two degrees. The other is the flour...."

"How do you know that?"

"It's the temperature of the air."

"Of course."

"These two factors added together, plus the temperature of the water should equal fifty-four degrees Celsius." So, if the air was two degrees, and the flour was two degrees, the water would have to be fifty.

"Hot," I said.

"Exactly." The water from the tap was steaming. Bob filled the carton.

I asked, "Bob, you don't use a thermometer?"

"No."

"Do you own a thermometer?"

"No." He considered. "You know, I might."

In a notebook, I wrote: "Water + air + flour = 54 degrees."

Bob poured the warm water into the basin and started an apparatus attached at the top, a mechanical kneader. It wasn't really "mechanical," not in the modern sense of the word. It appeared originally to have been operated by turning a crank, and at some point had been upgraded with a washing-machine motor. Two hooks, looking like prosthetic hands, scooped up the dough very slowly.

"It is no faster than if you did this with your own hands," he said.

"Then we take some of last night's dough." *La vieille pâte.* It was brown and cakey, wrapped in plastic film. He pinched a bit between his thumb and forefinger and tossed it into the basin. He took a second pinch, scrutinized it, thought better of the quantity, and tossed in half. This, in effect, was his "sourdough," yeasts still alive from last night that would be woken up in the new batch. It wasn't the only source. I knew enough about yeasts to know that here, they were everywhere. You could peel them off the walls. You could scrape all you needed from underneath Bob's fingernails. Here, your breath had texture.

I looked around. There were heaps of coats on a hook or rammed into a stone windowsill. On every available surface, there was an unwashed coffee mug. Fabric *couches* (looking like still-damp beach towels from last summer) were draped across wood poles. They were for shaping baguettes. A lightbulb dangled from the ceiling. Another one sprouted from a socket. There were the flickering blue lights of the ovens. The darkness put you on your guard. You could trip here and die. It wasn't a place that reminded you to wipe your feet before entering it. But maybe, in the perverse way of these things, this room, with all its sacred history, was what Bob's baguettes tasted like.

He stopped the kneader and tore off a piece of dough. It was ready. It was thin and elastic. "You can see through it," he said, laughing as he stretched it across my face like a mask.

I thought: I know this moment from making pasta. As you roll out pasta dough, its texture changes and it seems to glisten. You keep rolling until the grains of the wood board underneath start to appear: when, in fact, you can see through it.

Tonight's dough would be ready the next afternoon. The morning's baguettes would be made, therefore, from last night's.

"Let's get breakfast," Bob said. An off-track-betting bar opened at six.

The coffee was filthy, the bread was his but stale, and the clientele might be flatteringly described as "rough" (phlegmatic one-lunged hackers knocking back sunrise brandies, while studying the racing odds), but, for Bob, they represented companionship. His life was solitary nights. These people were members of his first society. He was at ease among them. He introduced me as the guy who was working in the boulangerie to write about him.

The French language happened and didn't. I seemed to be speaking it (up to a point) but often didn't understand it when spoken back to me. I dreaded the phone. I could order a taxi but didn't know if I had been told it was coming or when or that I needed to pay cash. The boys understood everything but rarely spoke. People had said, "Your children will pick up French in no time," and they didn't, not really. Once, Frederick was worried and addressed Jessica: "Mamam, there is a word following me. I don't like it. It follows me everywhere."

"What is the word?"

He whispered: *"Soldes." Soldes* means "sales." (In France, retail sales are allowed only during a prescribed four-week period when every merchant puts out a sign: *"Soldes."*)

The boys were assigned to an *orthophoniste,* a specialist in *"ré-éducation du langage,"* an austere, skinny woman with a scarf and perfect posture who had been engaged by the school to help students pronounce the French language properly. Every child's speech was subjected to her scrutiny. During our time there, she was made so busy that she rented an office directly across the street, with big windows that offered a clear view of who had been summoned for re-education, including many native French families. Everyone was challenged by the language, its subtle sounds, its muted vowels. When she examined our children, she became provoked when they claimed they didn't know the word for "spanking," which is *fesser* (from *fesse* for "butt"). She thought she was being made fun of. Implicit in her indignation was the assumption that *all* children are spanked. They probably are—in Lyon, we'd seen plenty of spanking—it just wasn't something we did.

Our children were diagnosed with a malady known as *bilinguisme,* and the *orthophoniste* demanded that Jessica come to her office immediately. Jessica's speech was then examined and found to be exemplary. The *orthophoniste* prescribed a treatment: Jessica was ordered to speak only French at home. The instruction didn't apply to me.

Was my French improving?

No.

Did my French even exist?

Meh.

I had a bad episode with *"four"*—not the number in English, but the word in French for "oven" (pronounced as if someone has just hit you hard on the back). It is the same sound if the ovens referred to are in the plural (*fours*). And it is, of course, what Bob bakes his bread in, the blue-lit, glass-door contraptions on the ground floor.

One afternoon, there were two people in the back at the boulangerie: Denis, Bob's then number two, and me. Denis, his only full-time employee—blond, thirty, with closely cropped hair, and dressed in white like a proper baker—was upstairs. I was below, making dough. When I bounded up to retrieve a sack of flour, Denis asked: The bread—was it still in the oven (*au four*)? At least I think that this was what he said.

He repeated the question, and this time it was more like "Don't tell me that the fucking bread is still in the oven, is it, you moron?" I still didn't understand. What I heard was strong emotion (anxiety, mainly) and *"four."*

"Four," I said to myself. *"Four.* I know that word."

Yes? Or no? I could hear the kind of answer that was expected. (I thought: fifty-fifty chance. Should I just pick one?) Instead, I repeated the word to myself: *four.* I was sure I knew it. Why wasn't it coming to me? *"Four?"* I said, aloud this time, which was provoking, probably because it wasn't "yes" or "no."

"Au four? Au four? C'est au four? Le pain!"

Denis bolted down the stairs in what seemed to me like histrionically high distress. I heard an oven door being "slammed" open and a bread tray yanked out on its rollers.

"Oh, putain!"

For me, still upstairs, the door was the prompt. Of course. *Four!* It's "oven"!

The bread was ruined. Thus, the *"putain!"* (*Putain* means "whore." *"Pute"* is also "whore," but *"putain!"* is what you say when you've burned fifty baguettes.)

We were expected to register at the prefecture. Bob knew the procedure. He had been there with his Cuban wife.

"It will be horrific," he said. "You haven't suffered this kind of humiliation before. Arrive early."

We were summoned as a family, with photos and all our French Consulate documents, and were to be interviewed; if "approved," we would be directed to an immigration medical facility (near the city prison). If "approved," we returned to the prefecture, with new photos and bank statements, and were issued a temporary residency while our portfolio was dispatched to an office outside Paris, which would tell us, if we were really "approved," to return to the prefecture for a proper *carte de séjour,* entitling us to stay for one year.

I went on my own, showing up just after six, and was twentieth in a line that would number in the thousands. I had told Jessica to bring the boys once I knew what the wait would be.

Around eight-thirty, she texted readiness ("ordered taxi").

Soldiers arrived, bearing weapons—the crowd-control factor. Promptly at nine, the doors opened, the nineteen people in front of me were rapidly dealt with—*very* rapidly—and suddenly I was, too quickly, sitting in front of a representative of the French government.

[Jessica? Where are you?]

As I was pulling out the documents, the representative asked, "And your family members?"

"Running a little late," I said. "I'll just check."

[*Me, texting*]: "Shit. Am in. Status?"

[*Jessica, texting*]: "Taxi a no-show."

[*Me, texting*]: "FUCK!"

"They're almost here," I said. "Children, you know how it is. Gloves, coats, scarves."

"Pas de souci," the representative said. No worries. She proposed that the two of us go through my bank statements while we waited. I pulled out each document, checking and double-checking that it was correct.

My phone vibrated. "Excuse me," I said.

[*Jessica, texting*]: "Reordered taxi. On our way. Finally!"

It was nine-fifteen. Rush hour.

"Any minute now," I said.

To her credit, the representative seemed helpfully meticulous, very, very meticulous, and we were, both of us, scrutinizing each document intently, confident that we were going to spot an error. But eventually—it took ten minutes—we reached the last statement. There was nothing left. She arranged the documents in a pile, banged them gently on the counter, and bound them with the clip that I'd delivered them in. She was about to hand them back, when I blurted out: "Lyon is the gastronomic capital of the world."

It is true, she said, and laughed, the Lyonnais like their food.

"It is why I am here."

"Really?"

I wondered if she had a favorite *bouchon*.

She did.

"So you're a true Lyonnaise?"

"I am Lyonnaise."

"Would you mind writing down the name for me of your favorite *bouchon*?"

"Not at all." She seemed pleased to be asked. She tore a piece of paper from a notepad, whereupon I went instantly to my phone.

[*Me, texting*]: "Update?"

[*Jessica, texting*]: "Terrible traffic."

She handed me the paper.

I wrote a book about the Italian kitchen, I said. "Can I give you a copy? It's in French." She seemed impressed that I'd brought it along and (to my surprise) agreed to accept it, whereupon I asked if I could sign it ("And could you write out your name for me?"). I told her that I was working at a boulangerie (*"C'est vrai?"*) and asked her if she knew it, "Bob's on the Quai Saint-Vincent."

"Bob's?" she asked, confused, whereupon I explained that it wasn't his real name but no one knew his real name, and I urged her to go there ("Best bread in Lyon"). I offered to write out the address for her.

She thanked me and took it.

She now needed to see the next person, she said. If my family wasn't here, she couldn't process our case. I would have to go to the end of the line.

"I am sorry for my French," I said.

"No, your French is good."

"No, it's not. I know it's not."

"Yes, it really is. You make yourself perfectly clear."

I thought, despite my panic and unease, that something unusual was taking place and that I would do myself a service to note it. I had just conducted a sustained piece of linguistic stalling with a government functionary in this new second language. I had made progress. *And* my stalling had been effective. I had almost pulled it off.

I made a last pitch. "Couldn't you process my case only and do the others later?"

"No. I'm sorry. You have to go outside to the end of the line."

I stood up. I thanked her. I pulled out the folded sheet of notepad paper that I'd put in my shirt pocket, and thanked her for the name of the *bouchon*. I said I would go there. I stuffed each file back into my bag, and imagined the stress that Jessica must be suffering in a taxi, with children, in traffic, when, miraculously, she appeared, my family, in the last possible seconds, a thrilling sight, *ma femme avec les garçons.*

We finished at two-thirty.

After our visit, Bob seemed to regard me in a new way. We weren't Americans on a gastro safari—tourists don't go to the prefecture. We were committed—manifestly—to being here.

"Tomorrow, we do deliveries. It is time to meet the real Lyon."

Bob delivered bread via an ancient tanklike Citroën that he hadn't washed—ever. On the passenger seat were Casino plastic sandwich-wrappers, a half-eaten quiche, a nearly emptied family-sized bottle of Coca-Cola, and editions of the local paper, *Le Progrès,* that had been opened at such specific spots and then tossed on the floor as to suggest that this is what Bob did while driving—he caught up on the news. He pushed it all to the floor and invited me to sit. Inside was a fine white cloud, as though the air had reached a point of molecular flour saturation and none of it would quite settle. I found a place for my feet, maneuvered a sack of baguettes between my legs, and buckled in. The car seemed to explain why Bob so seldom bathed: Really, what would be the point? (In the wintertime, Bob had the appearance of an old mattress.)

He drove fast, he talked fast, he parked badly. The car, by force of habit, reminded him that he was late and put him in an instant accelerating delivery mode. L'Harmonie des Vins was the first stop, on the Presqu'île, a wine bar with food ("But good food," Bob said). Two owners were in the back, busy, preparing the lunch service, but delighted by the sight of their bread guy, as if a friend had popped by unexpectedly, even though he came by every day at exactly this time. I was introduced ("a journalist who is writing about me"), quick-quick, bag drop, kisses, out.

Next: La Quintessence, near the Rhône (narrow street, no place to park, so he didn't, cars backing up behind him, none of them honking), a new restaurant ("Really good food," Bob said, pumping his fist), husband and wife, one prep cook, frantic, but spontaneous smiles, the introduction ("writing about me"), the bag drop, kisses, out.

We crossed the Rhône, rolled up onto a sidewalk, and rushed out, Bob with one sack of bread, me with another, holding it between two arms like a hug, trying to keep up: L'Olivier ("Exceptional food"—a double pump—"Michelin listed but not pretentious"), young chef, tough-guy shoulders, an affectionate face, even if too busy to smile, bag drop, high-fives, out.

One eating establishment after another: *in*—fast, joy, bread (still warm), introductions ("a writer"), two-person kitchen, sometimes one—then *out*. Many seemed less like businesses than improvisations that resulted, somehow, in dinner. Chez Albert: created on a dare by friends. Le Saint-Vincent, with a kitchen no larger than a coat closet (and formerly a toilet).

Bob drove south, in the direction of the football stadium—the deliveries would take two hours, two dozen drops (in itself a tribute to his bread), and took me to a city more varied than I had known—and into the seventh arrondissement, industrial, two-up/two-down housing, gray stucco fronts, with an improbable bistro on an improbable corner, Le Fleurie, named after a Beaujolais *cru,* as accessible as the wine. "I love this place," Bob said (*J'adore*): a daily chalkboard menu on the sidewalk, twelve euros for a three-course meal (lake fish with shellfish sauce, filet of pork with pepper sauce), polemically T-shirt-and-jeans informal, the food uncompromisingly seasonal (i.e., if it's winter, you eat roots).

Bob walked straight to the back, forthrightly in a swagger, a sack of bread on his shoulder, the familiar routine, the joyful effusions, the easy smiles, which I, too, was enjoying, so infected by Bob's ebullience that I felt not that I was a member of Bob's team, but that somehow I had become part Bob.

The day's last delivery completed, Bob asked after Olivier, the chef, and was directed to the bar.

Olivier Paget, Bob's age, was born in Beaujolais, father a carpenter, grandfather a farmer, cooking since age sixteen; normal chef stuff, including stints with *grands chefs* making fancy food, like Michel Rostang (yet again!) and Georges Blanc, where Daniel Boulud had trained. But Paget, his training complete, didn't do fancy. He located himself in a remote far-from-the-action working-class district, called it a "bistro," made good food at a fair price, and filled every seat, every lunch and dinner, every day: tight.

This, Bob said, is my idea of a restaurant.

By way of explanation (Paget pouring us both glasses of Beaujolais), Bob confessed to his loving the idea of *"grande cuisine"*—the term for cooking of the highest order by a *grand chef*. It was his dream fantasy, he said, and he still hoped that one day he would experience it. "I tried once"—a meal at Paul Bocuse's three-star Auberge, with Jacqueline, Bob's wife.

No one could have arrived with higher expectations. Few could have been more disappointed.

It wasn't the food, which Bob doesn't remember. "We were condescended to." Waiters sneered at them for not knowing which glass was for which wine, or for grabbing the wrong spoon, and served them with manifest reluctance. (Jacqueline is black; that evening, there was one other black person: the restaurant's footman, at the entrance to welcome guests, dressed up in a costume uncomfortably reminiscent of Southern plantation livery.) The bill was more than he earns in a month. It had been a mugging.

Bob knocked back his Beaujolais, and Paget poured him another, and as I watched them, the easy intimacy between them, I believed I was starting to understand what I had been seeing all morning: a fellowship, like a fraternity, recognized by a coat of arms visible only to other members. Everyone we dropped in on today belonged to it. They knew that Bob's bread was exceptional. They also knew that the bread was more than just bread.

Bob confirmed a table for Friday, a lunch with friends. He was always arranging large meals for friends—they were like board meetings for the kindred—including a seasonal *mâchon*, the all-day Lyonnais "breakfast" practice (starting at nine, and featuring every edible morsel of a pig, limitless-seeming quantities of Beaujolais, and loud, sloppy parades of singing men who, by then, are trying to remember how to get home. I feared it). Friday's lunch was less ambitious. "Just ten people," Bob told me. "You should come, too."

The chef, a guest at his own restaurant, was among the kindred, and joined others who "lived food" pretty much all of the time. (And wine. They also very much lived their wine.) Three were in the trade—a cheese guy, another restaurateur, someone who arrived with a rope of *boudin noir*—but not everyone. There was a schoolteacher, a violinist. It didn't matter. Everyone suffered the same affliction: an inability to think about much else except the meal you're having now and the one you're having next. They were eaters all. They were all devotees of Bob.

Lunch arrived in courses and now exists in my mind as a Beaujolais blur—salads, a pâté, a lake fish, a platter of something (meat?) with sauce (it *was* France), all of it family-style—but it was the bread, Bob's bread, that was talked about. At Le Fleurie, it is the first item on the table, a whole baguette, sliced, in a basket.

"Bill, *regarde*"—look. Bob directed my attention to an older woman on the far side of the room, well dressed, gray hair in a bun, eating by herself. She was removing a baguette from the basket and meticulously putting it into her purse, piece by piece, where there appeared to be a napkin to fold it into. She had come prepared—or else had also stolen the napkin. In either case, there was premeditation in her filching: She arrived for lunch knowing that she would go home with something for dinner.

She closed her purse, and put her hand up for a waiter's attention.

More bread, please— *"Plus de pain, s'il vous plaît."*

I turned to the chef. He looked as if he had been caught out. He hadn't been—*she* was the one caught out—but he tolerated the filching. He was not about to walk over and ask her to empty her purse. "Besides," he said, "she is not the only one."

The waiter refilled her basket.

"Others eat so much bread they don't want our food." It was a simple, baleful confession. But he wasn't about to stop offering bread. "Everyone here counts on *this* bread."

Bob was familiar with the complaint. "Each place has a bread thief. I tell them: Don't serve it fresh. People can't resist it when it's fresh." This wasn't a boast; it was a matter of fact. "Leave it for a day. Day-old bread is still good. It's just not *as* good."

No restaurant, so far, had heeded Bob's advice, but who would? The man who makes your bread delivers it to you within hours of its being baked, and you're going to stash it in a cupboard until tomorrow?

Bob here was different from the Bob I had seen before. He smiled— normally, he rarely smiled. His face was animated. He laughed. (I hadn't appreciated until now just how unrelaxed he was in a normal day. His informal *"que será será"* manner hid the fact that, for him, there was urgency in every minute.) Also, he was at a table with friends. Bob, for everyone there, was a gift—they understood him—and their gratitude for having Bob in their lives made Bob more Bob-like. He was the chairman of this informal board. He had an authority that was new to me. He never said, "I'm only a baker." He was *the* baker. He was more: He was the baker-philosopher. He was confident, at ease, even self-mocking ("People eat too much bread—look at me").

"Mon Dieu!" he suddenly declared. "Look around the table. Do you realize that everyone here is one generation from the farm?"

None of them had grown up on farms, but their parents had. Bob's father was a baker in Rennes, in Brittany. Olivier Paget's father was a carpenter. But the worldview of both their fathers was shaped by plows, and seasons, and their children, who knew farming by visits to their grandparents, also had a connection.

"Don't you remember how the farm was the heart of Frenchness?" Bob asked. "It used to be everything. We are the last generation to have some connection." He used the word *transmettre,* with its sense of "to hand over"—something passed between eras. I repeated the word to myself, *transmettre.* Everyone at the table was the beneficiary of a knowledge—call it "earth knowledge"—that had been handed off, from one family to the next, for millennia. "After us, it is gone," Bob said matter-of-factly. The sense was: Enjoy it while you can.

At the end of lunch, Bob drove me back to the boulangerie.

I asked him: "Is it the yeasts? Are they what make your bread so good?"

"Oui," he said very, very slowly (as in *"Oooouuuuweeeee"*), meaning, "Well, no."

I pondered. "Is it the all-night leavening?" Slowness, I'd heard over and over again, is essential to good bread.

"Oooouuuuweeeee."

"The final resting?" Bread gets its deeper flavor in its last stages, people say.

"Oooouuuuweeeee. But no. These are the ABC's. Mainly, they are what you do *not* do to make bad bread. There is a lot of bad bread in France." (Bob calls it *pain d'usine,* "factory bread.") "Good bread comes from good flour. It's the flour."

"The flour?"

"Oui," he said, definitively.

I thought: Flour is flour is flour. "The flour?"

"Oui. The flour."

ONE PIG

Visitors are always surprised by the habits and character of our people, but would be less so if they understood that Lyon, "capital of the provinces," is first and foremost rural. It is surrounded by farms and is more like an enormous town than a city and is the only large French populace that doesn't have a port. All its roads end in fields. Those who travel back on them into our rich city—from the Dauphiné, Bresse, Burgundy, Savoie—and arrive to make a living from it or a life in it, are farmers or sons of farmers. And country people, as we know, do not easily change their ways. So look no further to explain their rudeness, their mistrust, their no-nonsense attitude which seem at odds with the aristocratic and sumptuous history of the city.

HENRI BÉRAUD, *VOUS NE CONNAISSEZ PAS MON PAYS*, 1944

TRANSLATED BY JESSICA GREEN

I got myself invited to a pig killing. Actually, I worked for it: I begged, I promised faithfulness to the cause, I declared my carnivore integrity, until, finally, I was rewarded with a nervously proffered invitation.

Boudin noir, blood in a piece of pig's intestine, was ubiquitous in Lyon—few foods went better with a *pot* of Beaujolais—but it was sold already cooked, even from your local butcher: Go home, reheat, and serve. The *boudin noir* we planned to make after killing our pig (along with other, principally tubular porcine expressions) would be steamingly fresh. It was said to be nothing like the commercial stuff.

I had some crude logistical curiosities, like how you got the blood out of the pig and into an intestine: which was cleaned—how exactly? Or was there a lingering stink that the Lyonnais regarded, characteristically, as a flavor enhancer? I was also attracted to the visceral reality of killing an animal (how—with our hands?) that you would then eat (the sanctity of the act). Mère Brazier used to make her own *boudin noir*. So, famously, did Fernand Point.

As it happened, the farm that hosted the *boudin-noir* making was not far from where a certain Menon had raised the orchard-fed pigs whose blood Point coveted. It was a gravelly hilltop on the other side of the Rhône River from La Pyramide, among what could well have been orchard fruit trees—hard to tell in midwinter, stark trunks, everything dirt brown, under a silver-white sky that was huge and very cold. As in Italy, the French slaughter and cure their pigs only in the winter. Refrigeration is a modern contrivance, and pig curing is not modern.

I was taken to the farm by Ludovic Curabet, the only member of the team prepared to share his last name.

Ludovic was in his thirties—dark hair, fit, youthful—and committed to continuing the old ways. He was, in effect, a pig intellectual. He knew how pigs were cured in Spain, the Po Valley in Italy, the Alps, and especially here, the Rhône. He was also among the few people who still practiced (and admitted that they were practicing) a local rite called *la tuaille*. *La tuaille* translates as "the killing," but, in the Rhône and the south of France, it refers to the ritualized seasonal slaughter of a family pig, and includes some early-morning drinking, the eating of abundant freshly made *boudin noir*, followed by some midday drinking, some early-afternoon drinking, and then some late-afternoon drinking. Around Lyon, you see black-and-white photographs of *tuailles*—pictures pinned to the wall of a *bouchon*—featuring tired and bespattered people, often cross-eyed, but very happy.

What we were doing was legal, although there was a belief that it wouldn't be for long. The European Union tolerates old-fashioned pig killings, provided they are for farmers' private consumption. But such is their fear of the European Union, many farmers believe that they are the last generation. In fact, Ludovic asked if we could film the killing. He wanted to record it for his children.

The other two members of our team were both named Claude. One was the farmer. One was a butcher.

"Farmer Claude" was in his early seventies, tall, lean, slightly stooped, a long face, busily expressive white eyebrows, which, in effect, "talked" much more than he did, since he said almost nothing. He seemed bemused by our endeavor, ideologically committed to it but nervous about the possible fallout. Ludovic had persuaded him that I could be trusted.

Farmer Claude escorted me into a dirt courtyard adjoining the house, where Butcher Claude was waiting for us. He talked even less than Farmer Claude. Five words. Maybe less. He was about fifty-five, a little hefty, and in a white coat, as though he had just driven up from the shop in town. He was standing over a rectangular wooden pallet, pulling apart a bale of hay, and piling it on top. This was for a bonfire. After the animal was killed, Ludovic told me, she would be set alight to burn off the hair. (The pigs we eat are either sows or castrated males. The meat of a fully testicular male? Disgusting.) You burn off the hair to get to the skin. Pigs are the only farm animals not normally skinned, because their fat isn't integrated into the muscle, but resides between the muscle and the skin. If you skin a pig, you risk losing the fat, and the fat underneath translates into both belly cuts and the creamy white fat that goes into sausages.

Pig fat, Ludovic said, is good.

Boudin noir has its modest literature—in the *Odyssey,* Homer describes a stomach filled with blood and fat being roasted over a fire, and Apicius, the first-century Roman epicurean, has a preparation enriched by eggs, pine nuts, onions, and leeks. The origins of the word itself are obscure but probably hark back to a now lost colloquial usage during the Roman settlement of Gaul. (The *boud-* of *boudin* may be derived from the Roman *bod-*, which is "to inflate or bulge," just as the intestines fill up.) The preparation is among the oldest on the planet, older than the Romans or the Greeks, and probably dates to the earliest days of animal domestication (circa 10,000 B.C.), if not before—i.e., circa the discovery of fire—if only because it satisfies the universal philosophical imperative understood by every premodern farmer and hunter lucky enough to have an animal to eat: Waste nothing.

Butcher Claude continued building up the bonfire. Ludovic chopped onions and cooked them in a sauté pan over a Bunsen burner while Farmer Claude assembled an antique-seeming cast-iron kettle. It was like a very large teapot that he half-filled with water and set upon a three-legged stand like a barbecue. He stacked kindling underneath and lit it. The fire crackled, a lazy morning smoke, smelling of pine. This was where the *boudin,* once made, would be cooked, here in the cold, open air.

In the obvious absence of small talk, I wandered around the courtyard and came upon an animal pen—a low wooden door, a window with iron bars. How curious that I hadn't noticed it before. I stooped to peer inside. I saw our pig. The pig saw me. It was a startling moment. The animal was suddenly so there, and much larger than I expected. Two hundred kilos, about 450 pounds. It was furry, not pink, with white hair and brown spots.

I dropped down to look inside again. This, I couldn't help myself from observing, was a beautiful animal.

Pigs are the most intelligent of domesticated livestock and interpret their surroundings more efficiently than other animals. They also panic easily, and the panic often expresses itself in the taste of the meat.

In an instant, I realized why everyone had been so quiet. They were trying to be invisible.

The pig began to squeal.

Did I just do that?

The others hadn't looked. For them, there was no pig: We're just farmers going about our business, ho hum, a normal morning, big animal in a dinky stone pen, no big deal.

But I had looked and, like that, I had hit the squeal button.

Wow. It wasn't a squeal. It was a wide-open, high-volume, high-pitched cry. It didn't enter the brain; it pierced it, or at least it seemed to, my brain anyway, and with such an intensity that I wanted to do something about it. Urgently.

The squeal said: I am in danger!

It said: Run!

It said: Find me, help me, save me.

On and on and on.

Pigs had figured in Daniel Boulud's childhood. They were like storybook companions, more like dogs and people than cows and sheep. (The observation is not mine, but of the animal anthropologist Juliet

Clutton-Brock.) Boulud loved his pet pigs. But every year, when he was in the house eating breakfast, he'd hear the squeal. *This* kind of squeal. By then, as he was irrationally sprinting toward the sound without entirely understanding why (since he knew he was already too late), the pig was dead.

Was my pig so smart that she could see my thinking about her being dead? (Had I been?) Because, no question, the pig now knew she was going to die.

Fifteen minutes later, the farmer opened the pen door. The butcher put a rope around the animal's neck and snout. The pig wouldn't come out.

Butcher Claude and Farmer Claude pulled her from the front. Ludovic and I got in from behind, pushing her butt. She resisted with all the strength and adrenaline of her considerable 450 pounds. The ground was half frozen, and her hooves plowed shallow rows in the hard dirt. When she was next to the pallet, she was toppled over.

The back legs needed to be secured at the ankles. I was surprised by her strength, four of us on top of her, trying to get her limbs to cooperate. The squealing never stopped, until finally the ankles were secured, and I relaxed my grip, and the pig went quiet. She turned her head—she had to twist it round—and looked at me. Her gaze was intense, and it wasn't easy to turn away from. It said: Don't kill me.

"Get the bucket," Ludovic told me. He pointed. It was nearby. "Now kneel, there." *Là.*

I got down, just in front of the animal. She lurched and bucked, but the movements were small.

"As the bucket fills, stir," Ludovic said. "Steady and quickly. To keep it from coagulating."

Butcher Claude relaxed the rope. I glimpsed the knife briefly. He had kept it hidden—I hadn't known it was there—and had come up to the throat from below, just out of the pig's vision, and slit the artery below the Adam's apple.

I thought: I could never do that.

There was no reaction. The pig didn't seem to feel the slice. The deed was done.

Ludovic began working a front leg, up and down, like a pump—the pig continued to squeal but the squeal was diminishing. Blood streamed into my bucket from the gash, bright red. It steamed. I stirred. To stop the coagulation? Then I understood. Yes! To stop it! The blood was forming into strings, quickly and densely.

"Stir," Ludovic said. *"Remuez. Vite."*

I thought: I'm going to ruin it. The whole day has been structured around *boudin noir,* which we now won't be able to make because I didn't understand coagulation.

The threads were now wrapping themselves up and down my fingers. The surface of the blood looked normal, a little frothy, but underneath a plastic spiderweb was forming.

"Vite. Vite."

Faster. Faster. Faster. And then, finally, the threads began to dissolve, and then, once they started, they finished dissolving, and in seconds—some threshold having been crossed—they were gone.

The pig sighed. It was deep, like a yawn. It was the sound of a big person about to go to sleep.

She sighed again.

I looked down. The blood came about halfway up the bucket. Shouldn't there be more? Such a big animal. There was more than a gallon, but not much more.

She sighed again, a smaller sound.

I looked at her. Her face had gone pale. I thought: Pigs, too, lose their color. Her eyes went milky. She was dead. We were done.

Butcher Claude gave me a ladle. *"Goûtez,"* he said. Taste.

I was confused. He keeps a ladle in his back pocket?

Ludovic said, *"Non. Il faut l'assaisonner."* It needed seasoning. He fetched salt and pepper.

"Now. *Goûtez."*

I got up off my knees. The hairs on my arm were matted red. My shirt and jeans were splattered.

"Goûter?" Really?

"Oui."

I dipped the ladle into the bucket and tasted. It was warm. Rich. It was thick and weighty on my palate. The seasoning was almost obtrusive, but also welcome: It was intensifying.

I dipped my ladle back into the bucket.

The men laughed. "More?"

I was trying to identify the taste. Frankly, I was also getting a serious buzz. Was that the blood? Or the overwhelming fact of everything, this animal, the intimacy, the killing, the coagulation, the courtyard, this morning. I dipped the ladle back into the blood. I was flying.

The men were laughing hard.

"You like?"

"I like," I said. I liked it a lot. The blood tasted pure. Can something taste red? This was red. It was *invigorating,* in every obvious sense.

The bucket was put in a shady corner. The bonfire was lit. The pig burned until it was charred and black. We scrubbed the skin. The hair came off. The head was removed, the body cavity opened up, the stomach expanding as though having been buckled into too-tight pants. The entrails were removed. And then everything began to slow down, the particular business of honoring every organ and muscle and joint of a just-killed animal.

I was given the lungs.

"Blow them up," Ludovic said.

And I did, a pair of pretty pink balloons (a remarkable hue, unused to air or light), and I tied them (like a balloon), and Ludovic nailed them to a wooden post to dry out.

We yanked out intestines, the upper ones, a long hose, fifty feet, maybe more, and squeezed out their brown contents by pulling a segment between a thumb and forefinger and moving the solids toward an opening. Ludovic had the hose. He gave me an intestine and asked me to blow into it to open—it was warm against my lips—and he rinsed it out. He then rolled it up in a ring on the ground.

(I thought: Really? Is that it?)

He removed the bladder, and squeezed out the liquid, like water in a balloon, a steamy stream.

"Here, this is for you to blow up, too." He held it out in two hands, very reverential. "This, too, is an honor," he said.

The others stopped and watched.

An honor, eh?

I took a deep breath. The wet mouth of the entry (salty), my wet lips. I blew hard.

Nothing.

The men laughed.

I took a deeper breath. I blew harder.

Nothing. More laughter.

I took a really deep breath, my face changing color—probably to something between red-pink and purple—and the bladder yielded.

I closed the passage with my thumb and forefinger, Ludovic looped it into a knot, and nailed it, too, to the post to dry out.

"For the *poulet en vessie*," he said.

Ludovic mixed his sautéed aromatics into the blood, tasted, added salt and pepper, tasted again (like a chef finishing his sauce), added more pepper. I inserted a funnel into the mouth of an intestine, and Ludovic poured. We twisted the intestine sausage-style at six-inch intervals, tied it closed, and looped the rope into a straw basket. When the basket was full we walked it over to the kettle—a hot vapor cloud when we opened the lid, not boiling, not even simmering—and eased a length of *boudin* inside.

A poem about preparing *boudin noir* was written by Achille Ozanne, a nineteenth-century chef and poet (he wrote bouncy poems about dishes he cooked for the king of Greece), and finds a loose rhyme between *"frémissante"* and *"vingt minutes d'attente." Frémissante* is "trembling." It describes the water: hot but not quite boiling. *Vingt minutes d'attente*— twenty minutes—is the approximate time that you keep the *boudin* submerged. It is akin to cooking a custard. It is done once it is only *just* done. You boil a custard, it curdles. You boil blood, it curdles. Ludovic pricked a casing with a needle. It was dry when it came out. The blood had solidified. He removed the boudin. I cooked the next one.

We carried our basket into a kitchen, and found a dozen people already there, preparing the accompaniments: roasted apples, potatoes, salad, bread, bottles of the local Côtes du Rhône, made by someone down the road, no labels. The room was warm, the windows were fogged up, and we ate, the *boudin* like a rich red pudding, spoilingly fresh, complexly fragrant of our morning pig, and we drank, and afterward went back out into the courtyard, feeling stiff and sleepy, to make sausages and other preparations that needed aging.

It doesn't take long to kill a pig. But reassembling it into edible forms would take until nightfall. We had killed a beautiful animal. The food from it would last for months.

Henri Béraud, a novelist and journalist (as well as a fascist and an anti-Semite—and, nevertheless, an astute observer of the city where he grew up), describes Lyon as oddly situated. There is no port or nearby sea. Only farms and the roads that lead to it. And dairies as well and vineyards and rivers and mountain pastures.

ONE EVENING, CHRISTOPHE, OUR NEIGHBOR, APPEARED AT OUR DOOR, bearing a large envelope. He reminded me of the matrimonial squabble that had occurred during our *apéro*.

"My father," he said, "is an amateur historian. He spends a lot of time in the Archives." The Lyon Archives, which date from the year 1210, hold the raw documents of Lyon's (often tragic) history. "I mentioned our conversation to him," Christophe said, "and my father made a copy of a document that he thought might interest you." Christophe would become a good friend. He would drop off ducks that he shot during hunting season, and once invited me to join him. He now had a sly, quiet smile. It said: So—there might be something in what you were saying.

In the envelope was an account of a meal prepared for sixty visiting ambassadors from the cantons of Switzerland on February 25, 1548. It was a financial reckoning of an ambitious evening: the acquisition of plates (288 of them), German knives, and wineglasses; twelve musicians; wine from three suppliers plus four hired servers; the ingredients for each service—*entrées, plats principaux* (the main courses), salads, and desserts. Since the feast was held on a lean day, the ingredients included pâtés of trout, frogs, and anchovies, the lake fish that the Swiss and Lyonnais would have in common (like *lavaret* and *omble,* for which no exact translation exists because the fish never leave the region), and exotica like tortoises and whale tongue. But no meat.

At the time, most French banquets were simpler, more medieval (the reference cookbook, routinely reprinted in Lyon, was the fourteenth-century *Le Viandier* by Taillevent): a rotisserie for meat, a pot over a hearth, a lot of boiling. Meals were eaten mainly in one course, either by hand or with a *tranche,* a stale piece of bread used as a trowel, and with the aid of a knife (the fork, a feature of the Italian table, hadn't yet caught on).

The meal prepared for the Swiss ambassadors was different and more typical of the Italian Renaissance, bright and celebratory, a *festa,* an illustration of *convivium,* the Roman word that translates loosely as "coming together over food" and that ultimately makes a meal among the greatest pleasures in a person's life. I feel compelled to describe the meal as more "Italian" than French. The date is interesting, too: the winter of 1548. In the fall, Henri II and his wife, Catherine de' Medici, would make a famous and famously Italian entry into the city.

There was magic in the message that Christophe conveyed to me, a world of eating and drinking that was both proximate (many of the suppliers—the butchers, the fishmongers, the wine merchants—may have lived on the very streets of our quartier) and so far away as to seem unknowable. The place had become intriguing and mysterious.

One afternoon, I don't know why, I found myself thinking of Dorothy Hamilton and her urging me to attend cooking school. No, you really don't need to, I still believed, provided that you are without financial obligations or children, are able to throw yourself absolutely into the kitchen, are fourteen years old, and, with a mind as flexible as your youthful body, have a capacity to learn just about everything, every station, every dish, very quickly.

For the rest of us, we need to be taught. Dorothy was right.

I looked up the admissions director of L'Institut Paul Bocuse, Dorine Chabert, took a deep breath, and phoned. I was a journalist who had worked in kitchens, I said, and wanted to attend the institute in some capacity, I wasn't sure how or what. Would she see me?

We made an appointment for the next morning. I left a message for Bob. I would be in after lunch.

L'INSTITUT is housed in a turreted late-nineteenth-century "castle," in a wooded park, just outside of Écully, a historic village four miles north of Lyon. Madame Chabert seemed happy to meet me but declared outright that she had no idea what she could do for me. The school then offered a three-year course to about three hundred students. And although it was not unfamiliar with visiting journalists—there was a media changing room (you are not allowed into the *zone culinaire* until you've been fitted out in a paper lab coat, sanitary booties, and a tight-fitting shower cap)—*l'institut* had no experience of someone who was both a cook and a journalist. Or, to be more precise—and my mistake was probably in being more precise—the office had no experience of someone who wanted to learn to be a cook in order to write about what he had learned.

At one point, Madame Chabert declared, "*Des chaussures de sécurité!* You don't have a pair, do you? You are not really a cook if you don't have them."

These are heavy, high-platform, waterproof, electricity-proof, slide-proof chef clogs that are good for nothing except standing in one place and protecting your feet. As it happens, because of the nature of my appointment, and in the hope that it might include a kitchen visit, I was wearing a new pair. I pointed to my feet.

Madame Chabert didn't believe me and rose from her chair to confirm. She was impressed. Then she was distressed. She had never met a writer with *chaussures de sécurité*. Now she had a new problem, because by now she really wanted to be obliging but really didn't know how.

"Ha!" she declared. "I will phone Alain." And "Alain," evidently intrigued by the prospect of my presence, approved it.

"Alain" was Alain Le Cossec, MOF, the executive chef and director of culinary arts at the institute. The MOF after his name stands for Meilleurs Ouvriers de France (Best Workers of France). Once you've earned the honor of being among them (every four years, a nationwide competition is held in many disciplines, including pastry and bread making), the MOF initials are attached to your name, and your neck is forever adorned by the colors of a French flag instead of a normal collar. The flag tells everyone you meet that you are the most badass alpha dog in the pack and can kick the butt of anyone else in the kitchen. (MOF, in French, rhymes with "woof.")

The normal routine for students was a week in a kitchen, followed by a week of theory in a classroom. With "Alain's blessing," Madame Chabert invented a crash course for me, consisting of only the kitchen curricula, and it involved my jumping into whatever cooking class was being conducted at whatever level, which, at that moment, happened to be a weeklong session at Saisons, the school's gastronomic restaurant.

"You don't normally begin at Saisons. You're meant to earn your place," Madame Chabert said. "And it will be with first-years." She looked at the calendar. "And you will be there for the Valentine's Day dinner. Chef Le Cossec's Valentine's dinner is reserved a year in advance. Shall we do it?"

Shall we do it? Yes! I was about to be in my first restaurant kitchen since arriving in France.

I signed a contract, agreeing to pay tuition on a class-by-class basis (a week in Saisons was 1,000 euros), was given a locker ("Never arrive in the clothes you cook in"), a five-page glossary entitled *Vocabulaire professionnel de cuisine et pâtisserie* ("The words you need to know *before* your first class," Madame Chabert said), and a copy of the school textbook, *La Cuisine de référence,* a 1,040-page large-format, floppy paperback (35 euros). "The bible," she said.

I would start the following Monday. I needed to tell Bob.

Bob, I reflected on my way back into the city, had introduced me to a Lyon that no guidebook would have shown me.

I learned about its eating societies. I learned that there *were* eating societies, a proliferation of them: one for the real (*les véritables*) bouchon-owners; another for the real *bouchon* eaters. One for the true (*les vrais*) bistros, and another for the modern ones. There was a Society of Eight, which, by the designation of its members (Le Fleurie was one), included the eight coolest, philosophically unfussy kickass restaurants in Lyon. Its counterpart was the Club de Gueules (which might be translated as the Den of Gluttons), a round table of chefs and restaurant patrons who met to eat and drink with purposeful abundance. Three societies were committed to hosting a real *machôn* (whose members did gather early in the morning and ate and drank until nightfall). And there were serious grown-up societies, like Les Toques Blanches—named after the tall white toque—whose members were the grandest of the region's grand chefs.

Through Bob, I began seeing Lyon from the inside, as the Lyonnais saw it. When I crossed the city, I now met people I knew. I was comfortable. I was starting to feel at home.

I was now about to quit. I stepped into the boulangerie.

"Bonjour, Bill."

"Bonjour, Bob. Bob, I have decided to go to cooking school."

Could I have been more blunt?

He was behind the counter. I was where the customers come in. He took a step back as if he had lost his balance. He whispered, "I knew it was too good to be true."

What had I done? I quickly tried to explain, how I needed to learn kitchen skills first—

"Of course."

—and that I would be back soon. If he would have me. That there was so much more that I wanted to learn from him. "Like your touch. The way you make bread without fingerprints, that lightness. . . ."

The air seemed to be leaving him in my presence. His shoulders sloped. He was just a baker, his posture said. He was Bob. Just Bob.

"You've been accepted to L'Institut Bocuse," he said. In Lyon, there is no other cooking school. In France, there is (effectively) no other cooking school.

"I have been accepted."

Bob whistled.

"But I will be back."

He didn't believe me.

We stood like that. His gaze then slid over my shoulder. He seemed to be thinking.

"At L'Institut Bocuse, you will learn *la grande cuisine,*" he said forthrightly, with energy, like a fist pounding a table.

"I don't know."

"Of course you will. It is Bocuse." He seemed excited. "Maybe, for the first time in my life, I will eat a grand meal and enjoy it. You will make me something from the repertoire of *la grande cuisine.* It will be like Bocuse but without all the Bocuse."

"Of course I will."

He smiled. "I'm going to eat a grand meal, I'm going to eat a grand meal, a grand meal, a grand meal."

On Sunday evening, I prepared my clothes—chef's jacket, kitchen trousers, and apron. I didn't have a toque, which concerned me, but I would be given one when I arrived. (Today it is made of paper, with nothing on top—a curious feature, as though it were purporting to be a hat but isn't one; it isn't, in any case, something you wear outside in the rain.) I also didn't have a kitchen towel, which didn't concern me, because every kitchen has stacks of towels.

Instruction by Paul Bocuse

You, Madam, don't like cooking because it's a tedious chore, end-lessly repeated; it is beneath your intelligence. . . .

Permit me to respectfully disagree. Have you forgotten that cooking is the antechamber of happiness? Cooking is an Art; it satisfies our psyche by striking our senses; it is not unworthy of you. It is exactly like painting or music. . . . Cooking as you under-stand it no longer exists: It has become the Art of Gastronomy.

But is it appropriate for me, a man of science, a physiologist, to teach you an Art? Yes, since at the foundation of all art is science. And it is science that one teaches to make an Art understood. To understand music, you study physics in the form of scales, har-mony, counterpoint. To understand drawing, you learn perspec-tive, anatomy. To understand the Art of Gastronomy, an educated person must learn the science that this Art is based upon.

For this science, I have proposed the name "Gastrotechnique." It is a simple thing that consists in the application of six elemen-tary principles of physics and chemistry that you already know:

Boiling

Frying

Grilling and roasting

Stewing

Binding with starch

Binding with egg yolk

ÉDOUARD DE POMIANE, *VINGT PLATS QUI DONNENT LA GOUTTE*
(*TWENTY DISHES THAT GIVE YOU GOUT*), 1938,
TRANSLATED BY JESSICA GREEN

S aisons was a Michelin-listed restaurant, popular among in-the-know Lyonnais gastronomes and regarded by them as their dining secret. There was nothing about the food that seemed "student-made" in the least. Chef Le Cossec protected the restaurant's reputation and oversaw every plate served. He was in his fifties, tall, thin, with a boyish smile and an equally boyish gap between his two front teeth. He had straight gray hair, cut pageboy-style with a forehead fringe. He looked like a monk and had a manner that was more butterfly than barking dog. He was also so peculiarly light on his feet that you rarely heard him when he entered a room. The effect, since he was in charge and entering rooms with liberty, was that he seemed fleetingly omnipresent. He was almost always amused, which was a peculiar quality in a head-honcho type. Chef Le Cossec was responsible for what might be called "culinary grace." He was very easy to like. Or maybe he was just the "good cop."

His colleague, Chef Thomas Lemaire, oversaw the students and was responsible for lessons in kitchen rigor. He was a very mature-looking thirty-one—square face, glasses, unsmiling, with dour, thin lips—and had the classroom charisma of a resentful tax inspector. His first words to me pertained to a button.

"Your top one. It is undone."

He stared at my crotch. "Your *torchon*" (the French word for "kitchen towel"). "Where is it?"

The regulation uniform, I was informed, includes an apron held in place by a cotton belt, your towel tucked under it, falling on your right hip. It is always on your right hip, so that you know where to find it.

You don't, I would learn, ever use the towel for its normal towel-like characteristics, which, when I finally bought myself a stash, I couldn't help doing, since it *was* a towel, and my fingers *would,* in the course of preparing food, become wet and greasy, and when I thought no one was looking, I did, I admit, reach down and give them a little wipe. (In the event, there *was* someone looking: Lemaire, who had been waiting for the moment, having identified me as a likely nefarious kitchen-towel abuser, whereupon I was roundly rebuked.) Instead, the towel is to be used for its *oven-mitten* qualities, even though a towel is *not* a mitten and has none of its qualities and is only a rectangle of very absorbent cotton (and there is only one kind of *torchon,* the regulation *torchon,* which has two light-red stripes down its length and is so thin that, after repeated washing, it tends toward transparency).

In fact, on any given day, there will be a situation when your towel will be inadequate, since it continues *not* to be a mitten, and you will count on adding someone else's towel, urgently—as in "Hot, quick, you, *your torchon—please!*"

Once, I tucked two towels under my belt, both draped across my right hip, an obvious no-brainer, I thought. Why, when you are hunched down before an oven door, should you call out to the kitchen at large behind you, hoping that someone will appear and miraculously produce an extra towel before you get burned?

Lemaire spotted my two-towel transgression. He pointed and sneered. No words, just a high-pitched hoot of contempt. I felt that I'd been caught out trying to open a car wash.

On another occasion, I was spotted dipping my salsify fries into an eggy batter *with my hands.* I had no idea this was such a flagrant crime. In Italy, you get your hands dirty and are proud of it—it's a way of being in touch with the soul of the food. (Or something. What do I know? Maybe there was a towel shortage.) In France, you use two spoons. It was, I had to admit, more hygienic, and, afterward, you don't have to go searching for a container of water to wash your hands in. (And, duh, you then don't have to use your towel.)

I had a cooking partner, a nineteen-year-old woman named Marjorie who was the second-most soft-spoken student in the entire *institut*. (The most soft-spoken was her best friend, Hortense: In the three months there, I never once heard her voice.) One morning, Marjorie, making conversation, asked me (in her barely audible fashion) why I was here. I began by saying that I had once worked in Chianti. My intention was to say that, having learned northern-Italian cooking, I now wanted to learn the cooking of Lyon.

She had never heard of Chianti.

I said *"Toscane."* I said it loudly (maybe too loudly), to compensate for the softness of her voice.

She had never heard of *Toscane*. I tried *"Toscano."* I tried "Tuscany." I scored with "Florence." I conveyed that I had once worked in Florence, which I hadn't, but it didn't matter; besides, I still hadn't answered her question.

Lemaire knew where *Toscane* was. He knew the word "Chianti." I wondered if, in his eyes, I had put myself forward as an Italian expert. The know-it-all writer-guy Italian expert.

Later, Lemaire asked Marjorie and me to help him with his "cannelloni," which were meant to be rolled around braised beef cheeks. The trouble was the pasta sheets. They kept sticking. Lemaire had poured olive oil into the boiling pasta water to keep them apart. We were given tweezers. The sheets were overcooked along the edges, cakey in the middle, and everywhere olive-oil slimy, and you couldn't separate them without tearing.

"You can assume that I know how to cook pasta," Lemaire said to me. Why did he want me to know he could cook pasta?

"Of course," I said.

"The Italians," he added, "are not the only people who make pasta, you know."

I agreed.

"The French also make ravioli."

"Yes," I said.

"Ravioles. They invented them."

"But it's such an Italian word," I couldn't stop myself from saying.

He corrected me. "No, the French invented *ravioles."*

I then wondered if this might have been a test (and another of Lemaire's lessons in rigor), never to disagree with a chef.

"Of course," I said.

I was reminded of the spat between our next-door neighbors. Why did the idea of Italy put the French on the defensive?

During the break between lunch and dinner, I took a bus back into town. I had been told there was only one place to buy the two-red-striped regulation *torchons*: Bragard, on the other side of Lyon. Bragard was also *the* place to update my kitchen wardrobe, which, evidently, was in need of attention. I picked up the boys en route.

A chef was already in mid-acquisition when we arrived, slowly refitting his entire staff. We waited. Within seconds, the boys were bored. Within a minute, they were lying listlessly on the floor.

When it was my turn, I asked for a dozen *torchons*. I mentioned, in passing, that I was at L'Institut Bocuse, but not that I was a student. The manager's manner changed. She insisted that I try on the *institut*'s official chef jacket ("the one Paul Bocuse wears"). It was a flap-over with snaps instead of the blocky straight-up-and-down with buttons. It was smooth—the thread count was like that of an expensive bedsheet—and only a little stiff, and surprisingly comfortable. Chef jackets, especially the double-breasted kind promoted in the early nineteenth century by the legendary cooking impresario Antonin Carême (he is often seen as the father of the French kitchen look), are wonderfully contradictory: heavy and fire-resistant, but aggressively pristine white (like purity itself), on an assumption that they actually will never be soiled. This one, I touched it and vowed: I promise, dear coat, that I will never dribble on you.

I tied a silky white apron around my waist—the luxury model, the kind that circles the legs and comes down to the floor—slipped a pressed towel over the belt, and snugged it tight. The manager, who, I now concluded, must have thought that I was a distinguished chef visiting from America (my gray beard, my shiny pate, my conspicuous lack of youthfulness), climbed onto a footstool and put a toque on my head. She added a white kitchen neck-scarf and tied it from the front. ("I give you the scarf for free and insist you wear it. You are too elegant.") I crossed my arms. I was a giant in white.

The effect on the three-year-olds was immediate. They stood up and wowed. I admit: I had hoped for their wows. It was why I had picked them up, to share the theatre of my dressing up in chef whites.

I called for a taxi—by now outright tardy—dropped off the boys, and drove on to the institute. When I reached the kitchen, Lemaire was already so distressingly deep into the evening's batch of "cannelloni" (and possibly so embarrassed about being found there), that he didn't rebuke me. He must have known that he had added way too much olive oil this time, but nevertheless had the forethought, just in case, to cook way too many noodles. In the effort to unstick them, most were ruined. The small number that survived were just enough to wrap the braised beef cheeks.

The trick, by the way, is not oil. It's a wooden spoon. To keep your pasta from sticking? You stir it.

A staff member appeared and addressed me: "Chef Le Cossec wants to see you."

I had been invited to dinner. At a table, the two of us—alone in a dining room, attended by two servers—ate a meal that arrived in three courses. A sommelier poured wine from a decanter. Red Burgundy. The *plat principal* was duck with a red-cherry sauce. It felt as though I had been invited to the private chambers of a ship's captain. I pictured the meal that my wife was having with our children at our wobbly kitchen table: a plate of *nuggets de poulet* heated in a microwave. I then recalled a friend who, on learning that I had come to Lyon to learn French cooking, had written me—"imagining you getting your butt kicked by all those French bastards." In the locker room, earlier, I had listened to a message left by Daniel Boulud's assistant—"The chef wants you to know that no one in America is doing what you're doing—it is so hard-core."

My glass was refilled.

Le Cossec was curious. What did I want?

"To learn the skills of a chef. I have no illusions about my becoming a *grand chef.*"

I had learned the distinction. *Grand* translates as "great," in the way that you might say a "great baseball player." But *grand* combined with *chef* is its own designation. It was invented (again) by Carême. He was also among the first to describe cooking as an art. (The cooking classes at L'Institut Bocuse are described as instruction in *"les arts culinaires."*)

Grand chef is, in effect, a title akin to nothing else in any other country, because no other country accords such a lofty status to the person making your dinner. We don't have the same thing in English. If you are mad enough to tell people that your aspiration is to be a great chef—as in "I am a student at L'Institut Paul Bocuse so that I will become *un grand chef*"—you will be dismissed as silly and deluded. But for many of the students at *l'institut,* that was exactly their ambition. They wanted to be Marc Veyrat. They wanted to be Paul Bocuse. Why? I don't know why. A time-honored, highly inculcated reverence for dinner? It is, whatever the reason, at the very heart of Frenchness.

But for the rest of us, there was French cooking, which we wanted to learn how to do, and that was plenty.

One morning, I was sharpening a knife, running it up and down flat against a steel.

Le Cossec interrupted. "Yes, you may start with the blade flat, but finish at an angle, moving up and down lightly, like a breeze." (*Comme une brise.*) The angle hones the blade. When I touched it, I felt the fragility of the edge and its danger.

I asked to cook the steaks.

"Regarde," he said.

He put a sauté pan on the fire, waited, and confirmed the heat with his hand just above the skillet.

"Listen to the butter."

He dropped in a spoonful—"Not much." He paused. "Do you hear? It is singing." *(Il chante.)* The sound was like a muted babbling. "You hear this singing just before you add eggs to make an omelet. You hear it just before you set meat down on the pan." If it is too hot, the butter steams and burns. Too cold, and the protein sticks to the surface. He leaned over the pan with his ear. "You want it to sing."

He left the butter there.

It carried on with its soft tune—the temperature hot but not too hot—until it frothed up.

"This is a mousse."

He gave the pan a shake. He turned down the flame. He waited. The butter changed color. "This is *beurre noisette.*" Brown butter.

He poured the butter from the pan and started over. He dropped in butter, it sang, and he added the filet. It had been bundled up with a crisscrossing string to keep its shape and looked like a small parcel. He added more butter. It melted quickly, and he spooned it over the top of the meat.

"This is *rissoler.*"

Rissoler means to cook an ingredient in a small amount of liquid, usually fat. The technique is an item in the *vocabulaire culinaire*. In practice, it involves a lot of spooning. You cook your ingredient from underneath by direct heat (in a pan; in effect, sautéing it) and from above, indirectly, by ladling the fat over it. Once the ingredient starts to brown (*colorer*), you turn it over. You see the technique in French kitchens, in movies, and in a parody: someone tilting a pan, pooling up hot juices along the lower rim, frantically spooning.

Le Cossec corrected my posture. "Stand tall and make small, deliberate movements. Be easy in your body when you cook."

He showed me how to complete the rösti, the Swiss mountain preparation that renders potatoes into a crispy version of a fried hairpiece. They are cooked in a very large rectangular pan until one side is browned and crunchy. There is only one way to turn the rösti over: a flip.

"Picture the rösti landing on its other side. Think of nothing else."

"*Un. Deux. Trois.*"

I flipped. The potato was airborne. ("Yikes!") It landed. I was surprised. Le Cossec wasn't.

For the Valentine meal, he set out two goose livers and put on a pair of gloves to remove their veins.

I asked if I could do one.

"Really? Have you deveined liver before?" He looked bemused.

"No."

He gave me a pair of gloves.

A goose liver is impressively and massively brown, and the veins are gnarly. A long one runs north to south. The other runs east to west. They meet somewhere in the lobe's northern hemisphere.

I followed Le Cossec's lead.

He dipped his hand into the liver—no hesitation, he simply knew where the veins met (and there is nothing on the surface that tells you where to drill down)—and pulled them out. It could have been effected with a scalpel. The liver looked undisturbed except for a light scratch on its surface.

A quick intake of breath, a rough aim, and I plunged in feelingly with my fingertips.

Nothing.

I dug around. (You don't want to have to dig around.) The tissue was startling in its mushiness. Then I had one, I felt it, a vein—it was like a twig in mud—I grasped it and tugged. The rest, all connected, seemed to be coming out with it. It felt as though I were pulling out the plumbing underneath a street. Success! But the liver looked decimated. I could have been installing a sewer.

The messiness of my mess didn't matter. It was a lesson in the behavior of fat—a goose liver is overwhelmingly fat—and how, under heat, it reforms itself. For the Valentine meal, the foie was encased in puff pastry, and the result was smooth and luxurious and actually—no other word seems quite adequate—rather transporting. (The other menu items included a *carrelet*—plaice—served with a sauce made of the liquid it was poached in; guinea hen, beef fillets, and a cabbage *embeurrée,* made with butter and pork and, yes, more foie gras. It was not an easy kitchen to arrive hungry in.)

In pastry, I was told, "Water—essential to fruit, but its enemy in the kitchen." To clean a strawberry: never soak and always use two bowls (quickly in and out of one to wash, quickly in and out of the other to rinse). "Water dilutes flavor. In the kitchen, you want to enhance it."

I was told, "Air—essential to life, the enemy of conservation." Everything is stored on "contact," a piece of plastic film on top, the air pushed out.

I was told of the three lives of vanilla: fresh (first use) for intensity; dried (second use) for stewing and infusions; then, dried again (third use) to be stored with sugar.

The egg: never cracked on the rim, only on a flat surface, once sharply, so as not to be contaminated by the shell, which is unhygienic.

I was corrected on how to stir ("from the bottom up, circling, cleaning the sides as you go"), which I assume everyone else knows but which I never seemed to get right. I was corrected on my whisk ("limp wrist, figure eight, hitting four points of the bowl as if it had corners"), which I hadn't known and which is both efficient and actually rather flash (you can reach exhilarating speeds).

I learned all the pastries and, with my classmates, made them in student-body lunchtime quantities (e.g., 350 chocolate tarts). My favorite, without question: *pâte feuilletée* (in French—or "puff pastry," in English). Both terms, the French and the English, describe the preparation (large amount of butter enveloped in a small amount of dough rolled out and folded over many times and in several directions) with remarkable physical specificity. *Pâte feuilletée* describes the pastry before it goes into the oven. *Feuilleter* can mean "to leaf through a book," and if you slice firmly through the uncooked dough with a sharp knife it will look something like the neatly cut pages of an old novel. "Puff pastry" seems like a bad translation but is a good description of what you eat. In a hot oven, the pastry puffs: The butter melts, the water content evaporates, and the evaporation creates a hot blister between the layers of dough. What ought to be the world's heaviest food tastes, confusingly, like one of the lightest. For me, the English "puff pastry" captures its crunchy and ethereal contradictoriness—if cooked to perfection, if the fat is completely rendered—and, at the risk of my being eternally censured by L'Institut Bocuse, is the term I swear by, will use in this book, and urge the French to adopt.

Puff pastry is an absolute blast.

Pastry was all about the rules. The French kitchen was about rules: that there was always one way and only one way (like trimming the gnarly ends off your beans—with your fingertips, never a knife). And I liked the rules and how they were never questioned. Correction: I loved the rules.

I liked how my days started, which now included an iron that I purchased on the way home one night at Monoprix, the French everything-store, after Le Cossec had appeared unnoticed and shouted across the kitchen where I was working, *"Mais, Bill, regarde ta veste"*—your chef's jacket! (And everyone stopped and stared at me.) "Are you sleeping in it?"

I now woke at six and pressed it. The jacket was heavy and the sleeves needed extra attention. I pressed the apron, a luxurious swath of white fabric, like a piece of extravagant formal wear. I pressed the double-red-striped cotton towels, four of them, one after another. (There is, I confess, wonder in a pressed towel.) I folded everything into a tidy bundle. The activity took my brain to a happy place that it hadn't known: everyone else asleep, the repetition, the hiss of the iron's steam, a cup of coffee nearby, having only the day ahead to think about.

I fetched my knives and clogs and set out before seven, carefully, so as not to wake the boys, whose room was by the front door.

When I began at *l'institut,* the mornings had been dark, but each day the sun arrived a little earlier. I crossed the Saône on the footbridge, my shoes clacking on the slats. It took four minutes from my front door to the stop for the number-19 bus. Thirty-five minutes later, it arrived in Écully: a walk through the woods, another coffee at the bar, and then—boom—the fast high-focus intensity of physical labor in a French kitchen.

Classes were small, no more than eight people. My schedule tended to include a group from the second year, starting with its stint in a restaurant called F&B (short, alas, for "Food and Beverage"), which was daringly student-run and aspired to feed a sophisticated French lunch to everyone—faculty, staff, friends, visitors, about four hundred people—in two shifts.

The idea: Each student was the chef for a day, prepared a menu, ordered the ingredients, drew plating diagrams, and, creating a *brigade* from among their colleagues, executed the meal. The dishes included a vegetable terrine *en gelée,* a salmon in puff pastry, and a duck confit with an unctuous red-wine sauce made with fifty kilos of duck carcasses roasted by yours truly.

The reality: The menus *never* worked (not once). Between principle and reality were Paul Brendlen and Édouard Bernier. Brendlen fixed, Bernier implemented. Nothing was more seat-of-the-pants.

Brendlen, the top dog, was strong, stocky, unstoppable. You felt the stress of his kitchen the moment you walked in: Bang! Seven a.m. and everyone, including Brendlen, was sweating and running. Routine was impossible, and there were injuries—a slashed finger, a hand, a limb—and Brendlen, irritated, impatient, would seize the maimed piece of anatomy, examine it fleetingly, blood dripping on the floor, give it a shake, and dismiss it. It was not so bad.

"Oh, pas grave."

Someone was burned. The kitchen smelled of toasted skin.

"Pas grave."

A server dropped a tray of food, broken ceramic everywhere.

"Pas grave."

José Augusto was making the lunch on a Wednesday. He had endeared himself to me for his (largely clandestine) love for Italy. Augusto had persuaded the authorities to let him go to Italy to do his *stage*. (Every student has to do three *stages*, apprenticeships, at established restaurants. They *were* at the heart of the curriculum.) Augusto—he is still amazed that he was allowed—chose Dal Pescatore in Mantua. His F&B menu, not surprisingly, was Italian.

For a starter, he planned a plate of antipasti—vegetables (artichoke hearts, zucchini, carrots), a slice of prosciutto, a chunk of Parmigiano, and an olive-oil-and-balsamic-vinegar dressing. He prepared one in advance—in effect, a "demo model"—and set it on a counter for Brendlen and Bernier to approve.

They stared at it, their arms crossed. Brendlen turned his head to one side. *"C'est une catastrophe,"* he said to Bernier. "What are we going to do?"

"It's after ten o'clock."

"Oh là là."

Brendlen addressed Augusto. "The starter is your diner's first impression. You don't get a second chance at making a first impression."

Bernier explained: "This is not good. You have ignored the three principles."

The three principles of a French plate are *color, volume,* and *texture.* They are rules of presentation. If your dish uses *color* strategically, *volume* (i.e., has height), and *texture* (mixes soft and hard, or juicy and crunchy), then it will appeal to a diner.

Of the three principles, Augusto's plate had none.

"*Regarde la couleur,*" Brendlen said.

Apart from the carrots, the plate was green (the zucchini—thick slices overcooked) or gray-green (the artichoke) plus a bit of straggly brown (the prosciutto). It was like a lawn at the end of a very hot summer.

"*Regarde les dimensions.*" The dish was flat. It was unclear to me where anyone would find a third dimension. How do you teach a flat slice of zucchini to stand up?

"*Et la texture! José!*" Brendlen made a masticating sound, because everything was the same in the mouth, slightly slimy or squishy soft.

I wondered: Shouldn't someone have had a word with Augusto before he ordered forty kilos of zucchini?

"How much time do we have?" Brendlen asked.

"An hour."

Brendlen and Bernier continued studying the plate, hoping to Frenchify it.

For color, Brendlen proposed burying the artichoke.

"It will be a surprise, hidden, like the heart," Bernier said.

But how?

"Bread?"

"Toasted?"

"Grilled."

"But cut thin, so that it snaps when you bite into it, and shaped into an oval," which was the approximate shape of the artichoke heart. If you then propped the toast up against the artichoke, the dish would gain a height element (the elevated toast) *and* a new texture (grilled crispiness).

Bernier suggested that there was potential in the *green* zucchini and *orange* carrots—this time sliced thinly rather than roughly—and arranged in a semicircle.

"Can we make a zucchini mousse?" Brendlen wondered. The textural possibilities of a gourd were not infinite.

"Not enough time," Bernier said.

Brendlen turned on Augusto. "Why didn't you make a mousse? What is wrong with you?" It would be the last time that Augusto was addressed directly. The dish was no longer his.

"Let's cut them lengthwise with the meat slicer."

"Paper thin," Bernier said.

"So you can see through them."

Sliced thus, it could even be taught to stand up.

There were about five kilos left.

"There is also prosciutto," Bernier said.

"Another problem."

What do you do with a gangly slice of cured meat? If you're in Italy, you pop it into your mouth with your fingers. But here you don't do things with your fingers.

Brendlen picked up a piece—with his fingers, as it happened—and popped it into his mouth. "Good fat," he said. "Maybe it could be sautéed with some carrots and the rest of the zucchini *en brunoise*" (diced into uniformly small cubes).

"Plus tomatoes. A summer ragoût."

The tomato introduced both a new color and yet another texture. A ragoût was different from the other vegetables—it was cooked and not slimy, and could be spooned atop the artichoke-leaning toast.

Within ninety minutes, the dish was reconceived and reorganized (Parmigiano crumbled on top), and plated, although it was tight: The last one hundred or so were being finished as the first two hundred were being served.

I admired the finished plate. It made me want to eat it. It wasn't Italian. But it seemed instructively French, or was at least an illustration of what the French might do to a plate of antipasti if they ever invaded Italy and took it over.

I wondered: Is creativity more easily expressed in rigorous structures?

On the last cloudy day of winter, walking from the bus stop to the school, I noticed snow flurries and wondered when spring would come. The next day, washing up my bowls in the pantry of a pâtisserie kitchen, I looked out on the grounds and saw daffodils, and the day was bright.

On the first day of spring, there is a parade at the boys' school, *un défilé*, for *la fête des pentes*. A pile of leaves is set alight, to drive away the last of winter, and the children, dressed in homemade costumes, march through the quartier—barriers along the pavement for onlookers to stand behind—and climb up the *pentes*. The *pentes* are steep inclines that lead to the high plateau of the Croix-Rousse. You mount them on zigzaggy stone steps that were built centuries ago by the monks. Then the parade returns to the square by the boys' school, the Place Sathonay, and lunch. It was jubilantly festive, Jessica told me, because of course I missed it. I was making profiteroles. But I saw the pictures, and would see the parade the following year, our children dressed up like rosebushes, wearing wool hats for the still very cold March morning, and sunglasses for the unequivocally springlike glare, each holding the hand of another student.

Alfredo Chávez, a third-year student from Mexico, wanted to talk to me about the Medicis. He had written a paper for a theory class. The argument was a variation on the Catherine de' Medici thesis. According to Chávez, it wasn't Catherine who had influenced French cooking. It was her cousin, Marie de' Medici, who sixty-seven years after Catherine arrived in France became the wife of Henri IV. It was a novel take, but not entirely without merit.

Henri IV, from Béarn, at the heart of the kingdom of Aragon in the French and Spanish Pyrenees, was mainly famous for his effort to end the sixteenth-century wars between the Catholics and the Protestants and for the abrupt end to his twenty-year reign, when he was stabbed in the ribs by a religious zealot. In matters culinary, he was famous for his love of *pot-au-feu,* which encouraged the acceptance of a simple dish— meats cooked in a pot over a low fire—at both grand and simple tables. (Italians, incidentally, have long claimed that the dish was theirs—in Italy it is called *bollito misto,* and, as it happens, there were Italians in Henri IV's many kitchens.) Henri IV, "Le Béarn" as he was called, may have also inspired *sauce Béarnaise*—at least its name. And in matters of love, he was notorious for his sexual appetite, his impressive frequent-flyer account at several brothels, and his many, lavishly kept mistresses. Marie de' Medici, apart from being the second Italian woman to marry a French king, hasn't been dealt with sympathetically by history ("the fat banker's daughter," according to one mistress), but it is true that, like other Italians before her, she brought wealth and high culture to a France that was still lacking in both.

Chávez's paper was dismissed as a reckless piece of cultural propaganda. If he ever advanced the ideas in it again, he was told, he would be kicked out of the school.

"Kicked out? Really?"

"Really," he said. He sent me a copy. It was like a samizdat text. "But don't tell anyone."

Lyon has always had Italian connections—at least since the Romans first occupied it, in 43 B.C., named it Lugdunum, and made it their own—and has been a home to settlers from the Italian peninsula long before there was an "Italy" with modern fixed borders. Until the late sixteenth century, cities were still more important than states, and Lyon was among the most influential on the Continent, positioned at the confluence of two great rivers and between both Northern and Southern Europe and Eastern and Western capitals of commerce. (The loose idea of France, as it was then defined, ended on one bank of the Saône.)

There was no denying that the Italians were, in fifteenth- and sixteenth-century Lyon, very prominent. Wealthy Italian families not only profited from the *foires,* the two-week-long goods fairs held every three months or so on a religious holiday, they effectively created them. They also opened the first bank in France, developed a facility for loaning capital and exchanging currencies, created the first stock market, and became so conspicuous, in their worldly success and influence, that, fearing local resentment and retaliation, they appear to have changed their Italian names to sound French. (The Gadagne family, one of Lyon's most prominent, were Florentine exiles; their real name was Guadagni, which, in a coincidence of history, is derived from the Italian verb *guadagnare*—to earn or gain, with a sense of "rake it in." Thomas Gadagne, the richest man in Lyon, was wealthier than the king, who was a major debtor of his.)

The headquarters of the Italian banking operations, an august edifice with Roman columns in an open square (Place du Change), still stands, as do the homes of the Italians themselves, walled villas with courtyards, arches, statues, and other flourishes of the flourishing Renaissance. Viewed from the hills, its red terra-cotta tile roofs just below, the quartier Vieux Lyon (Old Lyon), could be mistaken for one in Florence.

At it happens, it was in Lyon that Marie de' Medici met Henri IV. (He missed the wedding in Florence, which was conducted by proxy.) And as it happens, their "second wedding" was also conducted in Lyon. And Marie de' Medici, a generous cultural patron, who, like many of the Italians in France, missed the food of her homeland and, as it happens, also employed Italian chefs in her kitchens.

Lyon, I was coming to believe, really was where you might see evidence of the Italian influence on French cooking, if such influence had actually existed. Did it? I didn't know. And it was, in any case, a long time ago. What was intriguing was the eccentric defensiveness that I kept witnessing, which seemed to betray chauvinism and—what?—fear, maybe? Would you really kick out a student because he was investigating the influence of a Medici queen? Was there *that* much at stake? Could an instructor be so naïve as to believe that the French had invented ravioli? Maybe it was just an enduring resentment: After, all, how could Italian cooking, which is rustic peasant food, have anything to do with French cuisine, which is civilization itself?

I was in the *Zone Culinaire*, watching a class through a glass partition. They were being examined. I hadn't really been examined. It seemed not to be a feature of the program that Madame Chabert had designed for me.

The students were from the first year, and I recognized them as the ones I had cooked with, including shy Marjorie and silent Hortense. They were making omelets.

A student presented his omelet. The instructor poked it and shook his head. He didn't bother to taste it; he tipped it into the trash. An omelet wants to be soft in the middle, pillowy to the touch. It should have bounce. This one was hard.

I was joined by a member of the faculty, Hervé Raphanel. I had been introduced to him before. He watched with me.

The next student's omelet was too big: big in the sense of too much volume. The instructor remonstrated him. It was like watching a movie without sound. His gestures said: "Why did you use a whisk?" *Un fouet.* "I told you a fork."

The class was kitchen basics. A whisk aerates the protein. It is what you use to make a soufflé or a meringue. An omelet gets its tenderness by being mixed, not whipped. You want the egg whites quiet and small.

The omelet was thrown away.

"How old do you think those students are?" Raphanel asked.

"Actually, I know," I said. "Most are nineteen. Two of them might be twenty." It was an unusually young class. Half the students at *l'institut* come from abroad, and most of them were older, career changers.

"Exactly," Raphanel said. "They are twenty years old. When I was twenty, I had already earned my first Michelin star." He reflected. "And they'll be twenty-two when they graduate? By then, I had my second Michelin star." The tone wasn't boastful. It was one of exasperation.

Another student presented her omelet. This one was too runny; it was seeping out at the ends. The instructor re-enacted pressing the back of a fork on the eggs in the pan. When the tines leave an impression, your omelet is ready to be rolled. Not before. The instructor wiggled his finger side to side—no, no.

"Look at how those students are standing. They are so removed from the food, pushing it around at arm's length. Where's the love?" *L'amour—où est-il?* Raphanel sighed. "They should be breathing *in* their ingredients." He simulated dipping into a plate and *in*haling the aromatics. "A chef needs to be transported by his food. If they don't have that love now . . ."

The next day, I learned about a new class, and exams, demanding exams, daily exams, with a full day of them at the end, were an essential feature. I wanted in.

Willy Johnson had been talking about it in the bar. Willy was the other American at *l'institut*. My pastry chef used to run out into the foyer and shout for Willy whenever I did something that the chef ascribed to my not being able to follow his French. Willy was twenty-nine, sandy hair, lightly freckled face, with something of a West Coast surfer's manner. He also spoke good French and was working as a private chef in the affluent homes in the hills above Lyon.

"The class," Willy said, "is fish." Just that. "Fish." It had been offered once before, in January. "It is brutal. It is also the most expensive class in the school—three thousand dollars. It uses more fish than you've seen in your life. There is no teaching assistant."

And the teacher?

"Éric Cros, a fanatic."

I knew him. He gave the impression of living in the present tense and of always being out of breath. He was exhausting to look at.

I found him and asked if I could speak to him.

"You have five seconds," he said.

"May I join your class?"

"Yes."

FISH. Two years before, Cros had been teaching "modernist gastronomy," but was alarmed by his students. They didn't know the basics. How can you be experimental if you don't know the basics? He dropped modernist cuisine and started a new class. Fish was the vehicle. Cros was on a mission. Time-honored techniques were no longer being passed on and were in danger of disappearing: The issue was urgent.

Cros had five assumptions that amounted to a philosophy.

1. You learn the old stuff before you try the new stuff.
2. You learn the old stuff in order to do the new stuff.
3. The old stuff is not easy.
4. You are not yet good enough to be creative: Don't even think about it or you'll be punished.
5. A recipe is only an introduction. It is the beginning of your relationship with the dish. (After Cros demonstrated one— quickly, breathlessly, talking so fast that he stopped to wash his face to cool down—he left. He didn't want your questions. He might not return for an hour. There was plenty of fish. If you failed, you tried again.)

"You can make fun of him," Willy told me, "but he changes lives. The people who take his course? They are different at the end. You don't know how lucky you are to be admitted."

I thought: I know friends who would fly to Lyon tomorrow, and pay much more than 3,000 euros, to get this kind of instruction.

I thought: This is why I've come to France.

The man himself looks surprisingly normal. He has a robust physique—broad shoulders, strong arms, maybe a little squat—and a familiar physiognomy, more Irish than French: a square head, bushy eyebrows, turned-up nose. He would have been bored in school, good at sports, played rugby. He was probably loved by his mother. But Cros isn't normal. He is, in the words of one of the teaching assistants, "damaged by food." He was on the far side of obsessiveness. Cros, chitchatting? Impossible to imagine. In the school hallways, he always had his head down, not wanting to waste a minute, running. I didn't know anyone else who ran to class. He was a maniac.

We began by preparing five hundred sea bass. It was an exercise in *mise-en-place,* a kitchen expression, to have everything in place before you begin the service. For the sea bass, we needed a plastic garbage bag, a cutting board, two trays (one for skins and guts, the other for bones), a pair of scissors, a scaler, a knife, and pliers for plucking out the bones.

With the knife, you didn't "cut" as such. You used the back to scale the fish and the tip for removing the eyes ("Never present a fish that is staring at the client") and for poking into the anus and slicing (a delicate wiggle-wiggle) back up the belly, being careful not to pierce the intestines. To skin, you made an incision just before the tail, pressed down with the side of your blade, and yanked the skin off in one go. (I loved the skinning. It seemed so flash.)

Cros examined my work. I had completed fifteen fish, lined up on my cutting board, looking, I admit, a little beaten up. The guy next to me had done thirty. Cros picked up a fish.

"Yes," he said, "this one is okay. We can serve it." He picked up another. "But this one, no." *Ce n'est pas correct.*

I looked at it. I couldn't see the difference.

"You trimmed off some belly, didn't you?" The bass's belly (which, frankly, doesn't have a lot of tissue) is covered by a nearly invisible fan of threadlike bones, and it's true, rather than pluck out each one, I sliced off the whole flap.

"We can't serve it," Cros said, and threw the fish into the trash.

I was stunned. You threw away my fish?

He picked up several others—"These, too, *pas corrects*"—and tossed them. I followed their trajectory into the bin.

He lingered, arms crossed across his chest. "Why are you so slow?"

"I don't know, Chef."

He studied me from behind.

I picked up a fish, clipped off its fins, and scaled it. I snipped out the gills. I skinned and picked up another fish.

"*Mon Dieu!* You're not still doing *that* with your knife? No one taught you?"

I thought: What exactly am I doing with my knife? And whatever it is, yes, I am obviously still doing *that*, whatever *that* might be, and, no, it is equally obvious that no one has ever taught me.

"No, no, no," Cros said. "Once you start with the knife you finish with it. No one ever told you that?"

"No," I said. I wasn't going to be apologetic. This was why I came to France.

"You *never* put your knife down and pick it up again." *Jamais.*

I've since come to think of the practice as "Assembly Line Knife Technique." What I should have done was set myself up as a single-person factory: Clip off *all* the fins and gills of *all* the fish at my first heavy-scissors station; scale them at the next station; and stack them up until every fish was completed: Then (and only then) I pick up my knife. I gut all of them; I cut off the heads of all; I skin all; I bone all. Then (and only then) I put my knife down. The technique's efficiencies are self-evident to all of humanity, even if they weren't to me, including the obvious one that, if you do the same thing thirty times, it's going to go a lot faster after the third time than the first and can be done at a magician's mindless blitz by the thirtieth.

Never pick up your knife until you know you won't have to put it down. There was such simplicity in the instruction: Would this change my life forever?

I then had my first test.

The assignment: Poach a fish in vegetable broth, stew vegetable slivers in the poaching liquid, make a sauce from it, and steam potatoes in the English style (*à l'anglaise*).

It had been demonstrated. The fish was a *colin*. In the fish morphology, a *colin* is in the "round with two fillets" category. It is white and meaty and, according to my dictionary, called a "coalfish" in England, or a "pollack" in America. I had no memory of eating one, and had certainly never *ébarbed, écailled, dépouilled, éviscéred,* or boned one (fish has its own culinary vocabulary). For me, therefore, a *colin* is and will always be a *colin* (whatever that is). The sauce was a *beurre Nantais*— a butter-and-cream sauce in the style of the city of Nantes. I say that as if I knew both where Nantes is, and why anyone would name a sauce after it. The only thing I knew about the sauce Nantais was that it was different from the one from Bercy, which doesn't have the cream.

I presented my dish. I hadn't tasted it. I was two minutes late. I was in a fluster.

Cros began with the potatoes. I had made three. He had a bite of each.

"This one is correct," he said. "The others are undercooked."

He tasted the fish. "Overcooked."

He picked up a selection of the stewed vegetables (a carrot, a leek, and a celery twig) and inspected them, resting on the tines of his fork.

"The size is okay, almost."

He tasted.

"It needs to be seasoned." (I had seasoned the broth; I hadn't seasoned the vegetables.)

He bit the carrot.

"Hmm . . . crunchy. Oh, that's right, Americans like crisp vegetables, don't they?"

"*Oui,* Chef," I said, thinking: Crunchy carrots, soft carrots—do you really believe that I am so in command of what I am doing that I have any inkling how my carrot twig is going to turn out?

He tasted the sauce. It confused him.

It was based on a beurre blanc. Many fish sauces are based on a beurre blanc, a white butter sauce: shallots, white vinegar (reduced), then white wine (reduced), plus butter. This one, being the one from Nantes, also had the cream plus some fish stock (reduced). The sauce is both acidic and lightly fatty, and a piece of lean seafood seems to taste better with some acid and a light fat.

"The butter, the *montée*," Cros said, shaking his head, mystified by the wrongness in his mouth and searching for an explanation. "The consistency of it, yes, the *montée*—it's not good enough."

The verb for adding butter is *monter*. You "raise" the butter. You "mount" it. You first reduce and concentrate all those good liquids, then build them back up, whisking in the creamy fat, and the whole pot seems to swell, the liquid becoming rather wonderfully thick and full. It becomes a sauce.

Mine: not so wonderful.

"*Pourquoi?*" he asked.

I couldn't say. I didn't know. Now I know. I had rushed it. I was running late. I didn't incorporate my butter one piece at a time. I dropped it in by the chunk, gobs of it, and then boiled the fucker, whisking wildly, a human blending machine on top speed, trying to make up for lost time. And Cros could taste that, could he?

He had another spoonful. "Actually, there isn't enough butter, not for the amount of cream you've used."

Nantes: I don't know why a beurre blanc from there has cream. I still haven't been to Nantes. Were there a lot of cows in Nantes—was that it? (A *beurre Bercy,* the one with no cream, is finished with beef bone marrow. Does Bercy have a lot of slaughterhouses?)

Cros had another spoonful. "It's too thin, isn't it?" *N'est-ce pas?*

"*Oui,* Chef."

"And the acidity," he said, tasting it again, "well, actually, it's almost okay."

"*Merci,* Chef."

He dipped in his spoon again. "But why doesn't it have more taste? It should have more taste." *Plus de goût.*

"*Oui,* Chef." I made a note: "Next time more taste."

What seems to produce a successful sauce is the balance between acidity and fat. That was my supposition, anyway, because I made three more sauces that day, and I never got the balance quite right.

For the sauce that went with a trout dish, there wasn't enough fat. Cros said that I hadn't added enough cream, until he realized that I had forgotten it entirely.

"*Excusez-moi,* Chef."

I cooked *raie*—i.e., skate, the dish that I'd once prepared in its sous-vide form in Michel Richard's kitchen. I then made the sauce, but the issue, this time, wasn't the fat; it was the acidity. Cros said that it needed much more acidity, and then asked: Where is the lemon?

Oh, fuck, I said (blurting out in English). I'd forgotten the lemon.

"*Excusez-moi,* Chef."

The day ended with sole *à la bonne femme* (back in the day an affectionate name for your home cook), poached in white wine, a fish stock, and six mushrooms. The sauce is again made from the poaching liquid, reduced and finished with butter and cream plus a citrus kicker. This time, I remembered the kicker. I tasted it. I liked it. It definitely had kick.

Cros ate the fish ("overcooked, but so was everyone else's"), spooned up the sauce, swallowed, and lurched sideways so suddenly, twisting his torso, seeming to double up, that I thought—well, I didn't know what to think. Had he slipped?

He regained his balance and stared at me, astonished, eyes bulging slightly.

Damn, I really thought I'd nailed this one.

He had another taste. He looked like he might spit.

"*Mon Dieu!* Taste the sauce before you add the lemon. You don't have to add it if there is enough acidity already. Oh là là. *Taste* it. *Please!*"

"*Oui,* Chef."

He had another spoonful, and grimaced.

After lunch, I found Willy in the bar, having a coffee. I wanted him to explain Cros. "What's up with the mini-exams?"

"He does them so that you will learn how much you have to learn," Willy said. "You think you know these dishes. The exams prove you don't know diddly-shit."

Once, midmorning, I was absent briefly. I hadn't paid my bill for Cros's class, and slipped out. Cros had already taken me to task for an unscheduled pee break. ("In America, they don't really take cooking seriously, do they?") This, evidently, was more serious.

I apologized. I explained that I had to pay for the class.

Cros was irritated by having to suffer an explanation.

"When you were not here, I taught four recipes."

I tried to look regretful and self-abasing.

"There are now four recipes that you don't know." His speech was clipped; it seemed to be the speech of a man who wanted to be swearing at me but whose pedagogical position prevented him from letting rip. He named what I'd missed: a fish clarification, a fish sauce, and two mussel dishes. "The class knows how to make a *moules à la poulette*. Do you know how to make a *moules à la poulette*?"

"No, Chef."

"Do you know what a *moules à la poulette* is?"

"No, Chef."

"You should learn how to make it."

"*Oui,* Chef."

"It could be on the exam."

"*Oui,* Chef."

"And if it is, you will fail."

Panic. Was I the only person who had never heard of a *moules à la poulette*?

On the bus back that evening, I studied the *moules à la poulette* recipe. It had been among the day's handouts. It didn't give a lot away. Cros's recipes weren't really recipes; they were inventories of ingredients and (sometimes) quantities. The rest was up to the student.

What does it even mean—a *moules à la poulette*? A *poulette* is small chicken. Can the word be used as an adjective? Chickeny? Chickeny mussels? The dish involves cooking the shellfish in white wine and draining the liquid afterward. The liquid, *le jus,* was the basis of the sauce, which was mixed with a roux (flour and butter cooked together as a thickener), cream, shallots, a lemon, white pepper (Cros fails people for using the wrong pepper), and an egg yolk. A yolk in the sauce? It *was* chickeny mussels. It seemed like a lot to take in.

By now the days had stretched to fifteen hours. ("There is so much to get through.") I was home by nine-thirty. I ate; I showered; I went to bed; I got up at five to catch the bus back. How was I going to practice the dish? I couldn't.

I met up with Willy for a coffee after lunch. I wondered aloud about Cros's affect. "It's so indifferent."

"He notices only performance," Willy said.

I had another coffee. I needed to get back to class, but I wasn't ready. It was going to be a long afternoon. In fact, the class was finishing early tonight, Cros promised, at eight o'clock, because our big exams were the next day. The Practical, the cooking test, would start at 7:30 a.m. Theory would be after lunch. We all had the same thought: *Merde.* We had been so committed to the food that we had forgotten the theory. When was anyone looking at a textbook? Or the handouts? Between now and exam time, we would be memorizing recipes. At some point, we would also have to start brushing up on the philosophic properties of round fish, flat fish, and sideways fish.

I asked Willy, "Do you remember what you were asked on your exam?"

"Of course."

I sipped my coffee. "What was on it?"

"The questions may not be the same."

"I understand."

"In fact, I am sure they won't be."

"But what were they?"

Willy sipped his coffee. He took another sip. I had made him uncomfortable. "Do you really want to know? I mean, does it matter?"

"I'd like to know."

"Okay." He looked at me to confirm that I knew what I was doing, and started in on the list—eagerly, it turned out, with the relish of someone who had survived a tough trial but, until now, had never had the chance to talk about it (because, after all, who else would care?).

Not everyone was asked to make the same dishes, Willy stressed, but everyone was asked to make the same *kind*. There were two sauces based on a mayonnaise, two with a clarified butter, and two with a beurre blanc. "Do you know what a *sauce Choron* is?" he asked.

"Yes."

"Wow. I didn't. I got burned on that one. I couldn't keep it straight in my head."

"There was a PDT." PDT is kitchen shorthand for *pommes de terre:* potatoes. They were to be done either as *cocottes* ("turned"—snub-nosed, oblong, skinny like a rocket, and sautéed) or *à l'anglais* (snub-nosed, oblong, very fat, and steam-roasted).

There were two ways of cooking a fish, *à la bonne femme* (poached in stock) or *à l'anglaise* (fried).

I was surprised by how much I knew.

"And a shellfish dish."

"Which one?"

"À la poulette."

"Really?"

"The one with the egg."

"The bastard."

I got up at four, to review the recipes. It wasn't the Theory that worried me—I knew how to cram. It was the Practical: the clock ticking and my making food for a panel of seen-it-all world-weary French chefs whom I had never met before. (Cros wasn't allowed to be a judge.)

I arrived. There was confusion. Cros—excited—redirected everyone to an auditorium for a practice run of the Theory test. Until now, Cros had been easy to understand, even for me, because his speech was always so purposeful. Most of my notes are in French. But Cros was excited by the exam, he clearly *loved* exams, and there was a complication (the fish hadn't shown up!), and it had rendered him incomprehensible.

It would turn out that I had misunderstood his instruction. It wasn't a *practice* Theory. It was the *real* thing, the one I had planned on cramming for during lunch. When I was then eating it with Augusto, and flipping through my now useless flash cards, he finally had to ask: "What are you doing? The Theory exam was this morning."

"It was?"

(I bombed it. I hadn't looked at a single page of text. *Poisson d'eau douce,* for instance. Sweet water fish? What could *that* mean? It means "freshwater fish." It is a good thing I hadn't known that I'd bombed it and could then enter the Practical exam full of misplaced optimism.)

The practical commenced at 10:00 a.m. I drew a folded slip of paper out of a toque that determined the exam I would take, A or B. I got A.

1. Make a *sauce Béarnaise.*
2. Make a *beurre à la maître d'hôtel.*
3. Make PDT *cocotte.*
4. Prepare a *merlan à l'anglaise.*
5. Prepare *moules à la poulette.* (Cros was a dick.)

Except for the *moules à la poulette,* it wasn't too bad. On paper, I knew the items.

I took five minutes to write out the ingredients, plus crude reminders ("Fish—don't overcook!") and a schedule.

At 10:45, I got ready to present my first dish, the *beurre maître d'hôtel,* to the two chefs waiting for it behind the worktop. One had conducted the omelet-making lessons. I couldn't remember his name, but I liked what I'd seen of his manner, firm but gentle. The other was my judge, Hervé Raphanel, the one who had watched the omelet-making with me. I had been used to seeing Cros behind the worktop, uncompromising, indifferent, tough. It was comforting to see these two faces. They looked so soft.

A *beurre maître d'hôtel* is butter fluffed up with a wooden spoon into a *"pommade,"* then salted and acidified by a squeeze of lemon. I presented it to Raphanel.

It was okay. *"C'est bon."*

PDT cocottes were the snub-nosed rockets.

They were okay. *"C'est bon."*

A Béarnaise.

It was okay. *"C'est bon."*

It was while frying the fish that my mind wandered. *Merlan à l'anglaise* is basically fish and chips without the chips. In France, however, there are rules for fish frying, going back at least to Escoffier, and if you didn't follow them the result would be *pas correct.* Like the portion of fish: It should be 62.5 millimeters in length. (That extra half-millimeter killed me. Really? People used a ruler; I didn't, I couldn't, it was too ridiculous.)

The egg mixture, the first thing you dip your fish into, is supplemented with a splash of milk and olive oil (really) but is never seasoned.

The flour, what the fish is dipped into next, *is* seasoned, and the seasoning must be mixed in with a whisk. (You got that?)

The breadcrumbs, the fish's last stop, are made with sliced white bread (only), fresh, the crusts removed, pulverized in a blender, and sifted through a sieve. And they are not—*ever*—seasoned. They look like a moist powder, less crumb than dust.

Michel Richard's brain popped into mine. He used a sieve, too. What he didn't use was the bread dust. He used the chunky stuff left behind: It was irregular, had texture, produced crunch. He would have learned the rules for breadcrumbs—everyone in a French kitchen learns the rules—but became engaged by what was left over in the sieve. (I had earlier noticed some of his other, modest pieces of rule breaking. In the kitchen, caviar is scooped out on a piece of plastic film tucked tightly around the rim of a bowl. You spoon the caviar off the film to plate a dish. Richard took the idea and made it into floating caviar. Or that *raie*. To this day, I have never seen a boned *raie* in France. Richard's was boned.)

Raphanel liked my fish: crisp, but not overcooked. It was very good. *"Très bien."*

I was buzzing. The mussels were last.

My knowledge of the dish hadn't advanced since my bus-ride contemplation, except that, since then, I had done dishes with eggs and knew that, if I added one to a hot pot, I needed to remove the pot from the direct heat first. Then I would mix everything rapidly, a quick figure eight, knocking the whisk against all sides of the pot: in effect, cooling the liquid just enough to prevent the yolk from coagulating.

While the mussels were in the sauté pan, I cooked my shallots and made my roux. Three minutes. I added the cream to it. At five minutes, the mussel shells opened. I set a sieve above my pot of creamy roux, tipped in the mussels, the *jus* running into the pot, added the egg, and whisked the fucker into a froth. It worked. It didn't curdle. Look at that! I then reheated it briefly on the flattop, poured it back onto the mussels, and walked the pan over to Raphanel. I found myself marveling at what I had done: It seemed right, yellow and creamy and smelling of the sea, even though I had no idea that it was going to look like this.

Raphanel touched a mussel with a fork. "It is plump," he said. He seemed surprised. He touched it again. "It is moist. Perfect."

He brought it to his lips. "It is warm. Juicy. Again, perfect." He really looked delighted. (*Molto, molto grazie, Italia*. I had learned my mussels chops in Italy.)

He regarded the sauce. "It is yellow. Deep. Once again, perfect." He tipped the pan. "Oh, but it is runny." His shoulders slumped. "You forgot to reduce it. What a shame." *Quel dommage*.

I had been so preoccupied with the egg that I forgot to allow the roux to do its work and thicken.

But I wasn't displeased. The tests are on that 20-point scale. I hoped only not to fail. Passing was 10. I got 16.5. I was levitating.

In the event, the result was an average of both tests. I was lucky to have done well on the Practical, because I had categorically crashed the Theory. (Pretty good + disgrace) ÷ 2 = barely passing. But "barely passing" was still passing. It was the worst mark in a class that had miraculously outperformed itself. (Willy was right: Cros changes lives.) But I had passed. I got 11.0.

On the bus, relieved, I felt I was finally learning what I had come for. The French kitchen no longer frightened me. I had much to do, but I believed it was within my ability. On the way home, I resolved to find a restaurant to work in: the next day.

IV

In a Historic Kitchen

The "saintly *mères lyonnaises*," who hardly exist anymore, are one of the favorite nostalgic subjects of old gourmets around here. Ah! The *mère* Fillioux! Ah! The *mère* Brazier! The *mère* Blanc of Vonnas! All those who tasted her *poularde à la crème* talk to you about it like the angel Gabriel had kissed them on the lips. . . .

What these mourners of the saintly *mères* miss is not, I swear, the blue-footed Bresse chicken. Go to the *mère* Blanc's son in Thoissey, go to her grandson in Vonnas: The chicken will melt in your mouth just like in the good old days of Grandma Blanc. Or forget about the Blanc family altogether, go to Paul Bocuse, come to Alain Chapel's, and you will see their little chickens have white, sweet thighs as satiny as those of the king's wench. The creamy Bresse chicken dish hasn't changed. What the mourners miss is the simplicity: the roaring coal stove, the wax tablecloth, the heavy platter under the pile of crêpes, the local wine of that year taken from a barrel, counted by the *pot*.

FROM *CROQUE-EN-BOUCHE* BY FANNY DESCHAMPS (1976),
TRANSLATED BY JESSICA GREEN

I showed up at La Mère Brazier mid-morning. I asked to see Viannay. I told him, in French, that I'd spent the last few months at L'Institut Bocuse.

"We all respect L'Institut Bocuse," he said. "It is very serious."

"It is," I agreed. "And now I've come to ask you to take me on as a *stagiaire*. Not long. Seventeen days. After that I'll be gone."

"Seventeen days?"

"Seventeen days."

He looked at a calendar. "Do you have insurance?"

Yes.

"You'll need to send me an e-mail, promising that you won't hold the restaurant responsible if you get hurt."

"Happily."

"Seventeen days. And then you'll be done? *D'accord?*"

"*D'accord.*"

We shook hands. "*N'oubliez pas l'e-mail.*"

"*Oui,* Chef."

"The kitchen starts at eight."

I'd done it. I was in. I turned. I walked out. I rounded a corner and punched the air.

I called Willy. He was gratifyingly impressed. Everyone wants to work at La Mère Brazier, he said. "Half L'Institut Bocuse would drop out today if they could get in. It is *the* place."

I didn't mention that I would be booted out after seventeen days. What mattered was I was in the kitchen. I was in *the* kitchen.

Sylvain Jacquenod was the sous-chef, the guy I would answer to. On my first morning, he was beginning a preparation involving chicken thighs. They had been in the oven for an hour, cooking in fat at a low heat.

"We'll do it together," he said, insisting that I call him by his first name. "But first you must wash your hands."

I was embarrassed that I needed to be told but liked that I had been.

He pulled out the tray, four dozen thighs, bubbling thickly in the fat, and handed me a pair of latex gloves. He was telling me what to do next—in fact, he was in mid-sentence of an instruction—when I suddenly blurted out, "It's like a duck confit!"

He paused, only a moment, a slight flicker of incomprehension, but just long enough for me to wonder: Why did I say that?

"Yes," he said, "it is a little like a duck confit." He seemed confused about why he had been interrupted. "Except that a duck confit is made with duck. This is made with chicken."

"Yes," I said.

"A chicken is different from a duck."

"Yes."

It was my French. I spoke like a four-year-old. I was, therefore, talked to like a four-year-old.

"But all birds are really the same, aren't they?" Sylvain said, trying to be reassuring. "The breasts always cook fast. The legs slow." These—he indicated the tray of thighs—were left over from dishes that had used only the breasts.

We put on our gloves.

First, he said, we remove the skin, working it loose from the thighs, trying to keep it intact. Torn is no good.

He held up an example—the skin had a distinctly testicular shrivel—and dropped it into a bowl. "We'll use them in a moment. Next we bone the thighs."

They were hot—almost burn-your-fingers hot—but because of the heat the bones came out easily. We put the meat in another bowl. It was oily and not much to look at but scrumptious-smelling. (A kitchen can be a punishing place not to be eating.)

Sylvain got a clean tray and emptied the boned meat onto it, still steaming, and we pressed it down with our hands. It made a squishy sound. It was a meaty wet brick about an inch deep.

"Now the skins," he said.

He turned them out onto a cutting board, and showed me what to do, scraping off occasional gobs of fat, cutting away stray gnarlinesses, then trimming each skin into right angles like small squares of parchment that could be stacked in a pile.

Had I been to Burgundy? he asked.

I hadn't.

"Then *that* is where we will go." He smiled. "The vineyards, the hills, the wine. Once the weather warms up."

He retrieved a block of foie gras from a fridge and sliced slivers off it and spread them atop the now only warm brick of thighs. We patted it down with our latex palms. The foie gras was soft, like butter.

"We'll go on a Sunday. With our wives."

Ophélie, Sylvain's wife, was pregnant with their first child, he said. His smile was huge, like a cartoon smile.

The parchment skins went on top of the foie gras: neatly, each square aligned. They were the roof of the dish. The tray then went into a hot oven—briefly, a flash blast, to melt the foie gras and crisp up the skin.

Had I eaten at Georges Blanc yet?

I hadn't.

"Oh là là! Ça n'est pas possible!"

Did I have a car? Sylvain asked.

I didn't yet.

"No? We will go there, too. Maybe on our way to Burgundy. An outing, and I'll introduce you to Georges."

Sylvain, who grew up in a suburb of Paris, moved to the gastronomic capital at the age of nineteen to work for Georges Blanc. (In Lyon, there are two royalties: Bocuse and Blanc. Bocuse = king. Blanc = an aspirational regional governor, with lots of property.) Sylvain remained with Blanc for five years, slowly climbing the ranks until he was *chef de partie,* the chef of a station.

He was twenty-eight. Almost everyone in the kitchen was about the same age—late twenties, early thirties—because no one older would have tolerated the pay (bad) or the hours (extreme), and because no one younger would have had a prestigious enough CV to be a candidate for Viannay's team. The restaurant had high ambitions. The cooks had high ambitions. They were a specific type: *Michelin cooks*. They had all worked at places with Michelin stars, and every one of them aspired, one day, to have a Michelin-starred restaurant of his own.

But Sylvain was, I was starting to see, like no one else I had met in a kitchen. He put me at my ease. He made me feel safe, which was not a feeling I had expected to have on my first day. It wasn't just the informal manner or the chattiness. It was that he smiled, and not just a little but pretty much constantly.

He had a modestly receding hairline, a military buzz cut, broad shoulders, muscular forearms, and impeccable posture, and was unforgivably trim. Later, at the staff lunch, Sylvain ate nothing. Lunch was called *le personnel,* served precisely at 11:00 a.m. On my first day, it consisted of sausages with a mustard sauce, boiled potatoes, and a salad of greens and foie gras. I, driven unstable by a morning of kitchen smells, devoured it. Sylvain had a double espresso. Nothing else. I would rarely see him eat, perhaps once a week, twice at most (and when he did, he ate with relish, which was scarcely surprising, since he had to be very hungry).

Later, I asked him why.

"La rigueur," he said.

"Rigor," except in French the word (I knew by now) has so much gravitas that it seems more like a branch of philosophy than its English equivalent. Sylvain gave the impression of being afraid of his own spontaneity.

Except, of course, when he smiled, and when the skin around his eyes instantly crinkled into mini-folds of happiness.

There wasn't a lot of smiling in France. My wife smiles a lot and was regularly taken to task for her evidently irritating cheerfulness. Once, when we were having dinner at our local bistro, Potager, a diner at the next table complained: Do you really need to smile so much? But a restaurant kitchen is even more severe. No one smiles there. Ever. Except Sylvain.

He removed the tray of thighs from the oven, set it on a worktop to cool, and told me to follow him to the *chambre froide*—the "cold room," the walk-in fridge—where he pulled out a large plastic container filled with a viscous liquid the color of black tea. It was meat jelly. Sylvain's weekly duties included making it (a shank of beef simmered overnight in two bottles of red wine, plus several gelatin sheets), because it was used in the restaurant's *pâté-en-croûte*. Once the pâté inside the pastry cools, and contracts, the jelly is poured in through a chimney built into the crust and fills up the space. (Once upon a time, I did not like meat jelly, its irritatingly wobbly texture. Now I eat it by the bowlful.) *Pâté-en-croûte* was also Sylvain's responsibility. When he was away—and this was later, after his wife gave birth—someone else made it. It was cakey and dry and difficult to swallow. Plates were returned from the dining room, untouched except for a first bite.

"Come," Sylvain said. *Viens.*

He led me to a narrow corridor in the back, where a dishwasher worked, Alain, and where some very tall shelves held every piece of the restaurant's kitchen equipment. Sylvain was looking for a *"chinois à piston."* A strainer is a *chinois,* a "Chinese," because, turned upside down, it looks like a Chinese conical hat. A *chinois à piston* has a valve that allows you to control the flow of the liquid—like, for instance, the thick, slow-moving jelly that he was about to spread evenly over a tray of neatly arranged thigh skins.

When it set, the tray was shiny and smooth. You could see your reflection in it. It had a peculiar appeal: like a tray of brownies, with a hard chocolaty top, and, like brownies, it would be cut up into small bite-sized morsels. They were the evening's amuse-bouche.

Popping peas was next and involves pushing a pea out of its delicate skin: not the pod, which is thick, and which you slit open with a thumbnail to get to the bounty inside, and a lot of fun to do, but the virtually translucent membrane of the pea itself, which is actually no fun at all. I hadn't known that people did such a thing. But for Sylvain, a pea, undressed, had more flavor than one still wearing its membrane. It was, he said emphatically, the true flavor of France (*le vrai goût français*).

I thought of Italy, though I didn't want to (and in general I tried not to), but the mind can be a slippery entity to manage, and mine was mischievously imagining itself in an Italian kitchen, making an earnest proposal to my colleagues there to start popping their peas, and being met with raucous, belly-wobbling hilarity. In the long history of Italian cuisine, you will not discover a single popped pea.

To pop a pea, you drop it in boiling water, very quick, drain, and ice. For many people, this is also how you cook a pea. After a few seconds of boiling, the pea is barely "not-raw," and the instant icing preserves its bright-green color. And, also for many, you don't do anything else, unless you want to add salt and pepper, maybe some olive oil, and a squeeze of lemon.

What I hadn't known is that the same action—hot bath, ice bath— loosens the vegetable's membrane so that, when you then give the pea a squeeze, gently between thumb and forefinger, the whatsit pops out. (What do you call the inner-pea? Is it, perhaps, just that—an inner-pea?)

The squeeze, I feel compelled to note, really has to be performed carefully. If it's done with too much force, the inner-pea splits in half. Half of an inner-pea is no good. You can let a few through—accidents happen—but if there are a lot of split peas, then the whole batch is thrown out.

Inner-peas—sautéed lightly in butter, with a small ladle of veal stock, and finished with lemon zest—accompanied the sweetbreads, the calf's puffy thymus glands, which, when done properly, have the airy texture of a slowly roasted marshmallow. But each serving involves a staggering *150* inner-peas. It takes a long time to pinch-press *150* inner-peas from their pea-membranes and not split them.

We flicked off the pointy bits of asparagus stalks. I was familiar with the concern. It was the stalk's tough outer skin. I had learned to skin it with a peeler, especially if the vegetable was to be grilled.

"You lose too much," Sylvain said. (In France, the skin of vegetables is highly respected, and you remove it at the cost of its flavor. Other elements are preserved in the skin as well—like nutrients and complexity of texture—but the only one that really matters is the flavor.)

Sylvain illustrated the asparagus flick technique with a paring knife. You start at the bottom of the stalk and spiral your way up flickingly to the floretlike head. The pointy bits are little triangles. They look like mini–artichoke leaves, and flick off pretty easily (until you get to the top, I discovered, where the easiest thing is to lop off the floretlike head in its entirety, which isn't the idea).

"I want to go to New York," Sylvain said.

"Why?"

He thought for a moment. "I don't know."

I don't think he had ever considered the question.

"I just know that I want to be in New York. Would a French chef find work there?"

It would be a recurrent theme, not just for Sylvain, but for most people in the kitchen, although none more often than Sylvain. No one wanted to go to Spain or Japan or Denmark. (England? Never.) And it wasn't for cooking reasons. For instance, none of the cooks believed that New York had something to teach them in the kitchen. They wanted to go to New York because they wanted to go to New York.

Once, a Lyon monthly magazine (called, tellingly, *Lyon People*— French magazine, English title) put Daniel Boulud on the cover, photographing him on the hood of a New York yellow cab, arms thrown wide open, as though inviting his friends in Lyon to come visit. There was a copy at the end of the bar. The bar area was where we ate *le personnel*. There wasn't a single member of the *brigade* who didn't pick up the magazine, read every page, and then stare at the cover. The Lyonnais don't know Daniel Boulud. It's chefs who do. Boulud is the one who got away.

At least I knew how to prepare an artichoke, and this, finally, was a relief. Artichokes are Italian. Artichokes weren't new to me.

Sylvain was astonished. "Really? You can turn an artichoke?"

"You mean cut away the leaves and carve out the heart?"

"Yes. You can do that?"

"Yes."

"C'est vrai?"

"Yes, really."

I wasn't trying to prove that I was more than a novice. I wasn't trying to prove anything. I had worked in Italian restaurants. At L'Institut Bocuse I'd actually asked for an artichoke lesson, just to confirm that I was basically doing the right thing. Artichokes are important in Lyon. I'd learned that early on.

Sylvain conveyed that he was very impressed, in that exaggerated theatrical way of a grown-up talking to a toddler, and said something about my being more schooled than he'd realized. He was showing me—no question—an immediate new respect.

This made me uneasy.

He set up an impromptu artichoke station. He took a plastic bottle from a shelf above the sink—citric-acid powder—and shook some of it into a large bowl of water. The citric acid keeps the artichokes from browning. Then he pulled a street-sized trash can next to our worktop. It is astonishing, the sheer volume of leaves that you end up jettisoning just to get down to the vegetable's small and tender heart. Does no one dip them in butter and scrape them off with their teeth?

He fetched a crate. We got to work.

I can't remember what I did. If I try to conjure up my effort, an image comes to mind, but it is of a perfectly turned artichoke, two to three inches of stem, gently curved, the heart smoothly symmetrical, looking like a flower. I genuinely felt that I had achieved what I'd intended to do. I hadn't known that it was a failure until I showed it to Sylvain.

What I did at the time was this: I made him cry.

What I presented, evidently, was so mutated-looking that Sylvain burst out laughing: at it and me. He laughed so hard that tears ran down his cheeks. He laughed so hard that he buckled over. Everyone in the kitchen then stopped their tasks and started laughing, too, weakly at first, because unstoppable laughter is always contagious, even if you don't know why, until you then discover why, and, with your funny bone suitably warmed up, you, too, break out into laughter: pointing at the offending object and at the person who made it.

Eventually, Sylvain threw my artichoke emphatically into the trash and said—with difficulty, because he was still laughing—that perhaps I wasn't quite ready for turning artichokes.

Only one person wasn't laughing. This was Christophe Hubert. Hubert was the executive chef.

He had crossed his arms across his chest. He stared out with displeasure.

Christophe continued staring until, one by one, each member of the kitchen slowly brought his laughter under control.

In truth, I was to blame. I knew this, and suspected that Christophe was thinking the same: If I hadn't been there, with all my dysfunction, no one in his kitchen would have started falling about in hysterics.

The room quieted down. People resumed their duties. Christophe waited another moment, a long one. *"Merci,"* he said, with exaggerated gratitude.

In my modest culinary life, I have been terrified by the possibility of having to work *garde-manger,* the place where newcomers normally start. (*Garde-manger:* fussy and fast. Me: sloppy and slow.) At La Mère Brazier, the station had two people, Michael and Florian. Michael (pronounced the French way—Mee-KELL) worked hard and seemed to be always on the verge of a hissy fit. Florian worked harder and was permanently in a state of near-hysterics. Sylvain was Florian's godparent. He introduced us, folding up his arms and rocking them, recalling Florian as a nine-week-old infant.

Now there were three. *Garde-manger* was where I would begin.

Florian was nineteen. He was the youngest person in the kitchen. From time to time, there would be younger cooks—interns, including a student from a *lycée* (the equivalent of an American high school) who had a bedtime curfew and left early—but none were on the payroll. Florian got a check: every Thursday, from Viannay personally, who shook his hand and stared into his eyes with an intensity that seemed to say, "Boy, I own you." Florian was an official member of the *brigade.*

My first task involved assembling seventy-five highly elaborate lobster-and-fennel mouth-taste constructs. At the time, they were the most ridiculous pieces of food I'd been asked to make. Each one seemed to take ten minutes, which is impossible: The math doesn't add up, because Florian and I were both doing them, and it didn't take us five hours. But it took a long time. Worse, you can't make mouth-taste constructs too far in advance or they dry out. Therefore, you make them as late as possible, which, in a kitchen, was a very uncomfortable time to be doing anything.

The lobster constructs were erected in soupspoons, the familiar Japanese kind, white, ceramic, pretty, made in Limoges (in France, every precious food-related product has its place, and, for plates, it's Limoges), and small.

We poured panna cotta into the bottom—a thickish dribble. Panna cotta is an Italian dessert. It is a cousin of a French one, the custard, but made with cream instead of milk ("panna cotta" = "cooked cream"), and egg whites instead of yolks. This one, our version, was infused with fennel fronds, the green pom-poms that sprout from a fennel bulb. They were for color. At the last minute, sheets of gelatin were melted in. These were for wobble.

Next: lobster claw, only a morsel, sautéed in butter. It was placed atop the panna cotta as if afloat. The image seemed to be nautical. (Maybe it wasn't, but it was how I made sense of it.) The green panna cotta was the sea; the red lobster morsel, the seafaring vessel.

"Toothpicks"—meticulously carved out of the fennel bulb—were the masts. Each one had a crow's nest, too: a flimsy red baby-tomato ring, placed atop the fennel toothpicks. ("Land-ho!")

The challenge was the flimsy red rings.

Actually, everything was a challenge. I didn't have the right fingers. It was my genetic heritage. Some people: born to play nocturnes by Chopin. Me: born to pull out root vegetables in cold weather. I don't have fingers. I have stumps. A flimsy red ring is a torture to prepare with stumps.

To make a flimsy red ring, you roast a tomato—not the round cherry kind but the plum-shaped Italian one—until it is shriveled and dehydrated. Then you slice it, thinly and carefully, crosswise. You can't slice it too thinly. Anything thicker than too thin is too thick. When you brush away the stray seeds, you are left with several fine red circles—loops, really—like a miniature version of what you, if you were about six inches tall, might toss onto pins at a county fair to win a stuffed animal for your six-inch beloved.

It was a myopic labor. I was hunched over. Florian was hunched over. Two grown men, bent in half, doing itsy-bitsy-bitsies with their finger-tippy-tipsies.

"Attention!" Florian said sharply. He pointed to my nose.

A bead of sweat was swelling threateningly on the tip.

Johann appeared.

Johann was one of the pastry chefs. The kitchen had two. Both were named Johann, and, somehow, each one knew which Johann you wanted when you called out "Johann." One Johann was relaxed. The other was manic. The relaxed one forgot to wear his toque. His pants were falling down, low-rider style. He had a seashell necklace. He would rather have been in sandals than in clogs. The manic Johann looked medieval. He was like a court jester. He had a head like an egg, very narrow at the top, a massive Adam's apple, buggy eyes that gave nothing away, and he didn't smile, even though he was never serious. (He was also preternaturally competent and never used an electric device for making the restaurant's soufflés, because he could whip faster by hand than any machine.)

"*C'est très joli ça,*" the medieval Johann said from behind my back, ever droll. Very lovely.

I was repositioning a fennel frond. Yeah, right, I thought. Let's make fun of the Neanderthal.

"*Oui, oui,*" I said. "*Je sais, c'est super-joli.*"

I un-hunched, stood up, and turned. Johann wasn't being ironic, except that this was impossible, because he was always ironic.

I wondered: "*C'est vrai?*"

"*Oui,*" Johann said, (ostensibly) without irony.

I looked hard into his face. "*Non,*" I said.

"*Oui,*" he said, "*c'est vraiment joli,*" and he walked off in an impressively impassive display of his convictions.

I re-examined my soupspoons: not merely as expressions of narcissistic fussiness (as they will, alas, forever remain, in my pedestrian eyes), but also as, maybe, something pleasing. Where was the pleasure, exactly? I found myself analyzing them according to three criteria:

1. Color: the vibrant red, the shades of green.
2. Texture: the crunchy vegetable, the soft sponge of the lobster, the pudding-ness of the panna cotta.
3. And volume: the undeniable three-dimensionality of a lobster barge with a mast and a crow's nest.

I stepped back. No question: I was in a French kitchen.

Florian was, for his age, surprisingly good company, mainly because he was so transparently himself. He never tried to be better than he was, and, for all his teenage gawkiness, there was, between us, an instant camaraderie developing: two novices, one young, one not so young, hoping against hope to become masters.

He was skinny and tall, probably midway through a final growth spurt, with straight dark hair, big ears, a big nose, an unusually long neck, and lanky arms; he looked something like a giraffe, with the disposition of a Chihuahua. He talked to himself. (*"Le stress! Le stress!"*) He swore at himself. ("Florian! *Putain de merde!*") He hit himself: usually a smack, left hand striking the right. This was done to control a tremor. It came from nerves. Sometimes the nerves got so bad he hit himself with force, raising his hand high in the air, casually, as though in a stretch, and then smashing it onto a countertop (quickly, as if taking the hand by surprise).

Unlike my stumps, Florian's fingers were long and delicate. They could have been a pianist's fingers, except that he would never have been able to control their shaking. The nerves came from fear, he confessed. He was afraid, at the start of every day, that he was about to fail.

Sometimes he gaspingly clutched his chest as if in enormous pain. I first witnessed this when I showed up late for an evening service.

"I was afraid you weren't coming," he explained. He was hyperventilating and was bringing his breathing under control, with long, slow exhales.

(It was shaming that I was late, and I seemed always to be a little late. In the kitchen, nothing matters more than punctuality. But I was happy to feel that I was needed.)

One morning, having successfully diced a shallot, Florian thrust his fist into the air and cheered. *"Je l'ai fait!"* I did it!

I thought: So I am not the only one. Nobody tells you this, but in your first weeks, a shallot is a tricky tease. You have to produce so many of them in a French kitchen (only salt and pepper are more fundamental), but they are imperfectly shaped and so impudently slippery that, even though you believe you know how to cut one into a pile of perfect tiny cubes, they keep refusing to cooperate, and you know that it is taking longer to prepare than it should, and that everyone must be noticing.

Florian conceded, in his characteristically open manner, that he had already failed twice here. Spectacularly. He shook his head, remembering. He had started at the meat station, he said (in a tone of "Can you imagine?"). It was a disaster. Christophe had to step in. Florian was humiliated. (No one, in my humble opinion, was more efficient at the ancient practice of sucking out the confidence of a weaker creature like a straw than Christophe.)

Florian was given a second chance. The next night was worse.

"But I wasn't fired. I was given a third chance."

Six months later, Florian was still on probation, although "probably" nearing the end of it. He was treated by the others, and especially by Christophe, as a pet now trained enough (almost) to be trusted not to wreck the place.

In itself, Christophe's attitude toward Florian was exceptional. Christophe encouraged no one. Every now and then, he would ask Florian to get him a bottle of sparkling water (only Christophe was allowed to drink the sparkling water) and then, in a gesture of spontaneous magnanimity, tell Florian to get one for himself. (*"Oui!"* Florian would quietly say to himself, pumping his elbow.)

Once, Christophe patted Florian on the shoulder. Christophe touched no one. (His handshake was damp and reluctant and, for me, especially memorable for a last-second reflex that would leave me holding only his sweaty fingertips.) Florian beamed. He was going to be a chef one day.

Jessica secured our *Cartes Vitales,* the green plastic totems that guarantee health care—without which, frankly, it is impossible for a family to live in France—but only after highly confrontational visits to the Health Service Administration (called CPAM, for the Caisse Primaire d'Assurance Maladie) on a miserable street equidistant from the sordid Perrache Railroad Station, the sordid old prison, and the especially sordid Place Carnot. Jessica was unfazed by the surroundings. It was combat that she appeared to relish.

"There is no sport the French like more than arguing," she said when she finally returned, victorious.

She was more forthright than her New York City self, and struck back with wicked vitriol whenever she had suffered a rudeness. Civic officials, at least in our arrondissement, seemed not to have dealt with an American before, and did not understand why they should have to start dealing with one now. Regardless, no civic official, I am confident, had ever seen an American like Jessica once crossed. She had been emancipated by the French language. There is a quality about French rudeness—a self-righteousness, probably—that provoked Jessica to the point of rage, especially if she was the target: as when a diner (again, a man) crossed the very small restaurant where we were eating with friends to tell her that she laughed too loudly, or when a diner (a man, of course) at the next table at the Bouchon des Filles leaned over, after observing that she had filled my glass, and told her that, in France, it is the man, not the woman, who pours the wine. Jessica expressed exaggerated surprise, given that the woman in question was a wine expert, that she also consulted on the wine list of the restaurant, which was pointedly called Bouchon des *Filles* and was owned and run by women. (The man was witheringly silenced, and his wife spent the rest of the evening apologizing for the behavior of her spouse.)

In our family, Jessica both opens the bottles and pours them.

She dealt with the *grèves,* the strikes, which were regular and unannounced: You showed up at the school and the front door was closed, a piece of paper taped to it, announcing that the teachers had walked out, or the canteen workers, or both.

She surmounted the horror of no-school Wednesdays, having discovered a citywide program of alternatives, held at outposts of the MJC (Maison des Jeunes et de la Culture—House of Youth and Culture), which were so popular they filled up within an hour of opening for enrollment. Jessica, at the front of the line, found places for the boys at a branch of the MJC just behind La Mère Brazier. I then took to wheeling them over in their stroller, a brisk clip, needing to stop first at the kitchen to secure a cutting board before there were none left, the cooks uncomfortable to find toddlers in their presence, the incongruity of defenseless children in what was an unapologetically aggressive kitchen, both boys staring out wide-eyed, astonished: their fragility, their softness.

During the spring, four friends from Jessica's "tasting club" made the trek to France to see her and, in effect, to resume their studies. It was a telling tribute of loyalty. It was also an obvious field trip: We were, after all, situated within easy driving distance of several major grape groups.

Encouraged, Jessica signed back up to complete her WSET diploma at a teaching facility in Mâcon, about fifty miles away. The classes were small, and conducted over long weekends in French; Jessica made four very good friends there and only one enemy, a pompous (male) fellow student whose acts of condescension she had found herself incapable of allowing to go unpunished, and from whom she would eventually have to be physically separated. For the remainder of the course, Jessica and the pompous one were made to sit on opposite sides of the classroom. When both of them passed one class and enrolled in the next, the seating arrangement continued.

I had some bad experiences with the artichoke soup that accompanied an artichoke-and-foie-gras starter. You make the soup by cutting off the choke bottoms, half-submerging them in chicken stock, salt, and pepper, and slowly cooking the liquid to a thick green cream. During service, the soup was kept warm in a pot on a high shelf in a corner directly over the kitchen kettle. The kettle was where bones are browned, and stocks made; it was the shape of a child's coffin, and was always in use, bubbling away, generating steamy heat. The challenge was transporting the thick green cream from that pot—hot corner, large outsized ladle, duck-bone vapor in your face—into a small white porcelain cup, without sloshing.

If you sloshed, you smudged. If you smudged, the smudge didn't slide back down into the soup. It clung greenly and incriminatingly to the insides of the cup.

Garde-manger was connected to the main kitchen by a speaker and was largely out of view, and since Christophe rarely saw what we were up to, Florian had come up with a trick for removing the soup smudges by wetting his forefinger in his mouth and giving the inside of the cup a wipe. I don't know why—even though my self-image is Pigpen with chocolate sauce down his front—I couldn't bring myself to do the same. If I sloshed, I poured the soup back into the pot, got a new cup, and tried again. (Really: Would you want a soup cup that had been saliva-cleaned?)

Garde-manger's dishes had their own pass, a worktop on wheels, positioned next to the main pass (the *garde-manger* dishes were never assembled by the chef; they were delivered up, at speed, and whisked into the dining room). On the worktop were an olive-oil bottle and a bowl of sea salt, for finishing the artichoke soup: You dressed it at the last moment with six salt crystals and three drops of olive oil.

Once, I added a fourth drop.

I stared at it. No question. There were four drops.

It was busy. A table for six was waiting. I had a choice: take the cup back to the *garde-manger* room and redo it (and incur Christophe's wrath) or leave it (and *maybe* incur it). What would you do? You would do what I did. You leave the cup. It was only a drop.

It was early days, and this was the first time I was the recipient of Christophe's particularly personalized wrath. (The second time was when, for reasons I still don't understand, I left at the pass a soup that had only two drops.) When Christophe is disappointed, he uses the word *franchement*—frankly—in a series. As in, "Frankly, I can't believe you can be so stupid. Frankly, I don't know why you are here. Frankly, I don't know how you ever imagined that you were competent enough to work in a kitchen. Frankly, I cannot stand to look at you." *Franchement.*

He was a dickhead.

One night, Sylvain invited me to do plating at the pass with him. It was a generous gesture, one he could make because of his position in the hierarchy. But I didn't understand why I would be tolerated by others. More perplexing, I don't know why I said yes.

The kitchen, once you're there, in mid-service, between the ovens, was immediately much hotter than *garde-manger*. It was like jumping into too-hot water. Your body wants to jump right out again. The pores on my skin dilated in response, and my arms beaded up wetly. It was bright, the lighting, the heat lamps.

Viannay was doing meat. He never wore a toque and his long hair kept falling into his face and having to be tossed out of the way. Also the loose, open sleeves of his chef's jacket draped flamboyantly, swinging within millimeters of the food, but were never soiled. It was like a dare. It hadn't occurred to me how much he liked the pass—the heat lamps could have been spotlights—but, being always in the back, I rarely saw him onstage.

Christophe was doing fish. I would be taking his place, Sylvain told me, and he urged me to study the line. (Christophe clearly didn't understand why I was at the pass, and was demonstrably irritated that I was anywhere near him.)

One dish was *filets de dorade de ligne*—sea bream—that was served with vegetables, grilled spider crab, and a sweet-and-sour sauce. A cook prepared the *dorade* and passed it down the line on a platter. Another cook sautéed the vegetables, grilled the crab, and poured out a quantity of the sauce, which were added to the platter and passed to Christophe, who assembled everything on a plate: no hands, all spoons, the vegetables arranged just so, the sauce spooned atop lightly, like a dew or a spray: i.e., barely. Every dish had its embellishment.

In the event, I did plate a couple of dishes, although I am not sure what I learned, because I was so worried that I would dribble erratically that, in the actual act, I tried to think of nothing. With effort, I can picture my hands, or a spoon, or the peripheries—like Christophe, whom I couldn't see but heard, hyperventilating.

I then returned to *garde-manger* and got shit from everyone there. Just who did I think I was?

Klaus, a Dutch *stagiaire* nearing the end of his stint, was in the back doing prep and openly jealous.

"I was never allowed to stand by the pass," he said, "even though *that* was why I came to Lyon—to watch Mathieu Viannay plate." He asked me, with ferocity, "Have you studied his *travers de porc?*"

The dish was pork ribs with a citrus glaze. It was among the dishes I'd been taught at L'Institut Bocuse. Viannay's version was a puzzle of shapes. The pork, its ribs removed, was a perfect rectangle. A foie-gras bonbon, served with it, a perfect cylinder. Yes, I'd seen it, but, no, I hadn't analyzed it.

"You should be more attentive," Klaus said. "Viannay's plates could be paintings."

Klaus was still agitated the next morning. He had almost completed his *stage* and would be returning to Holland and still couldn't believe that I had been allowed into the front kitchen.

"In Amsterdam," he said, "no one makes sauces. You buy them from a wholesaler. There are green sauces, brown sauces, white sauces, and red sauces. But you never know what they are. Here they make every sauce themselves. Have you tasted the veal stock? It takes two days."

Klaus confided in a whisper, "I'm keeping a notebook of Viannay's sauces." Then he got worried: "You won't tell, will you?"

The next morning, Viannay sought me out.

I was in the back. He leaned in close, elbow on the counter, face-to-face, a private conversation in a public space.

He asked me a question.

I didn't quite hear it. I apologized and asked him to repeat it.

He did.

I caught a phrase: *"combien de temps encore."* I apologized again. Could he, possibly, say it one more time?

He did.

My distress must have been manifest.

He tried a different syntax: *"Tu restes ici encore combien de temps?"*

(Meanwhile, a little voice in my head was hectoring: Why can't you understand this guy? You understand others. Is it because you're afraid?)

Sylvain jumped in.

"Combien de temps," he said to me, very slowly. *"Tu veux rester combien de temps encore?"*

Oh! *Je reste combien de temps?* How much longer do I want to stay? *Oui!*

You mean I can stay? As long as I want?

Oui!

I'd actually forgotten that I'd been given seventeen days. "Well, damn, forever? I mean, *toujours?*"

Saturdays weren't merely "days off." They were better than a birthday, better than Christmas, and with many more gifts. Saturdays were light and sky and spring and the river and children and a wife and family and clean sheets and lazy cups of coffee and bare feet. On one, I was preparing strawberries for breakfast (prepping them as I had been taught, washing before hulling, then hulling them deeply with the point of a knife to remove the less flavorful pulp), and thought, Oh, what the hell, and dusted them with sugar.

The boys appeared, and Frederick declared: "George, look, *fraises au sucre!*"

Of course, this is what they were, strawberries (*fraises*) in sugar (*au sucre*), but the way he identified the preparation, in French, seemed to locate it in their school canteen, where they would have first eaten it. In Lyon, I hadn't yet served them strawberries.

Another Saturday, an omelet, as I had learned to make it, and young Frederick observed: "I didn't know you knew how to make *une omelette,* Dada."

I stared at him, unpacking the assumptions implicit in his observation: that he had already been introduced to omelets (they eat omelets for lunch?); that he knew omelets as a French food and only in their French version (a thin-skinned, rolled, soft-in-the-middle preparation— preferably *nature,* without anything inside, and pronounced *"une omelette,"* coming down hard on the two "t"s); that he was surprised, therefore, that I, his father, the American in the family, would know both the food and how to make it; and that, like many fathers of French children, I was called "Dada."

The canteen menu was posted each week outside the school's entrance: three courses, plus a *produit laitier,* a milk product—yogurt or cheese. There were no repeats, a feature so radical that I am compelled to repeat it: No menu was ever served twice during the entire school year. (Jessica, who had become a member of a parent-teacher executive committee, discovered that, at strategic intervals, certain foods are repeated— turnips, kale, beets—to help children become familiar with them.)

The first course would be a salad—say, grated carrots with a vinaigrette, George's current favorite (*"Carottes râpées!"*), which he asked his mother to make for dinner. The second, the *plat principal,* might be a *poulet* with a *sauce grand-mère* (made from broth that the chicken had been cooked in). There was a cooked vegetable (maybe Swiss chard in a béchamel sauce), and a fruit or dessert. The boys' favorite had been *moelleux au chocolat,* hard on the outside, like a brownie, and soft in the middle, with a warm chocolate meltingness.

L'École Robert Doisneau was an underfunded, overcrowded public school. It had roof leaks, an asphalt playground that was breaking up and weeds growing through the cracks. In its confidence that eating could be taught, it wasn't exceptional. Daniel Boulud grew up on a farm, never ate in a restaurant or bought food in a store until he was fourteen. But he had been thoroughly trained in French cuisine: by his farmer family, of course, but mainly by the school canteen. Every French member of the Mère Brazier *brigade* had grown up the same. The food our boys ate made them different from their parents.

Another Saturday, after I had put the boys to bed (the only night I could), Jessica and I were having a simple meal—leftover chicken, a salad, a bottle of Beaujolais.

Jessica asked me, "Did you know that the boys get a grade for how they eat and behave at the canteen?"

There they eat their food in silence. This is to encourage them to think about what they're eating. They are served each course at a table by women who know how much the children want. They are not obliged to finish their food. But if they don't, they don't get the next course.

Jessica refilled our glasses. "America seems so far away."

It was true. We never thought about "home."

"No one who visits France knows it in the way that we are starting to understand Lyon," she said. She paused, taking the measure of the idea that was forming, wanting to articulate it, the relationship of food—to what?—to everything? "People don't do what we do." She was excited. Her eyes glistened. "I don't even know how to describe it—this what-ever it is, this place we find ourselves, the culture, our home, our place in it. It just seems very big."

A FARM NEAR MORNANT, TWENTY-FIVE MILES SOUTH OF LYON. Our family was invited by Ludovic Curabet to attend a tasting of the char-cuterie that he had prepared from "my" pig. Had we been *à la campagne* yet? No.

We stopped to pick up bread from Bob, who was fast-talking on a busy Saturday morning, excited to share his latest new loaf, one that had been inspired by our friendship, a mix of American and French flours—a hard durum wheat from South Dakota with a soft white from the Auvergne. ("It just needs a name," Bob said. "Lafayette?") When we told him where we were headed, he asked us to bring back a *saucisson,* and filled up a four-foot paper sack with the loaves of his repertoire.

Ludovic was waiting for us, along with two other families. A table, white butcher paper on top, had been placed on the gravelly hilltop crest. Ludovic put out variously proportioned but consistently tubular expressions of pig—only one large piece (known as a *Jésus*), otherwise small *saucissons,* no two the same size, each tied capriciously by a string, but no *jambon,* the French answer to prosciutto, because the leg needs a year to age, and no belly cuts, the *poitrine,* which would have to hang for another three months in Ludovic's cellar. There were two cheeses—a Brillat-Savarin, the creamy raw cheese from nearby Burgundy and named after the writer, and a Comté, a hard variety from the Jura, at the foot of the Alps—and bottles of a no-label red. He had also bought what appeared to be forty kilos of cherries—four crates, in any case, of Burlats.

"Cherries are the fruit of here," he explained. "They are in season now. Do you understand? They are at their best at *this* very minute of *this* very Saturday." Lyon has many varieties, appearing over the course of the late spring and into the summer, and starting with the Burlat, the first to ripen and the juiciest and sweetest of them all. Cherries were harbingers of spring. They seemed to have the same flavor and sweet-and-acidic spectrum as the Syrah grape, also the pride of the area, its northern- most home (and where scientists now believe that it may have been "conceived," the issue of two grapes from the Alps and the Ardèche). Charcuterie—made from a local pig—goes exceptionally well with both the local wine and the local cherries.

I surveyed the table, which seemed fragrant with possibilities and connections. Aged meats are among the earth's mystery food prepara- tions. They seem primordial, more ancient than history, and, since they are not cooked but dry out and ferment, according to what is available (the weather, the ocean, smoke, the sun, salt, yeasts in the humid air), they can seem as fundamental as nature.

For the boys, it was their first taste of home-cured French pig. "Mmm," Frederick said (and then noticed the breadbasket, lost interest in meat, and walked off with a baguette). George, the curious carnivore, took a bite and then promptly stacked slices in his palm.

I picked a floppy example, the size of a pancake, from the peculiarly named *Jésus,* the casing of which was the large intestines, four inches across. The slice felt wet. I rubbed it between my thumb and forefinger. It was squishy. It was very dark red.

Was it a failed cure? Or, being so big, had it just needed more time to age? It clearly wasn't ready. It was probably only for display. I hesitated—for reasons of mouth feel, if not hygiene, you really want your *saucisson* to be dry, not wet—and noticed that people were staring at me. I obviously couldn't *not* eat my piece of *Jésus*.

I popped the whole thing in.

"Mmm," I said loudly, and added, *"C'est très bon, non?"* People chuckled, and I exhaled the proverbial sigh of relief, while also struggling: The piece was too big to swallow.

"Très, très bon," I repeated, my mouth full. I was looking for a way to spit it out without being noticed. I was also in denial: that my brain was refusing, probably for reasons of politesse, to accept a message that my mouth was sending. The issue was the taste, one that might take my getting used to. The Lyonnais, it appeared, like to know that their pigs were unequivocally of a farm and a place. They liked them wildy and stinky and very piggy.

Afterward, we lingered languidly. The day had been gray when we started out, and rainy on the road. But the rain hadn't reached the farm. The boys were in the grass on the edge of a wheat field. The sun was out.

There were sheep, unshorn puffballs, like enormous mobile comforters. The boys, urban lads since birth, had never seen an animal close-up and went straight for them. The sheep ran.

Frederick asked the sheep if they would come back, please.

The sheep returned.

George joined him, approaching on tiptoes. The boys then talked to the sheep, making hand gestures and mime as though in a game of charades, and the animals gathered round and watched the boys closely and appeared to be listening. One allowed one of the boys to climb on top. There was a lot of laughing.

I put Frederick on my shoulders.

"Let's walk." I hadn't strolled down a hill of wheat before.

We proceeded slowly, the four of us. It was more amble than walk, no destination other than a vague descent. High clouds, blue sky, a warm late afternoon. Jessica was in a summer dress. The boys and I were in shorts. Jessica took off her shoes. The wheat came up to our waist. We didn't talk.

I reflected. We had never been so relaxed. It was seven months since we had arrived. Were we actually having a bucolic moment?

We hadn't come to Lyon for the bucolic. We weren't here for the cantaloupes, or the violet asparagus, or the lavender, or the peaches of the farmers somewhere farther south. We hadn't come for the south.

Nevertheless, our day had been pretty jolly, at least according to the basic agrarian, stick-close-to-nature benign view of the universe. The pork: cured by hand. The bread: made by Bob. The cherries: sold from stands outside the orchards where they were picked. The wine: bought by the barrel from a vigneron and bottled in the farmer's cellar. And now this wheat field beckoning from below, with its undulating summer grasses.

Lyon is beautiful, and rare, but it is not this, it is not nature. In Lyon, the rivers make everything built near them—bridges, *quais,* pastel-painted sixteenth-century homes, random Roman ruins—into performances of light and darkness and reflection. But Lyon is also a throwback city—wiseguys, corrupt cops, unbathed operators working a chance, the women, mainly Eastern European, working their trade. Friday nights are rough: The after-hours clubs across the Saône from our home open at 11:00 p.m. and close whenever—Elody's Pub, Fiesta, Bootlegger, New Ibiza. Saturday nights, remarkably, are rougher than Fridays. You wake on Sunday and there is a drunk guy leaning against your door. A vehicle that had been parked in front of the apartment has been torched. Farmers arrive early at the market to hose away vomit.

At school, George got into fights. During recess, boys from a Gypsy family—the "Roms," migrant Romanians and Bulgarians who lived in plastic tents on a vacant block on the outskirts of the city—pinned down a child and cut off his eyelashes with scissors. A babysitter twisted Frederick's ear until it changed color and he cried. During the vacation in April, at a day-care facility run by the city, young George got a backhand across the face because he wasn't standing in a straight line. Everybody seems to hit their children. They spank them on subways, in streets, at a playground, in restaurants, and at Sunday school. They smack boys on their ears and slap them across the forehead, one-two-three, pow-pow-pow (because little Sébastien is slow getting off a bus). A substitute teacher got so frustrated by one of the boys' friends that she lifted him out of his chair by his ear, and strangled him. (This was a mistake on many levels, especially because the boy's mother was a lawyer, and, to give the school its due, the teacher was dismissed.)

I had come to Lyon to learn how to cook French food, but I hadn't come on my own. This changed the enterprise. The family stuff mattered. During our first six months, each member of our small family had come to doubt the wisdom of the project. Ours clearly wasn't a pastoral pilgrimage. It wasn't a cultural one. We still hadn't been to Paris. L'Orangerie and the Impressionist painters weren't on our to-do list.

We reached the bottom of the hill. Jessica's legs erupted in hives. My ankles had a scattering of red dots, which I had been scratching unreflectingly and were now smears of blood. We looked back up the hill. It was much steeper-looking than it had been from the top. (Why do hills do that?) George asked if he could be carried, too.

We started back up. The earth began collapsing under our feet. Mole tunnels? The dirt was crumbly. Jessica gave up on going barefoot and put her shoes back on. Frederick was holding on to my ears for support.

This field, I said, tricked us. It had looked so enticing from afar. But close-up, varmint burrowings, stinging nettles, spiders, ticks—who knew what was crawling around underneath? It was menacingly alive, this wheat dirt, and seemed to have decided that we were edible.

Our host, the farmer, was of the generation that never used pesticides, not for any ideological reason necessarily, but because pesticides were expensive. Boulud's father, Julien, asked me: Why do we need them when we never needed them before? Their farms are organic because they always were. Boulud still resents having to weed the garlic field during the spring break, and being unable to play soccer with his nonfarming friends. Most farms in the Rhône Valley are smallholdings.

I wondered: Is this the kind of wheat field that Bob's flour is milled from? I hadn't been to the Auvergne, but knew it by its reputation, the wild place, backward, with a rich lava dirt from the many volcanoes there.

It would be a long time before we had another bucolic moment. But for now, owing to the nature of our being in nature—this pause—we found ourselves in a happy place. We were surprised by how right it felt to be exactly where we were. From the wintry end of autumn, to the summery end of spring. And then, on a Saturday afternoon in June, something unexpected occurred to us. We had arrived. We liked it here. We wouldn't be leaving anytime soon.

V

Stagiaire

"I am an illusionist with my hands full of truth. Put me in the middle of a dozen bored people, and you will see these sad folks awaken, break into smiles, and their eyes widen in anticipation of the marvels about to come from me. The most gnarled will recover, at the sight of my toque, childhood expressions of delight. This is why I always wear a fine toque of pressed cotton. I wear out as many as a bishop, but nothing in the world could make me wear an industrial paper toque, a throwaway toque like a Kleenex. It's possible you can't even tell the difference, to look at it, but me, I would know. I'd be afraid I'd lose half my magic power and so remove half the illusion for those watching me."

ALAIN CHAPEL QUOTED IN *CROQUE-EN-BOUCHE* BY

HIS AUNT, FANNY DESCHAMPS (1976),

TRANSLATED BY JESSICA GREEN

My new role—now that I, too, was an official *stagiaire*—was clarified for me by Frédéric. Frédéric and Ansel worked the fish station. Frédéric, the *chef de partie,* was in charge. He was tall and lean and stiff, with pale eyes and a rectangular, expressionless face that conveyed menace and danger almost all of the time. Ansel was squat and sturdy, with strong arms that seemed disproportionately long for his trunk (they swung), and, covered with body hair, had one of those five o'clock shadows that kick in just after breakfast. Quite apart from the take-no-prisoners attitude that they both shared, Frédéric and Ansel made a formidable team: something like Frankenstein's monster and an ape.

I had been sweeping the floor before the service—one of my new duties—and knocked my broom against Frédéric's kitchen clogs. They were as long as skateboards. I apologized and made a joke out of my clumsiness.

"You think you are a fancy writer."

"No, no, no, no." (Perhaps Lurch, I thought, studying his face, more than the monster.)

"You think you are funny. You are not funny. You are not a fancy writer. You are here to suck my dick." He waited. The intensity of his gaze was impressively hostile.

"*Oui,* Chef. I am not funny. I am here to suck your dick."

He relaxed and seemed satisfied. (I thought: At least we've got *that* sorted out.)

The next day, a new *stagiaire* appeared, a woman. There were no women in the kitchen. Since the restaurant had reopened, there hadn't been a woman (a situation that the ghost of Mère Brazier might have been looking upon with a less-than-amused sense of historical irony). There were also very few women anywhere else: Viannay's assistant, in a small office on the second floor, which she never left and whom we never saw, and two waitresses, who, unknown to me, were both about to hand in their notice. They would be replaced by two other women—I never got their names, because they, too, quit before I learned them. Afterward, in what must have been an oh-fuck-it decision, Viannay replaced them with men.

Sylvain brought the new *stagiaire* to *garde-manger* to introduce her. This was where she would be working, he said.

"Hortense?" I blurted out loudly.

Hortense was the pale, slight, straw-blonde, adolescent-looking, mute-seeming twenty-year-old from my first week at Saisons. What was she doing here? It seemed radical of Viannay to take her on and of Hortense to be taken on. She hadn't changed—she was as self-erasing as ever. But what did I know? She was obviously timid, but not intimidated. She was here.

There were now four in *garde-manger:* Florian, Michael, me, and Hortense.

The station probably didn't need more people. It just needed one who was in charge. That was a fundamental of the Escoffier *brigade* system: a clear hierarchy. Even a small station, like fish, with two people, had one head person, a *chef de partie.* I realized the problem with *garde-manger* when a consultant appeared one morning during our prep. He stood on the step, out of the way and, with a view of everything and, like God, with a clipboard, watched the "team" at work. He never introduced himself or confirmed his role. He never said, "Hello, your boss is paying me to find out why you are all so dysfunctional."

I found myself seeing us as we must have appeared to him: a hyper-ventilating Florian, a sullen Michael, an older balding American never quite sure what he should be doing next, and a mute Hortense, trying hard to hide her unease.

She was, understandably, uncomfortable: a confined space, shoulder to shoulder with men, most with testosterone-excess issues. It was as if she had been the victim of a clerical error, and, rather than being dispatched to a famous French kitchen where she would witness the higher expressions of culinary culture, she had landed in an all-male penitentiary.

The kitchen was also uncomfortable with her. For two weeks, she was addressed only as "Mademoiselle"—as in "Would Mademoiselle prepare the asparagus, *s'il vous plaît*?" or "Might Mademoiselle cut up some tomatoes?" The effect was to increase the spotlight. Every time members of the kitchen heard "Mademoiselle," they thought, Alert, there's a woman in the house! It made them giddy.

The giddiness passed, and Hortense became invisible; the routines of the place—and the normal sexual banter, which had been briefly suspended in honor of her presence—resumed.

I wonder if Frédéric then had a conversation with Hortense akin to the one that he had had with me, clarifying her role. He said something I didn't hear, but she was immobilized by it and suddenly afraid. She once referred to him as a "Michelin type"—a tough-guy persona who worked only at grand restaurants, training for a Michelin-star future— and thereafter visibly tensed up in his presence. Frédéric, for his part, had developed a practice, whenever Hortense passed in front of him, of pretending to mount her from behind.

Klaus returned to Amsterdam on a Friday. On the following Monday, Sylvain introduced me to Jackie Chan, another new intern. I recognized him, too: from L'Institut Bocuse, a third-year, about to graduate once he completed his last requirement: a *stage*, this *stage*. For Sylvain, what mattered was Jackie's kitchen experience. He had worked on the line at a respected restaurant in Burgundy, and would therefore start at the meat station. *Stagiaires* don't normally start on the line.

He lasted two days.

It was not entirely surprising. The three previous people who had tried to work there, including Florian, had failed and been kicked off. In Jackie's case, he wasn't kicked off permanently—it was more like a public rebuking—because there was no backup. (The restaurant—and there were other signs that money was tight—needed another cook, but didn't want to hire one. It got lucky. It got a *stagiaire* with evident qualifications.)

During his temporary demotion, Jackie popped peas with me in the back, as members of the *brigade*—Christophe, Viannay, Ansel, even Johann (the court jester Johann)—went out of their way to seek out Jackie and remind him of his disgrace. Sylvain told Jackie that he was a *putain* and had brought dishonor on the restaurant. "I hope you are thinking about what you did wrong," Sylvain said.

I asked Jackie what he had done.

"I underseasoned the meat."

"Not enough salt and pepper?"

"Not enough salt."

Christophe had said that Jackie wasn't tasting the food. "But I was tasting. My palate is different from his." Jackie paused. "I'm from Jakarta."

"Your name is not Jackie Chan, is it?"

"No, Jackie Chan is a famous actor. He is Chinese. I'm Indonesian." A droll pause. "We all look alike." He smiled. "My name is Hwei Gan Chern," he clarified. "You can call me Chern."

I'd got "Jackie Chan" so firmly in my head—it was the only name used in the kitchen—that it was an adjustment to think of using "Chern."

"You prefer to go by your real name?" I asked.

"Well, yes. Wouldn't you?"

"Of course. I don't know why I asked."

Chern was allowed to return to the meat station the following week.

"Jackie Chan, this is my crate of carrots," Ansel said. "This is your crate." The day's vegetables had just been delivered; each crate held five kilos.

"Let's race, Jackie Chan. Here is your peeler. Here is mine. Go!"

Ansel hated everyone, mainly because everyone was slow.

"Faster, Jackie Chan. Faster!" Ansel, as it happens, was very good at peeling carrots. "Jackie Chan, are you lazy?"

Ansel finished his carrots. He walked over to Chern's station, and stood over him. Chern had a lot of carrots still to do.

"You are very, very slow, Jackie Chan." Sweat had beaded up on Chern's forehead. "Why are you so slow?" Ansel crouched lower, to get within Chern's field of vision. "Why don't you answer me, Jackie Chan? You're a girl, Jackie Chan. You will never be a chef."

"Ansel is an asshole," Chern told me during *le personnel*. Chern hated Ansel possibly more than Ansel hated the rest of the world.

The next day it was potatoes.

"You're no good, Jackie Chan. Maybe you should look for a job as a waitress."

The day started at eight and finished around midnight, except Friday, which finished at 1:00 a.m., and the pace was always on the verge of what could be called "running." Nothing was more important than speed.

I was preparing red peppers—removing the skins and seeds, nothing fancy—for a bright-red savory sorbet that went with cured fillets of *merlu*. (Or "hake"? Is that right? Whatever it might be in English, it was now *merlu*.)

"Have you finished yet?" Sylvain asked me. The service was about to start.

Ten minutes later: "So—nearly done?"

Moments later: "The peppers?" Sylvain stood over me to see what was going on.

"Ah, I see now. It's your hands."

I stared at my hands.

"You must never cross them. Here," he said, rearranging the items around my cutting board. "Put peppers on your left, knife on your right, trash bowl there, too, and the tray for your finished peppers, in the center."

(Was I the last person on the earth to discover that not crossing your hands made a difference?)

Sylvain beamed his Sylvain smile. Then Christophe appeared.

"What are you doing," he said. *Qu'est-ce que tu fais.* There was no way to answer the question since it wasn't one. (Christophe never swears. He never raises his voice. He says, *"Qu'est-ce que tu fais."*)

"I was teaching Bill," Sylvain said, falling into the trap of replying and stuttering on my name. "A technique. For speed." It was as if he had been caught out.

Christophe swept his hand in the air, which seemed to indicate that this guy "Bill" was a fly. "You're wanted at the pass, Sylvain, where, maybe, you'll do something useful."

You didn't waste time. You didn't walk and change direction. You didn't change your mind. You didn't make two trips.

In the morning, when the doors opened, you grabbed a cutting board from the cutting-board rack, and picked up every pot, pan, and utensil that you would need for the entire day. You didn't return until the end of service, when you hauled everything back (stacked totteringly on your cutting board, cautiously making your way through *garde-manger*, because you couldn't see your feet, and there was a step at the beginning and a step at the end). In between, you stayed put. You didn't, for instance, suddenly realize: Oops, I forgot something and I'd better go back.

Actually, you could return, but the passage was via a narrow alley with Ansel and Frédéric at fish, and then Michael and Florian in *garde-manger*, and Sylvain in the walk-in, and no one wanted to see you because your return meant you weren't organized and deserved rebuking. Florian (befitting his lowly position on the proverbial totem pole) was the most aggressive and had a way of becoming exaggeratedly tall and lanky, and wasn't about to get out of your way without bumping you, concentrating his face into an expression of filth and scorn, and calling you a *putain de merde*.

In the beginning, no one ever takes you aside and says, "Hey, let me tell you how this place works." Instead, built into the culture of the kitchen is a pathological intolerance of the novice and a perverse bully's pleasure in watching a novice's failed efforts to figure out a kitchen that everyone else there already knew. For them, it must be very funny.

Then Ansel announced he was quitting, which, in the small community of the kitchen, was a significant event. La Mère Brazier was a project—which we were all there to revive and all aware of what was at stake. Ansel was the first member of the original team to leave of his own volition.

He appeared in the back on his last night. He was working out his shift and had been told to help me. I was popping peas. I popped. He popped. We said nothing.

We finished and started on peeling potatoes. Ansel used a knife. I had a handheld slicer.

We said nothing.

We peeled.

It seemed evident to me that, in Ansel's eyes, I was a contemptible dog (which was probably fine, since, in my eyes, he was an ape).

"Do you think Christophe is a good cook?" I asked. Suddenly I must have wanted to make conversation.

"Christophe?" Ansel seemed startled, as if he had just discovered that the contemptible dog knew a trick involving human speech. "Why would you ask that?"

"I was curious."

"Christophe, a good cook? He might be. I have no idea."

I started in on a new potato.

"I hate him. Christophe." Ansel pronounced the name like something he had just coughed up. "I don't like being in the same room with him."

He finished a potato and picked up another. Ansel was very fast. "I don't like that I might end up breathing air that he has breathed," he added. "Do you understand? He is the reason I am leaving."

"You are quitting because of Christophe?"

"He makes me want to spit." He stuck his fingers in his throat.

"You're not leaving because you have another job."

"I don't have another job."

We were silent. It was a strong position.

"You should use a knife," he said, pointing to the potato in my hand.

"Yes. I know. I'm slow with a knife."

"It's the peeler that's slow. A knife is not slow," he said. "How many strokes do you have to do to peel your potato? You don't know, do you?"

I didn't. I carried on. Ansel watched me. He was counting.

"Twenty-five," he said. "It took you twenty-five strokes to peel that potato. Do you know how many it takes with a knife? Seven. Watch."

Ansel picked up a new potato and proceeded to shave it, beginning at one end and finishing at the other. Then he did a second shaving. With seven strokes, he'd got all the peel. He didn't have to go back and trim off any skin that he'd missed, because he had missed nothing, including the top and the bottom of the potato, which, with a handheld peeler, I always have to address with a bunch of mini-strokes.

Ansel held up his potato between his forefinger and thumb. It was a perfect heptagon.

"I used to keep an egg in my pocket. To practice."

I mentioned a potato-peeling competition that I'd read about in *Le Progrès*. It had taken place the weekend before, at the seedy Place

Carnot. The competition seemed so eloquently symptomatic of where I found myself—in Lyon, this self-obsessed capital of gastronomy. (I mean, *really*—an open competition to determine the fastest potato peeler?)

"Yes, I know that competition. I won it twice."

When I got home that night, I boiled up an egg, and carried it around with me for a day. I couldn't quite make it work, the motion, pretending to shave an imaginary potato with an imaginary knife.

I had better luck with the real thing. On Saturday, I bought a sack of potatoes and practiced on Sunday morning, before the family got up.

Ansel was a knife guy, and the knife, in the kitchen, is your essential tool. He taught me something that I thought I already knew about keeping your knuckle against a blade so as not to be cut by it. I did this, but only intermittently, afraid of pressing up against something so dangerous and probably because I had been cut so much and so badly. Ansel said that I was therefore an utterly stupid person. For his part, Ansel wouldn't cut butter unless his knuckle was against the blade. And, as for me—he who seems to have been regularly cutting himself since he walked into a kitchen—I have, after my session with Ansel, not cut myself with a knife. Not once. (To be clear, I still cut myself: I just figure out other, ingenious ways to do it.)

Ansel was an asshole. Chern was right. And I was happy he was leaving. But I was also happy I had finally talked to him. He was a good asshole.

The next day, Friday, Ansel's last day, was the day when Michael didn't show up. It had never happened—since the restaurant had reopened—that a cook simply didn't appear.

Michael was the most reliable, self-contained member of the kitchen. He tended to the morose, and his affect was of unrelieved misery, but he worked hard, kept to himself, was never late, and was rarely given to displays of aggression or histrionics (unless, I discovered, you accidentally crowded his cutting board).

Christophe waited an hour. At exactly nine o'clock he called Michael on his cell. No answer. He left a message. He tried again ten minutes later. He stared at the phone. He summoned Sylvain, who was doing the weekly inventory of the walk-in, and told him to move to *garde-manger*.

Sylvain, half-waiting for his own phone call—his wife was expected to deliver their first child—marched into the *garde-manger* kitchen and spat on the floor.

Michael was a *putain,* he said. No, he was worse than a whore. He was a dog.

Sylvain was revved. His speech was fast. It was clipped. "A dog," he said, "a filthy, filthy dog. A dog, a dog, a dog."

Did Sylvain know something that I didn't? I thought of possible explanations: illness, food poisoning, a family member in trouble, a malfunctioning alarm—the most plausible, I felt, if only because of the hours. The longest days, which ended between one and two in the morning, occurred when, without warning, Christophe inspected the stations and found that each one needed recleaning and then reinspection.

"*Pas propre,*" he would say.

"*Sale.*" The other word he used: "dirty."

"*Pas propre.*" He would point and sneer.

A smudge, a fingerprint, grease on a slicer blade, a dark dot on the grouting, a streak on the unforgivingly streaky chrome refrigerator door. "*Sale.*"

It took a long time for Christophe to get to "Okay."

I counted the hours, not without pride: sixteen to eighteen hours per day (with a short-but-not-guaranteed afternoon break) *times* five days. An eighty-hour week, plus or minus. At home, I left before anyone else got up and returned after they'd gone to bed. But my routine was easy: I walked there and back. Sylvain, both Johanns, and the guy who ran the meat station, Mathieu Kergourlay, drove home and had long commutes. Chern and Hortense lived in the dorm at L'Institut Bocuse, and waited for a late-night bus.

I had come to like the no-compromises, in-your-face totality of it. There was no morning team doing your work. You prepped, you cooked, you plated, you cleaned your station, you washed the walls, the floors, and the worktops, and then you started over and prepped the dinner. There was an honesty, even a philosophy—that making food was more than cooking it. I was liking the hours. They had a purity because they were so absolute. This is what you did. But if something went wrong— there was no sick leave, no backups—then someone, like Sylvain, had two jobs, his and Michael's.

Around 11:00 a.m., there was a call. Christophe missed it and listened to a voice message—no name, a friend, Michael had been in an accident, late last night, and flipped his car.

Sylvain was indignant. He seized a worktop with his hands. His neck muscles swelled alarmingly. I feared for him, the intensity of his rage, the unreleased power of it, his face turning red.

Sylvain knew nothing else except that, in some way that he didn't yet know, Michael had done wrong. He had violated the code. *La rigueur*— Sylvain used the word. Suck it up. Be hard. Don't let the side down.

Viannay used it. Once, I had been late, needing emergency dental surgery, and I didn't show up until after *le personnel* was finished. Viannay was waiting for me at the door, at the top of the steps, blocking my entrance, arms crossed.

I had left a message. Panic: Did he not get it?

"I heard it."

I apologized for my lateness.

He pointed to his watch.

I apologized again. I pointed to my jaw. "The pain." I tried to be jokey.

Viannay shook his head. "*La rigueur.* Do you understand? *La rigueur.*"

I apologized. He wasn't moving. He was blocking the door.

"You are with us, or you are not."

"I am with you."

Then he stepped aside.

Les règles. The rules. *Les règles* governed the food. *La rigueur* governed behavior.

After lunch, the police phoned. There had been a passenger, Michael's girlfriend. When the car overturned, she was injured, and was in the hospital, in intensive care. Michael had been drinking.

Sylvain slammed a fridge door with his fist and made a dent.

"Michael was intoxicated. He was over the limit," Viannay reported.

Michael showed up the next morning. Viannay asked to speak to him upstairs and fired him.

"He doesn't have the skills," Viannay told me. "The issue wasn't the drink. Do you understand? He wasn't good enough."

Why was Viannay telling me this? He seemed excited by blunt truth.

Viannay could do badass. And then not. He could go from warm to cold to hot in an instant. You studied him. We all did. ("Look at the collar," Frédéric whispered to me, referring to the MOF stripes, staring at Viannay, wanting to learn whatever it was that he had.) He was the patron chef. We were in his territory at his pleasure. The laws were his. You didn't feel entirely safe in his presence. Then you did, and he was your friend. Then you didn't, and you thought he might hurt you.

His rages were rare but focused, like a predator's. He became exceptionally quiet, tiptoe quiet, like a forest animal. Viannay never screamed. He spoke softly, unless he was very angry, when his voice was something like a sibilant whisper. He clenched his teeth, and the jaw seemed to elongate, and the face changed. He put me in mind of a wolverine or a mink, vicious, fast, mean.

One morning, I was in the middle of a particularly tedious activity, stripping delicate plants of only the perfectly formed examples of their foliage. Christophe demanded them. (He'd experienced a horticultural epiphany of some kind, and now believed that, by tossing perfect leaves hither and thither on a plate, the items on it—the meat, the veg, the sauce—were then connected aesthetically, or metaphysically, or maybe just physically.) Christophe had concurrently developed an intolerance for any leaf delivered to him that was inferior or damaged. *"Feuilles,"* he would bark over the loudspeaker. *"Feuilles"* is "leaves." Christophe wasn't calling for *feuilles*. He was expressing displeasure at the *feuilles* I'd just given him, because, invariably, I had delivered up ones that were both inferior *and* damaged.

Viannay came upon me while I happened to be having a little private tantrum, me and my crate of leaves, hurling them this way and that, the little fuckers, with nothing less than outright hostility. There were just so many, and they all were flawed—look there, a whole handful of bent stems—and I wasn't seeing a single perfect one, because nothing was perfect, and, frankly, even morally, nothing *should* be perfect, and I found myself longing for Italy and its happy acceptance of nature as nature, with all its bent stems.

Viannay froze. He stared at me. "What are you doing?"

It was as if he'd come upon me stealing from him (and maybe, on some level, I had been), and he passed from chef guy who seemed to be my friend to man in a rage: the teeth, the jaw, the carnivore mug.

Then he changed back. It was as though a cinematic cloud had just floated across the night sky, and Viannay's normal face returned, his having realized that I was American, and he had been to America, and knew that the people there are ignorant of the culture of the leaf and other matters important to a Frenchman.

"Let me show you," he said. "The leaves are tender. They need to be treated tenderly." *Doucement.* He proceeded to demonstrate: how you dip your hands into the crate of leaves, and then, with curiosity, even affection, you sort through them, one by one, putting the inferior ones aside, looking for the perfect specimen. Each promising leaf was like a possible romantic relationship ("This one? No, alas"), and Viannay's ever-changeable face softened.

"It takes a while to find a perfect leaf," he said. Then he had it. He laid the leaf on the palm of his hand. He stared at it so closely his eyes crossed slightly. Gently, he set it upon a paper towel.

"This is a good leaf."

In the evening, Viannay summoned Johann to the pass via the kitchen loudspeaker.

It was Johann the mellow who appeared, all happy and casual, toque slapped on at the last second, chef pants falling down.

"I want you to make me a dessert for Monday," Viannay said, "something with raspberries."

"*Oui,* Chef!"

Johann headed back to the pastry kitchen, flattered. He was smiling.

Viannay was partial to classic, established French desserts, rendered flawlessly. There was an implicit assumption—Paul Bocuse was probably the inspiration—that the items in the French repertoire were perfectly good, provided that they were perfect. On Viannay's menu was a Grand Marnier soufflé, with an especially intense orange flavor, and the Paris-Brest, the choux pastry shaped like a wheel, my unequivocal go-to favorite dessert from now to everlasting. In the appropriate spirit, Johann created a layered fruit construct called a *mille-feuille croustil-*

lant aux framboises—three planks of puff pastry, raspberries between them, held in place by a raspberry cream. It was red and white and pink.

Viannay crunched into it with a spoon. It made a satisfyingly firm "crackle." He had a bite. He chewed, and I could hear the snap in his mouth. He took another bite, a bigger one, and then another, and rapidly dispatched the dish.

Johann was pleased. It was obvious that Viannay liked it.

In fact, what was obvious was Viannay's hunger.

He wiped the corners of his mouth. He cleared his throat. Then he fired Johann.

"It is not good enough," Viannay said. And like that: There was only one Johann.

The other Johann asked if he could work out the week, and Viannay allowed him to. Johann had been surprised to be terminated but accepted his plight with a worldly equanimity. Viannay had been unequivocal: Your desserts are not good enough. Goodbye. Ice.

Sylvain spoke to Johann in a corner. Was it cocaine—*coco*? (Johann wouldn't have been the first chef who couldn't get through the long hours without some extra help.)

No, he said. There was no mention of drugs. It was simple. He said I was not good enough.

One day, Hortense was weeping. Just before the lunch service, she had gone out into the front kitchen to sweep the floor (now *her* job), and Frédéric, towering over her, had said something—I saw the encounter but didn't hear what had been spoken—and she fled back to *garde-manger* in high distress. Viannay was summoned. By the time he arrived, her face was puffy and sopping, wet like a towel, and she was struggling to get a full breath.

Viannay touched her shoulder to calm her. He got her to regulate her breathing. He leaned onto the worktop, huddling close, inches away from her. I was nearby, funneling jelly into a terrine, and was impressed by the instant bedside manner, the humanity of it.

The huddling was for privacy. He was whispering in a white hiss. He had no interest in the offense. It was the kitchen. You deal or you leave. You are with us, or you are not. And she confirmed that she was.

On Sunday mornings, I took the boys out as early as possible and for as long as possible. It was a pleasure. It was also Jessica's instruction.

Most of the Presqu'île closes on Sundays, except for the cafés and bistros near the farmers' market on the Quai Saint-Antoine. Our place became La Pêcherie. Its appeal was in its bountiful baskets of *pain au chocolat* (the boys each ate at least two), fine hot chocolate, and serviceable coffee. (An enduring French fallacy is café culture. French coffee is filthy, weak, incompetently made, and miserable-making to drink. The best coffee you get is the one you drink after crossing the border into Italy.) The Café Pêcherie was opposite a suburban bus stop and, on Sunday mornings, hosted stragglers after their festive all-nighters as they waited for their public transport, drinking a beer for breakfast, struggling to remain balanced on a bar stool, sometimes rushing downstairs to the toilet, aromatic curiosities whom my children stared at warily.

The boys and I then went to the market, and returned home by way of "the Amphitheatre of the Three Gauls," an ancient ruin, unearthed only in 1978. It had been built by the Romans to be an outdoor meeting place for the indigenous tribes of the Rhône Valley, and is so large it seems improbable that it had been buried so thoroughly by history that it took nearly two thousand years to locate. In its time, it was where hairy men (the Gauls, being famously furry) traveled great distances to get flat-out drunk. My boys became fascinated by the plumbing: so many places to pee, poop, and vomit.

We crossed the river and came upon Christophe, whom I was slow to recognize in his street clothes and without his giant toque. He was sitting with a woman—dark hair, pale complexion, loop earrings, red lipstick—at an outside table of the Wallace Bar, a Scottish sports pub known for its bad food, good beer, and many televisions. I had never seen Christophe outside of the kitchen. I had never seen him with a woman. I had never thought of his actually existing in normal life. I didn't look at them long—Christophe and I acknowledged each other by the most imperceptible of infinitesimally tiny nods—but the two seemed to be not entirely at ease. Was this a date? At the Wallace? Did Christophe's idea of courtship involve indigestion? (Was it possible that someone loved him?)

Frederick's feet bounced against my chest and George's small hand was in mine, and I was aware of a sudden unease. It seemed unsafe for me to be seen thus, with my progeny. In the kitchen, you become a different person from whoever you might be outside it. I was accustomed to being on guard there. Hard men, hard women. I didn't like being seen with my children by the person who ran the place. They weren't hard. They were vulnerable. I felt vulnerable with them in my care.

THE LOIRE VALLEY. The Loire is France's longest river, flowing up from the south and then, just before Paris, veering west to the sea. Its valley was where the capital used to get much of its wine, mainly because it was so close. It was also where kings and queens got away to, for hunting, or from the heat, or just to escape.

I drove there on a weekend. I left our home and headed straight north, the Saône on my right, the hills of Beaujolais on my left. After an hour, I reached the Rock of Solutré, a towering limestone formation that marks the beginning of southern Burgundy and that had once been home, perhaps as early as 50,000 B.C., to the region's cave dwellers (the Middle Paleolithic era, in "the Stone Age"). On hilltops all around are vines, white grapes, almost exclusively Chardonnay, the happy wines of Pouilly-Fuissé, Saint-Véran, and Mâcon.

I stopped for lunch in the town of Beaune, the heartland of Burgundy, and continued. At Dijon, the highway bends northwest, in the direction of Paris.

My destination was Amboise, once the home of François Premier, the king of France from 1515 to 1547 (and the father-in-law of Catherine de' Medici). The town is on the Loire River and along a famous fifty-mile stretch of castles. These are the Valley's architectural miracles—Chambord, a twenty-eight-year building project begun by François Premier that appears to have been designed by two Tuscans; Chenonceau, reconstructed in 1515 and, from 1560, the home of Catherine de' Medici; Châteaudun—one ornately elaborate château after another, more than fifty of them. The turreted castle that Disney uses in its fireworks-exploding logo could have been modeled on the châteaux of the Loire: Even in the sixteenth century, this stretch was like a fairy tale, the châteaux having been built not as fortifications but, in effect, as dream statements, inspired by northern Italy's noble residences, many designed by northern Italy's architects or decorated with Italian fireplaces, staircases, and tapestries. In the same spirit—and it amounts to a French longing for what the Italians had already achieved, a Renaissance of their own—François Premier, an Italian speaker, shortly after having been made king, invited Leonardo da Vinci to move to Amboise, then the royal home. It wasn't without precedent. The king sought out Italian artists to patronize—like Benvenuto Cellini and Andrea del Sarto—and they were welcome at his table. But Leonardo? It was an astonishing gesture.

More astonishing, Leonardo accepted.

The following year, at the age of sixty-four, he embarked on the journey to his new home, probably crossing the Alps from Italy (there is no record of how he traveled), bearing modest belongings on his pack animals, including two just-completed paintings. He was installed, grandly, in the Château du Clos Lucé, a vast "enclosed" property that included lawns, streams, and woods. It was a short walk from the king's residence, so that the two men might have meals and conversation together, which they did almost daily.

I had been to Vinci, where Leonardo comes from—*da* Vinci—in Tuscany. Leonardo is the undisputed genius of the Florentine Renaissance. Just about everyone knows this. What I hadn't known, even when I was visiting the village where he grew up, was that he would die, in 1519, effectively a Frenchman. The detail is seldom mentioned in Italy. It seems to be mentioned less in France, even though Leonardo's most famous painting, the *Mona Lisa,* is hanging in the Louvre because it was one of the canvases he brought with him. The other was *Saint John the Baptist.*

Just past Chablis, there is a junction—Paris to the north, the Loire to the west—and I joined a long arching highway that crosses the middle of France, traversing the plateau of la Beauce. You never see it, unless you have to drive through it, and I, in my effort to discover why a king would have persuaded an aging Leonardo to move to France, was now in the middle of it.

I hadn't anticipated the flatness or its size, four thousand square miles, a vast alluvial plain, formed by the ancient sediments of two rivers, the Seine in the north and the Loire in the south.

The harvest had been completed, and the soil tilled. From one horizon to the other, there were uniform rows of turned earth, an exacting symmetry. It was hot. It was soporific. I put on the radio. I turned up the volume. I drove fast, no vehicles in front, an empty highway. There was nothing to look at, no habitation, no leaf, only the sky, brutal blue, and the endlessness of plowed fields, their unmitigating brownness. I spotted an owl on a fence post.

La Beauce is called *"le grenier de la France"*: its granary, its breadbasket. This is where the nation's flour comes from. Every year, the wheat, once harvested, is threshed and milled, becoming, with each day, month, year of its indifferent storage, less and less a food and more a neutral, characterless starch. The plant is ripped out and replanted, refertilized, nitrogens added to stimulate growth, redusted with pesticides, regrown in what is basically a fake soil. When Bob talked of *la farine,* he was not thinking of one milled from the wheat grown here.

Bob's flour came from the Ardèche. In fact, he bought a lot of flours, but a farm in the Ardèche was his main source. The Ardèche is south and slightly west of Lyon and is rarely mentioned without an epithet invoking its otherness. It is *"sauvage"*—wild—with cliffs and forests and boar. It is untamed. Its mountains are formed by volcanoes, like so many chimneys, still cup-shaped, still menacing, though dormant.

I hadn't visited Bob's Ardèche source, but, once, on an August Sunday morning, I drove through a valley nearby, with Daniel Boulud. We were on our way to the far verge of the region, to meet with Michel Bras. Bras is an eccentrically original chef with a restaurant on an eccentrically unspoiled hilltop. To get there, we had to contend with a chain of volcanic domes. Either you went over them or you drove for hours to get around them. We went over them, and each village we then encountered seemed to take us farther from modern France.

In Félines (a river, a waterfall, a church—altitude, 3,000 feet; population, 1,612), we bought charcuterie at a boucherie. The village had two. Few places celebrated the pig more than the Ardèche, Daniel explained.

At La Chaise–Dieu, we bought more charcuterie (it was different—fattier, more coarsely prepared, more rustic). When we got back into the car, we were blocked by several hundred residents on a march. We

waited; there was only one route through town. At the top of a mountain there are no side streets. The crowd was on its way to church. Where
else does a whole town go to church together?

In Saint-Didier-sur-Doulon, our passage was blocked. The mass there
had just finished.

We crossed a pass, and the land flattened. The route was again blocked:
by goats.

In Bob's boulangerie, there was a picture of a goat on a steep Ardèche
hill. It was kept by Bob's farmer friend, the one who grew the wheat that
was then milled locally into a flour that Bob used to make his bread. The
picture was the only information Bob's customers needed. Who needs a
label when you have a goat?

What made that wheat so special?

"Oh, I don't know. The dirt, maybe?"

"The dirt?"

"The Ardèche is volcanic! No dirt is better than volcanic soil. It is the
iron heart of France."

ONCE, I ASKED VIANNAY HOW HE WOULD DESCRIBE HIS FOOD. It was a
journalist question. But by Viannay's reaction—he seemed to freeze and
was momentarily unable to answer—I saw that my role wasn't entirely
clear. I wasn't really here as a writer, not at this point, but as Viannay's
stagiaire and cook.

"*Néoclassique,*" he then said, emphatically. "My cooking is *néoclassique.*"

Neoclassical? I repeated the word silently. Who today uses such a
term?

Viannay seemed pleased with the effect.

"I am a neoclassicist," he added as though for clarification, and turned
and went upstairs to his office.

I got back to work, thinking: Yes, there would be a classic period in
French cooking—probably several. Is that what Viannay was doing,
neo-versions of them?

On another occasion, we were having a coffee at the bar after *le personnel* and I asked where he was from.

"Near Paris," he said, "Versailles. But"—he added quickly, appearing
to recognize the implications of my question—"my grandfather was

Lyonnais." In Lyon, there is an assumption that only a Lyonnais knows how to cook Lyonnais.

I made him nervous. I was asking him basic journo questions because he made *me* nervous, and I felt uncomfortable (with him, my French, my role, whatever it was) making chitchat.

"I knew two *New Yorker* journalists," he said suddenly, seeming to recognize my unease. "Neil Sheehan and Susan Sheehan."

"They are both Pulitzer Prize winners," I said. Both had filed pieces when I was an editor at *The New Yorker*. "They are famous."

"They were the parents of Catherine, my girlfriend. I remember hearing their typing upstairs. They were always writing." He paused, seeming to recall clickety-clack sounds.

"You had an American girlfriend?"

"Not just a 'girlfriend.' More serious than 'girlfriend.'"

"And you lived in the United States?" I couldn't help myself: I knew so little about this man, the journo questions kept popping out.

"We *were* intending to live there, Catherine and I," he said, and then, like last time, seeming to convey that he had said too much, he bolted upstairs.

Viannay wasn't easy to be with, in any role: so guarded and then seeming to let the guard down and then rushing to put it back up again. I was intrigued by his speech, in its pauses and unexpected stresses. Viannay had a stutter, I now realized, one that he had almost entirely mastered—it was really an almost-stutter—and it gave him a complexity that I hadn't appreciated, and a vulnerability as well. He gave so little away, he seemed to try so hard to hide his interiority, that when it broke through it was impossible not to be engaged by it.

Viannay would eventually tell me the story of Catherine, four years later, over a glass of wine. (Spoiler alert number four: Viannay would become a friend—or, rather, I believe he became one; it won't be surprising if I admit that, with Viannay, I was never quite sure.)

His basic bio is blah-blah-blah aspirational chef familiar: In 1987, his *formation* (cooking school, *stages* at two-star restaurants); in 1998, first job as chef (Les Oliviers, the place Bob delivered bread to); in 2001, first restaurant as patron and chef (M); the MOF in 2004; first Michelin star in 2005; la Mère Brazier in 2008; that second Michelin star in 2009:

boom, boom, boom, boom. But there was a gap, when Viannay abandoned his aspirational chef role and left France to be with his girlfriend
in the United States, during which his career became so derailed that it
would take him ten years to get back on track (an absolute cliché of a
metaphor, but one that would turn out to be absolutely apposite). The
derailment wasn't in the love element. It was in his becoming a sandwich maker. To be fair, he also made croissants. What he didn't make
were neoclassic plates of anything.

To get to America, where Catherine was about to start Wellesley College in Massachusetts, Viannay came up with a loony lark of a scheme
that involved his betraying his trusting, impeccably just, and loving
father (a professor of physics at the University of Angers), borrow-
ing a large sum (around $35,000 in today's money), and spending it
all in two months. "He pretended to go to Johnson & Wales in Rhode
Island, an 'American cooking institution.' He even got a friend to join,"
Sheehan told me, when I reached her in Washington, D.C., where she
now works for the FBI. "Mathieu never went to class. He got kicked
out."

How did you spend the money? I asked him.

"Drink," he said.

Disgraced, he set out to pay back his father by making sandwiches.

His first venue: C'est Si Bonne, a lunchtime bistro, in Greenwich,
Connecticut.

Second venue: C'est Si Bonne in Chicago. Such was Viannay's gift,
the owners asked him to open a branch there.

Then he was summoned to do his French military service. But even
this was curious (one might say, a little "off the rails"). The careers of
many chefs—Michel Richard, Jacques Pépin, Éric Ripert, and even
Escoffier—began in army kitchens. Viannay volunteered not for the
army, but the air force, and not as a chef, but a sniper and a parachutist,
stationed in the mountains of the Languedoc. Had he forgotten his calling? ("Mathieu didn't have to sign up for that," Sheehan said, still bitter
about Viannay's *Boys' Own* fantasy indulgence. "Uzès was the nearest
town! Uzès! Do you know how hard it is to commute to Uzès from the
United States?")

Afterward, Viannay went back to sandwiches, in Paris now, at the

Gare du Nord. "When I was a child," he explained, "I dreamed about being the *chef de gare,* the stationmaster who runs the trains. I got a job as *chef de la gard.* When I told people, they were always impressed, and I had to say, no, what I do has nothing to do with trains. I make the sandwiches served at the station." He was at the Gare du Nord for two years.

His next venue? Gare de Lyon-Part-Dieu. There he made sandwiches for four years. But he was, at last, in the gastronomic capital. (Viannay is obviously very good at making sandwiches.)

THE POPE

The Dombes has changed a little. But it is still in the key that I
love. Wetland skies, with soft, changing colors. Charms, birch trees.
Swamps fringed with weeds and, sitting on top, water birds and
multicolored ducks floating like toys. Up high, seagulls, white
in the sun, gray at dusk. Nothing sumptuous. Nothing flashy.
Good French countryside, made to be lived in every day and
contemplated in autumn, when the woods take on all the colors of
the feathers and fur of the game animals, and the evening fog, rising
from the swamps and flooding the distance, takes on a painterly
melancholy.

CROQUE-EN-BOUCHE BY FANNY DESCHAMPS (1976),
TRANSLATED BY JESSICA GREEN

One day, just after *le personnel,* I was having a coffee at the bar and venting, expressing my frustration that I hadn't met Paul Bocuse to Stéphane Porto, the tall, immaculately dressed maître d'. I hadn't shaken Bocuse's hand. I hadn't exchanged a word. I couldn't get to him.

There were photographs of Bocuse on the walls, from when he worked in the Mère Brazier kitchen.

I had been told I could reach him through his people. A wife, a daughter, a son-in-law. I wrote them all. The daughter was outright disdainful. The tone was: How dare you think that you, lowly writer guy, would have anything to say to Monsieur Bocuse that was even remotely worth his time?

Viannay was standing behind me.

"You want to meet Bocuse?" he asked.

"Yes."

"Come in early tomorrow. Seven. Be on time. I will introduce you. Don't be late."

Viannay drove me across the Rhône River and into the third arrondissement to the indoor food market, Les Halles de Lyon Paul Bocuse. I spotted the great chef's vehicle, a massive black Jeep Wrangler (American), with all the doodads: spotlights on the roof, a winch, and wide off-road tires (Michelin). It was parked on a sidewalk, in front of the hall entrance. The sight confirmed two Lyonnais rumors: (1) Bocuse did indeed have a daily morning coffee at Les Halles, and (2) the police knew his vehicle and never ticketed it.

For our part, we used a conventional parking lot, and paid for it, entered the hall, and stopped at a vendor, Chez Léon, which has been selling shellfish at Les Halles, or one of its earlier incarnations, since 1920. We had a platter of oysters and a glass of Muscadet, a bracing breakfast. Viannay leaned over and whispered: "Chez Léon. Remember the name; it is where you will buy your oysters. Do you understand?"

We made our way to Le Boulanger, an informal café opposite the stand of La Mère Richard, the city's famous cheese lady, where Viannay paused to point out the quality of what was on display. ("This is where you buy your cheese. D'accord?")

I looked across the aisle. There he was: Paul Bocuse, sitting by himself, finishing a coffee.

He was slumped slightly in his chair, and wearing a black Pringle Polo cotton shirt, a worker's cotton jacket, black trousers, and sneakers, and looked like a regional train conductor at the end of his shift. On spotting us, he stood up. He had shrunk considerably since I'd seen him last. Then again, that last time he had been in a towering toque and heavy-heeled clogs, and doing that erect-chef posture routine. Without the gear, he was, frankly, a little naked. He seemed, to me at least—and it is startling for me even to utter the thought—to be almost normal. He was a man.

Except he wasn't, in fact. He was, in fact, a deity.

There was a lot about him that I didn't know, I realized instantly. Actually, on reflection, I knew nothing. Or at least now—me, alone with the deity himself, without a handler—I felt that I knew nothing. I hadn't yet eaten at his three-star place, and was now angry with myself that I hadn't taken myself there.

And here he was, shaking my hand, *the* Paul Bocuse, and, damn it, startled to find myself in this situation—among the greatest meetings in my life—I went irrevocably shy. Me, the gabby-gabby talker, the intrepid give-it-a-shot guy: I went mute.

I spent twenty minutes in Bocuse's company. I said nothing more than *merci* (or its variations).

He told me to follow. *"Viens,"* he said gently.

"Merci, Chef."

He wanted to give me a tour.

"Viens," he repeated.

"Merci, Chef."

Since Bocuse knew everyone at Les Halles, and since everyone obviously knew him, and since it was an early hour and few shoppers had shown up yet, and since the place had been named after him, our slow passage through its aisles was surprisingly intimate. It was like being given a tour of his home.

"Here the charcuterie is very good," he said, not unlike the owner of a large estate showing off his roses. "This is Chez Sibilia." Sibilia was an imposing no-nonsense woman with ten employees, all women, all looking like no-nonsense mini-versions of their patroness.

Viannay whispered: "You will buy your charcuterie nowhere else. *D'accord?"*

"Oui, Chef."

Sibilia and Bocuse did kiss-kissy *bonjours* and produced slices of rosette for me to taste, the dried local sausage that Lyonnais crave whenever they leave town. They both stood there studying my mouth, waiting for a verdict, as if such a tasting were a matter of great importance. It was a shtick, of course, their PR routine. I knew that. They knew that I knew that. He'd done it many times; he had done it with her many times. But, meanwhile, the overwhelming fact was this: Bocuse, *the* Paul Bocuse, was hand-feeding me a *saucisson*, and I was remarkably okay with that.

"*Merci,* Chef."

Across the aisle was Les Volailles Clugnet, a bird vendor. The proprietor ("*Bonjour,* Pierre"), on seeing Bocuse, handed over a white bird unsolicited. Bocuse seized it between his two large hands and slapped it around, firmly but with affection, as though the puppy of a favorite hunting dog.

"The best chicken is the white breed from Bresse," Bocuse said. "*Tout le monde le sait.*" Everyone knows this.

He handed it to me. It was heavy. Full. The French don't gut birds until they sell them. (This keeps them longer. It now seems wrongheaded that, in the interests of "hygiene," the USDA insists on evisceration.)

I held on to the chicken and looked at it politely. Bocuse riffed quietly on its features, the red wattle draped across my thumb, the white feathers, the dangling blue feet, and the many qualities that make the *poulet de Bresse* a rare and scrumptious creature.

Viannay whispered: "Les Volailles Clugnet. Do you understand? The only place."

"*Oui,* Chef."

Then, like that, bang: Bocuse said goodbye.

Leaving already? It was—I can't deny it—a moment of shocking disappointment. So soon? After such a long wait? I hadn't even asked a question. (Then again, who could blame him? Why hang out with a guy who never talks?)

"*À tout à l'heure,*" he said.

"*Merci,* Chef."

I thought: *À tout à l'heure?* Really? See you soon?

We made our way back to the parking lot, but paused first at a charcuterie stand. "Do you know Bobosse? You should know Bobosse. It is the only place for *andouillettes.*"

Viannay said, "Let's go for a drive."

He drove me back to the Saône, traversing our *quartier* in the first arrondissement, and headed upstream. This part of the river, zigzagging in the direction of Beaujolais, is outside the city, but very much its folkloric heart.

The drive was slow and pretty: the river on our left; steep hills, almost mountains, on the right; and the foliage, dense and out of control, everywhere, like a rain forest. I hadn't been here yet and felt transported to another country. The buildings were few, but crumbling-grand. Many had been church properties, seized during the French Revolution: monasteries, a convent, Île Barbe in its entirety—a fifth-century abbey built on a rock formation in the Saône.

An estate appeared on our right, reminiscent of an Augustan English country house. "Ombrosa."

So *that* is Ombrosa.

It is a bilingual school, suggested for our children before we got here. It has a privileged, leafy tranquillity. We couldn't have afforded it. Besides, I liked where we had ended up.

We crossed a bridge (the Pont Paul Bocuse) and drove briefly downriver to a flat building with an old clock tower. Viannay pushed on the front door, which was unlocked, and led the way inside, turning on lights as he went, a long hall.

The building, originally a monastery property, was called L'Abbaye de Paul Bocuse. Our footsteps echoed. Viannay was mute but amused. It felt like trespassing. Then, entering a large bright dining room, I got the point: I had been secreted into an enormous Bocuse confection.

The dining room had a name (Le Grand Limonaire), a stage, a floor-to-ceiling "Orgue Gaudin" (a mechanical pneumatic organ), and a chorus of marionette cancan dancers. Viannay flicked a switch and music started, and a version of Paul Bocuse as a life-sized doll conducted it with a wooden spoon. *Limonaire* is "hurdy-gurdy." Viannay flicked another switch and many *limonaires* all kicked in at once. The room dazzled, literally, with shiny kitsch and was red, green, and gold, like an enormous candy cane. It was confusing to look at because there was so much to look at—it was crammed with stuff—including the space above our heads, which was crowded with low-hanging ornate chandeliers.

"It seats four hundred," Viannay said.

It was a private dining room, but more public than private, and promised not just dinner but time travel: to a late-night all-night Toulouse-Lautrec France where everyone was expected to behave badly.

Viannay suggested that we get back in the car.

I paused, taking in the preposterous venue. You don't walk into it and think: I have arrived at a solemn temple of high gastronomy. You think: Party!

We drove back past the bridge to the main Bocuse restaurant, L'Auberge. The word normally means "inn." Bocuse's "inn" is a massive three-story box of a mansion that he also calls home (the restaurant is on the ground floor) and looks like an outsized birthday present for giants: improbably square, with red shutters and green walls, decorated with eight-foot-high paintings of food, including of course *poulet de Bresse,* and the name PAUL BOCUSE built across the roof all in caps. The man from the Ivory Coast—the livery suit, the top hat—was the same front-door opener who had welcomed Bob and his Cuban wife.

Outside was a *"rue des grands chefs"*—a passage of culinary murals, arranged like windows, each a glimpse into one of the great kitchens in French history. It started in the nineteenth century. It ended with Bocuse. (Bocuse's view of history might be described as greatness improving on greatness, culminating with him. Modesty wasn't a feature of a Bocuse worldview.)

I stared at the first panel. It portrayed Antonin Carême in a kitchen, looking like Byron, dressed not in a chef's jacket but in a robe, the "inventor" of *"grande cuisine"*—the guy whence the whole shebang started—leaning on the windowsill, looking contemplatively into the middle distance. (In the background, Napoleon and Josephine rush in to grab a bite to eat.) Was Carême a Bocuse model?

We know that Carême came from a large family. What we don't know is when he was born (probably 1784) and if he was one of fifteen children or of twenty-five. At the age of eight (or twelve—our source for Carême is Carême), he was abandoned at a tavern door and taken in by the patron. (Probably true.) At seventeen (or sixteen), he was accepted as an apprentice at the most renowned pâtisserie in Paris. In no time (or, at most, four years), he came to be regarded, especially by Carême himself, as the greatest pastry chef since the discovery of sugar. By then, he was cooking everything, savory and sweet, but always flamboyantly, mainly banquets, and mainly for princes and heads of state, including the slimeball Talleyrand. (Talleyrand was Napoleon's foreign minister; he conducted diplomacy over dinners made by Carême, his young employee, whom he had famously instructed never to repeat a meal.)

Carême and sugar: the foundations of French cooking. You hear it often: Pastry chefs have driven French cooking. The Italianists, who now probably included me, recognize that the Italians taught the French *grande cuisine.* But it was sugar, and the scientific kitchen that could make things with it, that may have been the basis for what French cuisine would become.

What intrigued me in the mural was the tool in Carême's hand. It was a quill.

Carême is the most important chef in French culinary history because he wrote books. He was the poet of the French kitchen. You can't taste his meals today, but from his writing you can get enough instruction to imagine what they might have been like to eat, and maybe, in theory, make approximate versions of them (as long as you prefer wood to gas, have no electricity, pluck your own birds, churn your own butter, and have *commis,* apprentices, servants, and other members of elevated slave labor housed in a bungalow nearby).

I had begun reading Carême and found the sentences, even in my rudimentary French, to be vivid and accessible nearly two centuries after Carême wrote them—except, I learned only recently, Carême didn't write them. Carême, the first historian of French cooking, wrote nothing. He probably couldn't write, at least not well. (He was taught how to read in the pastry kitchen at sixteen.) But he was savvy enough to recognize the value of the written "performance." He was living in a time when food described on a page was as important as what was served on a plate. Kitchen books mattered, they made reputations, and Carême "wrote" several of them, but none more influential than his magnum opus: the five-volume, fifteen-hundred-plus-page *Art of French Cooking in the Nineteenth Century,* one of the most ambitious projects in the history of cooking, marred modestly by the fact that Carême died (aged forty-eight, maybe) after completing volume 3. He wrote the last two volumes posthumously.

Carême was both a master impresario and a master self-mythologizer, a larger-than-life commando of *le spectacle,* unmatched in the magical relationship between self-invention and self-promotion until—well, who? There hasn't been anyone else in the world of the kitchen, I was thinking, not on Carême's scale, until, possibly, Paul Bocuse—when, unannounced, Bocuse himself silently padded up from behind and appeared alongside me. I jumped.

"I thought you were at Les Halles," I said idiotically, since, obviously, there was no reason for him not to be here: "Here" was his home.

I tried to catch Viannay's eye. How did he pull this off—with less than a day's notice, getting me the guy no one else could reach? I was grateful. I was impressed. And I was also aware, or at least strongly suspected, that it had been Viannay's intention to impress me. The undisguised show-offy clout of it all. He may not have been from Lyon, but he was very secure in his place in it. He was a member of the "club."

Bocuse, meanwhile, was looking at a mural—the one devoted to Mère Brazier, appositely enough.

She was in the foreground, stately and authoritative and square-shouldered. Gaston, Brazier's long-suffering son, was in the back, mixing something in a bowl and looking, somehow, not quite like her offspring: head down, fearful, the tentative eyebrows of a dog who knows that he is about to be kicked again. (Off to the side was the legendary Mère Fillioux, Brazier's former boss, rounder, softer, more maternal, doing that wizard thing of boning a chicken with a spoon.)

"What was Brazier like?" I asked Bocuse.

"You know, her cooking was simple," he said, understanding my question to refer to her kitchen and not her person. "It was based on the good products that you find here. We are fortunate." (*Nous sommes heureux*—and he made a sweeping gesture with his hand.) Bocuse was deliberate in his sentences and had a quiet way of uttering them. "The fish, the birds, the pigs. But, frankly, they weren't sophisticated, her dishes." This wasn't a slur, just a fact. "It was country cooking. The food was good, but it was about the ingredients."

"Ingredients?"

Ingredients? This is how Italians talk.

"The rivers and lakes, the swamps of the Dombes, the mountains. That's where our food comes from. It's like nowhere else."

"Brazier screamed at her staff," Viannay added. "She didn't care if anyone was listening. She beat her son in front of the diners. Her kitchen was her home. No one was going to stop her from being herself."

Bocuse nodded, but the nod seemed to be a courtesy. Implicit in it was, for me, a modest realization. Viannay was repeating what others had said. He hadn't been there. Bocuse had been.

We made to return to La Mère Brazier. I had a proposal. I wasn't sure when I would be alone with Viannay again.

I had been at the restaurant for four months, in the back, preparing amuse-bouches, searching for perfect salad leaves, making starters. I could be counted on. Viannay had no reason to change the arrangement. But I needed to change it. I wanted to be moved into the kitchen.

I wanted to work on the line, and I was going to ask him to put me there.

My nervousness surprised me. I reflected: Whatever I do now, including nothing, will have a consequence.

What if Viannay says yes and I end up suffering an even longer catalogue of humiliating and spectacular failures?

I stalled. I said nothing. The idea of not asking was appealing. I could always ask later.

"Chef, I was wondering if you would consider a request."

"Of course." (He sounded so friendly.)

"I want to work on the line."

There was an audible intake of breath—ouch!—and a long pause. During it, I wondered: I have been deluded, haven't I?

"You're a good cook," he said.

"Thank you." This was cheering.

"But you're always late." This was true.

"And slow," I said.

"Late," he corrected. "Frankly, I worry about your punctuality."

He was looking for a parking place and not finding one.

"You will have to prove that you can make food and not be late making it. I will ask Christophe if you can cook *le personnel.*"

The staff meal: cooking French food for French cooks. It was an intimidating prospect. It frightened me. It excited me.

"I would be honored."

There was another intake of breath. "You must never be late. If the meal is not ready at eleven o'clock, the staff doesn't eat."

"I understand."

"Okay. I will ask Christophe. Christophe will have to approve."

This seemed unlikely. Christophe couldn't really approve of my being moved to the kitchen, because, fundamentally, he disapproved of my being in the restaurant. I could easily imagine Christophe's response: "This is a joke, right? No, please. Tell me you're not serious."

But, evidently, Christophe agreed.

The next morning, a Thursday, I went to the main kitchen and reported for duty.

Christophe blew me away with his hand.

"Yes, yes, Mathieu told me. I am not happy. You will start when I am ready for you to start."

I returned to *garde-manger*.

On the Friday, I popped my head into the main kitchen, and Christophe wouldn't look at me.

On the Monday, I didn't bother—I went directly to *garde-manger*—and was then summoned. Christophe didn't greet me. He studied my person, up and down, my eagerness. He looked at me, without question, with contempt. He expected me to fail.

"Pork belly," he said.

"Pork belly?"

"Yes. In the walk-in." *La chambre froide.*

I thought: I have just been told to make pork belly for thirty people?

"You'll find onions upstairs."

"Onions."

"And potatoes."

"Potatoes."

"And your sauce?" Christophe asked.

"My sauce?"

"Yes. What is your sauce?"

I didn't know what to say.

"What sauce will you make with pork belly?"

I turned uncomprehendingly to Mathieu Kergourlay, who ran the meat station.

He tried to be helpful. "What would you make at home?" *À la maison?*

I wondered: What sauce *do* I make at home when I'm serving pork belly?

"Oh, maybe something with a meat stock," I said, "a *fond*." I did make sauces sometimes, usually based on a stock—chicken, fish, the bones of whatever meat I was serving—and then reducing it down and adding wine. I read it somewhere: Elizabeth David? A British newspaper column? But I was stalling. I was really thinking: (1) I have never cooked pork belly at home, and (2), if I did, I wouldn't make a sauce.

"No," Christophe said. "The *fonds* are expensive." *Trop chers.* The stocks—and all of them made in the kitchen (veal, chicken, duck, fish, lobster)—were too precious for a staff lunch.

"What about a beurre rouge?" Mathieu Kergourlay proposed.

Yes, I thought. I should know how to make that. I know how to make a beurre blanc. I'd done it at L'Institut Bocuse. But how exactly? I wasn't panicking, but my Institut Bocuse database was suddenly uncomfortably inaccessible.

"You don't know how to make a *beurre rouge*?"

"No, I do. I just may not have made it yet. That is, I've made the white one, the blanc, but don't remember if I ever got around to doing the red."

Later that morning, Viannay reminded me that the salad needed a vinaigrette. I didn't know that I had to make one.

"Yes, you have to make the vinaigrette."

A reflective pause.

"And how exactly do you make a vinaigrette?" I asked.

"You don't know how to make a vinaigrette?" Christophe looked at Viannay, with a heavily inflected expression of incomprehension. And, yes, again, I basically knew how to make a vinaigrette, I'd made it, just not often. Besides, weren't there twenty different kinds? I had no idea what was made here and what everyone expected. (At home—"*à la maison*," as Mathieu Kergourlay refers to it—our salads are dressed with olive oil, lemon, and salt. *Basta.*)

"Two parts oil, one part vinegar, plus mustard," Viannay said. "And salt and pepper."

To make a beurre rouge, Young Mathieu explained, you chop up shallots fine (*émincer*), sweat them in butter (*suer*), don't let them brown, add a liter of red wine, reduce slowly until it's a syrup, and build it back up (*monter*) by whisking in a half-kilo of butter, bit by bit.

"At that point, I'll help you."

My shallots, I am pleased to report, were excellent. I sliced them on a cutting board that I had to borrow from another cook (because I had shown up after eight—not a lot after eight, but a definitive five minutes after eight—and by then there were no boards left), and I eventually found a makeshift worktop (i.e., I balanced my board above a trash can, because, by then, all the counter space had been taken). The counter-space scarcity I understood—the kitchen was cramped. But why weren't there more cutting boards? Every day started with twelve people fighting for ten boards. They are not expensive. (Why? Because everyone then knows who the late guy is—the moron who spends the first hour of his morning trying to persuade someone to lend him a board.)

Unfortunately, as beautiful as my shallots were to look at—small, perfectly formed, crisply purplish—they took nearly an hour to complete. Though I didn't know a lot yet, I knew that an hour to cut up some shallots was an unforgivably long time.

I put a saucepan on the flattop to heat. What I didn't know was the flattop's temperature. It was correct that I should now be getting to know the kitchen's fundamental heating instruments—the ovens, the burners, how long it takes to boil a liquid, and the flattop. I felt confident in wanting to be here. It was right that I had asked Viannay.

I tossed in my butter and shallots—to sweat them. The point is to reduce the shallots' raw intensity. You want them still white, maybe a little creamy. Brown is bitter. White, creamy shallots, halfway between uncooked and cooked, constitute one of the fundamental flavors of French food.

But oh dear. Something was wrong. There was an alarming hissing sound, and smoke.

"*Merde,*" Christophe said.

"You're going to burn them," Viannay said.

"Shit," I said.

"You have five seconds." Christophe was unquestionably delighted.

What could I do? Was I going to have to do my shallots all over again? I took the pan off the heat.

"That's a start," Viannay said, slowly. I looked up, needing direction. Viannay was studying me and my steaming pot with what I can only describe as "clinical calm." "You need to reduce the heat by adding something to the pan," he said. "It's too early for the wine. More butter. But quickly—"

I grabbed some butter and dropped it into the pot, and swirled. I scooped up another spoonful. I was about to scoop up another—

"Stop," Christophe shouted. "You're going to give us heart attacks" (a peculiar fear, I felt, given that another half-kilo was yet to be added).

I added the wine. I reduced it. And I then added that half-kilo of butter, whisking it in bit by bit until it emulsified with the by then very concentrated wine (it was smooth and velvety, like a purple fabric). Mathieu Kergourlay came over to taste it.

"Pas mal." He added salt and pepper. He tasted it. He added red-wine vinegar. He tasted it. He turned and removed a jar of mustard from a shelf and added a spoonful. "But only a spoonful. *Très chère.*"

(Mustard? Expensive?)

He whisked, tasted, added another vinegar splash, whisked, and tasted. It was ready.

He gave me a spoon. It wasn't what I expected. It didn't taste of butter. There was fat, obviously, but it was textural (a rather luscious roundness), and fruit (from the wine), and an appealingly bitter acidity (from the shallots, the vinegar, the mustard). The sauce hit so many happy spots on my tongue that it didn't matter if it was healthy or not. It was delicious. It was a meal, except that it wasn't. You wouldn't want to drink a mug of it, but a spoonful or two dribbled across some chunks of pork belly (sautéed with potatoes and onions) was a definite package-enhancer.

Except that the package was late.

At ten-fifty-five, Christophe, seeing that lunch wouldn't be on time, reached down into a lowboy and pulled out a tuna steak, sautéed it, and took it to a table to eat it by himself. I finished up the lunch, intermittently catching sight of Christophe through the small window in the swinging door between the kitchen and the bar. I had failed.

But I wasn't fired. It seemed that I was being given a second chance. Tomorrow I'd get a frickin' cutting board.

But I didn't. I was late.

I woke up thinking, Whatever you do, arrive on time—and then didn't. Viannay was right: I did have a problem with tardiness or focus or a vaguely ADHD organizational dysfunction. All week long, I was late. To be fair, the lunches themselves were never *very* late; they were just always a little late, and everyone, except Christophe, was only a little bit unhappy. Circa 10:55 a.m., Christophe was apoplectic.

Friday, I was really late. Fridays, it turns out, are leftover days. Before, when I was mere eater rather than the lunch maker, I hadn't noticed. Christophe must have assumed that no member of his kitchen could be so clueless as not to recognize a leftover. Or maybe (likely) he was just perverse. I hung around, waiting for him to tell me what the day's ingredient was going to be, the morning getting later and later, until, finally, I asked and was informed that there wasn't one. Go to the walk-in, Christophe said. "There you'll figure out what we're eating."

I stared at the shelves, trying to determine what was a leftover, and then wondering what I was going to do with it that would feed thirty people. This is Hell, I thought. It was the first day when, after I prepared the lunch (I don't know how late, I've repressed the time, just as I have no idea what I made), I didn't eat it. I ran upstairs to the bathroom, took off my chef's jacket, and wrung it out. The sweat filled the sink. I stood there, half undressed, trying to cool.

On Monday, however, there was a remarkable turn of events: Christophe ate *with* us. Lunch was served at 11:00 a.m. On Tuesday, Wednesday, and Thursday, it was also served at 11:00 a.m. (Friday was late *again*—it was now fully established as the worst day of my week—and Christophe resumed dining on his own.)

The modest achievement was effected by my taking what would turn out to be an unacceptable shortcut. I didn't do a sauce. I'd intended to, at least on the Monday. The principal ingredient was skirt steak. Christophe presented it to me like a clue in a quiz, followed by what I now recognized to be the usual catechism. How will I cook it? (In sauté pans, several at once.) With what? (*Une purée de pommes de terre*—buttery mashed potatoes.) And? (Asparagus.) How? (In the oven, roasted.) And? (A salad with anchovies.) And the sauce? "Beurre rouge," I said, thinking, steak + red wine = eternal combo, etc. It wasn't a complicated meal.

I got to work. I cut up shallots, sweated them and added the wine. I set the meat out to bring it to room temperature, and seasoned it. It was the potatoes that subverted my schedule. Despite Ansel's whiz-kid potato tutorial, and the fact that I had been practicing at home, when it came to my going live with forty kilos of tubers, I lost my nerve; I didn't think I would yet be fast enough with a knife, and resorted to the old practice of the peeler. In fact, the peeler really is slow, and, if you're still using one, you should give it up. It is also maiming. The more I fell behind, the greater the pressure I felt to go faster, and the more I maimed myself. It was an angle problem—a big elliptical root vegetable in one hand, the T-shaped peeler in the other, and, if you're trying to move at speed, you can't reliably get your knuckles out of the way of that wide, badass razorlike blade as it comes sliding around the potato's southern hemisphere. Nicked knuckles weren't a big deal—you didn't stop to bandage them up—but they slowed you down: the shredded skin, and a bleating imperative from your brain, which I was unable to override, to stop hurting yourself.

Finally, the potatoes peeled, I filled a fifty-liter container with water to store them, put it on a shelf in the *chambre froide*, cleaned up my work-station, and went looking for a *tamis*.

A *tamis* is a sieve that looks like an Indian drum, round with a wooden frame. In pastry, it is a flour sifter. In the kitchen, it is a vegetable smoosher. You press boiled potatoes through the mesh, and a light, creamy starch streams out the other side, which you then mix with half its weight in butter (i.e., twenty kilos of butter). Chef Joël Robuchon made his *purée de pommes de terre* this way at his 1980s Paris restaurant Jamin, and ever since there has been a debate about the butter percentage, because most healthy people find the proposition of mashed potatoes made half of butter to be morally unacceptable. In this debate, I am now a witness for the defense and can attest that, in fact, yes, you can make potatoes with 50 percent butter. Just don't think about it. It's vegetable dessert.

The *tamis,* however, was not to be found. I checked with the dish-washer, the pastry chef, Florian in *garde-manger,* Christophe. Nowhere.

"Not important," Christophe said. "Do them *à la rustique*." Smashed.

"Of course," I said and returned to the *chambre froide*. The potatoes were gone. I rechecked my station: not there. I returned to the kitchen. Not there. I asked Florian if he had seen them.

"I took them," he said.

"You took them?"

"I needed them."

Wow.

I peeled a new batch. I didn't have time to peel a new batch, I still had to cook them, another forty kilos, frantic now, knuckle chunks flying in all directions. I heated up the sauté pans, hot, hot, hot, and threw the steaks on them, dropped the potatoes into a massive marmite, highest flame setting ("Boil, baby, boil"), made a vinaigrette, rushed back to the steaks, flipped them . . .

"Vite!" Fast! Christophe was in a fury. It was ten-forty-five. *"Vite! Vite! Vite!"*

"Vite!" Mathieu joined in. "This is not difficult. *Vite!"*

I was sweating. My arms were glistening. My hands were wet. I was talking to myself. "Don't be late."

"Vite!"

"Don't be late, don't be late."

"Vite!"

The sauce? The sauce! I checked it. The reduction was complete. It was a beautiful, deep midnight black-red, and deliciously viscous, but I hadn't mounted the butter. I hadn't even started. I looked at the butter. Question: Mount sauce with butter and be late? Or jettison butter and be on time? I killed it. Like that: gone. When I thought no one was looking, I poured shallots and wine down the drain. (This was naïve: Someone was always looking.)

When I set out the food, I declared that I'd made the steaks "Tuscan-style," with sea salt, olive oil, and wedges of lemon.

In France, no one dresses a steak with lemon.

Vlad picked one up. Vlad was a Russian émigré. He had been studying English from American hip-hop songs. "What fuck this?" he asked. "I no fucking eat no fucking lemon," he said, and then he threw a wedge at me. "Fuck you, muttafucka!"

But it was on time. Everyone served themselves, and went out into the bar area to eat it, and I stayed behind to clean up, and found the missing *tamis*—at Florian's station, hidden underneath a counter.

———

The following week I was summoned by Viannay.

"Christophe tells me that you are serving *le personnel* without a sauce."

It was true. I apologized.

Viannay confirmed that I knew that I was meant to make a sauce, that it was one of my obligations in producing *le personnel*. "My staff needs a sauce," he said. "It's possible that you don't understand the seriousness. *Le personnel* is an important part of their day." Viannay wasn't angry. On the contrary, he was patiently pedagogical. He was teaching me a principle about French food. "For me," he said, "*le personnel* is a contract with my staff. If they don't have a sauce, it's as though I am taking money out of their pockets. *D'accord?*"

"*Oui,* Chef. *D'accord.*"

"There must always be a sauce."

Meanwhile, Ansel the asshole was right. I wasn't going to use a peeler again. The next potatoes were *à la vapeur*. Christophe's directive. It was what he wanted to eat.

"How many will you need?" he asked. The quiz show.

"Sixty?" I was thinking two per person.

"Ha!" More bark than laugh. "Sixty?" He sneered. I was so utterly ignorant. "Two hundred fifty." He repeated the number slowly— "You ... will ... need ... two ... hundred ... and ... fifty."

Two hundred fifty? That is a lot of potatoes. It was an important instruction.

A potato *à la vapeur* is roasted in steam. It is also called an English potato—*pomme de terre à l'anglaise*—for no reason that I've been able to figure out except that, just after the brilliant food scientist Antoine Parmentier proved to the French in 1772, that the potato was edible and they instantly came up with two hundred ways of cooking it, the English borrowed the one called *à la vapeur,* because it was awfully good with roast beef, and made it their own.

To make, the PDTs are skinned and trimmed to the same weight (fifty grams), length (six centimeters), and shape, what is called *bombées*—ballooned, bulging in the middle. And they are to be "turned"—seven "planks," just as I had been taught by Ansel the Asshole. The ends are flat, not rounded.

It was a risk—the number of potatoes, the 11:00 a.m. have-it-on-the-table deadline—but, for me, one that I calculatedly wanted to be taking. My potatoes *à la vapeur* represented a modest rite of passage, my finally graduating to the knife.

They had, I reflected, as I made my way through a first batch, an unnatural natural beauty (a thing from nature rendered with a symmetry that you will never find there): the planks, the creamy yellow color, the visual harmony of each one looking exactly like the others. I was at the sink by the *chambre froide,* away from the urgencies of the main kitchen, my back to all of it, water dribbling from a faucet with the acoustic comfort of a stream, and the almost musical rhythm that you can sometimes find in a repeated task—the Zen of it.

I reflected on how the PDTs *à la vapeur* were tricky to cook (fat in the middle, narrow at the ends), reached doneness slowly, arrived at it briefly, and thereafter deteriorated to mush, and I made a mental note to be attentive when I cooked them.

I wondered: Why do the French make so many different kinds of potatoes? They can be done as batons, straw, matchsticks, hair, hazelnuts, waffles, and mushrooms, as well as your basic "French fry" (*mignonette*).

I wondered: Was it because when they were finally deemed edible—thanks to Parmentier—they were served not boiled in a bowl for a peasant to slurp up, but instantly incorporated into a highly developed cuisine? By then, there were a hundred ways to cook an egg. Why not two hundred ways to cook a potato?

I wondered: Had anyone else had this thought?

Today, I wonder, horrified: How could my mind have drifted so far from the kitchen?

I had been at the sink for a long time before an alarm was raised. There was no longer time to cook the potatoes. Mathieu Kergourlay put a pot of water on the stove. Menu change: pasta (without a sauce; just pasta, because there wasn't any time for a sauce). I began cleaning up frantically, to get out of the sink and back into the kitchen, peels and bits of potato everywhere, when Christophe began pacing behind me. He had come to rant.

"Your potatoes are shit," he said, and walked to the end of the passage.

"They are *pommes de terre de merde,*" he said, returning.

"We do not eat shit potatoes." He walked back again.

"Bill should take his shit potatoes home. Who knows what he was doing for an hour? He was making shit potatoes for himself. He should feed his children his shit potatoes. The shit potatoes are for *la maison de Bill*."

I didn't take the potatoes home. I stored them in two very large containers of water and put them in a corner of the walk-in, behind the cream, in the hope that Florian wouldn't find them. According to the leftover rules of the kitchen, one night of potatoes, in water, was okay. Two: never. I continued to think about my shit potatoes on my walk home that night: What was wrong with my brain?

Also—and this seemed telling—I was among the last ones to change into his cooking clothes in the morning. But I was *always* the last one, without fail, in the evening.

It got so bad that, toward the end of service, I started loitering by the stairway. I wiped a counter, I rewiped it. I wiped it again. I couldn't go up until Christophe gave the signal. He grunted, finally. I bolted. I was the first up. But then, for no reason that I understood, I was still the last to leave.

I began stashing my clothes in a corner of the pantry so that they would be ready to change into, and I wouldn't have to jostle by the lockers. Once again, the loitering, the signal, my bounding up the steps, except that this time I was focused and found my stash, set out my street clothes on a chair, whipped off my clogs, socks, pants, jacket, shirt, and was standing stripped down to my boxer shorts, just as the others reached the top of the stairs.

They were confused.

Why was I in the pantry without any clothes on?

Then Frédéric declared, "Look at how much weight he's lost!" He walked over and poked my stomach with his finger.

Attention! La panse de Bill! "Bill's paunch. It's not the paunch he had when he started." He poked again. He nodded approval.

Sylvain joined him. He, too, poked my paunch.

"You've lost weight!"

"A lot of weight," Frédéric added. He poked me again, tickled by his findings. "It's still soft, but not as soft as it used to be."

"In the beginning, you were big," and Sylvain did a Santa Claus pantomime, holding his belly in two hands. (The others nodded sagely.) "Now, Frédéric is right, you look okay." Sylvain straightened himself upright, stomach in, chin out, shoulders back, his military display. "You look like a chef."

I was frantically trying to get a leg into my trousers and failing.

"It's the hours, no, Bill? The work. The manly work." Sylvain was unable to hide his pride. *"La rigueur."*

They all then crowded into the locker space and changed; by the time I had tied my shoes, they were gone. I was still the last one out.

My mind, for whatever reasons, appeared to be host to infinitesimal, barely detectable, micro bad habits. What exactly was happening when I was taking off my clothes? Did my brain go skitty when other brains went straight? I could only imagine what a slow-motion video would reveal, my head bobbing this way and that as I noted the light from a window, the color red, remembered a childhood tricycle.

The next morning, exactly forty-five minutes into cooking my shit potatoes (at 200 degrees Celsius, on the "steam setting") Christophe peered inside the glass window of the oven and opened the door.

"They're done," he said.

I poked a potato with the point of a small knife.

"No," I said.

"No?" He scrunched up his eyebrows. The eyebrows said: "WTF? You're telling *me* 'No'!" He reminded me that the potatoes are only briefly done and thereafter ruined.

He returned ten minutes later.

"They're done. Take them out."

I poked. "No."

"I am hungry. You are going to serve mush."

"I don't think they're ready."

He stared at me. He went back to his cutting board.

I wasn't meaning to be confrontational—I didn't have the confidence. I was trying to arrive at a potato that I wanted to eat: *à la vapeur,* steamed, yes, and therefore not browned, but just a little bit crusty.

The meal was on time—how could it not be, when much of it had been prepared the day before? The principal ingredient was fish—cod, with white sauce, my first sauce in a week, a perfectly ordinary but surprisingly delicious beurre blanc (the fatty, rich sauce with the lean protein)—but for me nothing mattered more than the potatoes. Every one of them—all 250—were eaten.

Afterward, I was in the back, cleaning up, the frenzied period just before the lunch service. (Yes, I was doing *le personnel,* but I still had my day job.) Christophe walked by. He appeared to have sought me out.

"The potatoes were good."

It was my first praise. I was surprised by it, that Christophe could call my potatoes "shit" one day and "good" the next.

Just before the evening service, Viannay sought me out. Next week, he said, why not an American meal cooked by an American? Why not burgers?

I made fifty burgers: buns, red onions, tomato slices, and lettuce, a mayonnaise that I'd made by hand (surprisingly yummy) as well as a ketchup that I'd also made (utterly inedible). The fries were double-dipped: three minutes in hot fat, followed by five minutes in very hot fat, marred marginally by Florian's determination to crank up the heat on the first round. (He'd got crazy out-of-control excited about the prospect of fries.)

I had scored a case of Coca-Cola: in bottles. They went mainly undrunk, even if briefly scrutinized—kitchen people regarding the bottles as though they were test tubes of pesticide, their faces conveying confusion over why anyone would ingest a sweet liquid with a savory food.

Everyone ate, including people who normally didn't show up for the 11:00 a.m. lunch, including Viannay, and the sommelier, and the woman upstairs who did the photocopying. Several ate standing up. Among the many French rules is that eating is always done at the table. But these were burgers, and burgers were not French, and there was for everyone an undisguised thrill about eating like Americans. It was among the most blissed-out meals I have ever had a role in preparing.

"Good lunch," Christophe said, the second praise in two days.

Maybe this is all going to work out after all, I thought. But then, just as I'd had the thought, I dismissed it. Out of superstition, fearing bad luck.

———

I was carrying the pots, pans, and tools that I would need for *le personnel*, all of it tottering on a cutting board, and greeted my *garde-manger* colleague.

"*Bonjour,* Florian."

"*Putain,*" he said. He was crouched over a knife, his big lanky frame curled up like a congested question mark. He looked up at me. His face said, "How dare you interrupt me?"

After lunch, I re-joined *garde-manger*. I needed plastic wrap. It was on a shelf just behind the slicer.

"Florian," I asked, "would you excuse me?" I needed to get around him.

"*Putain.*" He didn't move.

I mimed having to reach over his shoulders.

"*Putain.*" He edged sideways, blocking me completely. I found some in the pastry kitchen.

Later, on my way back to the dishwasher to retrieve a whisk, Florian veered out of his way and stepped hard on my foot.

It was a Thursday. The cooks were different on Thursdays. Everyone was cheerful on Monday, but rapidly—by Tuesday afternoon, in fact—most people sank below their best. They deteriorated on Wednesdays. Thursdays, when most of the accidents happened, could be outright dangerous. Just about everyone was a different person on Thursday. It was the hours. But it *was* unusual for Florian.

The next day, a Friday, I was about to prep the asparagus for *garde-manger* and headed to the walk-in to retrieve it. The asparagus were kept upright, bound in rubber bands, the stalks half submerged, in a plastic orange crate with a snap-on lid. It was heavy because of the slopping weight of the liquid. Florian stepped in front of me.

"*Arrête!*" he said loudly. Stop! He pushed me aside forcibly with the flat of his hand. Several people were in the back, and they stopped what they were doing.

"Hortense, *attention,*" he declared, summoning her in a big voice. "Bill is struggling. He is old. Old people are weak. Bill is weak. Bill cannot lift heavy things. We need to help him.

"*Attention,* Hortense," Florian continued, boomingly. "*Le français de Bill, c'est de la merde.*" Bill's French is shit. "*Il faut* speak him English. *D'accord?*"

Florian went to lift the crate, but in his flamboyant haste he got a bad angle, the water inside slopped, and the crate swung up against a door and crushed his fingers. Later, I saw him discreetly sucking on his knuckles, which were bleeding.

What had happened to the guy who had cheered when he successfully sliced a shallot? Who had been open about his failures in the kitchen and his difficulty working under stress? I could see why Christophe liked him. I had liked him, too.

In two days, the nineteen-year-old I regarded as a friend had turned into Darth Vader.

At the start of the dinner service, Sylvain phoned. He wasn't coming in. His wife was in the hospital, giving birth to their first child. In France, a husband is entitled to two weeks' paternity leave.

I was helping on the prep. Moments after the phone call, Florian told me to stand in the corner.

It wasn't actually a corner. It was the step by the door, the one where the consultant had placed himself to see why *garde-manger* wasn't working. It was out of the way but with a view. In my particular case, I would be out of the way and *in* view. It was the culinary equivalent of being put in the stocks. Such was the vantage place of the step that I would be seen from two kitchens at once: *garde-manger* and the main kitchen, including the pass, where Christophe stood.

I stared at the step and thought: I'm not going to stand there.

Florian was watching me while working, flicking his head up (as though on a pivot) and then down. "Stand on the step," he said. He was on his own tonight. It was a big night. I didn't move.

"Stand on the step."

"No, I'm not going to stand on the step. I'm here to help. You don't have Michael. You don't have Sylvain—"

"*Trop de stress.* You make my hands shake. It doesn't matter. I don't have to explain. Stand on the step."

"No. Viannay won't like this." In the petty battle of tiny wills, I had just lost. I could have been saying, "You'd better behave, or I'll tell Teacher." I had no idea what Viannay would or wouldn't like, which is immaterial, since he hadn't appeared yet.

"Stand on the step."

Florian stared at me. I stared at Florian.

What would you do? I stood on the step.

Christophe, at the pass, saw me and didn't understand, and then seemed to get it. Then maybe I got it, too. Had Christophe become Florian's coach? ("Take charge, young man. Show that you're a chef!") It was a curious place to find myself, still being loathed by the guy who ran the kitchen and being bullied by a high-strung nineteen-year-old in what was probably his very first power moment.

Garde-manger fell behind. Tables hadn't received their amuse-bouches, starters weren't plated. Florian made to slice a serving of *pâté-en-croûte*. So much work went into making it—the flaky pastry, everything on the verge of falling apart but somehow staying together—and it was so precious (the foie gras, the meat jelly, the *poulet de Bresse*) that you must never be caught cutting it badly. Florian got it wrong. He grabbed his heart. He threw away the failure quickly before anyone else saw. He tried again. He failed. He hit his hand. He tried again. He slammed his hand on the counter. He tried again, and this time got it right.

Viannay arrived.

Viannay saw me and called from across the kitchen. "Bill, what are you doing?"

"I am standing on the step."

He could see that I was standing on the step.

I nodded toward Florian. "He told me to."

"Please, bring the amuse-bouches to the pass." Waiters were standing around, fiddly, nervous. *Garde-manger* was deeply in the weeds.

"*Oui,* Chef."

I stepped down and put eight amuse-bouches on a small tray.

Florian, hunched over, his back to me, turned. "No, you are not to take those to the pass."

Well, whatever. I picked up the tray, took it into the kitchen, and set it down. The waiters made to pick up the dishes, but were stopped by Florian ("No, do not touch them!"). He came running after flailingly—his hands in the air like flags—pushed me out of the way, grabbed the tray, and returned to the *garde-manger* kitchen, where he removed the eight dishes, put them on a new tray, and rushed back to the pass.

Viannay made a modest Oh-I-get-it nod of the head. He moved on. He wasn't going to intervene. (He wasn't?)

Was there a code that I didn't know? Christophe had done nothing, even though the station was badly behind. But neither had Viannay, who arrived when it was overwhelmed. Did the code have a name? Fights happen. People get pushed around. And top guys don't intervene?

I was still on the step when Johann, the remaining Johann, stopped en route to the kitchen, and said, "You are on the step."

"Yes, I am on the step."

I proposed to Florian that I go to the very back, near the sink, and help out there.

"That is an excellent idea."

In the back, I did whatever was needed. It was Friday night, and everyone was running out of stuff.

Chern, working the meat station, rushed back.

"*Persil ciselé, s'il te plaît.*" Parsley sliced longways, like chisels. "Quick, quick. Thank you."

He returned. "*Petits pois.* I'm out."

Fava beans, lemon zests, *feuilles.* (Always *feuilles.*)

Over the loudspeaker, Christophe was barking; *garde-manger* was still overwhelmed. I should do something. But how?

Without my noticing, the barking stopped. Once again, I'd got lost in the revelry of my urgent-but-not-so-very-urgent duties, the Zen of the repeated tasks, and eventually realized that I hadn't heard a bark for some time. The kitchen was still under pressure. New orders were being called out, but Christophe was no longer haranguing. I'll pop my head into *garde-manger,* I decided, and walked over, and discovered Viannay himself doing the starters, with Florian and Hortense standing behind. He was such an unexpected figure—I'd seen him in this confined, narrow kitchen only once before—that it took me a moment to adjust to the reality of his presence, the hair, the MOF white jacket, his stubble. I had no idea that he knew how to make the *garde-manger* dishes. He was moving with impressive speed.

"There you are," he whispered. It was the white anger. He had gone wolverine. "Where have you been? How could you have not known what was going on? You, you—" He hissed at me incomprehensibly.

He finished his plating and handed it to Hortense.

I stood there, stupid, too late, embarrassed, debating what I should have done.

Viannay paused and wiped his hands. "You say you want to work on the line. You can't work on the line. You don't get it. You will never work on the line. Never." *Jamais.*

Florian had a peculiar expression, not gloating, not quite smiling, more like a smile suppressed. He was exaggeratedly calm.

Johann was standing nearby.

"Did you hear that?" I asked.

"Yes."

"He said 'never.' Did you hear that—you will *never* work on the line?"

"Yes."

When I got home, I went to kiss Jessica good night and sat on the edge of the bed. It was true, I seemed not to be getting it. Suddenly it was all very difficult. I paused. Viannay had said that I would never work on the line. Never.

"The boys and I had dinner at Potager," Jessica said. "I told Franck what you were going through. He said, 'Tell Bill to come work for us.' You should consider the invitation."

UNEXPECTED MYSTERIES IN
A VINAIGRETTE

RENAISSANCE SOCIETY OF AMERICA CONFERENCE. The cultural magnificence of the vinaigrette was revealed to me in a paper read by Timothy Tomasik, an accomplished scholar of sixteenth-century French food, basically 1530 to 1560, during the height of the *foires* of Lyon and right around the time that the grand councillors of the city hosted their Swiss counterparts. The event, held on a rainy Saturday morning in Manhattan, was moderated by Allen Grieco, a research associate at the Villa i Tatti in Florence, the Harvard Center for Renaissance Studies. (Spoiler alert number five: We did visit New York City—twice; in fact, we would eventually return.) Tomasik's paper was on the history of the word "vinaigrette."

Since the withering humiliation of my having to ask how to make a vinaigrette, I had become a student of it and its many variations and its importance to the French kitchen (acid! wine! balance!). But the history? I had read Pasteur, but Pasteur was nineteenth century. Tomasik, then a friend (we met at another Renaissance food conference), was going to go deep into the word's very origins. I showed up jumping-in-my-seat excited, and was shocked, genuinely, to see that only six other people were in the audience in a room that accommodated two hundred. On a Saturday! New York is a big city. Where were everyone?

Tomasik's lecture was an effort to solve a puzzle. The modern sense of the word "vinaigrette" was first published in the *Dictionnaire de l'Académie française* in 1694, which describes it as "a type of cold sauce," *une sorte de sauce froide,* that is made "with vinegar, oil, salt, pepper, parsley, and chives." Since then, there have been variations on the essential formula, but the French Academy's remains the best definition.

But before 1694, it was a meaty sauce. The word first appears in the fourteenth century, in Taillevent's *Le Viandier,* one of the earliest surviving French cookbooks. It is perhaps less French than medieval, illustrated by his instructions for making *"une vinaigrette,"* for which you start with a pig's spleen, brown it on a spit, chop it up, add it to a pot with blood, broth, ginger, a pepperlike spice, saffron, wine, *and* vinegar (finally), and then boil. "It should be brown."

A sheep-based vinaigrette calls for the head, stomach, and feet. A cow vinaigrette insists on using all four stomachs.

During the Q&A, Tomasik, disarming in his honesty, admitted that his paper ("A Vinaigrette by Any Other Name") was a work-in-progress.

He had begun, Tomasik said, with what seemed like a straightforward problem of lexicography. In early French history, "vinaigrette" meant something that seemed appropriate for the food eaten at the time— basically, pot-in-a-hearth cooking. By the late seventeenth century, the word had come to mean something completely different, but was *also* completely appropriate for the food of its time: a light dressing for comparably lightly cooked vegetables, like haricots verts or artichokes. What he couldn't find was when the word changed. He had charted its usage in books published in 1536, 1539, 1542, 1547, and 1552. He expected to find something in the subsequent one hundred years, but hadn't yet.

He had the aw-shucks manner of the good student who had shown up to class with an essential problem in his homework not quite solved but one that he would sort out shortly.

I thought: Not a chance.

Those one hundred years: They represent the dark tunnel in French cooking. At one end, you find the food that you can cook in your fireplace; at the other the end, on or around 1651, when *Le Cuisinier françois* was published, a radical festival of ostentation and expertise. The book was written by a François Pierre de La Varenne. Though the title is probably a play on words (i.e., either *The Cook François* or *The French Cook*), there is no ambiguity in how it was understood and translated. It was a declaration of nationalist cuisine. *Le Cuisinier françois* said, "This is *our* food. It is *our* culture." In the approximately four-hundred-year span of recipes, manuscripts, translations, and culinary publications of any kind in French, no text had so forthrightly proclaimed its Frenchness. After *Le Cuisinier françois,* French cuisine was established.

But, in the eyes of many, there is virtually no record of what had been going on to effect the change. Something was happening, obviously (nothing comes from nothing), but who knew what it was?

Meanwhile, I was jumping up and down in my seat. I was very excited. I knew the answer! At least in relation to the vinaigrette! It was on the other side of the Alps, in Italy, a tract about salads, but I couldn't remember the name of the author, except that it was a quirky name, something like "happiness."

Grieco, for his part, was also jumping up and down, but he knew the name and had downloaded a text on his phone. The author was Costanzo Felici.

"Yes," I blurted out. I couldn't help it. "Felici! That's the guy!"

Grieco continued. "Costanzo Felici was a medical doctor and a naturalist in the village of Piobbico." Piobbico is east of Florence and almost to the Adriatic. "He had published tracts on aspects of natural history: the olive tree, the mushroom, the wolf, an agrarian calendar." Grieco, who was sixty-six and had a silver goatee and wore round scholarly spectacles halfway down the bridge of his nose, had the manner of a man accustomed to having to speak softly in libraries. Tomasik, half his age, was robustly broad-chested, and youthfully confident. Grieco treated him with careful respect.

Felici fell into a correspondence with one of the great botanists of the time, Ulisse Aldrovandi, at the University of Bologna. Aldrovandi asked Felici to describe the vegetables that were being eaten in his village, especially the salads and herbs, and how they were prepared: something like a field report. They were done in one way, Felici wrote: *con olio, aceto, sale, e pepe*. With oil, vinegar, salt, and pepper.

After Felici's death, his letters to Aldrovandi were published as a book. Grieco read a few sentences aloud, a reference to how the Italians had been regarded by the French, as indiscriminate salad eaters: *"il cibo dell'insalate—così dette volgarmente, cibo quasi proprio (dicono gl'oltramontani) de' Italiani ghiotti quali hanno tolta la vivanda agl'animali bruti che si magnano l'herbe crude—."*

I had come upon the passage before, in 2003, in a cultural history of Italian cooking by Alberto Capatti and Massimo Montanari that would be my introduction to the beauty and high achievement of the Italian Renaissance kitchen. The text is now quite famous, if only for its droll wit, including the word, *oltramontani,* to describe the French: i.e., the people from the other side of the mountains. Those people think *we* are the crude ones—they think *we* are the gluttons (*ghiotti*)—because we take raw grass out of the mouths of brute animals and eat it instead of them!

The French, Felici was saying, don't get it. They are the *ghiotti,* meat-eaters only, who don't understand the appeal of salad and vegetables, earth's bounty, the expression of its seasons. Felici wasn't to know that it would be only a matter of time.

Is there a paper trail that we can follow that illustrates how the Italians taught the French how to make and dress a salad?

Probably not.

But there is a footpath, seldom mentioned by historians, a mountain trail, and the traffic on it, in food and people and ideas, was steady and busy. It is pre-Roman. It is as old as walking. It begins in Susa, the town the Romans called Segusio, on the northwestern edge of the Italian peninsula, passes through the mountains, and emerges in Le Planay, a village where the French established an early customhouse. It wasn't the only way between Italy and France, but, in the early 1500s, had become popular enough for the king to see a tax-collecting revenue opportunity. In exchange for paying duties, traders were promised protection on the trail from thieves.

What attracted the Italian traders? The *foires,* those quarterly markets in Lyon, only recently re-established, and this transalpine trail, sometimes called *le chemin du Piémont,* led directly to them. Many of the products sold there (spices, silks, mortadella, the suddenly popular *"fromage de Milan"*—i.e., Parmigiano) were Italian; most of the bankers, importers, and wholesalers (Gadagne, Capponi, Manelli, Grimaldi, Sauli, Johanno, Bonvisi, and Cenami) were of Italian descent. The *foires* made Lyon prosperous. They also made it into a culinary hothouse; they helped create the cuisine that was developing there.

Later I traveled to Susa and learned the route has been protected by a customs pact for much longer than I had known. It is commemorated by a stone arch at the start of the trail, agreed between Caesar Augustus and the Celtic tribes of the Alps under King Cottius. The town no longer figures in guidebooks (with the construction of the Fréjus Tunnel, Susa is almost always bypassed), and since the Maastricht Treaty of 1992, the borders have been effectively dissolved, but for me it was an unexpected miracle—to stand there, in front of the portal through which so much has passed, back and forth: hunter-gatherers, soldiers, salt, Hannibal with his elephants, black pepper, the Apostle Paul, Julius Caesar en route to conquering Gaul, Charles VIII hoping to conquer Italy, François Premier (twice), Rabelais, Montaigne, Leonardo da Vinci, manuscripts, merchants, popes, eighteen centuries of monks, religious pilgrims, Charlemagne, Italian bankers, the Renaissance, the history of Europe, and, possibly, a salad dressing.

And, thus, this word "vinaigrette": I think of it like a crustacean's home, the shell. When its inhabitant dies, another creature moves in. Or like the peasant homes that you see on *le chemin du Piémont,* built from the stones of older homes that have been abandoned. Vinaigrette worked for a medieval stew. But it is a curiosity of history that when people stopped making the stew there was this great word that an oil-and-vinegar dressing could move into.

Foods are always crossing the globe. The pig, at the heart of the Italian and French diet, came from China. Turkeys, potatoes, tomatoes, squash, and chocolates came from the Native Americans in the New World. The quenelle, famous as a Lyonnais food, came from the Austrian *Knödel*.

But vinaigrette: This is of a different order. It is not an ingredient. It is a preparation. It is an idea, a way of eating.

I would rarely meet a French person who believed that the Italians had anything to do with the development of French cuisine. A phrase I would hear often was the lack of *"preuves incontestables d'Italienités"*—the incontestable proof of anything Italian in what became French food.

The evolution of the word "vinaigrette" is not an incontestable proof. But it invites one to consider the limitations that inhibit scholarly investigation. Culinary historians tend to work in the language of their specialization and rarely venture out of it—the Italians rarely speaking to the French, the French not going out of their way to speak to the Italians—none of which is surprising except that, in food matters, the two cultures are complexly connected. Jacqueline Boucher, a professor of sixteenth-century Lyonnais history, has written the excellent *Présence Italienne à Lyon à la Renaissance* (The Italian Presence in Lyon During the Renaissance). In her (admittedly abridged) bibliography, she lists forty-six works: Forty-two of them are in French, two in English, and one in Italian, a genealogy of the Gadagne banking family. How, I can't help myself from asking, can one write about the Italians without reading what they had to say in their own words? In our time in France, I attended a number of Renaissance food conferences, fascinated by what there was to learn, and, each time, was warned by an organizer: "Watch the Italians and the French—they won't want to have anything to do with each other." That big mountain range separating the two countries appears to be much more than a matter of geology.

That big mountain range itself is also misunderstood, informed by an anachronistic view that, in medieval and Renaissance Europe, a boat was more reliable than travel by foot or by animal, especially if it involved crossing the Alps, which was obviously too arduous for normal people to cross.

Well, it wasn't, and it isn't. And, in an era without reliable meteorological forecasting, it was much less dangerous.

I wanted to replicate that crossing, climbing up the steep side, with my young boys: to make the point that if *they* could do it—in, admittedly, the summer, the most favorable season for an Alpine crossing—so could cooks, artists, poets, architects, princesses, monks with their knowledge of bread and sausage making, painters, and the whole long train of the Italian Renaissance. The trail, I knew, wasn't in good shape. In 1803, Napoleon changed the route (he found a wider passage, suitable for his armies, that commenced in Lanslebourg, the next town up the valley from Le Planay, and that survives as a paved road, the D1006). After two hundred years, the original path is scarcely well maintained. We stayed at Lavis Trafford, the *chambre d'hôte* built on the premises of the original customhouse, and we tried the trail when the boys were five. In the morning, they walked a mile to the trailhead. There was a sign invoking the centuries of history that had made the ascent. The boys read it and said, "Nah." They were already exhausted.

We returned when they were seven. Encouraged by Marc Broyer, the Lavis Trafford proprietor, who mischievously described the walk as a "stroll" that wouldn't "take more than an hour," the boys and I, dressed in shorts and sandals (I never thought that they would actually reach the top), completed the hike. It took four hours. It wasn't that far—four miles?—but was steep, and the trail was washed out and rocky (George twisted an ankle, Frederick, terrified of bees, was stung), and we ran out of drinking water before the last challenging ascent. Meanwhile, both boys were being covertly coerced by their father, who promised them that, if they completed the walk, the event would be recorded with their names (George Ely Buford and Frederick Hawkins Buford) in the book he was writing. They considered the offer and concluded, okay, they would press on. When we reached the top, there was running water, a restaurant, and a paved road. But that didn't matter. Four years later, aged eleven, they did the hike again!

VITERBO, ITALY. Our family was traveling to a medieval walled town in Lazio, to attend a weeklong conference on food, wine, and olive oil. Viannay had approved my going, but the others in the kitchen, on hearing about it two days before I departed, were outraged. You don't take holidays unless the restaurant tells you to take one, and the restaurant permits them only when it closes—in August, and between Christmas and New Year—because there is no backup, and if you're not there someone else has to do what you do. For two days, I heard different renditions, varying in their degree of sarcasm and venom, of *"Bonnes vacances, putain."*

The Viterbo event was an alumni event, organized by Jessica, for a program called School Year Abroad, SYA. It was open to former students who had spent a year in a non-English-speaking country to learn its language. (Jessica, at sixteen, had lived in Rennes, in Brittany.) For most alumni, the year abroad had been a life changer. The conceit of this event was that the alumni would reconnect to that early life-changing experience not by the conventional totems of high culture, but by food and drink and by talking about both. The speakers my wife invited included Ruth Reichl, Harold McGee, Thomas Keller, Dan Barber, among others, and me.

Me?

Well, yes, she would invite me. I was her husband. But the effect of the prospect surprised me. I experienced it as a groggy piece of mental awakening. I was a writer, or, for twenty-three years, a literary editor. Without my realizing it, I had stopped thinking of myself as a literary anything. I was a kitchen guy in mid-training.

In New York, my profession had been my identity, confirmed pretty much all the time, in the day-to-day routine of appointments, meetings, parties, and social blah-blah. In Lyon, I didn't have those social confirmations. Neither did Jessica and the boys. Our identities weren't "stripped"; it was more that, without external reminders, they started to dissolve. In their school, the boys were still local celebrities, the *New-Yorkais,* but they were losing memories of their American home. They couldn't remember what our apartment looked like. After two years, their French was better than their English.

In Viterbo, we stayed in a modern hotel, together in a largish bedroom, and were ridiculously happy. Whatever was lost between my wife and me was gained in an intimacy among the four of us. We slept to the sounds of children sleeping. The arrangement—something like camping with room service—would become the model of our future travel in France. In the morning, my wife left early, and the children and I had breakfast. I was reconnecting with my paternity.

In the afternoon, I met up with Dan Barber, who had shown up clandestinely, stealing an Italian getaway with his girlfriend, Aria Sloss. His kitchen didn't know he was away.

I hadn't seen Barber since the white truffle supper at Dorothy's.

He asked me what I had been up to, and I said that I was doing a *stage* and cooking *le personnel*—nothing else, but I must have betrayed something in my face.

"Oh, I am so sorry," he said. The apology was solicitous and unexpected. I thought I might cry.

Barber's time in France turned out not to be so straightforward after all.

He had worked in two places, he said. The first had been Michel Rostang's. Barber spoke French, and was given a position on the line, because Rostang liked him, but Rostang was rarely in the kitchen, and the others, especially those who wanted to work on the line, made Barber suffer.

"I am familiar with the dynamic," I said.

"The second restaurant was rougher. It was in Provence."

"Where?"

"I can't say."

"What is it called?"

"I can't say."

"Oh, come on. I won't tell."

"No. It's famous. The chef was a maniac," Barber went on. "If we were slow, he closed the windows, locked the doors, shut off the air-conditioning, and made us work in the heat. It was summer in the south of France. It was one of the hottest summers on record."

"Two thousand three?" It was the summer when we were in Italy, and hundreds died in their apartments. I had heard of the no-A/C treatment.

"I used to get hit."

I couldn't imagine Barber's being hit.

"A lot. If I was slow. Or for no reason." He put a hand to his cheek. "I always had a big swollen knot here." He chuckled. Barber is long-limbed, bespectacled, and helplessly intellectual. The French kitchen types are brawny and big-armed and can be as stupid as a fence. His laughter about his time with them was self-deprecating and winning.

"One day, shortly after I started, the maître d' came into the back and said, 'I smell something. Is anyone else picking up the smell?' No one said anything. He returned to the front of the house.

"The next day, he wandered back into the kitchen. 'I smell it again. Really, no one else is smelling it?' He went back to the front of the house.

"The next day, he returned. 'I've got it. It's the smell of a Jew.' "

"You won't tell me the name of the restaurant?"

"No."

I was humbled by Barber. He had said that French kitchen training was invaluable, and that you could always spot the young cooks who had it. It was a complex message.

At La Mère Brazier, no one had been hit.

When I got back to La Mère Brazier, the banter resumed. ("Did you enjoy your *vacances, putain*?") But there was also a noticeable difference, an animation, a new energy. In the small, intensely felt, emotionally exaggerated place known as the kitchen, there had been changes in the duties of the members of the *brigade*.

First, Florian would no longer be at *garde-manger*. He had been promoted. He was going to become a line cook, doing fish, and work alongside Frédéric. Christophe had come through for him. Florian set up his *mise-en-place* at his new station. He was physically changed, taller, no longer stooped. For the whole day, he smiled.

Second, I was told that I, too, had been promoted, although it would take me two weeks to realize that I had been. I would continue to make *le personnel*, and I liked learning that, in my absence, it had been cooked by Chern and Florian, trading off, and everyone was still complaining about what they had to eat. But now I was to report, officially, to the meat station. No one said I would be cooking on the line, and after being savaged by a Viannay who had gone wolverine on me, I didn't even ask. In fact, that was exactly the prospect—*if* I showed that I was ready, *if* I then proved that I could do it.

Sylvain, too, had a new job—and this was the most radical news. He would be running *garde-manger.* It was now his responsibility with a much reduced staff; one person, in fact: Hortense.

Sylvain told me that when Christophe informed him of the change he closed his eyes and asked him to repeat it. His body shuddered. It was, for him, a clear demotion. He had started at *garde-manger.* He had then been promoted to sous-chef. People referred to him as *le cuisinier,* the guy who made the kitchen work. To go from the pass, at the front, plating the food, to *garde-manger* in the back: How could it not be a disappointment?

He rearranged his demeanor. "I'll use it to perfect my *pâté-en-croûte,*" he said. He smiled the giant Sylvain smile. "I'll practice for the *coupe.*"

The *coupe*—the cup—is held in Tain, the winemaking village between Lyon and Valence, to honor what is judged to be the world's best *pâté-en-croûte.* Makers—officially from "all over the world," but effectively from "all over France" (because where *else* would they come from?) and mainly from the Rhône Valley—convene and produce the most aesthetically thunderous expressions of meat inside of a piece of dough that you will ever see in your life. Sylvain was determined to compete. He was determined to win. It would be his ticket to whatever was next in his life.

One morning, early, just after eight, Hortense rushed into the front kitchen. Sylvain marched in right after her, in long, purposeful strides. He was wild with anger.

It seems that Hortense had fetched the wrong pot for Sylvain. There must have been more to it than a simple pot, but the pot, in its wrongness, became the proverbial trigger. Hortense, frightened, took cover behind a cooking island: a flattop stacked high with, as it happens, many pots. Sylvain strode up to it, pulled his arm back, and swept all the pots onto the floor. They made a cascading crashing sound—tops, a sauté pan, casseroles, everything stainless steel, very loud, and very bright, the metal under the kitchen lights—and all of it tumbling thunderously around Hortense. It was so unexpected and loud that, for a moment, I thought a structure had collapsed. Hortense hugged herself. She seemed to be trying to be small. She looked—her face, the flat-out terror in it—as though she was about to be killed.

Sylvain, hyperventilating, having crossed some line, now even more furious, picked up a pot and hurled it at Hortense. He missed. It clanged against an oven door. He picked up another and threw it. This missed, too. He picked up a third, a fourth, a fifth—fast, fast, fast—and missed each time. He seemed not to be trying to hit Hortense, only to scare her, although I'm not sure that Hortense was comforted by the distinction or even if, in the circumstances, it had occurred to her. For instance, it is not my belief that, amid all this banging and crashing, Hortense was thinking: Oh yes, these pots flying in my direction, they're not actually going to strike me in the head. No, I'm safe. It's just poor Sylvain I'm worried about—how he really needs to make noise.

Christophe, like the rest of us, watched until Sylvain was done. Then he got back to work.

There was another outburst. This one also involved a new *stagiaire,* a fifteen-year-old from a *lycée,* whom I called "Little Matty," since he was the third Mathieu in the kitchen. Owing to his age, his stint was limited: no longer than ten weeks, no later than 10:00 p.m. He'd had a rough start, and was treated badly, and the bad treatment was making him aggressive in turn. (He was like a petri dish of the workplace's toxins: He had arrived innocent, got roundly abused, and was now trying to find his place as an abuser.) He said something, a nasty tone, about how the sink had not been properly cleaned by the last person who used it, and was instantly airborne.

Sylvain lifted Matty by the throat, pinned him against a refrigerator door, feet dangling in the air, raised his fist—it seemed to be the size of a melon—and cocked his arm like a tightly compressed spring. I stared at Matty's face, his now big eyes, his delicate features, his small straight nose: about to be crushed.

Sylvain tightened his grip. "I hate you. I want to hit you in the face. I really need to hit you in the face." The two of them remained poised there, Little Matty and Sylvain with his big arm.

"Why?" Little Matty asked, high-pitched, uncomprehending. "Why do you want to hit me in the face?"

It was a reasonable question and showed, on Matty's part, an impressive clarity of mind.

Sylvain paused and, for a flicker of a moment, seemed confused. "I don't know why. I don't like the way you look."

"I'm sorry." *Je suis désolé.*

Sylvain stared into Matty's unsatisfactory face, breathing hard, wanting the pleasure of hitting him, and didn't hit him. He dropped him.

Christophe, standing off to the side, talking to the pastry chef, had paused. Once Matty had crumpled, a heap at Sylvain's feet, Christophe resumed his conversation.

I wonder now: Why didn't I intervene?

By the end of the week, Sylvain had another outburst.

The artichokes had just been delivered and were by the service door, and were of two sizes, medium and very large. The medium-sized chokes were for the soup. Would I mind breaking off the stems? Sylvain asked. He regarded me now as a member of the meat station.

I was grateful for the courtesy.

There were three crates. I got through them. Then I don't know what happened—I fell into the rhythm of the labor and got lost, or I disappeared into the reverie of being by an open door, or my brain did that Zen walkabout thing—because I proceeded to stem the large artichokes as well. The very big artichokes were not for soup. These were prized. They were to be carved carefully as the centerpiece of a starter.

Sylvain checked in on me. He stared in silent astonishment. Then he picked up each artichoke and hurled it into a wall. I was in a corner, between the door and the artichoke boxes. I was trapped. The display was for me.

I felt that I knew Sylvain enough to know what was going on in his mind: namely, that each artichoke being smashed against the wall wasn't an artichoke. Each one was my head. Sylvain was hurling my head against the white tile wall, making a splattery green spray.

In his defense (and I like Sylvain and am happy to defend him, even if he was momentarily overcome by an urge to obliterate my head), he had plenty to be frustrated about. Some of his frustrations arose out of the restaurant's not-ever-quite-clear use of *stagiaires*. Viannay liked them because he didn't have to pay them or, at least, have to pay them much. (Most *stagiaires* get a weekly stipend, except, of course, yours truly.) For my part, I was happy to be one because I now regard the arrangement—cooks in training exchanging their labor to work in a celebrated restaurant—as the best way to learn French cuisine. Sylvain, for his part, didn't want a *stagiaire* at all: Couldn't he at least have a trained cook he could count on?

Then there was Florian. What did he want from a *stagiaire*, now that he had been promoted to a line cook? Evidently, a slave or an elf or a small animal he could kick every now and then. It was, I hasten to add, a perfectly comprehensible need, and it might, one day, make Florian, who had obviously been abused and humiliated in his time, into a better cook and—who knows?—maybe a loving human being. Because the fact is that Florian, even though he was now at the fish station, was in my face more than ever.

The next morning, he dropped a sack of potatoes on my worktop, the moment the staff lunch was done. "Peel them."

It was for his purée: the fish station's responsibility.

"Asparagus," he said, before I had completed the potatoes, dragging over the large plastic orange-crate. "Clean them."

I could see what Florian was doing. What I couldn't figure out was how to stop him. I hadn't been bullied since fourth grade and had developed strategies for never getting bullied again: charm, wit, jokes, and then—and only if every tactic of good humor had failed—outright evasion. But it wasn't easy. The kitchen is a small space.

"Carrots. Peel them."

ONE DAY—and I remember the date, July 14, Bastille Day (when, unlike most restaurants in Lyon, we were open)—I saw something in Christophe that seemed to enlarge my understanding of him. It didn't make me like him, but I felt a quality verging on respect.

The occasion was a sauce. Christophe had ordered chipolatas for *le personnel*, 180 of them. They are a long and skinny sausagelike entity, gnarly and fatty, with bits of bone and cartilage that get stuck between your teeth while you eat them, and smell like roadkill on a hot day. They are disgusting. The Lyonnais loved them.

I resolved to roast them in the oven (sautéing would pollute the kitchen; the sausages also exude a black glue that is difficult to scrub off the pans). For the sides: boiled potatoes, smashed with butter and salt, and red onions, sliced thin, braised with red-wine vinegar (like a relish, with a bracing acidic bite: very good, I hoped, with bad fat).

Christophe interrupted me. He wanted to know what I was preparing for a sauce.

"For chipolatas?" I asked.

"There is a sauce." He told me to go upstairs for a bottle of Port.

I followed his instructions. Shallots, a little butter, a whole bottle of Port, reduce. It was purple and rich and smelled of plums and of a place that wasn't here.

I got on with the rest of the meal, checking every now and then on the Port, until it was about an inch deep.

"Monter," he said. Build it with butter.

I thought: A beurre rouge with Port. I built it, whisking, whisking, whisking.

I checked on the sausages. They were done (i.e., they looked like Halloween, bony fingers retrieved, scorched, from a fire). I covered them with foil, and put them on a high shelf.

I returned to my sauce.

"Three slices of prosciutto," Christophe said. He had a stash in a lowboy.

"Three?"

"Taste," Christophe said.

I added salt and pepper.

I tasted the sauce again.

"Vinegar?" I said.

He took a jar off a shelf and handed it to me.

"Moût de raisin," he said.

"As in wine?" *Moût* is grape must, the skins that remain after fermentation and can be distilled afterward into a spirit, like grappa (in Italy) or marc (in Burgundy). Or made, evidently, into mustard. I opened the jar. The *moût* mustard was black and grainy; dense, like tiny caviar.

I added two spoonfuls.

"Taste."

The sauce now had bite. I liked it. I added more pepper.

Hortense appeared with a salad. Outside, in the bar, waiters were setting the tables. It was ten-thirty-five.

Christophe looked in a drawer and pulled out a wedge of duck demi-glace, a verboten wobbly (*"trop cher!"*)—a meat stock reduced until it is a brick of gelatin and flavor. (In such moments, everyone in the kitchen makes *"whoopee"* noises.) A demi-glace, added to whatever you've been fussing with, instantly intensifies everything: more body, a richness that is both fruity and savory, a meatiness that doesn't taste of meat.

The result was like an edible liquid expression of purple velvet: sweet because of the Port, and faintly (but only faintly) meaty, maybe because of the prosciutto, or the demi-glace, or both. The shallots and the mustard added sharpness. But the sauce also had a textural quality that I hadn't expected, like a fabric, and was pleasing to look at.

On the weekend, I tried chipolatas on the boys.

I happened to have a leftover sauce, which I'd frozen, no idea what. I smelled. Maybe chicken? The demi-glace Christophe gave me was whatever he'd had on hand. What the hell? I tossed it in.

The boys liked the dinner. They didn't stand up and sing "La Marseillaise." But they did say "yum" and finished their food, each one scraping up the leftover Port deliciousness with a fork.

Before bed, I browsed a copy of Escoffier. I had assumed that Christophe had made the sauce up, except that he seemed to be adhering so faithfully to an itinerary, one item after another, as if it were a known thing. It was the prosciutto slices that seemed so eccentric. I found it, not exactly as we did it, but among several salty-sweet preparations.

I had a glimpse of Christophe's basic mental kitchen database, and of the thousands of sauces that could be found in it. He'd plucked this one out of his head because he knew that a sweet-savory thing would go with a salty, disgusting one. I was impressed by the command. It seemed both old-fashioned and rather profound.

After lunch, Christophe and I were changing out of our kitchen clothes together. He alluded to having seen me several weeks before with my children—"a father with his boys," he said. It was the first personal thing he had said to me that hadn't been done with mocking irony. I wondered: Can I trust what I'm hearing?

We chatted, which was also novel. I mentioned the *lycée* student, Little Mathieu. He had completed his ten-week *stage*. (He had also complained to his teacher, a big no-no, and, worse, the teacher had phoned Viannay, who then took the boy, looking very solemn, out into the courtyard—we were all watching from the kitchen—and seemed to give him a lecture on *la rigueur,* as well as on the basic axiom that what goes on in the kitchen stays there.)

Christophe's face looked stricken. "Ah, *petit* Mathieu," he said. "That was a mistake, bringing in someone so young." He paused, seeming to reflect on the error of having agreed to take him on. "I regret it."

It was a complex confession. Christophe wasn't necessarily objecting to what went on in the kitchen—which seemed like a given—but that Little Mathieu had been too young to be subjected to it.

In the days after, my 11:00 a.m. staff meals seemed, somehow, not to matter so much. I continued to make them but they were no longer a test. Without my entirely knowing how, I was sliding into becoming a member of the line.

NO FOOD ROAD MORE IMPORTANT

In summer, I can't sleep, my head full of the voices of guests dining under the linden trees in the garden. What magic. It's the middle of the 1970s: Charlie Chaplin comes to dinner, as do Serge Gainsbourg, Jean Piat, many others. The tablecloths, the carts—everything is sumptuous, like a fairy tale. Planted on my balcony, I see Jane Birkin's bare feet, the elegance of the guests, the exuberance of the artists. People stop to see us because they're on the way to the Côte d'Azur on the Route Nationale 7. Salvador Dalí is often here. (There he is, drawing little things for my brother, as Dalí's wife keeps a watchful eye.) When there are violent storms, the wind lays waste to everything on the terrace. The guests, with their napkins on their heads, protect their skirts and suits and retreat into the restaurant. They have to be reseated, the cooking stops, everything has to be redone. There are howls. So gigantically stressful. I feel sorry for everyone, but no one panics. Service gives rhythm to our life. I wait for the guests to leave, swinging in the garden amid the smells of wet earth and thyme.

ANNE-SOPHIE PIC,

TRANSLATED FROM THE FRENCH BY CLIO DOYLE

Daniel Boulud came to Lyon just about every two months, and each time he seemed completely different from the person I'd once known in New York. There, he had been as hard and as assertive as the city. In Lyon, he was a pet puppy: soft, empathetic, sometimes self-doubting, solicitous, humble, introspective, and uninhibitedly honest. It would take me a full year to feel brazen enough to ask him about the change. We had eaten lunch at Potager, and afterward I drove him to Les Halles to pick up fish to cook for his parents in the evening, "because they are farmers and never eat it." They lived in the village of Saint-Pierre-de-Chandieu, twenty miles southeast of Lyon, amid pastures and vegetable fields. Just as he was getting out of the car, I put the question to him—Do you know how different you are when you're here?

"Yes," he said.

"You do?" I was surprised. (I'm not sure why: that my perception had turned out to be sound, or that he was so aware of it?)

"Yes, yes, I know I'm different, but I've never known the words to describe how or why."

He had in his face, at that moment, a purity of expression that was rare to see in an adult. He was here, in his home, with his mother and father, his siblings, his nieces and nephews, his chef buddies, and would be spending the night in the farmhouse where he had been born (and where his father and grandfather had been born) and that had been owned by his family for at least 180 years, and nothing else—no restaurant enterprise, business prospect, banquet, urgent phone call, no piece of New York business—was going to complicate what lay ahead of him, the simple prospect of making food for his parents at their kitchen table and making them happy. He seemed whole.

Boulud began his career when he was fourteen, a difficult adolescent ("a handful for my parents"), made restless by school and bored by the farm ("He was allergic to hay," his mother, Marie, told me—"how can you be a farm boy and allergic to hay?"). He declared, suddenly, that he wanted to be a chef, even though he was unclear about what a chef did. He had never been inside a restaurant. He had never been to a grocery store. He had never eaten store-bought food. Everything came from the farm: milk, wine, cheese, vinegar, vegetables, salads, bread, pickled vegetables, pickled meat, cured meat, nothing frozen, plus chickens and ducks and the fatty bacon served cold at breakfast.

His parents tried to help, but they didn't go to restaurants, either, so they called in a neighbor, referred to by the Bouluds as "the countess." "Countess Volpi," as she called herself, was fond of Daniel. She also ate in restaurants and knew the chefs who ran them. She was a wealthy young widow who had moved to Lyon from Paris—single, modern, with long platinum hair, an American car (a Mustang convertible), an affluent surgeon as a lover—and she took up the young Boulud's cause. She phoned every three-star establishment she knew, summoning the chef by name and asking if anyone needed a *stagiaire* (Bocuse, La Mère Brazier, La Pyramide—nothing). She got lucky with Nandron, a family establishment, father and son, in Lyon, on the Rhône River, that made grand, elaborate nineteenth-century French dishes at a time (1969, just before the advent of nouvelle cuisine) when they would be among the last to prepare them. Boulud knew Lyon only as the city where he helped out at his father's farm stand on Saturdays. Now he was, in effect, moving there. He found a room in an uncle's home in the city, and disappeared into the kitchen just after his fourteenth birthday. He would emerge later to take up employment elsewhere—Georges Blanc and Paul Bocuse—and, at eighteen, would leave Lyon forever.

Boulud's Lyon started in a kitchen and ended in one. It was, for him, a time-warp city, the most intense four years of his youth, most of it spent indoors, and then he was gone—the south (with Roger Vergé); the southwest (with Michel Guérard); Denmark; Washington, D.C.; New York. Sometimes it seemed that he was trying to retrieve what he missed or, at least, a version of what his life might have been if he hadn't left.

In 1989, he almost succeeded. He resolved to return to Lyon and open a restaurant there. He had a newborn and wanted to raise her in Lyon, had been worn out by New York, power and business and money, and missed his home city, the enduring appeal of a place where nothing was more important than your next meal. He scouted venues, met with city officials ("Grand Lyon," as the city's administration calls itself, owned and still owns a portfolio of beautiful historic properties), but couldn't raise the money. People were confused by him, Boulud told me, this guy who said he was Lyonnais—but, then, why was he living in New York?

He was still trying to get back. He had promised Gregory Stawowy, a former chef at Daniel in New York, that they would open a restaurant together. I visited potential sites with them. A brasserie opposite the Pont La Feuillée, the gateway into the raucous Vieux Lyon. ("Too much like a pub.") A sixteenth-century mansion and library on the Saône, one of the properties of the ancien régime that the city of Lyon would assume ownership of and was now trying to exploit. ("Too grand and commanding," and Boulud shuddered at the prospect of having to work again with the city's property people.) But there was a *bouchon,* La Voûte Chez Léa (built on the perimeter of a former monastery, in the original arch or *voûte,* and opened by Mère Léa in 1943), that appealed: not too big, but historic, with at least a partial view of the river, and, with its *mère* connections, expressive of good, basic Lyonnais cooking. He submitted a bid, 350,000 euros, and then returned to New York. But he was being played. The guy conducting the sale didn't know Boulud ("A Lyonnais in New York?") and had always intended to sell the property to Christian Têtedoie, one of the city's rising stars; he had needed someone to up the price with a bid.

It wasn't so easy being a Lyonnais in New York. I puzzled the prospect afterward, Boulud and Stawowy, and it was hard not to wonder at the psychological complexity of their partnership, the younger chef trying to complete what the younger Boulud had longed to do.

Boulud, when in town, always saw me. It was a privilege.

It was also true that Boulud had in me someone that he had never known before. For more than thirty years, he has been telling Americans about Lyon, the gastronomic heart of French cooking, and no one was interested. The food was meant to be heavy, they told him. The Lyonnais are famously unfriendly, they said. And it's a city. Its outer boroughs, *les banlieues,* were ugly and industrial. It's not Provence. It's not the Côte d'Azur. And now, in me, seemingly out of nowhere, he had someone who seemed to get it, or was at least putting in the time, and who had moved here with his family and seemed prepared to stay as long as it took to understand the place.

He kept a respectful distance, as though an intervention might impugn my apparent intention to make my way on my own, which, of course, only appeared to be my intention because, alas, I *did* have to make my way on my own—with the help of my linguistically gifted and supremely organized better half. Boulud became the person who filled in the gaps.

Boulud saw Bocuse every time he came to the city—it was a promise to himself to do so—and often called me at the last minute. "Come quick, I'm at Bernachon"—the *pâtisserie* and *salon de thé* owned by Bocuse's daughter and son-in-law, on the Cours Franklin Roosevelt, in the sixth arrondissement—and I would rush over, half dressed, sometimes with the twins, and arrive either just in time to say hello or a little too late. One extremely rainy Saturday evening, a monsoonlike summer deluge, Boulud called—I hadn't known that he was in the city. "Come quick, you must meet Pierre Orsi." Orsi, who had started in Bocuse's kitchen, was one of the grandees of the city. That night, I didn't make it, but I would meet him later, once again with Boulud, a long, digressive evening in the back—chef gossip, Bocuse stories, dishes. Orsi was among the gentlest people I've met in the kitchen.

Boulud and I are the same age, but he had been in the city when he was a teenager and learned a Lyon that few of us have any chance of knowing.

He was uncomprehending that I didn't know how to mount *écrevisses*. *Écrevisses*—"crayfish" or "crawfish" (if, like me, you're from Louisiana), a ubiquitous dish adornment in Boulud's time and you prepared them by hooking their tails underneath their jaws as if they were sitting in a chair.

I had to tell him: "Daniel, times change. No one pokes a crayfish on a toothpick into their food. It isn't done."

"*C'est vrai? Non, ce n'est pas possible!*"

Or that I didn't know how to turn a mushroom, a particularly challenging way of carving the cap so that it looks like a finely ribbed miniature parasol for fleas. "What do they teach you at L'Institut Bocuse?" he asked.

Me (again): "Well, they didn't teach turning mushrooms, because no one does that anymore."

He shook his head. He didn't believe me. In his eyes, I hadn't been fully trained.

Once, he alluded to Route Nationale Sept—the National Route 7. I didn't know the reference.

He was horrified.

When I found out what it was, I, too, was horrified, although I also discovered a good reason for my not immediately knowing it, since it no longer exists. (Again the time warp.)

For centuries, the route (small, rural, rarely paved—originally a Roman road, when Lyon had been the capital of Gaul, then a royal one in the sixteenth century) was the principal way to reach the Mediterranean from the north. It gets its name from being among a dozen established routes, radiating from the capital and leading to a frontier. (La Route Nationale Cinq, for instance, leads to the Alps.) "La Sept" leads you down the country's eastern corridor, passing near many of the principal winemaking regions of the southeast, and has come to represent the core of French cuisine, if only because, in the eternal way of things, when there is good wine, there is usually good food.

But since the 1970s, the "RN7"—the universally recognized shorthand—has been slowly supplanted by what would become a massive motorway, the A7: a six-to-eight-lane monstrosity locally called L'Autoroute du Soleil that, at the height of summer (*"Alert rouge!"*), becomes a bumper-to-bumper parade of campers and station wagons with bicycles on top, rear windows obscured by beach balls, umbrellas, children's paraphernalia, and leading to everyone's beach-holiday fantasy. You can still follow the National Route 7 by superimposing an old map on a modern one, and will discover an ancient, simple two-lane road, sometimes framed by historic plane trees, and sometimes with only the occasional edifice—a café, a village bistro, a post office, a winemaker, a home—built right up to the edge of the road, as it would have been from a time when transport was done by animals. Many of the restaurants—and it breaks the heart to see how many small family restaurants are still there (*just*)—hark back to the nineteenth century.

For Anne-Sophie Pic, born in 1969, the daughter, granddaughter, and great-granddaughter of a line of venerable chefs (including André Pic, who is celebrated in Curnonsky's *Lyon: The Gastronomic Capital of the World*), La Sept has an aura of magic. Her family's restaurant was in Valence, about sixty-five miles south of Lyon, and is, like all the old establishments, built on the route's very edge. In her view, La Sept was the foundation of French cuisine, *la véritable épine dorsale,* its spine. Her father, Jacques Pic (born in 1932), was a member of the nouvelle cuisine generation, which was mainly scattered along the National Route 7. "They were musketeers. In pictures, you always see Pierre Troisgros, Paul Bocuse, and my father together. Alain Chapel is there too, as well as Roger Vergé."

On one of Boulud's Lyon visits, he asked Viannay if he could take Jessica and me to lunch at Alain Chapel's restaurant in the Dombes: not, technically, on the old RN7, but an established detour from it. (I had thought, No chance, Viannay won't agree—and then was surprised by Boulud's sway. He asked; it happened.) It was the first of what would be many culinary forays, in which Boulud tried to share with me his fragile, just-on-the-verge-of-disappearing Lyon.

The trip taught me the Dombes. It is said that if you don't know the Dombes you don't understand Lyon.

The Dombes is a sunken plateau, a geological peculiarity, situated between two mountain ridges, the Alps and the high hills of Beaujolais, and less a valley than a vast spongy footprint. On a map, the Dombes looks like the bayou—fifty miles of ponds and streams—except the bayou is at the mouth of the Mississippi River, and the Dombes is near nothing. It could be a dinosaurs' playground. The land is half water, largely untamed, and empty. The wild foods that you eat in Lyon come from the Dombes: ducks, geese, wild pigs, *brochet,* frogs, hare, crayfish, trout, woodcocks, deer, rabbits, and freshwater eels. The farm that Mère Brazier grew up on is in the Dombes. It is also where Alain Chapel—regarded by many as the greatest chef of his generation (born in 1937)—grew up, an intuitive swamp-botanist, observing it like a scientist in training.

Chapel was insistent, obsessed, introverted, mercurial, troubled, big-hearted, and a genius. He was bookish, an unusual quality in a chef, a scholar of French cuisine, with a legendary library; he spoke rarely, walked the Dombes with his dog daily, listened to Schubert obsessively, loved to join hunts but never shot a gun, was full of rage that he vented privately (and then personally repaired the doors that had splintered in its expression), and ran a kitchen that was like a Carthusian monastery in its tranquil, silent intensity. He wrote one book, *La Cuisine, c'est beaucoup plus que des recettes* (*Cooking Is Much More Than Recipes*), 510 pages, a polemic and a poem and, despite its title, a give-it-all-away collection of groundbreaking preparations. He extracted small livers from an improbable bog creature called a "freshwater monkfish." He juiced the farmers' first lettuce of the season and cooked his spring peas in this liquid. When, on a trip to Provence, he discovered wild thyme, he imagined not cooking with it, but raising rabbits on it, and then cooking *them*. His food was regional in the extreme.

"This was where I used to hang out," Boulud said, speaking about when he was working nearby, at Georges Blanc in 1973, and had a car. "On my way home." Everyone knew that Chapel, in the village of Mionnay (the population then fewer than four hundred people), was at the epicenter of what was going to happen next in French food. Boulud knew the cooks, and often stopped here for the atmosphere of promise, the feverish feeling of the kitchen, the perfect food, when Chapel was only in his early thirties and everything seemed possible. Boulud's eyes came alive at the recollection. His eyes asked: Do you know enough to know how exciting that time was?

And then, in 1990, Chapel died, *"crise cardiaque,"* at fifty-two, the same age when his father had died, also of a *crise cardiaque*.

Daniel would introduce me to others. Each visit was a little bit like Christmas: Régis Marcon, the three-star chef, MOF, and master mushroom forager, in the mountains above Condrieu; Michel Bras, a high priest of the kitchen, in the treeless foothills in Laguiole, the Auvergne; Michel Guérard (three-star chef and an MOF), in Gascony, who was the most naturally inventive chef I would meet in France (he opened Le Pot-au-Feu in 1965, in an unglamorous, rough suburb of Paris, where he tweaked and twisted and improvised on the French classics, making them better, lighter, more fun, and became the embodiment of the nouvelle-cuisine mantra, "Make it new"). After Gascony, Boulud and I made our way back to Lyon, and he made a proposal.

He was completing a cookbook, which he thought of as his take on French cuisine, but something was missing that he believed the two of us could provide. He was wondering if we might cook together in New York, side by side, making the dozen or so preparations that he regarded as essential to his formation as a chef. These dozen or so dishes were, in some elusively poetic way, iconic for him. They had made him a chef. It would take time to assemble. It was a wonderful prospect, and I agreed to join him.

By the time I flew over, I had been away three years. New York was disconcertingly familiar, its conveniences, its deliveries, its bright winter blue, the English language, which seemed soft and easy. I stared at people's mouths when they spoke. I was lost in our small apartment. Where did we keep the plates? How did we make our coffee? I retrieved my knife bag, and reported to Daniel's very French, very Lyonnais kitchen, where I was, to my surprise, instantly at ease.

The roster of dishes was high and low, haute and farmhouse, and therefore very Lyonnais: veal head (rustic) but done in the shape of a tortoise (haute); a roast chicken (farmhouse basic) but completely boned and reconstructed so that it could be eaten by the slice (haute, and very flash). A leg of pork cooked in hay (what, frankly, could be more peasant?); a turbot done as a soufflé. I was intrigued by Chartreuse, a dish that Boulud said had somehow got lost and dropped after the nouvelle-cuisine revolution. (It was a Carême specialty, inspired by the non-meat-eating Chartreuse monks, a game dish with the game hidden inside of what looks like a vegetable birthday cake.) Or a coulibiac, an import from Russia in the nineteenth century, when the Russians and the French were culinary cousins.

My account of the dishes appears in *Daniel: My French Cuisine,* and I won't describe them. But there are two that warrant attention because they would occur later, in Lyon, in a conversation that would be illuminating for both Boulud and me, although in different ways: the "ham in hay" and the flashy boned chicken, called a *volaille à Noelle.*

Boulud first ate the ham in hay at the Auberge de Paul Bocuse, when he was seventeen years old and had just completed a short stint there.

Boulud had no idea that you could cook with hay: "It was what we fed the animals." In the confusion, and excitement, of finding it on his plate in a three-Michelin-star restaurant, he betrayed his divided upbringing: His rustic had been really rustic (except for the electricity in his home and the use of petroleum-powered engines in the farm vehicles, he could have walked out of the nineteenth century). His idea of travel was going to a country fair to sell garlic. But his "haute" was very *haute*. At Nandron, he learned to make foods that, in the eyes of his family, could have come from Mars. Daniel's grandmother, who made the meals chez Boulud, had never served Martian food.

The hay recipe wasn't a Bocuse invention. It appears in country cookbooks and publications from the eighteenth century, a genuine farm preparation in which "hay" is used like an herb, an aromatic to cook the ham in. In Boulud's re-creation, he made a hay brine and soaked the ham overnight in it. He used a penetration-and-probe device to pump more brine into the meat's tissue. He wove tightly wound hay cords around the leg.

The two of us smelled like a stall, and had to change clothes after the morning prep. When the ham was done, we pried off a pastry cap and breathed in the results. Had the hayness dissipated? Maybe, but it was what it was, and we were happy.

The *volaille à Noelle* is based on the conceit of a bird, entirely boned, that has been refilled with vegetables and truffles and the meat, and that is then, in effect, reinflated to look like the real bird. You eat it by the slice.

It was my new skill: turning a chicken inside out and removing everything except the beak and feet.

The preparation was the creation of Joannès Nandron—aka Nandron, Sr., the father of the father-and-son team—and since he never wrote a cookbook, the instruction was more than a little vague. Also, by the time that Boulud was there, aged fourteen, the old guy had effectively retired (and, according to Boulud, was usually drunk). Asparagus made an appearance, Boulud remembered, and the chicken stuffing was prepared as a mousse. There is also a video, Nandron, Sr.'s only television appearance, that had been retrieved by the Musées Gadagne for a gastronomic exhibit. (It depicts a rotund, impatient man of zero charisma, a round face, and a short-haired caterpillar mustache, who is bored and imperious, and possibly drunk, tossing together a dish that he has made a thousand times, stuffing a saggy bird with a mousse that looks like slop, some carrots, a fistful of peas, and gobs of butter.) For this dish, Boulud was pretty much on his own. The result was crisp and golden on the outside, a piece of art within: a miracle to behold. The bird was also, alas—which I say trepidatiously, if only because I now regard Daniel Boulud as my unofficial mentor—a little disappointing, dry mainly, and evidence, yet again, at how such dishes are not recipes but lifelong relationships. (I also wonder if there was something to Nandron, Sr.'s drunken preparation, with its fistfuls of dairy fat, to give the filling an unctuous richness that it might need.)

QUENELLES. They were not on the Mère Brazier menu. But a quenelle was such a fundamentally Lyonnais dish, and Brazier's version had been so famous, that you had to wonder: Why wasn't Viannay making one?

I asked a chef to teach me how to make them, one of my new friends, Alain Vigneron, at Café Comptoir Abel, a *bouchon* farther down the *quai* from our home, a bus ride. It is an arcane, dark, elaborately shuttered structure, embedded in a stone arch of a ninth-century monastery, and with rooms like an old English pub: low-ceilinged, a fireplace in each, history nailed into every wall space, no two rooms alike. As an eating establishment, it dates from at least 1726, and quite possibly earlier. I spent Saturdays there. The quenelle recipe was a theft. It was Mère Brazier's secret. (Brazier did grant interviews to Roger Moreau, a food journalist who produced a 1977 book based on them called *Les Secrets de la Mère Brazier*. But the quenelle recipe that you find inside is a blah-blah filler text, because obviously Moreau could not *not* have a quenelle entry, but it is nothing like what she served.)

The real recipe was smuggled out of her kitchen when it was being run by her son, Gaston.

"All of Lyon knows that Gaston was abused by his mother," Abel's chef, Alain Vigneron, told me, as if in explanation when I asked how he came by the recipe. "All of Lyon knows how he was crushed by her"—he pressed his toe into the floor and swiveled it—"like a bug." (Gaston was a man, his daughter Jacotte remembers, who wanted only to please but, in his dealings with his famous mother, managed only to infuriate. He became her sous-chef, and still he provoked her, his attentive presence, his respect, his number-two-ness.) Whatever the source, and Viannay later confirmed for me that the recipe was indeed the real one, Vigneron—early fifties, sturdily built, a head of brown hair, a soft, tolerant face, born in Lyon and cooking at Abel for four decades—appears to be the only one in the city still making the dish as *la mère* made it eighty years ago.

LINE COOK

You learn to cook at the meat station by doing it. There is no further instruction. "You must cook and be seen to be cooking," Mathieu Kergourlay told me, in a whisper. Kergourlay was the number-three cook in the kitchen. I was standing between him and Chern.

"I just jump in?" I asked.

"Yes. Jump in. Now."

So I did. I jumped in: with sweetbreads, as it happens, *ris de veau*, which was the first ticket item.

"Remember. You are being watched."

I nodded. Viannay and Christophe were both standing nearby.

"You will always be watched. Nothing you do will go unnoticed."

I seasoned the sweetbreads, put a sauté pan on the flattop, and added butter.

Viannay instantly called out from across the kitchen, *"Tu les fais rissoler"*—You cook them *rissoler*. "Do you know what *rissoler* means?"

"Yes."

"Really?" He looked doubtful. "Most Americans don't."

In fact, I *did* know what it meant—*rissoler,* to cook in a way that allows you to sauté and baste at the same time. I'd learned it with Chef Le Cossec. (It could be said that I'd watched it being done more than done it. To be strictly accurate, it could be said that, on balance, Viannay's doubts were warranted.)

The butter in my pan went instantly brown.

"It's too hot. Show him, Mathieu."

Kergourlay poured off the pan, gave it a wipe, set it back down, this time near the edge of the flattop, and added a wallop of butter.

You need plenty of fat, because it is what you spoon over the protein, the basting action. (It is drained off when you're done.) You can use butter or oil, or both butter and oil, but butter has the advantage of alerting you when the pan is getting too hot by changing color—it is like a temperature alarm. You then pour it out and start over. You don't want the pan too hot; it upsets the equilibrium of the technique, cooking from below and above. In fact, it is the same temperature, more or less, at which you cook an omelet. You want, as Le Cossec said, to hear the butter singing.

The whole time, spooning, spooning, spooning.

The spooning is easier when you tip the pan toward you, letting the fat pool up along the rim. Spooning, spooning, spooning, or, in my case, splattering, spraying, splashing, and every now and then spooning, which, surprisingly, seems to be only marginally less efficient than everyone else's efforts except that impressive quantities of fat land outside the pan. You can always tell when I've been doing *rissoler,* because the kitchen floor shines.

In itself, *rissoler* seems to mark a simple difference between the French kitchen and the Italian, where meat is either cooked hot or braised slowly in a liquid. *Rissoler* is somewhere in between.

Once the sweetbreads are golden and puffy, they go into the oven for five minutes, and finished in a new pan, and new quantity of butter. Chern prepared the garnish, a mound of sweet peas and fava beans. Kergourlay finished the sauce, veal stock reduced so much as to be almost spicy. It had thick, savory black intensity. The sweetbreads, however, were like air.

I reflected on the exchange that I'd had with Viannay. I had seen that he was looking at me. I expected a protest, an objection to my audacity, asking by what arrogance I had planted myself on the line during service. But his remarks were matter-of-fact—most Americans don't know how to sauté with a spoon. No one was doubting my competence.

The mornings, Kergourlay told me, would now consist of both prepping the lunch service and making *le personnel.*

"Really?" It was inconceivable that I could do both.

"Really."

It seemed like two jobs. I involuntarily took a breath, as though about to dive into a very deep body of water.

And then: "Turnips. Do them."

"No, Florian, I don't want to do your turnips."

"Do my turnips."

They were white baby turnips that needed to be "turned," the French trick of rotating a vegetable in your hand, both peeling and shaping it with tiny knife-flicks, transforming it, in the case of the baby turnips, into a Christmas ornament. It was round and white, with a green stem at the top. I knew how to turn turnips. But I didn't want to turn Florian's.

The next day it was asparagus again.

Florian was in the front kitchen, at his fish station, and I happened to be in the back, in *garde-manger,* preparing *le personnel.*

"Bill!" He had to shout for me to hear him—there was a wall between us. "Do my asparagus." I heard him. So, too, did the rest of the kitchen, as well as anyone walking by on the sidewalk outside.

"I can't. I'm pitting cherries." I, too, had to shout.

"And after?" *Après.*

"I'm peeling potatoes. For *le personnel.*"

"Et après?"

"I'm boiling the potatoes."

"Et après?"

"Florian, this is ridiculous. I'm making *le personnel.*" Sylvain was standing next to me. He had stopped what he was doing to take in the exchange. For all I knew, everyone else was as well.

"Et après?" Florian said.

"After I make the staff meal?"

"Oui."

"Well, then, like you, I'll be eating it."

"Et après?"

"I am preparing for the lunch service."

"Good. Do my asparagus first."

"You want me to do your asparagus before I start setting up for lunch?"

"Yes. Do my asparagus."

I wondered: Was Florian showing off? Proving that he had me at his beck and call?

Sylvain turned to me. "You have to go in there and hit him."

"Florian?"

"Yes. You have to hit him."

"Really?" Sylvain was an authority in the kitchen. A guy in charge had just told me to walk into the adjoining room and hit a person there.

"Yes," Sylvain said. He was firm. "Now. Go and hit him." Sylvain was angry. He made a fist and smacked it into his palm. "Like that. Hard. Knock him down."

"I can do that?"

"Yes."

The situation was suddenly rather complex.

"I mean, it's allowed—for me, to hit him?"

"Yes. Please. Hit. Him. Now."

This was really quite a lot to think about, the implications flipping through my mind fast.

For instance: Wasn't Sylvain Florian's godfather? Hadn't he known him since he was a baby?

And: I liked Sylvain's anger. It was akin to having a friend backing me up.

And: Was it possible that, though everyone in the kitchen had been silent, they had in fact registered that Florian had become a certified basket-case bully?

And: Where do I hit him? Do I march over to the fish station, and then—what exactly?—roar?

I have hit people (twice?), but not for a long time, and only when there was an issue, and have come to believe that, in general, hitting anyone, including those who deserve to be hit, wasn't a sensible practice.

"Hit him, please."

I had another thought. My book, this book. I had a book to write. I wondered: Would this be good for the book, my hitting Florian, *if* I ended up hitting him? Yes, absolutely. The incident would be what we in the trade call "good copy."

Okay, I said. I'll hit him.

I didn't hit him.

It wasn't that I decided *not* to hit him. It was more that I decided to hit him *later*. There was another issue. When I pictured how the exchange would play out, my walking big-chested to the fish station, my arms swinging slightly, taking him by surprise (I hoped), and quickly smacking him (maybe a head butt—since he was so tall?), I came to suspect that someone (me, perhaps?) might get hurt.

Frankly, I didn't like where I found myself. I didn't like that Florian had put me there: that, by crossing a line of acceptable behavior, over and over, he had made me, and the others around me, believe that I had no recourse, that I, too, should cross a line of acceptable behavior, I should hit him.

I didn't want to hit him. I didn't like that I was expected to.

What I hadn't realized was that, by then, Florian had become wacko. He had always been unstable—jabbering, mumbling, hyperventilating, chest-clutching—but, without my knowing it, he had been getting wobblier by the day. Chern told me that he and Florian had been working through the afternoon together, skipping *la pause,* in order to get through all the items in their prep (and doing, therefore, a seventeen-hour day without a break).

"In the beginning, I helped him finish his *purée de pommes de terre,* so that we could get out and have something to eat before the service. But after a while I was always helping him. I wasn't *finishing* the *purée de pommes de terre.* I was *making* it."

It was the pressure, Chern said. "He kept saying, '*le stress, le stress.*'"

Normally, the more often you do a task the faster you get. "Florian got slower," Chern said.

Is it possible that Florian's asparagus demands were convoluted calls for help?

After the lunch service, on the day when I'd been instructed to hit Florian, I joined an artichoke-trimming circle, all the cooks including Christophe pitching in to help Sylvain get through a stack of boxes. Florian then appeared just as I was finishing an artichoke heart, which I showed Christophe for approval and dropped into a bowl of acidulated water.

Florian grabbed a choke, whipped through it at an ostentatious speed, his knife flashing, and tossed it into the bowl like a basketball shot. It made a splash. In an unspoken way, it seemed that the display was for me—putting me in my place. Or at least that was how I had understood it. I had asked for Christophe's approval; Florian hadn't.

He picked up another choke.

"Qu'est-ce que tu fais?" Christophe asked. What are you doing?

"I am turning an artichoke."

"Show me what you just did."

Florian pulled it out of the bowl.

"This," Christophe said, holding up the hastily completed and (to be fair) slightly lopsided carving job, "is unacceptable." He threw it in the trash. "Do it again."

Florian dropped the choke that he'd started on and walked off, muttering that he had better things to do. (The behavior was not necessarily unacceptable—preparing artichokes was optional and verging on a social event—but the episode created a bad feeling. For my part, a voice began chanting quietly in my head, "Na-na a boo-boo.")

Florian was again corrected by Christophe, just before the evening service, another hastily completed task.

"No."

"No?"

"No. I am not going to do it again."

"Yes, you are."

"No, I'm not."

Florian undid his apron and threw it to the floor. *"Casse-toi!"* he said, which might be loosely translated as "Get the fuck out of my face."

He walked out. And like that: Florian was gone.

He returned to the restaurant once more, to collect his paycheck (greeting no one, rushing past the kitchen and up the stairs two steps at a time). Some time later, his mother called.

"Florian?" Christophe said in exaggerated bafflement. *"Oh, pardon, madame.* Yes, Florian. Now I remember. No, he hasn't been here since he walked out before the dinner service two weeks ago."

For me, life without a taunting nineteen-year-old was liberating. Without my knowing, I had been walking around, in effect, with a wedge of glass jabbing into the bottom of my foot. Now it was gone.

It was curious, I thought, reflecting on the episode, that Florian had been tolerated. Except that it wasn't curious. It was a feature of the kitchen. What was curious *was* the kitchen. The only thing that mattered was that meals were made on time and well. Everything else was left to the cooks to sort out among themselves. Christophe missed none of it. He also did nothing about it.

The consequence, for me, was to consolidate my position. I had not only survived being hazed, but I had survived the hazer.

The first night without Florian, Étienne, a new hire, only his second day at the restaurant, stepped up and took over his station, and was given a cheer at the end of the service.

The meat station became surprisingly tranquil—without Florian in the kitchen, it was bound to be—but the tranquillity was principally owing to what it was: in effect, its Frenchness. It could be fast and rude and rough—you could count on the adrenaline rush—but it also had an overriding sense of order. It was less physical than brainy. You had to concentrate.

Most of the cooking you did before the service. What you did then, mainly, was assemble it, and the assembly often required all three of us working together. A duck dish was like a puzzle: the stem of a Swiss chard that had been poached midday to serve as a platter to place the breast on; or the thigh, boned to look like a savory popsicle, the meat crunched up at the end, that had been cooked confit in the morning; or the rich purple cherry sauce, prepared the day before; or a potato plank "Maxim," named after the legendary Parisian restaurant, made by yours truly while preparing *le personnel*.

The results were modest works of culinary beauty.

The soul of the kitchen: birds. We did snails, frog legs, crunchy pig ears, bone marrow, pork, sweetbreads, and beef. I put lobsters asleep by petting them behind the head: after four strokes, the claws drooped; two more, they drooped more deeply; two more, they were out and were slid, comatose, into a hot oven. (They figured in a version of surf and turf.) But we were in Lyon, and Lyon was about birds, especially the famous ones from Bresse.

We didn't cook them as one might at home. We didn't think of them as one might at home, because we never cooked one bird: We cooked two. In the kitchen, all birds are two birds, white meat and dark meat.

One is cooked quickly (the breast); the other needs long and slow (the legs). One tastes of nothing if cooked too long; the other, impossible to chew if cooked too fast. The simplest fix: Remove the breasts, snap the thighs off, and cook each separately. The *suprême* is the breast poached in chicken stock, heated in a sauté pan, and served with a creamy beurre blanc enhanced by a splash of white Port (a Viannay secret that is transformative, rendering the already rich confection into an ethereal-tasting mouth luxury). The leftover thighs: any number of ways, as long as they are not rushed, like those that I helped Sylvain make on my first day, the "brownie tray" with foie gras and a meat-jelly glaze.

"Roasted" *poulet de Bresse demi-deuil* is also two birds. Actually, it is a trick of presentation to make it seem as though it were one. It also isn't roasted.

It is poached in chicken stock, with black truffles under the skin (the widow in mourning, etc.), until the breasts are *almost* cooked. The bird is then put in a "roasting pot," presented to the table, and whisked back to the kitchen for a rushed piece of culinary surgery. First, the breast is removed: sautéed, sauced, plated, and returned to the dining room. Then the legs (which are almost raw) are removed, popped back into the "roasting pot," and carry on being cooked with some extra fat. When they are finally tender and juicy, they are reproposed to diners as a final course, served on a salad.

Evidently, Mère Fillioux, the greatest of the *mère* chefs, didn't treat birds' legs and breasts differently. Like Viannay, she poached them in chicken stock—the more birds in her pot (kept only hot enough to raise a ghostly vapor across its surface), the richer the stock. Unlike Viannay, she appears then to have left the birds there until both "meats," breasts and legs, were inexpressibly tender. Thus, her table trick of carving with a spoon. In effect, Mère Fillioux—bless her—reconciled a bird's eternal contradiction by pretending there wasn't one, and, with all respect for the great chef's achievement, I must nonetheless declare that, as delicious as those thighs must have tasted, the breasts had to be ruined. Breasts don't like a long, slow cook: It soaks out their flavor. They tasted of nothing.

LA SAUCE BÉARNAISE

CONDRIEU, RHÔNE-ALPES. This town of four thousand people, across the Rhône from Vienne and La Pyramide and a little farther downriver, is famous for its lusciously floral white wine and the local Viognier grape that it is made from. One Saturday evening, the boys' favorite sitter, Stephen, having agreed at the last minute to babysit the boys, Jessica and I stopped at a hotel and restaurant there, on the very banks of the Rhône, Le Beau Rivage, no plan, no reservation, and found what we had been seeing at every other place we had tried since driving out of Lyon. The place was raucously full. (What we had actually discovered was that the prewar French summer practice of following the old National Route 7 from Paris to the south, stopping at hotel-restaurants en route, was very much alive.) We studied the dining room—there appeared to be only one table available—when a maître d' greeted us and asked if we were staying at the hotel, and, by now hungry and distressed, we abandoned scruples and said yes, of course (and, alas, displaced a couple who showed up twenty minutes later). We ordered a bottle of the local wine (well, two bottles, actually—a Condrieu, from the hills directly behind us, and a Côte Rôtie, from the very steep hills three miles upriver), and ate a surprising meal, the highlight of which was a massive turbot, the flat, shellfish-munching bottom-feeder (with its eyes floating arbitrarily on one side of its scaly, weird head—a special category of marine delicacy, fabulously ugly and fabulously delicious), carved tableside on a trolley and served with a fluffy Béarnaise. It wasn't dribbled atop or poured over; it seemed to settle alongside like a perfumed mysterious fog.

Until now, I hadn't thought about the sauce. It was what people ate with roast beef. I hadn't eaten it with a meaty fish. I also had never tasted a version so perfectly rendered, with a brightly vivid vinegar acidity that seemed to wrap itself around every round molecule of the sauce's fat. I liked, too, that it was different from most other French sauces, which are wine-based and can be manipulated to match the food they are served with. A Béarnaise doesn't have to match. It's just there. It could be its own food group.

I now regularly embarrass myself by how much I openly love it. By no reckoning will it ever be deemed to be good for you.

French cookbooks regard making a Béarnaise as a no-brainer, or at least they seem to, but since our meal on the banks of the Rhône, just about every sauce I ordered at a restaurant was a disappointment: overcooked, thickened with flour, unpleasant, having been neglected during a busy service. A Béarnaise is an emulsion—a way of getting two incompatible elements, liquid and fat, to bond (actually, the secret code of French cooking—its flair—seems always to involve getting two incompatible elements to live with each other).

Christophe regarded the sauce as tricky. It became an issue between us, after I'd declared, during one of our *personnel* catechisms (because I was still making lunch), that, for *la sauce,* I wanted to prepare a Béarnaise, and he said, "No," flat-out.

"A Béarnaise is difficult," he said.

It was a perfectly responsible position. Christophe wanted to feed his staff.

"Have you even made a Béarnaise?" he asked.

"Yes."

"Often?"

"No."

"Then why make one now?"

"Because that is why I am here."

He was confused.

"To learn. I am here to learn." *Je suis ici pour apprendre.* It seemed obvious, but obviously it wasn't.

Christophe uttered a faintly audible "huh." He got it. I wasn't going through an initiation rite to become a French chef. I was here only to learn what a French chef does.

The following week, the protein was steak. "Go ahead," Christophe said. "Make your sauce."

"Ah, the perfume of the *mignonette,*" he said, entering the kitchen after I'd got started on "my sauce" (which was, I admit, encouraging). *Mignonette* describes the infusion, the dark tropical spice of black pepper, the licorice fragrance of tarragon, in a bracing white vinegar, simmering slowly. The infusion is one of the three components of a Béarnaise, which on paper looks straightforward. The other two are egg yolks and clarified butter.

I removed the infusion from the heat and let it cool. It was pretty concentrated.

For twenty-five to thirty people, I needed two kilos of butter, which you let melt into a liquid state, whereupon the solids sink unappealingly to the bottom. It's the bright-yellow liquid on top that you want: You pour it off into a container, careful to keep the solids back. (The kitchen is so hot you never have to melt the butter as such; you just leave it out on a shelf.) I used eighteen eggs, and separated the yolks, with Christophe looking over my shoulder to make sure that I wasn't cracking them on a rim but tapping them authoritatively against a flat surface. In fact, if you're me, you've been practicing that authoritative tap for a long time: too little authority and you have to tap a second time (whereupon it often goes splat); too much and . . . well, it definitely goes splat.

Both Béarnaise and Hollandaise are at the heart of the French kitchen. Hollandaise, which may or may not have come from the Netherlands (akin to how a Béarnaise may have come from Béarn but probably didn't), is one of Escoffier's five "mother sauces," the fundamentals you build many variations with. The others are béchamel, velouté, tomato, and espagnole, the wonderfully intense veal-tomato combination that is said to have been conceived by a Spanish cook at the wedding of Louis XIII and Anne of Austria in 1615—and, if so, a glimmer of innovative activity during the long period when French cuisine was just being born, *maybe,* even though no one thought to record the event definitively. Hollandaise and Béarnaise are basically alike, differing mainly in their particular acidity: A Hollandaise is lightly enhanced with lemon, a Béarnaise, emboldened by the vinegar reduction. Some cooks cut the vinegar with white wine. In Lyon, the Béarnaise is done only with vinegar and only with the most in-your-face version of it, *white vinegar,* based not on a wine but cellulose (i.e., tree bark) and what housekeepers use to clean with. It is a sauce that bites back.

The first time I made it, at L'Institut Bocuse, I marveled at how, with my whisking, the sauce foamed and frothed and mounted in my pot into something insubstantial-seeming. The difference between a Béarnaise and other emulsified preparations, like, say, mayonnaise, is that in a Béarnaise you are also heating up the eggs while whipping them and hoping to land on that awkward custardy temperature that is *pre-*

cisely between raw and scrambled. How hot? Well, according to Harold McGee, it should be fifty degrees Celsius. But according to L'Institut Bocuse's textbook, it's sixty degrees Celsius. And according to Joël Robuchon, sixty-five degrees. And all the figures are useless, because you're not about to poke a thermometer into your pot while you are wildly whisking away, afraid that at any moment it's going to break. I use my finger, quickly, and if I burn myself, I know I'm in trouble.

A failed Béarnaise is a liquid mess. Some describe it as scrambled eggs. It's not. It's barf. It is awful to look at. I know this because, for reasons that I never understood, my efforts at home sometimes failed. But then, sometimes, they succeeded, and I didn't know why. Thus, my determination now: I wanted to know that I could nail the sauce and understand it.

This time, my Béarnaise appeared to be working, and after it frothed up impressively, I slowly added a golden thread of the clarified butter, whisking, whisking, whisking, as the sauce, like a metaphor of its maker, seemed to defy gravity and puff up.

I tasted it. I added salt and pepper. I tasted it again. I added lemon. It seemed to be missing something.

Christophe tasted it. "What does it need?"

"Vinegar," I said.

"Vinegar?" He looked at me, stupefied. "Vinegar, really?"

The sauce already had a lot. I knew that. I don't even know why I proposed adding more. I just said it. I tasted it, and thought: More, please.

I added some vinegar, Christophe looking powerfully doubtful.

We tasted again.

"You were right," Christophe said.

It was a good moment.

Then it was a bad moment. As we were standing there, the sauce broke. It failed. It was barf.

"Look at that," Christophe said. "It's broken."

"Why did it break up?"

"I have no idea." He seemed very amused.

To fix the broken sauce, put cold water in a pan, not much, a glass's worth (plus an extra glass nearby in case you need it), heat it, and add your ruined sauce by the spoonful, whisking it in, as though it were a piece of butter, and then another spoonful, and so on. "The trick is the water," Christophe said. "You want to get the sabayon right."

"Sabayon." Of course. Someone had used the same word at L'Institut Bocuse: "You're making a sabayon." I had been thinking that, as with every other sauce, you reduce it as tightly as possible, concentrating it. Like a great veal stock: Take five gallons and reduce it to five ounces. Or fruit sauce: Take a container of orange juice and reduce it to a test tube. And then you build it up. But maybe Béarnaise wasn't French.

A sabayon is a foam sauce as much as it is an emulsion. As Harold McGee points out: Yolks will foam pretty well on their own, but they will foam *spectacularly* with water. Mine had failed because they didn't have enough water. I had reduced it too much.

Dictionaries describe the French word *sabayon* as having appeared in the French language in 1803, even though the technique was probably in place long before. It comes from the Italian *zabaglione* (sweet wine, Marsala usually, the water element, plus egg yolks, whisked and cooked). It appears in two centuries of cookbooks, beginning with Maestro Martino in the fifteenth century. Martino was the gifted, flamboyant Renaissance chef who wowed Platina, a Vatican librarian who sampled his cooking while staying at a cardinal's summer retreat. Platina then wrote a book that was among the first to treat cooking like works of art. It also plagiarized about half of Martino's recipes—the manuscript of which is held at the Morgan Library in New York City—and created thereby an international best seller (of a kind) that would be translated into many languages, including French. (In many ways, it was the first book to export the Italian culinary Renaissance to the rest of Europe.) Might the origins of a Béarnaise be found there, in Platina? There is also a recipe from 1570, by Bartolomeo Scappi, regarded by many as the greatest Italian chef in history. Scappi's recipe includes savory elements, like chicken broth, and is, frankly, not so different from a Béarnaise. Might the origins be there? Is there incontestable proof that the Italian chefs were introducing some of the sauces that would later become the fundamentals of French cuisine? Is there proof that the reverence for "the sauce" itself—its importance to a meal—actually originates in Italy? No, not that I've found . . . yet. But it seems highly likely.

Incidentally, the trick to keeping a sauce from breaking up is, yes, not to allow your infusion to reduce too much—you need the water element—but also to take your time cooking it. You can achieve a consistency that you might believe the sauce should have by heating it over a medium flame and whisking like a mad Italian. It will take five minutes. But, in my experience, the emulsion hasn't quite set, and the sauce might later fail. You'll have more success if you approach it like a custard, slowly raising the temperature, for ten minutes, fifteen, whatever it takes, whisking the whole time, not in a frenzy, but with a measured steadiness, like a Frenchman.

LEFTOVERS

"Ah! If I were a poet! I would put all of this splendor in verse.
Because I'm just a peasant, I put it in salad."

ALAIN CHAPEL AT THE MARKET, QUOTED IN
CROQUE-EN-BOUCHE BY FANNY DESCHAMPS (1976),
TRANSLATED BY JESSICA GREEN

EVENING SERVICE, WHENEVER, A THURSDAY, MAYBE. We were about to run out of plates. I had to get some from the dishwasher in the back. It was urgent. The prospect? Ugly. The route? Nothing but obstacles—Christophe, Viannay, waiters, the pass, orders being called out, shouting, people hurtling back and forth from *garde-manger*. I clamped my elbows into my sides. I tilted my head slightly forward. I took a breath. In my mind, I was a robot on roller skates. I was off. I deviated in nothing: no head movement, no flickering of the eyes, nothing. I grabbed the plates. I rushed back.

It was an exaggerated version of how people move in the kitchen, what I thought of as the "Frankenstein sprint." I was doing it in parody. But was I?

From a faraway corner, I heard my name, and a cheer.

It was Sylvain. He looked happy, which was rare. In fact, he looked very happy. He was shouting: "Bravo, Bill! Bravo! You finally learned!" (I was confused, and then, slowly, I wasn't, because, slowly, I got it: My joke wasn't a joke?) "Bill, welcome to the kitchen!" He was very excited. "Do you have any idea what you looked like in the beginning?"—whereupon he did *his* parody, of a rag doll with its scatty eyeballs, bobbing up and down, looking this way and that, whatever, everything—and he laughed loudly. He could laugh because he was confident that I was laughing with him.

And I pretended to (ha, ha, ha), while marveling: Really? That was what I looked like?

I knew that I was slow. And there was actually merit in Sylvain's observation: I *had* been trying to discipline my brain, not to change it, but to train it, like a client at the gym. I regarded it as blobby.

It wasn't obvious during service, because service is fast and buzzy. A dish is ordered; you make it. A table of dishes is ordered; you make them. It feels that you have a dozen items in your head at once, each at a different stage of preparation. In fact, you probably don't. The orders are ordering your brain.

Prep was harder.

The worst? The day we returned in September for *la rentrée* and reopened. Frédéric poked my stomach when I appeared in the changing room, declaring loudly, *"Qu'est-ce que tu as fait, Bill? Tu as mangé tout?"*—what did you do when you were away, eat everything? I was told to make *le personnel* for eleven-thirty, which confused me until I understood. We were closed. There was no lunch service. It would take a full staff and fifteen hours to get ready for reopening—*everything* had to be prepped—and without the adrenaline of service, the day was arduous. I missed feeling that what I did mattered, right now, as well as the fundamental joys of making food that people were going to eat, right now. I couldn't keep up.

How to be faster? I purposefully reviewed my lessons: Sylvain's, not to cross my hands; Cros's, how to use the knife. I watched Étienne, the new guy, dicing shallots, how he prepped each one, slicing it vertically, then horizontally, the tic-tac-toe board, and how he then arranged them so that he could slice down from the top without having to put his knife down. I admired Étienne's patience. It was slow but fast.

"*Vite! Vite! Vite, Billou,*" Christophe said. In the kitchen you never stand still. (I now had a nickname, Billou.)

I began by wanting always to know what I was going to do next. I don't know why it took me so long. I don't know where I got the idea from, except that it is obviously obvious. And, to my surprise, it resulted in a modestly enhanced concentration. Then, the second task completed, I stood wondering: What now?

"*Vite! Vite! Vite, Billou!*" (Did he really have to repeat "*Vite!*" so many times?)

That moment, standing there, wondering "what next" was my clue.

I added another task. While working on task number one, I quietly repeated to myself the two that were coming up. The result was striking. No question—I enjoyed a new level of clarity.

I tried to keep five in my mind, and the effect was even faster because I seemed to race to get to the fifth task, just to be relieved of having to think so hard about remembering all five. Five was exhilarating. I had to be fast. I had a lot of things—five of them, in fact—to get done. It was like an act of accelerated meditation.

When I reached the last item, I paused, exhaled, and briefly relaxed. Then I compiled a new list.

I told Jessica about my discoveries, as if they were real discoveries, how, in the kitchen, you need to know what you're doing next, and what you're doing after that, and you have to keep them in your mind, because you can't write them down—your hands are busy, the surfaces are full of your work.

(And she looked at me, no questions, with loving but undeniable pity, as in: Oh, poor thing, you've only come to realize this now?)

My historic slowness must have been in the pauses, things that I'd forgotten and had to retrieve, the sloppy organization of not knowing what was coming next. I was fast with a knife. I knew my cutting board. I had the technical skills. I just needed to contain the wayward ways of my digressively civilian mind.

I now think that I was picking up clues from the habits of those around me. I've concluded that my Frankenstein sprint wasn't a joke: In effect, I was trying it on, to see if it might work. And it did. And the outcome was this: I came to love speed.

What did I most enjoy in the kitchen? Making *le personnel* on Fridays, the one that had no menu, that was entirely improvised, the make-it-up-on-the-spot-with-whatever-you-are-lucky-enough-to-find end-of-the-week lunch. Once it crushed me; now it thrilled me. And the thrill wasn't in the leftovers in the *chambre froide*. It was in the ingredients that might not last until Monday, and there was a very elastic zone of judgment governing what constituted a food that was about to go off.

Around nine o'clock, stashes started appearing, urgently passed to me like contraband, described sotto voce, some delicacy that hadn't spoiled "yet" but was clearly "on the verge." Squid, herring, lobster claws, squabs, foie gras, langoustines, a single spider crab. By ten o'clock, more foods had unexpectedly deteriorated and were deemed unlikely to last the weekend. Once, I was handed a quantity of caviar. ("Oh là là, this has probably already gone off," Frédéric observed. "We really should eat it right now.")

Once, at ten-thirty, he gave me four chicken legs.

"What am I meant to do with these?" I asked. "And what are you doing with chicken in the first place? You work the fish station."

"This is *poulet de Bresse*." They were wrapped anonymously in butcher paper, which, his back to Christophe, Frédéric peeled away to show how beautiful they were, the famously faint blue tint in the sinews. "If you don't cook them, they are trash." *Poubelle. Tu comprends?*

I stared at them. "I don't have time to cook chicken legs."

"Why not?"

"Why didn't you give me these earlier?"

"Earlier they looked okay. Now they look as though they might go off, don't you think?"

I added them to what I was doing, my last mad thirty minutes, six sauté pans at once, and three items still in the oven, including a *gratin de pâtes* that I had made just in case and that was browning but not yet crusty.

Mathieu Viannay had told me: "I made you cook *le personnel* because you were always late. I hoped it would teach you to be on time." It did.

I was loving speed.

On Fridays, there was now a feeling of collaboration between me and the others, of making the lunch into a *fête*. They knew I could cook. There was no hazing or mocking.

Johann made a wild-blueberry tart. Cheeses appeared. Multiple salads. Leftover desserts. Sylvain made dishes, too: one week, a perfect Spanish tortilla; another week, a quiche Lorraine. (They were also statements. He hadn't said they were coming or introduced them; he only morosely dropped them off and returned to *garde-manger*. The tarts said: I made this while running my station by myself. Don't you see that I am in the wrong place?)

Fridays taught me the French philosophy of the leftover, codified (I later discovered) in my Institut Bocuse textbook and older books, such as the 1899 *Art of Using Leftovers*. There were rules—never store a leftover in a serving dish or a cooking vessel; never store a warm liquid in a closed container without cooling it first; never reuse a preparation made with raw egg; never keep anything for more than three days; and, the most important of all: Never, under any circumstances, use a leftover twice. A leftover has one chance: to be made even better than the original.

I made celeriac rémoulade, repurposed from the morning's mayonnaise. I made blanquette de veau repurposed from a veal roast.

And, once, just after 10:00 a.m., Sylvain dropped a quantity of raw tuna on my worktop without explanation. *Il y a du thon,* he said ("There is tuna"), and walked away.

I studied it: considerably more than a kilo, not insubstantial, but not enough to feed everyone if cut into steaks and sautéed. I had a thought. In the pantry, there would be soy sauce. In the walk-in, chives, shallots, and lemons. I asked Johann if pastry could spare the bread rolls. I was making tuna burgers, Michel Richard's tuna burgers.

I made lemon mayonnaise, adding a squeeze of the juice at the end and mixing in the zest (six minutes).

I made a marinade: shallots, chives, soy (six minutes).

I cut the fish by hand. Christophe—who was watching, because he was always watching—would call this *thon au tartare,* tuna done like a steak tartare (six minutes).

I put four sauté pans on the flattop.

I put my hand-cut tuna in a bowl, added olive oil, and smashed it with the back of a plastic spatula, making a squishy pulp, emulsifying the oil with the fats of the fish, binding it (three minutes). I added splashes of the marinade and shaped the emulsified pulp into twenty-four burgers (six minutes), sautéed them (quick—I wanted them rare)—forty-five seconds on one side, thirty seconds on the other—removed them to cool, inserted them in buns, dressed them with the mayonnaise, and stacked them up in a clean roasting pan. They looked eminently grabable. *Franchement,* they were sensational.

After lunch, Frédéric stopped me. He was sitting on a worktop, eating his second burger. "Delicious," he said. "How did you make the mayonnaise?"

"Lemons plus the zest."

"Ah. The zest." He nodded, appreciative.

"I learned it from Michel Richard."

"Richard? Hmm. I've never heard of him."

I returned to the kitchen.

"Excellent," Christophe said. "You know, you can also use eggs. To bind the tuna. You add egg to the tuna."

Yes, I said, but then wondered: Why would you do that? With eggs as a binder, you can't cook the tuna rare. People don't like raw egg.

In an instant, I understood Richard's preparation. The French practice: Bind with egg. But then your tuna needs to be cooked through. Meanwhile, the world has discovered seared tuna, barely cooked tuna, sushi-grade tuna, and no one is interested in an overcooked tuna with egg.

"I learned the technique from Michel Richard," I told Christophe.

"Richard?"

He, too: bafflement.

It was everyone's favorite *personnel.* But the credit for it went unjustly to me. And I didn't want it. The credit was wholly owed to the restlessly reinventing Michel Richard.

Jessica woke in the night with a migraine. A bad one. She couldn't keep anything down and was writhing.

I phoned the kitchen. No answer. I left a message. "I will be late." It seemed dangerous to leave her alone. "I will come as soon as I can."

I arrived after eleven. The staff lunch, which I hadn't made, was just finishing. I apologized to Christophe.

"You are very late."

"I know. I am sorry. Jessica had a migraine. I left a message."

"I got the message."

I knew the drill. *La rigueur*. In the kitchen, you never have a reason for not showing up.

"I didn't believe it was safe to leave."

Christophe nodded. "You were missed, Billou."

"Thank you," I said, and then played his reply over in my head. You were missed. *Tu nous as manqué.*

I was at La Mère Brazier for six months, just as the restaurant was entering its second year. There was no official send-off, because, when I left, it was to attend to a piece of business (I made two one-hour films for the BBC about my time in Lyon called *Fat Man in a White Hat*). I intended to resume my place when it was done. The films took longer than expected. I stopped in on Viannay every now and then to confirm my intention and just to check in. Once I found a space in the back, to practice a dish that I had watched his making: fois gras and artichoke hearts rolled up as a cylinder in a boned *poulet de Bresse* and served, sliced, crosswise, with that intense veal-cherry sauce that we made at the meat station. In the summer, I produced it for friends who had a son the same age as George and Frederick. They, and especially the boys, devoured it. (The secret, I think, was the sauce.)

In the interim, Hortense was gone. She had broken her foot and didn't return. Chern was gone. He had earned the credit he needed to complete his degree. Frédéric was in Japan, a chef's job. And Sylvain had left to work at Bocuse's Brasserie Le Nord. ("Monsieur Paul is there every Thursday at eleven.") It was nearby, on the Presqu'île. Sylvain's job title was *chef de cuisine*. Was this a step down? Le Nord didn't have a Michelin star. It wasn't *"grande cuisine."* And Sylvain wasn't an executive chef, or a sous-chef, but he wasn't, at least, the guy running *garde-manger* single-handedly.

"Viannay wouldn't submit my name for the Pâté en Croûte World Cup," Sylvain said. "I needed a sponsor. He refused."

Sylvain had embarked on a career based on the traditional kitchen assumptions of hard work and fair rewards: that if you were rigorous, disciplined, punctual, and attentive; if you had deep knowledge of the French repertory—your Escoffier, classic dishes, pastries, sauces—and that if, as well, you secured a job at a fine establishment, such as the three-Michelin-star Restaurant de Georges Blanc, then you could count on rising up in the hierarchy. You would be rewarded with increasing responsibility, prestige, and a reasonable salary. You could raise a family. It was for life.

Was Sylvain competent? Absolutely. Rigorous, disciplined, reliable? No one more so. The classic training? Definitively. But there was a new element he hadn't prepared for—creativity. Was he innovative? Possibly not. It had never been assumed that you needed it.

At La Mère Brazier, Sylvain seemed to have lost his future. He had the manner of a man betrayed: not just by the restaurant, but by the culture of the kitchen, by France.

I asked Viannay about him.

"Sylvain was not good enough," he said. He looked at me hard to ensure that I got the message. "He wasn't what Christophe needed. Sylvain is a bistro chef."

I had a word with Christophe. I will be back, I promised.

"You will be welcome."

But I didn't see him for nearly a year.

VI

Dinner

At the table, the Lyonnais are intolerant of sparkling water. They drink dry wine. When, on a whim, they dilute it with a bit of water, it is only the good water of the Rhône. They know it is pure and of good quality.

The Lyonnais do not like eating fast. In this they prove their passion, because, by controlling the urges of their stomach, they can savor the varieties and pleasure of their food. . . .

The Lyonnais do not give away their recipes. They protect them. They never ask for the recipes of others, because they never want to have to return the favor.

In Lyon, they do not eat with music, even if they are passionate about the art. They don't like, in fact, to mix their joys and be distracted from one of the most important functions of life, eating their meal.

Traditional Lyonnais take their coffee and liqueur at the table to prolong the pleasures and the time there. . . .

In politics, the Lyonnais know that it is with good dinners we govern mankind and that the best political document is in a very well-written menu.

FROM *LA CUISINE LYONNAISE* BY MATHIEU VARILLE (1928), TRANSLATED BY GEORGE ELY BUFORD

Lᴛᴏɴ, ᴄʜʀɪsᴛᴍᴀs. My mother, seventy-seven years old and a recent widow, flew from Florida, changing planes in Washington, D.C., and Frankfurt, where her flight arrived late and she missed her connection and didn't know how to make her cell phone work. Finally, unflappable, she appeared in Lyon to visit her grandchildren for the holidays and check in on their parents, who had told her that they would be staying in France six months but had already been there much longer and had no apparent plans to leave. On Christmas Eve, I phoned Brasserie Georges to confirm they were open. (I didn't know; our first Christmas didn't involve going anywhere.) The restaurant, built in 1836, has high ceilings, red leather banquettes, waiters in tuxedos, children under four for free, a birthday song on the *limonaire* every quarter-hour, as proverbially busy as the train station next door, and room for two thousand covers a night—with, in my opinion, an exceptional steak tartare made tableside. It is a throwback establishment—the kind of place you read about in history books but never survive—and evidently was where Lyon went on Christmas Eve. Yes, they were open, but the waiting list was already so long that no more names would be accepted. We had never, in our many visits to the place, been turned away. It seemed a physical impossibility. I had thought that Lyon was now ours, that we knew its customs and its practices, but we hadn't been here long enough to know its family practices on Christmas Eve, the rituals of dining in the historic Christian city.

We settled on a popular bistro, not in our quartier but not far, and walked there on what had become a brisk, still night, cobbled streets full of many more people than I had expected to find.

George began singing a song and, after a refrain, was joined by Frederick:

Qui a la barbe blanche
Et un grand manteau?
Qui a la barbe blanche
Et sa hotte sur le dos?

It was the first time I'd heard it. When the boys reached the refrain, strangers joined in. A guy on the corner smoking a cigarette. Couples on their way somewhere. All adults, and no children in their care. They stopped, stood still, and sang. My mother hadn't noticed, and I told her to listen: a chorus led by two elfin American children, their perfect French, their fragile soprano voices.

Qui descend du ciel
Une fois par an?
Qui descend du ciel
Pour tous les petits enfants?

C'est le Père Noël
Père Noël
C'est le Père Noël
Pour mon joyeux Noël.

Applause echoed off stone walls and the cobbled street and from around a corner.

French had come easily to the boys, but not as fast as we expected. But when, finally, they became fluent, they were deeply fluent. Jessica and I can date the moment, a full year after we arrived, an evening when we had arranged for Stephen, their rambunctiously energetic "sitter," to look after them. The boys let him in.

"Hello, George and Frederick."

"*Bonjour,* Stephen," they said, in an impeccable accent, and Stephen, after a glance at us, replied in French, and they, in turn, did the same, and, from that arbitrary-seeming moment, they never spoke to him in English again. It was as if they had managed to twist their brains and (*click!*) the French one was now in the front and in charge, and the English one was a backup in the back. Now, if you woke them in the night, they emerged in another language, from French dreams.

When we walked home after dinner, the bells were ringing for the midnight service, all of them in close proximity, the historic churches, a reminder that the city had often been under siege. Midway through the French Revolution, on May 29, 1793, Lyon had declared its independence, and Robespierre, indignant, declared that the city should be exterminated (*"Lyon n'est plus!"*). He hired sixty thousand mercenary troops to surround it, bomb it daily, starve it, and the bells rang in defiance, until many of the churches were leveled and, two months later, the city capitulated. The guillotines were on the Place des Terreaux, and some of the 1,684 corpses (each one named and numbered, since the Revolution was nothing if not *punctilious*) were stacked in an improvised morgue in the chapel nearest our home and by Bob's boulangerie. The bells in Lyon are always a little mournful, even on the eve of a day celebrating a birth. They seem to fortify the Lyonnais in their Lyonnaisness.

Christmas morning was bright and intensely blue. When young Frederick saw that Père Noël had left him a gift, he rushed to the window, with its long view of the Saône and the skies over Beaujolais and the Alps, hoping to catch a glimpse of him, as if the bearded guy's visit had only just been completed. The expression of high expectation on his face has played over and over in my memory, like a rebuke for our manipulating a child's innocence: Or maybe it's just the nostalgia of a moment in France when everything was finally seeming right and good.

I went out to Bob's, who had told us only the day before that he'd be open on Christmas. He had pulled an all-nighter. The display of breads and cakes was vast and unprecedented. There were baguettes in what appeared to be every possible variation, including *flûtes,* which were long and unwieldy, and *ficelles,* the little ones like a string, and *bâtards,* the fat ones, and both the "short" four-footer (a *joko court*) and the long one, the six-foot *joko long.* There were braided breads, and winemaker loaves, plus pastries and the *pains au chocolat* that George and Frederick couldn't do without. I had never seen Bob make such a variety. It expressed expertise and a sense of history.

But the shop was not crowded. In fact, there was only one customer: me.

"It is my fault," Bob said. "I hadn't made up my mind to open on Christmas until the last minute, and no one knew."

I bought a tottering armful—simply a ridiculous amount—and made my way back home, dropped them spillingly on the kitchen table, and went looking for a magnum of wine that I'd been saving for the right occasion—a red one from the Rhône—rushed back down the stairs, and presented it to Bob as a gift.

I knew that I would be returning to work for him, and that, for my own selfish purposes, I needed to complete my stint there, if only because it completed a list of what I thought of as "French essentials"— not "haute cuisine" but, rather, the rustic fundamentals of foods that had been made here for thousands of years, fashioned from the land: cheese and *saucisson* and bread. Bob was skeptical. In his view, I was now on to other things. Even so, we had become close. Our family was so often in his shop that it came to seem like an extra room in our home. Bob was family.

Bob had an agenda, and he trusted me enough to know that I would want to understand it. He grew up with an idea of what a boulanger did. He had a refrain: Everyone deserved good bread. But there was more to it. It was like a calling or a social imperative: A boulanger can be counted on by the people he feeds. Opening on Christmas Day was, somehow, one of his duties.

Recently, I contacted Steven Kaplan, a historian of the boulangerie. His *Good Bread Is Back* helped me to understand a rage that Bob felt at how factory breads—the kind, in fact, that La Mère Brazier then served (half baked, then reheated, with mixing tricks and chemicals to simulate the bounce and yeasty aromatics of an old-fashioned loaf)—had deprived a whole generation of French people from knowing what real bread should taste like.

I told Kaplan about Bob, how his bread was recognized in Lyon to be the best around. "Bob," I wrote, "says that the flavor is all in the flour. He has a guy in the Auvergne whose wheat he swears by, and I don't know if it's the farmer who mills it or someone else, but the flour is fresh, especially in the summer, and arrives not in bulk but every few days, and there's a goat, on the wheat farmer's property, Bob has a picture in his window, named Hector."

Kaplan wrote: "Wow. Your fellow Bob is very unusual." There are many good bread bakers in France now, but he didn't know anyone who was getting his flour directly from the farmer growing the wheat.

It's not much, a loaf of bread. Flour, water, and the dough left over from yesterday. It seems scarcely to exist. Let it rise, weigh it, shape it, proof it, slash it, bake it, and ask for 90 centimes. Maybe the secret really was the flour.

COOKING IN A PIG'S BLADDER

At the market, Fernand Point told us, "I am not difficult.
I am happy with the best."

CRO*Q*UE-EN-BOUCHE BY FANNY DESCHAMPS (1976),
TRANSLATED BY JESSICA GREEN

VIENNE, RHÔNE-ALPES. In a reasonable approximation of Fernand Point's original and outrageously luxurious recipe, Henriroux makes his *poulet en vessie* by first loading up both bird and bladder with luxury ingredients: truffles, foie gras, a couple shots of a good Cognac, and a glass of Condrieu, whose golden grapes can be seen growing on the other side of the Rhône. (Point also added Madeira and Champagne, of course, being a lover of the beverage.) The preparation is another illustration of the Lyonnais high-low thing: the rustic bladder, the flashy ingredients.

Then you truss it, which struck me as highly unnecessary.

I appreciate the virtues of trussing, which tucks in the extremities, wings and legs, and keeps them from cooking faster than the rest of the chicken. It also makes for a more attractive presentation, a poultry parcel rather than wings splayed out like a pair of wonky boomerangs. But I've never been entirely clear about the textbook trussing method, and was reassured when, later, in Boulud's kitchen (trussing birds), Jean-

François Bruel, Boulud's top chef, also didn't know and wasn't bothered that he didn't. He had his own way—until he was stopped mid-truss by his boss.

"*Non!*" Boulud said. "That's not how it is done! What's wrong with you?"

In fact, there are *two* official trussing methodologies—one involves the trussing needle's poking into the chicken; the other, no poking—but I couldn't keep them straight, and I persist in stabbing my way through just about everything, sometimes two or three times, with double loops and extra knots.

But a chicken in a *vessie*? Didn't the *vessie* do whatever a needle and string were meant to accomplish, and keep the extremities tucked in and the poultry package tidy?

The *vessie*, when it is rehydrated (you buy dried *vessies* at a butcher shop—they look like Frisbees), has the features of a small rubber sock, and appears too small to put a whole chicken in. It's also thick and opaque. With a faucet running, you stretch it, first with your fist, rotating gently, being careful not to tear the mouth. The chicken has to go through the mouth. Melted butter on the chicken's skin helps. You hold it firm with a rubber glove, and eventually you get it in there, not with a sense of "plop," just "whew."

You tie the bird shut. A double knot doesn't work. You need to tie it up as though it were a balloon, very simply, tucking it into its own loop, so the increasing pressure tightens it.

To cook, you bring a pot of water to a simmer, slide your chicken-filled *vessie* across the surface, and start ladling. The ladling has the effect of heating the bladder from above as well as below. This also keeps it moist. If it dries out, it explodes. Some chefs use a pot of chicken broth, which is a waste, because none of it is getting inside the *vessie*. For very good reasons bladders are not normally porous.

After a few minutes, the bladder expands, slowly at first, but then quickly, becoming suddenly and alarmingly very big. You ladle, ladle, ladle, starting to worry. After twenty minutes, the *vessie* is transformed: No longer thick and opaque, it has the appearance of a beautifully golden, nearly translucent beach ball that some maniac is still insisting on pumping more air into. Also, you can see the chicken!

I was stunned by the sight. It seemed so foreign, to find a globe so large in the kitchen and with a bird inside, that I spontaneously declared, "Man, imagine how much pee that thing must hold!"

Five or ten minutes later (ladling! ladling! ladling!), the bladder is at its maximum expansion. It is a test of your preparation. If you made the mistake of using a double knot, it will slowly start to loosen, and there will be nothing you can do to stop the mouth's opening, and the foie and Cognac will pour out in a cloud of brown sludge. Likewise, alas, if you failed to truss the bird, you will witness—through the now very capacious transparent golden membrane—the extremities slowly opening up in the perpendicular. There will be nothing you can do to stop them until they puncture the *vessie*. Once again, the Cognac, the foie, and brown polluting ooze.

Now I truss.

The chicken, once you open up the bladder tableside to share fully its emancipated aromatics, is overwhelmingly sensual—in the sense of all your senses being activated: the steam, the meat, the rich flavors of the Rhône. The embellishments—truffles, foie, wine—render a dish that is smooshy and rich. I can see why Henriroux tried to dissuade me from it. It is not light. But what a celebration of pleasure!

After my session, I lingered.

Point died here at La Pyramide, at the end of winter in 1955, at the age of fifty-eight. The restaurant, remarkably, continued as though Point had never left, owing to the care of his widow, "Mado," who directed operations, her husband seeming to whisper in her ear.

The kitchen still looked as it did when he was alive. It has since been renovated, but I was there before the upgrade: cracked white tile walls, blocky wood-frame windows circa 1930, elementary four-legged worktops, like a spare table at your grandparents'. It was premodern prewar dowdy. I had expected a narrow space, cramped and dark, where two people passed each other with difficulty. But the actual kitchen was roomy and light, and I was able to picture Point moving around in it. It was a professional establishment, but also like the generous kitchen of a family home in the country.

I stood still and tried imagining the food then being made here, so exceptional that it led people to believe that Lyon, and the region around it, was the world's gastronomic capital. French cuisine was then held in such esteem that, if the best cooking in the country was found here, then it was, therefore, the best food in the world. (That had been the premise of Curnonsky's 1935 *Lyon, capitale mondiale de la gastronomie*.) And maybe it was. Young Paul Bocuse came here to work after four years at La Mère Brazier. Young Alain Chapel trained here before taking over his father's inn in the Dombes. The Troisgros brothers trained here before taking over their family restaurant in Roanne, sixty miles to the northwest. These then young cooks were members of the first generation of nouvelle-cuisine chefs. Their approach—it could almost be called an "ideology"—was said to have been fashioned by Point. What did he teach them?

I reread Point's book while sitting in an alcove of the restaurant, a museum of Point artifacts. The recipes are brazenly laconic. Commentators cite the understatement as proof that Point was writing for professionals and didn't need to spell out the how-to. A recipe for *tête de veau à la tortue,* a veal's head done in the shape of a tortoise, was no more than a short paragraph. Normally the preparation is immensely complicated. What Point did describe—a strong herb infusion, a cup of Madeira added to the sauce, a garnishing of olives and rooster kidneys and combs—were his unique embellishments. Otherwise, everything was according to the *règle*—the rule. And that phrase—*selon les règles*—might be the proverbial window into Point's culinary soul.

It was a modest epiphany. *Selon les règles*—not many phrases are more French. Everyone working for Point knew the classics, just as I had, by now, learned many of them. Actually, the word "classics" isn't accurate. They knew the repertoire. They knew the way dishes were made. Such was their training. Point's recipes describe only the deviations: the subtle ways in which the received dishes were, in Point's hands, made differently. Thus, his role as the godfather of nouvelle cuisine: He didn't just perpetuate the old dishes; he was provoked by them; he made them better. It didn't take much, but nothing he did was entirely conventional. Michel Richard had once told me that the secret to Point was not in what he said. And in that secret was a definition of nouvelle cuisine: not new for the sake of the new, but the old—the French "repertoire"—

rendered a little bit new. After all, in an orthodoxy, even the smallest deviations are acts of rebellion.

LESSONS IN PASTA MAKING

You are told by Lyonnais that they are used to appearing cold—to strangers, foreigners, visitors, you. They don't care whether they know you or not. You won't understand them. You won't get their city and will be put off by its gritty darkness, the sewage smells, the graffiti, the cobblestone streets with their broken stones, its low cloud of melancholy. You will dismiss its people. "Buttoned up," "reserved." True, the city conveys the impression of nights at *bouchons* and restaurants—and the Lyonnais, in mirthful jollity, can be found there on weekends (not talking to you), dining with focus and Rabelaisian determination, because they regard being fed and waited on as high privileges and will deny themselves nothing: wine, three courses, dessert, cheese, a glass of high-alcohol Chartreuse. Normally, the Lyonnais are eating at home, which you won't know, because they don't invite you. (Henri Béraud wrote in 1944: "Lyon does not host grand dinners. What am I saying? They host no dinners at all.") You will see them, returning from markets on the *quai* with their vegetables and chickens, and smell their meals being cooked when you pass by their apartments, the broths, the sauces, and, in the summer, their windows open, hear the sounds of their dinner. But you won't eat with them.

This, without our even realizing it, had been our Lyon, too.

The breakthrough was a long time coming. What's more, that breakthrough, our first Lyonnais invitation, wasn't a conventional invitation. It was an invitation in reverse: Our Lyonnais friends—and, yes, they *are* our friends (now)—didn't invite us into their home; they invited themselves into ours.

We were having a meal at the Bouchon des Filles, on a busy Thursday night, and Isabelle announced that she and her co-owner, Laura, were coming to our apartment for dinner. (I thought: I'm not understanding, but this sounds complicated.)

"Laura and I agree that you are going to make pasta for us," she clarified.

"I am?"

"Yes. It is time we understood pasta. You are going to teach us. Are you available next Friday?"

"Uh . . ." I looked to Jessica.

She shrugged: Why not?

Isabelle later confirmed that their significant others would be coming as well: Gérard (Laura's) and Yves (Isabelle's).

On Monday, Isabelle phoned to confirm that the *bouchon*'s business manager was coming, too. "We can't have a pasta dinner without her."

Of course, I said.

On Tuesday, Isabelle told us that two others were coming, Sonia Ezgulian (author, restaurateur, culinary consultant) and her husband, Emmanuel. In the event, ten people gathered around our IKEA-purchased dining-room table, including Stephen, who succeeded in putting the lads so soundly asleep (shortly after an antipasto and a pasta) that they wouldn't wake once in what would turn out to be the loudest night of our stay, so far, in our apartment.

I prepared five pasta courses—dried, handmade, filled (two different ravioli), and baked. Jessica lined up bottles of wine, including (to get everyone into the Italian spirit) two *double* magnums of a Morellino di Scansano, a Sangiovese from Tuscany's western coast, and assumed that everyone would drink, on average, about a bottle each, which seemed wholly contrary to our experience of the Lyonnais. (Except at *mâchons*, they are otherwise uncompromisingly moderate drinkers, and their moderation had long perplexed us—was it because they had grown up drinking so much great wine that another bottle of it was, you know, ho-hum? Was it a fear of drunkenness?) After an initial *apéro* of bubbles followed by a couple bottles of a light white to go with the first pasta (a *linguine alle vongole*), our guests started in on the Sangiovese and, without our noticing, finished both double magnums just after the second course. Whoa!

Other wines were found, the meal proceeded, and, true to my assign-ment, I explained how the dishes were made—the "soul" of the Italian ragù, of tortellini—but no one seemed particularly interested until I produced a plate of duck ravioli. The filling was a tight, almost dry ragù that I made by slow-braising the birds' thighs, dressed with an intense cherry-and-veal-and-duck-carcass sauce, another variation of the one I had learned at La Mère Brazier. Isabelle, skeptical that such food could be made by hand, insisted that I take her to the kitchen for proof (which, frankly, was a delightful challenge).

The room got warmer, especially for the cook, running in and out with each new course, plates carted back, washed quickly, returned, and the loud talk louder—chatter, clatter, patter about food and farms and dishes and who was opening the next place and who was about to close—and we adjourned to the living room and opened the doors onto our little balcony—the moon full, the river shimmeringly still— and I recognized, among everyone, a happy conversational buzz that, showing no prospect of diminishing, might carry us along for hours, when I looked at my watch. It was 4:00 a.m. Damn! In the morning (which of course it was already) we were intending to return to Lavis Trafford, that former customhouse in the Alps. I then did something that, militating against every code of being a host, I have never done: I told everyone they had to go home, and, I am grateful to report, they did.

What had happened?

We appeared to have done something almost inadvertently meaning-ful. We had played host to Lyonnais chefs and restaurateurs and fed them generously. For the duration of a nine-hour meal, we had made our table a happy place to be. In some fundamental way, we had dem-onstrated that, in feeding Lyonnais friends in your home, you cannot do too much. For them and you, there are few greater privileges. You cannot expend too much effort, splurge too generously, aspire too ambi-tiously to make the occasion a unique event. And we had confirmed for our guests, therefore—our now formally recognized friends—that we shared their commitment, almost like an ideology, to the culture of the table.

It wasn't the most ambitious meal I cooked. After all, pasta hadn't been high on the list of French dishes that I was skilling myself to nail. But it was the most consequential. It became a "founding dinner" for what would become a round-robin of festive meals at each other's homes, a kind of informal dining club—a Lyonnais practice dating from the nineteenth century. Ours continues to this day. The meal changed our relationship to the city.

In all this, there was also the overwhelming fact of the *filles*. I would like to say that, during our time in Lyon, we would see the gender balance in the kitchen readjust itself, and that the *filles* were somehow at the forefront of those doing the readjustment. But it's not really accurate. They were at the forefront of its being challenged. As backward as the kitchens in the United States or Britain might seem, they were rarely as outright Stone Age as the French. Even the *mère* tradition was less forward-thinking than it seemed to be. Yes, the chef was a woman, but with the understanding that she wasn't a grand chef. She was making local dishes—what she learned at home—while the man was often in the front of the house, the money guy, running operations. (Brazier was a complex exception.)

Isabelle and Laura met while working as waitresses at Café des Fédérations, owned by Yves, the man who is now Isabelle's partner. The café wasn't actually a café but an authentic museum-piece *bouchon* (pig paraphernalia, black-and-white photos of eating and drinking and picking grapes, an authentic pre–World War I stand-up toilet right by the kitchen). The café's approach to service, which depended on sassy waitresses, was flippant, back-talking, flirtatious, and always on the verge of being out of control, and informed by an implicit understanding that no one there talked about boyfriends or girlfriends, husbands or wives, or children, because its fundamental philosophy was that you were there to have a good time and behave just a little bit badly, and that nothing else mattered. For the *filles,* the time came when they thought: We could do this better. The *bouchon* they opened was a modest but conscious act of rebellion. The Bouchon des Filles is not merely a *mère* restaurant. It is one run by the daughters who know better. Their restaurant, its name, its practices, in a food city with a long history of women in the kitchen, was more than a witty conceit. It was a declaration of purpose.

In Lyon, the model is Anne-Sophie Pic. At L'Institut Bocuse, women students of a certain status (competent, ambitious, talented) longed to work for her. She was who they wanted to be. And everyone knew her story.

It starts in 1889, in a village in the Cévennes Mountains near Saint-Péray (seventy-five miles south of Lyon, where Bob's favorite white wine comes from), where the great-grandmother (Sophie) opened a *mère* café-restaurant, l'Auberge du Pin ("Pin" is pine). It ends, more than a hundred years later, after near financial ruin, a tragic death, banishment of a sibling, and a daughter heroically vindicated. Few stories illustrate the plight of women chefs in France with more pathos.

André Pic, the son of the great-grandmother, is a chef whom Curnonsky celebrated with a special enthusiasm ("PIN! PIC! Remember those two syllables!") and awarded the family restaurant three Michelin stars in 1935. André then moved it out of the mountains and into the city of Valence, on that still narrow stretch of the Route Nationale 7. But André, a charmer, was a financial incompetent, and in 1946, a Michelin star was taken away, among the few times in the *Guide*'s history that a three-star establishment had been diminished. He pressed on, stubbornly refusing to yield his position to anyone else, notably his son Jacques, who left home and learned his culinary skills elsewhere. André grew so obese he couldn't climb the stairs to go to bed (an elevator was installed) or stand at the pass (and a platform was built so he could taste dishes). He lost another star, and the restaurant was on the verge of bankruptcy, when in 1956, Jacques returned, and slowly and respectfully took over the kitchen, and directed the family's business out of debt. It took him seventeen years to earn back the restaurant's three stars and establish financial stability.

Anne-Sophie, understandably reluctant to follow her father, Jacques, into the profession—the kitchen, in the Pic family, was a place of great drama—went abroad and trained in business management, but in 1992 had an awakening—she was twenty-two—and returned to Valence to be taught by her father to be a chef. She adored him. She was in the kitchen, three months later, when Jacques, after a particularly arduous day, had an aneurysm and died at the stove, fifty-nine years old.

The *brigade,* all men, all "French-trained," had been employed at Pic for at least ten years. They regarded Anne-Sophie as a child. You don't start training at twenty-two. "The cooks wouldn't even consider the possibility that I should be there," she recalls in an interview. "I didn't have the courage to fight back. I became the receptionist." Her older brother, Alain, was made chef. For two years, she kept the books and saw that the restaurant was again in debt. Then it lost its third star.

There was a showdown. The grandfather was cited; their father invoked. The son lost, quit, and moved to Grenoble. He has been acknowledged since, but not often. In family histories, and on the restaurant's Web site (at least at the moment), he appears to have been excised. (One entry describes Jacques Pic as having only one child, his daughter.) Anne-Sophie Pic, without formal training, entered the kitchen and faced the same *brigade*. But she was stronger now (*"Je suis plus forte"*). "I am a woman, self-taught, the daughter of the *patron* who is no longer there. I am proprietor and apprentice."

Anne-Sophie was different from her male culinary peers, it seemed to me, when I first met her in Lyon, two years after she earned her third star (because she did, finally, ten years after taking over the kitchen, earn back the star that her brother had lost). She was spontaneous, easy in her skin, without any of the alpha-male social armor that most chefs wear in public. She didn't cross her arms across her chest. She read books. She liked words. Her accounts of her father, and the life she had growing up with him and her mother, read like poetry. She could be witty. She was savvy, quick, modern. She was then thirty-nine, with straight dark hair, a tailored chef's jacket, diminutive in stature, and an aw-shucks manner. She was a mother. Her son was the same age as our boys. We talked about children and food.

The following year, Jessica and I spent a weekend at her establishment, still built right up against Route Nationale 7. She was, to see her in the dining room, the same person I had met before, a recognizable high-achieving type, urbane, self-deprecating. You could imagine her running—well, just about anything.

But she was different in the kitchen.

I had made an effort to see her there, crossed a courtyard, and stopped. In the design of the place, the kitchen was visible from outside, and Pic appeared as a soundless, angry figure on view through a window the size of a village cinema screen. She was red-faced and, from the muscles in her throat, shouting, her posture erect, her arms and hands gesticulating indignation and fury. The members of her *brigade,* who in normal circumstances would have towered over her, drooped their heads in self-abasement. As the verbal drubbing went on, they seemed to droop more deeply. Pic is among the most articulate and civilized chefs I've met. Her kitchen persona was unexpected. In the restaurant, an hour later, she would resume her identity as an affable host. But I was glad to have seen the uncensored kitchen persona. It was reaffirming.

Pic describes her cooking as the food of emotion. It is exhilarating to eat because it is flawless. (It is also pricey—more expensive when we ate there than at Paul Bocuse's Auberge.) It is precise. The composition of the plates, the temperature of the food, the textures, the come-hither appeal: perfection. The emotions expressed in it must be many: longing, sadness, tenderness, loss. There is also rage. A rage against mortality. A rage against injustice, her fuck-up charming grandfather, a father's genius that has gone largely unnoticed, her brother and his entitlement. A rage against the kitchen and its knee-jerk prejudices. A rage that helped make her a grand chef.

One summer, on our way to Italy on a family trip, we stopped en route at an Alain Ducasse establishment in the Provençal Alps, near Verdon, the natural regional park. We were hungry—too late for lunch—and were greeted with a picnic on an outside table near the kitchen. A delivery arrived, meanwhile: crates of vegetable-patch-warm tomatoes, carefully arranged top side down, irregular, striped, ill-shaped, flagrantly evocative of a southern-French summer. We were surrounded by flowers and bees. Jessica and I had a glass of white wine. It was bucolic.

Then *crack* from the kitchen: *"Putain!"* Another *crack. "Qu'est-ce que vous faites? Eh?"*

The boys laughed covertly. To this day, they have not, within my hearing, said *putain.*

The kitchen roar continued, anger, fury, another *crack* (*"Mais vous faites chier"*—What you are doing is shit), culminating in a withering piece of name calling. *"Vous êtes des crapauds. Vous comprenez quoi? Des crapauds. Putains."* (You are toads. Do you understand? Toads. *Putains.*)

In the male culture of the kitchen, there are few put-downs worse than being called a toad by your kickass woman chef. It was too much; the boys erupted with laughter. The chef was Julie Chaix.

The women now running French kitchens seem tougher than the men. You know what they've been through to get there. If you let them down, they will humble you. They will call you a toad. But they won't throw pots at your head, or pinion you to a wall, or whisper pornography into your ear.

Why hadn't I intervened?

It could be said that no one was seriously hurt. No blood, nothing broken.

But it couldn't be said that people weren't damaged, their persons, their sense of themselves. Little Mathieu. I witnessed how, day by day, he was changed from a hopeful child to a nasty, snarling bully-in-training.

Hortense . . .

I am, by training, a journalist, and journalists *report* stories, not *change* them. But by then my journalist credentials had come to seem irrelevant. At Michel Richard's, everyone knew who I was. At La Mère Brazier, I became a member of a kitchen staff. I had crossed over, but, in the crossing, I appear to have left my conscience behind. In real life, I would have intervened. At the very least, I would have said, Stop! *Arrête!* A shy, modestly built woman in the kitchen where I was working, almost within my reach, was dodging pots being hurled at her head. I didn't step in. I didn't say, *Arrête!* I looked around, and found whoever was in charge, and looked into their faces for an instruction, and found nothing. Was I trying to learn the way? Understand the code? Or maybe I was just afraid.

SMALL BROWN COWS ON HIGH GREEN MOUNTAINS

Bruno did not like to think about practical problems. He never talked to me about debts, bills, taxes, mortgage rates. He preferred to talk about his dreams, or the physical intimacy he felt when milking, or the mystery of the rennet.

"Rennet is a little piece of a calf's stomach," he explained. "Imagine the part that enables a calf to digest its mother's milk. We take it and use it to make cheese. It's right to do so, don't you think? It is also terrible. But without this piece of stomach the cheese wouldn't form."

"I wonder who first discovered it," I said.

"It must have been the wild man."

"The wild man?"

"An ancient who lived in the woods. Long hair, beard, covered in leaves. Every so often, he appeared in the villages, and although people feared him they always put something out for him to eat to thank him for having shown them how to use rennet."

PAOLO COGNETTI, *LE OTTO MONTAGNE* (2016)

PRALOGNAN-LA-VANOISE, HAUTE-SAVOIE. It is still before dawn. I am a guest in a mountain chalet, nearly seven thousand feet above sea level, isolated, no trees, on the edge of a protected national park through which you would have to walk a long way to see another habitation. I have been dressed in white boots and rain gear, as though ready for a deluge. I am in a room that is pristine and rectangular. It has white walls, a red floor, and a heavy copper cauldron hanging from three black chains that have been filled with seven hundred liters of warm milk. I am about to witness one of the oldest and most miraculous acts of the already very old and very miraculous molecular process known as fermentation: the one or two minutes it takes to convert that milk into cheese.

Bob used to add a piece of dough from the night before, which housed all the yeasts he needed to make a whole shift's worth of baguettes. Here they use last night's milky, almost cheesy mixture (*le lait de la veille*). "It is called *lactosérum*," one of my hosts, Claude Glise, tells me. He fills up a bucket and pours it into the cauldron. The white liquid, the white overalls, the pail—he could be a housepainter. "What is *lactosérum* in English?"

"Whey." As in the nursery rhyme, with the spider and Little Miss Muffet. It is something like "cheese water."

"The *présure*," he explains, "is in the *lactosérum*. What is your word for *présure*?"

Présure describes an enzyme generated by the lining of the animal's stomach. French makes the distinction between the enzyme and the lining. In English, both are interchangeably described as "rennet." It is what nursing ruminants—calves, kids, does, antelopes, etc.—produce to help them digest their mother's milk. Humans have similar enzymes, principally lactose; it is what adults sometimes lose the ability to make, and then develop lactose intolerance.

Glise stirs his cauldron for a minute, maybe two. I'm asking him questions and don't notice what has happened: that his white liquid is thicker. The change is so quick as to make me doubt that it occurred. But in the next instant, it is even thicker. It isn't cheese, at least not recognizably so, but is no longer milk. It is more like yogurt. I want to drag my finger through it, which Glise seems to intuit. He picks up a wide-mouth trowel, fills it up thickly, and rolls the liquid out in slow waves. The sound is like syrup splashing.

"This is fromage blanc." The milk is starting to curdle. In the nursery rhyme, Miss Muffet is eating not just "whey" but "curds and whey." It now occurs to me that she is eating fromage blanc.

It is the simplest cheese you can get: the first expression of milk plus rennet. Uncooked, unaged, scarcely firmed up, undoctored. In Lyon, you hope to eat it when it's fresh, fresh, fresh—just from the mountains. It is served at the end of a *bouchon* meal. It was Rabelais's favorite. He ate it with cream. Others add sugar or jam. At their school, our boys eat it plain.

A "mountain chalet," I should clarify, isn't grand. It is often just a hut. It doesn't have Wi-Fi, and rarely has electricity or gas, unless you bring it up by the canister. Glise's place—with bedrooms, a kitchen, a *cave* to store wheels of cheese—is unusually large, and in the summer is where he lives with his wife, Caroline, and their two children. Claude and Caroline make Beaufort, the hard, "cooked" mountain cheese, something like a Gruyère. In the extensive literature about Beaufort, you will read that its peasant-family proprietors—and today there are eighteen—have been making the cheese for many centuries, passing on the know-how from generation to generation. The Glise family is an exception. Claude and Caroline were professionals with city jobs, which they abandoned to move to the mountains. I think of them as *nouveaux paysans*—not pejoratively. In fact, happily, there seem to be more *nouveaux paysans* every year in France, charismatic fanatics, all of them, and culinary heroes, like Bob.

The Glises make other cheeses—*reblochon* (raw), *tomme, sérac* (the French ricotta, which is double-cooked)—but their most prized is a

Beaufort called Chalet d'Alpage. It is the rarest (I have never seen it outside of France), the most expensive (but, oh my, is it worth the expense), and the most elegantly delicious. Like other Alpine summer cheeses, it is made from the milk of cows that have fed exclusively on wild grasses in the high mountains. A Chalet d'Alpage is not just of the high mountains, but among the highest.

I get a sense of just how high. After the milking, which was done long before the sun comes up, some of Glise's animals disappeared. He was not in the least worried, and so I was not worried, but I'm curious, and by the morning twilight start looking for them. When I finally spot them, they are the smallest of small brown flecks on a high vast green slope, the muffled ring of their bells seeming like an echo that has lost its way, and at an altitude that I discover to be nearly twelve thousand feet.

The cows remain here in the high mountains—they have to remain here; it's one of the rules—for a biblical-sounding hundred days. There are other rules, enough that it can seem that making a Beaufort d'Alpage is almost a pagan rite, including that the cheese must be made in situ—in the field or pasture or on the mountaintop where the cows were milked—*and* in great haste. No one else rushes as frantically from cows to cauldron (Claude hurled his milk containers into a pickup truck, sped down the steep slope, and then literally ran into his cheese-making facility), owing to the belief that you need to convert the milk to cheese at the veritable body temperature of the cow (which, frankly, is impossible unless you're milking in your living room) or else risk losing some of its delicate flavors.

The cows themselves are curiosities: only one of two breeds, either a Tarine or an Abondance. The names are meaningless until you discover that they are both quasi-worshipped and unique: small, with oversized lungs and muscular legs, and a striking capacity to eat on pastures verging on the perpendicular (a perplexing sight, to see an animal situated thus, at a right angle, grazing). They must be milked twice a day, in the dark early morning and the early evening. I tried the milking myself and, to the astonishment of my hosts, failed to persuade an udder to relinquish so much as a drop. (I also learned that each cow has a name, and comes when called, except Minette, who is mischievous and is always trying to get back into the milking trailer for a second round of reward pellets, and whom Claude asked me to chase away, and I failed at *that*, too, my useless two-legged milking stool still strapped to my waist, and he had to intervene and clap his hands threateningly.)

It is extreme, this Alpage cheese, which is why I came. I found myself wondering: How can you not love the French? Really. No irony. How can you *not* love a people who, isolated, in a field or a stable or a vineyard, far from normal society, no one looking, left to their own devices, obsess over their food or drink, worry it, and strive for an expression of purity that would be not just baffling but incomprehensible to their agricultural counterparts just about everywhere else in the world?

The fromage blanc, meanwhile, can now be made into a Beaufort by a simple process: by turning up the heat a further twenty degrees Celsius, and not via the agency of a device that has a knob. Here at seven thousand feet we stack up wood for a fire.

I pitch in, feeling awkward, an interloper in somebody else's efficient twice-daily routine, and fetch sticks from outside to stack underneath the cauldron. They light quickly. Claude stirs and rakes his thickening mush, trying to stay out of the way of the smoke. He finishes by submerging a large square of the appositely named "cheesecloth" beneath his floating curds and lifts them out by the cloth's four corners, water draining through, hundreds of gallons of it, sloppily, splashingly everywhere. Thus, the rain gear.

Afterward, Claude offers me a bowl of still-warm milk.

I go outside and find a flat boulder to sit on. It is adjacent to a sluicing stream and on the edge of a long green meadow. The green is very bright. The sky, too, has a peculiarly deep blue, as if outer space were showing through. Is it the thinness of the air? The open long-distance pastures without landmarks? Everything around me looks magnified, especially the sun and its dangerous-seeming Alpine light. The fast stream sounds like water shouting.

I have never drunk milk from a cow that has just been milked. Will it make me sick? I stare at it. Will it taste green?

Glise told me that there are sixty varieties of wild grasses growing here, in a single square meter. *"Là!"* he said, pointing to wherever we then happened to be standing. *"Les herbes sauvages."* These grasses, he said, are why he brings his cows here.

At my feet, there is an impressively knee-high flourishing: yellow flowers crammed up against white ones, pink, then red, then an outbreak of tall furry stalky things. Are there really sixty varieties? It seems possible, except that the "grass" looks like leaves, not grass, and the leaves are all different shapes. One might be wild arugula. What a thought: that the taste of Beaufort, among the most French of French cheeses, *le prince du fromage,* is derived from a diet of Italian salads that cows spend a whole summer eating.

This space, *"là,"* crowded and without a pattern, seems like a botany lesson in hyper-growth: Take a patch of ground, deprive it of light, bury it in snow, and then—finally, *now*—expose it to the extremes of an extreme high season. I have seen this before. It is a feature of both high mountains and high latitudes, where plants, as the earth tilts into the direction of the full-on sun, pass from germination to flowering to fruit in what can seem like hours. Extreme seasonalities, like the tropics, produce extreme foods. But the high-altitude flavors that you find here—in the proliferation of wild berries (straw-, black-, rasp-, blue-, cloud-, cow-, bear-), or the herbs and flowers, like my favorite *génépi* (*genepi* in Italian), one of the principal aromatics in Chartreuse, culled only in August and only at ten thousand feet and only for a single week—have an airy gentleness. They have qualities that are more subtle than what our conventional flavor vocabulary describes. They seem, somehow, to express "sunshine" and "gratitude."

I set my bowl on the boulder and slip off.

The ritual of taking animals to the high ground is called the "transhumance," a Latin word (*trans + humus,* "earth," "dirt"), harking back to an ancient peasant practice. The animals, dressed up with flower necklaces, extra bells, and colorful blankets, are paraded through the village and, with much hoopla and music making, up the mountain. After a recent trip to the Canadian Rockies—where the forest's wild ruminants, moose, bighorn sheep, elk, come down to the valley at the end of winter, but instantly go up to the high mountains to graze once the snow clears—I have come to suspect that the transhumance practice predates society, that it harks back to an era when aurochs roamed what we now call France, that wild animals have always known how and where to eat, and that it was early peasants who learned from animals and not animals that needed to be directed by peasants.

The appeal of a mountain myth—that rennet was discovered by a wild man dressed in branches—is that it is probably true. One of the earliest vehicles for cheese making is said to have been in Sicily: a baby goat's stomach. That is where the curdling takes place. And before? Cheese making was discovered by hunter-gatherers. It is the eternal principle of hunting: Eat everything. Cheese was in the tummies of the baby animals they killed. We learned our know-how of the process from them, the hunter-gatherers, the wild men.

Maybe it is altitude or the strange clarity of the light or simply that I haven't had much sleep, but I find that I am on the verge of making connections that probably aren't entirely logical or sensible, but feel, almost, as if they should be.

Like the fact that there are so many different kinds of cheese in France, more than anywhere else in the world, twelve hundred of the twenty-two hundred unique European varieties, according to Michel Bouvier, the former curator of food and drink at the Gallo-Roman museum near Vienne. And now, my hands still smelling of milk, I find it miraculous that there would be so many. The miracle isn't because France has a varied landscape with varied food-making practices arising out of it, although it does; it is implicit in the sheer antiquity of how long cheeses have been made here, each one originating out of a specificity of place that is probably pre-civilization, when the horizon was not much more than the perimeters of where you could walk in a day. Each cheese is necessarily unlike any other and could well date back thousands of years, to the hunters and gatherers and auroch slayers. And each cheese was essential to survival, especially in winter or in famine, an efficient piece of protein that met the caloric needs of a hungry family when there was nothing else.

What French cheese is now seems more complex, I find myself reflecting, because most families have enough food to get through the winter and yet, as though a rite, continue to end their meals with cheese. They are trained to end their meals with it. The boys do in their schools. It is a cultural imperative. Why? Is it that eating a piece of cheese is, more than any other food, akin to honoring a piece of place? Is it that, in preserving and continuing to cultivate twelve hundred unique and mainly handmade cheeses, the French express their respect for food and its relationship to the dirt it comes from?

Claude appears. I feel I am also seeing some kind of connection to extreme seasonality and the magic of this Alpine sun, and make an effort to share my ramblings with him. He seems to understand and even, possibly, to agree.

He then kicks a dense green-leaf outcropping nearby. The soil breaks up a little—it is less dirt than a network of roots—and he pulls out some plants with his hand. It is the soil he wants me to look at, the subterranean chaos of it. It is foamy, complicated, the fibrous stuff of decomposition.

"Humus," he says.

"Humus," I repeat. It is the same word in French and English and Latin.

Humus: It is the fertility of the soil. It is the capital of nations. It is how the earth dies and is reborn. It is, according to Albert Howard, now regarded as the godfather of organic farming (he died in 1947), what you find in unmanipulated nature, in the forest, in an open meadow, amid the high-altitude stretches of the *alpage,* and on rustic farms, where peasants "can tell by a glance at the crop whether or not the soil is rich" and where plant life—in what is perhaps Howard's most quirkily brilliant observation—develops "something approaching personality." Howard wrote mainly in the 1920s and '30s, when science, having discovered agriculture, was just setting out to make it more efficient, more profitable, and he witnessed firsthand the consequences of pesticides and chemical fertilizers and the disregard—the destruction, in fact—of humus: a slow poisoning of our dirt that is, in his description, "one of the greatest calamities which has befallen agriculture and mankind."

Humus. It introduced itself to Jessica and me, the boys on our shoulders, as we walked through that wild wheat field after our *saucisson* tasting, our first spring in Lyon, the messy dirt, full of sticky decomposing stuff, with insects gnawing at our ankles.

It figures in a film, *Natural Resistance* by Jonathan Nossiter, in a scene in northern Italy, featuring a winemaker, Stefano Bellotti, on a dirt road that separates two properties. One is Bellotti's.

"We are standing on the same slope of the same hill and these two soils"—Bellotti gestures to his land and his neighbor's—"are identical."

His neighbor's vines look like what we expect a vineyard to be. The rows between them have no weeds. They are tidy. The earth looks as though it could have been swept. It is appealing to the eye.

Bellotti's plot is a mess. A tumble of weeds and grasses.

"Let's take a shovel," Bellotti says. *Andiamo a prendere una vangata di terra.*

He walks to a spot between his vines and pushes the blade into the earth and turns it over. It is loose and red and brown and yellow. It is busy to look at: roots, straw, much of it decomposing, mulch, worms. "There are several generations of grass here." Last summer's, the year before's. "A kind of digestion is obviously at work," he says. Albert Howard uses the same word, "digestion."

"Let's look at my neighbor's," Bellotti says.

The cameraman follows and stops and asks nervously, *"Vado?"* Isn't this trespassing?

Bellotti shrugs.

He walks in among the vines and makes to slide the shovel into the earth. It doesn't budge. He steps on it, wiggles it, and then it breaks the crust. He turns it over. It is uniform in color and texture. It is gray. It is compacted. It looks like cement. Nothing stirs.

"Smell it," Bellotti instructs the cameraman. "It smells of laundry detergent.

"Wine is a cultural commodity," Bellotti explains, "and it commands an unusually high price." Bellotti, a small producer, working fifty acres of land, makes a living. He is threatened by his neighbors, he is harassed and fined for not using pesticides—"This year the fines might be as much as one hundred fifty thousand euros"—but he can get by because of the commercial value of what he produces.

"But grain farmers, they're more vulnerable."

An image comes to mind of my drive through the French "breadbasket," miles and miles of a mono-colored monoculture, arid, still, like death.

I finally sip my bowl of milk. It doesn't taste green. It isn't even obviously fatty. But it is good. I have another sip. It is long in the mouth, the milkiness lingering after swallowing. Is it a little fruity? It is certainly sweet. Mainly it is good because it tastes fully of milk. I am surprised by it. It seems to be healthy and alive and tastes overwhelmingly of itself.

I slide off my boulder and bounce. The dirt is spongy. I knock back the rest of the milk, and try to spot the cows on the mountain, and I can't.

PARIS

In one of my routine fantasies, Michel Richard flies to Lyon. We speak French. I bring him to La Mère Brazier, seat him in the bar, and make his dinner, perhaps the *caneton* with a thick dribble of cherry-veal sauce, or the *poulet de Bresse,* with the truffle under the skin. I put him up not at the Villa Florentine, because he would be provoked by its Italianness, but at Le Royal, on the Place Bellecour, where Bocuse students now prepare the breakfast. In the morning, we visit Bob—born in Brittany, like Richard—and discuss what it is that makes his bread unique. For lunch, we go to Paul Bocuse. In my fantasy, I show Richard that, inspired by him, I have made Lyon, and its kitchens, my home.

When I started at La Mère Brazier, I phoned him. I urged him to come. "Maybe."

I phoned again, around Christmas.

"Maybe in the summer," he said.

In August, he called. "I am coming," he said, but not to Lyon. Paris. "My hotel is always the George V," he said, grandly flamboyant. "And then we'll go to the Ardennes, where I grew up and first worked in a kitchen."

Richard landed at Orly, via an experimental all-business-class service in which Richard was the "visiting" chef for the season and was rewarded with first-class air travel. I stood opposite the automatic doors by the immigration and customs agents. The last time I had seen him, when he dropped me off at Union Station, France was an abstract and intimidating idea.

Richard appeared, dressed in a capacious purple T-shirt, a shoulder bag for luggage, the familiar smells of wine and sweat, a miraculous sight, fast-talking, thrilled to be in Paris, explosively effervescent. He was traveling with his business manager, Carl, who reported that Richard had entertained passengers with stories of his first *stage,* working for Monsieur Sauvage. "Michel didn't sleep," Carl said, "but, then, neither did anyone else."

We went to a bistro for dinner, Le Petit Marius, wobbly wood chairs, small tables, chalkboard menu, loud and hot and perfect. Richard, still in high performance mode, engaged every female within chatting-up distance: the waitress (complimenting her on her English), a woman sitting nearby waiting for a boyfriend ("How can he make you wait? Don't you know that every man here would abandon everything to spend the rest of his life with you?"), a woman at another banquette ("I am sorry, mademoiselle, but you are so beautiful I cannot concentrate on my food").

The diners, Parisians, were confused by Richard's outgoingness, his lack of inhibitions, his un-Frenchness, and his accent.

"Where are you from?" a man asked. (Richard had just sung an aria of weakness and infatuation.)

"From here! Like you!"

"But your accent. It's not Canadian, but it's not—"

"Yes! It's French, just like yours!"

I had never understood Richard's French when I was in his kitchen. In a language that I now followed, he was more fully dimensioned, as if I had known only half of him. He attacked the most hackneyed phrases with ironic vigor (how the staff at his hotel were *"très gentils,"* or the restaurant was *"très joli,"* and the wine *"très, très bon"*). I said *"Loire"* as "Lwah," without pronouncing the final "r," and Richard roared the word back at me with a full guttural roll at the end. *"Feuilletée,"* he corrected, when I told him how I was finally making puff pastry—"No, not *'foy'* like 'foil' "—and he did that thing that young Frederick can do, rendering what had seemed like a simple word into the multisyllabic aural equivalent of a caterpillar.

But when our *plats principaux* arrived, roasted chicken for both Richard and me (the test of a bistro's competence), and he asked for *"le plus grand,"* the biggest serving, and I asked for *"le meilleur,"* the best, Richard erupted in a high-pitched and joyous laugh.

"Tomorrow," he said, "we travel to the past."

———

We boarded a local train that passed the vineyards of Champagne, slate roofs, shiny-damp from a morning fog, the sad battlefields of World War I, and the famous Forest of the Ardennes. Richard hadn't been on this track in forty years. "My face then was covered in black ash when I hung my head out of the window." A steam-engine memory. The line ended at Charleville-Mézières, where Richard had his first full-time job as a pastry chef. We found it, and Richard boisterously introduced himself to the pastry shop's owner, startling him considerably, then tasted his chocolates (and then spat them out when he wasn't looking). "They're very hard. I wanted to tell him how to make them softer, with walnut oil for lightness, but what is the point?" He looked at a display case. It was messy, colors running murkily among ill-shaped stacks of macarons.

We rented a car and drove north, the river Meuse on our right, toward Belgium. Fumay, forty minutes away, a village on a cliff, was our first stop and where his family had moved to on leaving Brittany, surrounded by factories, "thirteen of them," all within walking distance. He pointed to windows on a top floor. "That was our home. A family of six that was about to become seven" (because his mother was pregnant again).

"That was where Father came home, walked to the kitchen, and started beating my mother, who was pregnant, knocked her down, and kicked her in the stomach. I broke a wine bottle and tried to stab him. I wanted to kill him." He paused. "I wonder if he had just learned that my mother had a daughter and a son before he met her. He probably had."

A square prefabricated building a few miles farther was once a disco where Richard, in a new collarless Sgt. Pepper–inspired Nehru shirt, showed up on a Friday night one October and met a girl named Monique; they danced, and they kissed, and they had "bong-bong," and he stayed the night, and they had "bong-bong" the next day, and more "bong-bong" the day after, and he returned to Charleville-Mézières because he was expected at work. She then tracked him down and announced that she was pregnant.

In Givet, Richard asked me to stop at the church where the two had been married on Bastille Day in 1967. We went inside, and he lit a candle.

Givet is where Richard remembered growing up—he was eight, when he arrived—a fortress town, on the border with Belgium. The factory where his mother worked was on the outskirts, a one-floor assembly-line construct, abandoned now, looking like an ancient monastery with a courtyard. There was a row of row houses. We stood by a low wall and looked into his childhood home from the back, the garden a bounty of summer vegetables with outsized lettuce, zucchini, eggplant, green and yellow peppers. From Richard's original telling—he described chickens, rabbits, ducks, fish caught from a stream across the road—I'd imagined a place on the edge of nature. The countryside wasn't far away ("My mother spotted rabbit tracks in the snow and would set a trap"), but it wasn't in the least country. It was more that his mother's economies (preserving green beans, strawberries, tomatoes, meat in Mason jars) were country practices that she knew and that could be applied in the city, a large family in a tough factory community, trying to make ends meet.

"There was a schoolteacher who thought that I had creeeeativity," Richard said, stretching out the word self-mockingly. "He lived here." He pointed to a house two doors down the street. Something in the window of the schoolteacher's former home caught Richard's eye, and he was momentarily lost to me. It was a kitchen table. Richard was staring at it and seeming to imagine his younger self sitting at it.

We got back in the car. Monsieur Sauvage was our next stop.

I asked Richard, "When did you realize that you had a talent that people were prepared to pay money for?"

"Oh, I don't really make so much money."

"But you have an ability to surprise, an inventiveness, a creeeeeativiteee that means you have something that others don't have, and you will always be paid to open eateries, feed people on trains, or airplanes. Your pastry shop in Los Angeles, your many restaurants—"

"It's true; twice, I've made more than a million dollars a year." He reflected. "You don't make much money as a cook. Or as a chef. You have to be a *patron*." He gave the word its strong French pronunciation. "When I came to New York for Gaston Lenôtre, I made seven hundred dollars a month. One month later, I was in Santa Fe, running my own pastry shop and making five thousand dollars a month."

He thought further. "Actually, it was Gaston Lenôtre. He showed me that I had something."

We drove on.

As we approached Carignan, factories appeared, built the size of airport hangars, now abandoned. When we arrived, Richard declared: "Where are all the people? On Saturdays, it used to be so crowded you couldn't cross the square. There were festivals and fairs and dances. Where did everyone go?"

We visited the original pâtisserie, now owned by a chain and run by a husband and wife. "This was my first *stage*!" Richard told them, forever exuberant, and they recoiled with alarm, as if at any moment he was about to produce a document that proved it was his place and not theirs.

Afterward, we sat in a parking lot, directly behind. The family was having lunch, and eyed us uneasily through a back window.

"I arrived on August 29, 1962." (Richard remembered every important day in his life with a preternatural calendar specificity.) "My first day was September 1. We started at seven a.m. and had to be in a little bed upstairs by midnight, with a jug of water and a bowl, no days off except a half-day on Sunday."

Léon, eighteen years old, was the chef. "He liked to hit me. You make a mistake, you get smacked. 'You burned your croissants!' Smack. 'You didn't clean this corner!' Smack. 'You cooked a meringue in a copper pot!' Smack. 'You ground the almonds too fast and the rollers are stuck! *Imbécile! Putain de merde!* You don't make mistakes!'" Education by humiliation.

"I was at my station, my back to the kitchen, and a knife flew by my head and pierced the wall in front of me. The chef thought it was funny."

Richard hit him on the head with a rolling pin and knocked him unconscious. Finally, the two had established a rapport.

"For three years, I never went home. I never saw a movie. I learned everything: *apprendre, apprendre, apprendre.*"

On September 3, 1965, Richard took his pâtisserie proficiency exams. The French system: You do an apprenticeship, you take an exam, and you are certified. He was now a trained chef.

"Monsieur Sauvage never did any work, except at Christmas, when we started at four a.m. and worked until ten at night. But Monsieur Sauvage loved me. He never said so. But I could tell." After Richard left, he phoned Monsieur Sauvage every year, just before the new year, thanking him for taking him on. "He gave me something. He passed on a body of knowledge." When Richard was in Los Angeles, by then established and very successful, he still phoned—"With best wishes for the new year and gratitude for being my first teacher of pâtisserie"—until, finally, he was told that Monsieur Sauvage could not come to the phone, because he had died.

The next day was our last day, and we were returning to Paris.

On the train back, I riffed.

I talked about acids in French foods ("In the United States, no one uses vinegar—in France, no one doesn't"), my new love of mustard, my children's love of *very* spicy mustard, their appreciation of mayonnaise, and how I now made it at home, and how Frederick, having eaten it so often at school, could smell my making it from the other side of the apartment.

"Can you smell mayonnaise?" he asked. (I panicked: What? You can't?) And he then added, quietly, "I add a little bit of crème fraîche at the end"—a tip, to which I, still in high-riff mode, managed to say, "Oh. That's interesting," and carried on babbling. How French food is built on making opposites work: butter sauces (suspending fat and liquid), or foams like sabayon (fat and acid), or the magic of puff pastry.

"I have a theory about when French food became French," I then said.

"Really?" Richard said.

"Nostradamus, in the 1550s. His treatise on jam making."

"Really?"

"Sugar," I said.

I described the flavor of the cherries of the Rhône Valley, their sweet-tart intensities, and the Mère Brazier sauce that went with duck, and how I then made a jam with the cherries afterward, fascinated by the molecular change that occurs before your eyes, the sugar ratio finally making the water hotter than boiling.

Richard nodded (and I thought: He thinks I'm off my rocker, doesn't he?).

I talked about my irritations.

"So much French cooking history is anecdotal and unexamined. Like, why does everyone stick a clove in an onion when they make chicken stock?"

"A clove in an onion?"

"Yes, you see it in every French chef's chicken-stock recipe. You peel an onion and push a clove into it. Why?"

"Oh, yes, that is true." He nodded, a small gesture, like a professor entertaining an overexcited student during office hours.

What was I trying to prove? I paused.

"Have you eaten at Alain Chapel?" he asked.

"Yes!" I said.

"Did you eat the foie blanc?"

Did I eat the foie blanc? I couldn't remember.

"Really? It is a famous dish. And what about Marc Meneau, in Vézelay?"

"Yes! L'Espérance!" It was where Jessica, a sixteen-year-old school-year-abroad student, had experienced her first meal made by a grand chef. We went there for an anniversary.

"And the foie-gras bonbons?"

"Yes!" I said, as if I'd got a quiz answer right.

Had I eaten at L'Auberge de Paul Bocuse?

I had!

"Did you eat the *bar en croûte*?" Sea bass in puff pastry with a *sauce Choron*.

"No, but I've made it."

"Really? Was the pastry cooked through?"

"Yes!" The pastry hadn't been the problem. It was its appearance. Like a massive prehistoric pollywog that had been stepped on by a dinosaur.

"What about the *filet de sole Fernand Point*?"

"No." I hadn't eaten it yet. I have since. The dish defies understanding in its deliciousness: perfectly cooked sole mixed in with fresh tagliatelle, plus copious quantities of butter. No one in Italy would do such a thing to a plate of pasta, and the idea, to an Italian, would be horrific. But trust me: genius.

"And you've eaten at La Pyramide?"

"Yes!"

"But it's not like it once was, is it?" Richard said. "The young man there—what's his name?"

"Patrick Henriroux..."

"Yes, Henriroux. He's fine. But he's not Point. Point was a *grand* chef." He drew out the word *grand,* rendering it with its fullest cultural heft. Richard then paused, as though in silent wonderment at the high mountain of achievement that had been Fernand Point.

"When you make your puff pastry," Richard asked, as though curious, "do you use water?"

"To make the *pâton?*" *Pâton* is the piece of dough that you fold the butter into. "Yes."

"I never use water. It's a rule. Sometimes a sweet wine like a Sauternes, or apple juice, or pear. I love pear."

I made a note in my notebook: Don't use water.

"Do you make it with butter?"

"The puff pastry? Well, yes."

"Sometimes I make it with foie gras." He paused. "You need to understand what is producing the effect in a recipe. What kind of flour do you use?"

"Normal flour, fifty-five-weight." In France, flour is sold according to its protein content. Pastry flour is the lightest (thirty-five-weight), bread among the highest (up to 110-weight).

"I use bread flour."

"Bread flour?"

"Because you want gluten development. You want the pastry to stretch and puff."

He continued.

"Fish sauce? It is better if you add mussel juice at the end."

Madeleines?

"Yes! I make them with my leftover egg whites."

"Oh, I also use the yolks. My measurements are one, one, one, and one. One egg. One cup of butter. One cup of flour. One cup of sugar. Baking powder?" he asked.

"No."

"Good. Are they booby?"

"Booby? Yes, I think so. They're pretty booby."

"Booby is good."

"Do you get the booby by whipping?" I asked.

"I whip only the butter. Sometimes I use a little bicarbonate."

I mentioned making a Béarnaise for *le personnel.*

"I make mine with olive oil and basil."

"Whoa. A Béarnaise with olive oil?"

Apples: He peeled them by dropping them whole into a fryer, then dipping the fruit in ice and removing the peel with a towel. "It is then a perfect apple, no knife marks. I do the same with cherry tomatoes."

I'd brought a book. I kept forgetting to show it to him. It was Gaston Lenôtre's first, published in 1975.

Richard stared at it. "I worked on this book." He continued to stare, as though afraid to open it. A tear beaded up on the lip of each eye, which he wiped away with the back of his hand. David Bouley had told me that Richard was a secret author. "I tested them all. I wrote many."

"Can you remember which ones?"

He considered. "No."

He slipped the book into his bag.

I had come to France, learned the language, attended a cooking school, worked in restaurant kitchens, and only now was I understanding Richard's achievement. In Washington, he had seemed like a magician. He wasn't. But he might be a genius.

I accompanied Richard back to the George V. The weekend marked *la rentrée,* and the city, so empty and beautiful when we left it, was now congested and loud.

What is Citronelle like now? I asked.

"Oh, you didn't know?" Citronelle had closed. The hotel was deemed unsafe—the sinking foundation, its tilting walls, its leaking roof. "We had to evacuate."

Citronelle closed? And I didn't know? In Richard's company, I had been so transported into another time, *his* time, that I never thought about his life in the United States.

"And David?"

"He is at Central." Richard's Franco-American bistro.

"But, Michel, you don't have a restaurant?"

"It's true. I will find something. I always have a restaurant."

VII

Italy (Obviously)

How to roast and garnish turtledoves and quails in various ways

Take the turtledove in season, which is from June through November, and, as soon as it is dead, pluck it clean and cook it briefly over coals without gutting it, then put it on a spit over a robust fire, turning it quickly so the fat does not drip underneath; and when it is almost done, dredge it in flour, fennel pollen, sugar, salt, and bread crumbs. When fully cooked, it should be served hot.

To tell the young from the old turtledoves, you need to know that the young have darker meat and whiter feet, and the older white meat and red feet.

You can roast quail in this same way when it is fat and in season, which starts in mid-August and lasts to the end of October. Even though in spring you see a lot of flocks passing over Rome, and even more near Ostia and Porto, they are not as good as they are in their season.

Sometimes fat quail are cured with salt and fennel pollen; you leave them in a wooden or earthenware bowl for three or four days, and then sauté them in melted lard with chives and serve hot with black pepper on top. You also can split them in half and marinate for a day or so, then flour them and fry in melted lard. Serve them hot with sugar and bitter orange juice or with the marinade.

BARTOLOMEO SCAPPI, *OPERA DELL'ARTE DEL CUCINARE*
(*ON THE ART OF COOKING*), 1570,
TRANSLATED BY JESSICA GREEN

When Jessica and I were living in Panzano, in Tuscany, and I was working at a butcher shop, I used to walk there in the mornings on a small road called Via Giovanni da Verrazzano. Verrazzano was the Italian explorer who discovered the water inlet now known as New York Harbor. Today the long suspension bridge connecting Staten Island and Long Island is named after him, traversing the bay where the explorer had probably dropped anchor. Verrazzano was born in a fortified castle overlooking the market town of Greve, ten miles north of the village of Panzano, and I enjoyed the connection between my Italian village home and my American urban one.

In Lyon, my walk to La Mère Brazier began with the walled mural across the street from our home, the *fresque* of the Lyonnais, a history of the city in pictures. One painting was eye-level with our third-story apartment, and I saw it every time I opened the shutters. It was of a bearded man with an ermine-lined coat, a compass in one hand and a globe in the other. Who was he? Eventually I discovered an inconspicuous square of text at the bottom of the wall. It was a legend to the pictures. The bearded guy, it said, was "Jean Verrazane, the famous Lyonnais explorer who discovered New York Harbor."

Verrazane? Is this a Frenchified Verrazzano? Was the hero of New York Harbor from a castle near my Chianti village, or a French guy from my newly adopted home in Lyon? He was both.

Just about all food historians are familiar with the aforementioned Catherine de' Medici myth: The Florentine bride made her way to

France, by land or by boat (the myth has different versions), and then embarked on teaching the lowly Gauls how to cook. There is a man on the moon, there is a tooth fairy, and there's the Italian Catherine, inventor of *la cuisine française*. The idea can't even be argued. It no longer warrants a footnote. It is dead.

Given its longevity—there are references to the idea dating from the eighteenth century—its passing is a relatively recent event. This occurred in 1983, the year when the American librarian Barbara Ketcham Wheaton killed it. Wheaton is the curator of the culinary collection at the Radcliffe Institute for Advanced Studies, in Cambridge, Massachusetts. In 1983, she published *Savoring the Past: The French Kitchen and Table from 1300 to 1789,* one of the first efforts to treat early recipes as historical documents, in which she deals with this Queen Catherine nonsense in a brisk, dismissive two pages.

How old was Catherine when she came to France? she asks.

Fourteen.

Who was she? The Medici equivalent of a princess: a *child* in an arranged marriage with a prince.

What, seriously, would she have known about the kitchen? And, at *that* age, from *that* family, en route to a *royal* wedding, she was also meant to have crossed the Alps? No, Wheaton says, enough mythologizing, I'm not buying it. Besides, she took a boat to Marseille.

It was a riff, but with enough conviction that it has been accepted as a historical truth and is now cited in reference books in both English and French, but especially in French. *Savoring the Past* was published in France in 1994, where it is celebrated in academic circles for its kiboshing of *the* myth. It informs *Un Festin en paroles* (*A Feast in Words*), a popular literary history of gastronomy, written by the late Jean-François Revel, a philosopher-journalist. His chapter on the Italians is entitled "The Ghost of the Medicis."

Now, after five years in the city, I have a different view.

Yes, actually, the Italians *did* teach the French to cook. But it wasn't only the work of the Italian queen, although she *was* demonstrably interested in cuisine and she did employ Italian chefs in the royal kitchens in Blois. She wasn't the active agent. It was her French father-in-law, François Premier, who wanted Italy—or at least its northern provinces—so much that he went to war three times to try to possess them. But it wasn't just the territory that he wanted. It was the Italian Renaissance. He wanted its culture, its buildings (all those ornate Italian-built châteaux on the river Loire), its music, its sense of fête, its spices, and its silks (he hired the two greatest silk makers, Turquet and Naris, in Piedmont, to move to Lyon, and rewarded them richly enough that one bought a residence in Vieux Lyon, at the end of an alley still called Impasse Turquet). He invited painters and poets and sculptors and architects, and housed them in his royal home, and spoke Italian with them at the table. And of course he made Leonardo—*the* Leonardo da Vinci—his immediate neighbor and friend.

In Catherine de' Medici, François Premier wanted (and got) the most sought-after Italian bride for his son. The marriage was the culmination of the Renaissance in France: and its future.

Lyon, for more than a hundred years, was already, in the words of one local historian, home to a colony of Italians. In 1467, some of them, mainly residents of Vieux Lyon, directly across the Saône from our home, gave themselves a constitution and declared themselves a nation: *la nation florentine de Lyon*. Only after my discovery of "Verrazane" did I come to appreciate just how powerful their influence on the city had been. By the time Catherine de' Medici arrived there as queen—eighty-one years later, in 1548, after her husband had been crowned King Henri II—Lyon was already extravagantly Italian. The city commemorated the royal visit with a week of feasting and drinking, with boat promenades on the river Saône (a barge dressed up as a fire-breathing dragon), publications of poetry, displays of fireworks, and performances of music and theatre so outlandish that merchants went bankrupt in the aftermath. In effect, the city celebrated the occasion by a very expensive pop-up version of a Frenchified Italian Renaissance. (Richard Cooper's extraordinary *The Entry of Henri II into Lyon* depicts, in itself, a Lyon so dominated, if not outright overrun, by Italians in their High Renaissance extravagance as to make it very challenging, today, to credit historians who dismiss their influence.) Or, as one foreign diplomat could be paraphrased to have said, in one of his letters home, having gone sleepless for three days during one of Catherine's (later) visits, "These Italian French sure know how to party."

These Florentine Lyonnais included members of the Medici family and the Medicis' rival, the Gadagnes. They established banking and foreign-currency exchange on a scale never before known in France. They enlarged the idea of a wholesale market, mainly by way of the *foires,* which they largely underwrote. Owing to Italian investment, hundreds of tons of spices (and silks and wines and foods) entered Lyon either by barge up the Rhône River or by pack animals through an Alpine pass from Turin. Because of the Italians, Lyon looked like a mini Florence with the sway of French Venice. It remains, like a movie set, a labyrinth of alleyways and teetering buildings and endless basement tunnels and secret villas with private gardens and red tile roofs and high stone walls evocative of an era otherwise unreachable—and honored by UNESCO as the largest example of Renaissance architecture in the world.

Venture capitalization, another Medici and Gadagne specialty, included funding wars. They also funded, or contributed to funding, explorations across the Atlantic, hoping to locate a passage to the Far East, or to stake a claim on a new territory. When Verrazzano came to visit them looking for funds to sail to the New World (and who like many Italians in Lyon had changed his name to sound French), the Italian bankers persuaded François Premier to fund him.

And the food? A review of the *pre*-Catherine chronology is illuminating.

In 1494, twenty-five years *before* Catherine was born, the *foires* were re-established.

In 1505, fourteen years *before* Catherine was born, a Lyonnais printer produced the first French translation of Platina—the plagiarist of the very gifted Maestro Martino. (Printing began in Lyon in 1473, and Lyon became the premier cultural printer in France until the Revolution.)

In 1528, when Catherine was nine, another Lyonnais printing house published an improved "translation" of Platina. (There was no copyright, and the publisher, effectively regarded as the author, could do whatever he wanted.) During the next twenty years, there would be many other editions. Tomasik, my American culinary historian, analyzed the *fourteen* different French translations of Platina, "each one an improvement." Each successive translation, Tomasik said, "drifted further and further from the original, and became more and more French, until finally the book ceased to be Italian at all." Platina became, bit by bit, one of the first important texts of the French kitchen. On the question of the Italian influence, it was both metaphor and evidence.

In 1532, when Catherine was thirteen, the medical doctor, poet, narrative impresario, and gourmandizing raconteur François Rabelais arrived in the city and published his first book, *Pantagruel*. It was a hymn to eating—you could call it "variations on a theme of excess"—documenting the original Lyonnais menu: pork, chicken, *saucisson*, including the new "rosette," and lots and lots of red wine.

In 1541, when Catherine dei Medici was twenty-two and now a French princess (now Catherine de' Médici), another cookbook was translated from the Italian: *Bastiment de receptes, nouvellement traduict de italien en langue françoyse*. Lyon—where the interest in food was, well, Rabelaisian—was by now the capital of books about cuisine.

In 1547, Rabelais, at the invitation of French Cardinal Jean du Bellay, attended a celebration of a prince's birth in Rome and wrote about the feast he witnessed—with multiple courses and flamboyant presentations—unlike anything that he had seen in France.

In 1548, that feast held to welcome Swiss ambassadors to Lyon was unusual enough in its ambition and its scope (the multi-courses, the flamboyance, the wit) that a record of the meal was made and published.

And it was also in 1548, on September 23 (just months after yet another "improved" edition of Platina was published), that Henri II and Catherine de' Medici first entered Lyon. Is it possible that, amid all this, Catherine's entourage, floating majestically down the Saône, included a boat of Italian cooks? Is it likely that, along the quai, a pack of donkeys marched in tandem, bearing panniers of the vegetables and cheeses and cured meats that Italians have alleged that she introduced to France?

No. Because they were already there.

BLOIS. On another trip to the Loire, I uncovered a secret possession of Catherine de' Medici.

We were in the Royal Castle in Blois for an unusually specific exhibit, "Les Festins de la Renaissance," about eating and drinking in the sixteenth century, the very period when the French kitchen was about to be born. A *festin* is a celebratory banquet or gala, a feast. Blois was the royal home of, among others, Catherine de' Medici and her sons. The exhibit was in the castle and gathered up two hundred years of kitchen artifacts, mainly from Italy and France: books, tools, dishes, menus. They illustrated how the French ate at the beginning of the period, with a *tranche,* a piece of bread for scooping, and then a knife for cutting (guests arrived with their own blades), and at the end, with early ornate examples of forks acquired from Italy, including one that could be kept in your pocket (you brought it with you when invited to dinner). The exhibition included a long kitchen scroll, on which Niccolò Alamanni, Catherine de' Medici's chef, wrote out family meals. It could almost be seen as "the smoking gun"—the chef (an Italian) writing out instructions (in Italian) of (Italian) dishes for the sons of an Italian mother and the future kings of France. The parchment was a wonder to come upon, the rich vellum, the care of the presentation, its flamboyant script, this act of feeding France.

We met the historian of the castle's museum, joined him at a Renaissance re-enactment lunch (guinea hen in a pot, carp in a sauce, fava beans in saffron, marzipan according to a recipe by Nostradamus), and were told that the exhibit was just a pretense. The real excitement was the conference occasioned by it. It would be the first time that historians gathered to discuss who had invented French cuisine: The French? The Italians? Or the French and the Italians?

"There will be no resolution," he promised. "The French don't listen to the Italians. The Italians won't listen to the French."

After lunch, I drove with my family downriver to Amboise to show them Leonardo da Vinci's home, where the boys ran in the gardens among the re-creations of his inventions. Seeing the two exhibits on the same visit—the treasures, largely Italian, of the French sixteenth-century kitchen, and the treasures, entirely Italian, of a Renaissance genius—was powerfully affecting. There were three paintings, historical reimaginings, of the king holding the hand of a weakened Leonardo in his last days. Leonardo, the almost incomprehensibly brilliant embodiment of the Italian Renaissance, died in a bed that François Premier had given him.

At the conference, I learned about the fifteenth-century Italian obsession with lemons. I learned, to my surprise, that Catherine de' Medici, during her ascendancy, introduced a breed of Italian cows to France and implemented innovations in animal care. Timothy Tomasik read another paper, on the many French translations of Platina. Marjorie Meiss-Even, a scholar at the University of Lille, read her findings from a kitchen inventory that she had discovered among the archives of the powerful Guise family, in which, bit by bit, Italian ingredients began appearing around the 1550s, some acquired at the *foires* in Lyon, some via travelers—asparagus, artichokes, shallots, citrus, even Parmigiano, so-called *fromage de Milan*—until, finally, they became essentials in the French diet. It was a stunning piece of research, and the room was reverentially still through the reading of it.

At some point, I found myself wondering how many *"preuves incontestables"* do you need before the proof is, in fact, incontestable.

In many respects, the conference was insistently about one figure: Scappi. Scappi was the ghost. He was there, and he wasn't.

Bartolomeo Scappi is—owing to a multi-volume book written in 1570, at the end of his working life (called simply *Opera, the Works, of the Private Cook to the Pope*)—universally recognized to be the greatest chef of the European Renaissance. It is nine hundred pages long and meticulously detailed—it is, in fact, the first known illustrated cookbook in history, an evocative celebration of what a grand sixteenth-century kitchen looked like—and has become a reference for how the food was cooked in it, and with what tools. It includes menus for three-day feasts, weeklong feasts, flamboyant no-meat feasts on fish-only Fridays, and a two-month-plus feast that began on November 29, 1549, on the death of Paul III, and ended on February 7, on the announcement of a new pope. Scappi's range includes cow udders in their many variations, testicles (stuffed and roasted), and peacocks (boned, reconstructed, re-"plumed," and served in slices, anticipating the now more modest-seeming Lyonnais *volaille à Noelle* that Daniel Boulud would teach me). Many of the sauces that are now the fundamentals of the French kitchen (such as Béarnaise and Hollandaise) and many of the techniques (such as *pâte feuilletée*) appeared in print, first, written by Scappi. What Scappi represented, more vividly than any other chef of the era, was dinner as spectacle, and the meal as an expression of high culture.

But he was never translated into French. There is no evidence the book even reached France, and for Florent Quellier, cochair of the conference, that lack of evidence was telling.

Quellier delivered the conference's opening remarks. He didn't give a speech. He delivered a tirade. It was like starting a prayer meeting by setting alight a pile of gunpowder. It was exhilarating. Among its several themes was the refrain, Where is Scappi? The assumption: If Italy really influenced the cuisine of France, then surely its most famous book should be an obvious influence. In fact, the argument puts rather a lot of weight on a book that was pretty late in the long queue of texts that had already made an appearance in French. But it *was* curious.

Quellier, from the University of Tours, was about fifty, looked about thirty, had cropped hair and black horn-rimmed glasses, and wore white cotton short-sleeve shirts, a tightly knotted narrow black tie, and a look of uncompromising purposefulness. For the duration of the conference, Quellier spoke to no one. He took notes. (He doesn't do chitchat, a colleague told me; he does mission statements.) In appearance and manner, he could have been an engineer or a mathematician. You don't look at him and think: Hey, why don't we have dinner and knock back a couple bottles? You think: Wow! Angry!

Barbara Ketcham Wheaton had dealt with the Catherine de' Medici myth by making fun of it. But she didn't have access to the cartoon version, an item in Quellier's presentation, a 1950s comic strip of Donald Duck as a fat, pizza-making Italian chef, his toque falling off his head, his belly slopping over his belt, instructing bewildered Goofy dog figures, standing upright and attentive in their French way, how to cook. The French dogs are baffled but grateful. It was the climax of Quellier's speech. It was very funny.

Quellier was a member of the anti-Italian faction. I'm not sure I'll ever find anyone as outspokenly or aggressively pro-French. His basic position is, yes, until the advent of La Varenne's book in 1651—*Le Cuisinier françois,* the text that changed everything—French cooking was still medieval. And, yes, it was influenced by the Italians—a little, he can't deny it—but it was also influenced by the Spanish, in table manners, for instance, and by the Belgians, and even the Germans. What he can't find, he said, is *"preuves incontestables"*—his recurrent phrase—that the Italian influence mattered more than anyone else's.

The proof, evidently, isn't in the many cookbooks translated from the Italian, or in the fact that the Italians had their Renaissance before the French one, or in the protocol of a meal's presentation—linens, the fork—that the Italians had first and the French imitated, or in the texts by Rabelais and the translations of Platina, or in the Italian chefs in the kitchens of both Catherine de' Medici and Henri IV, or in the popularizing of Italian ingredients at the *foires* of Lyon, or in the nearby Italian-built châteaux on the very river where we found ourselves, or in the fact that Leonardo lived nearby or that Italian was spoken at François Premier's table. The missing proof incontrovertible was in the one text: Scappi's *Opera,* the greatest book of Italian cooking, which was never translated into French.

La Varenne, the forefather of the French kitchen, is not Italian, Quellier said. Has anyone found a passage in La Varenne that acknowledges Scappi? A Scappi recipe, perhaps? An expression of gratitude to my dear friend Monsieur Scappi?

A Belgian scholar objected, which I found brave and rather risky. "There is Lancelot de Casteau's *Ouverture de cuisine*! The text is full of Scappi recipes!"

Quellier ignored him.

(The Belgian scholar is correct. The text, published in 1604 in Brussels, is among the first comprehensive attempts to codify a new French cuisine and includes the first description, in French, of *pâte feuilletée*. And, yes, there are a lot of Scappi recipes. In fact, there are also early versions of French preparations with Italian names: like *pâte Poupelin,* after the Italian pastry chef Popelini, or *fèves de Roma,* for the green beans now called haricots verts, or the *tourte genoise* for what might otherwise be called a "spinach tart.")

Quellier pressed on.

"Is there a translation of Scappi? Did anyone, in the sixteenth or even the seventeenth century, have a copy? Where is the Scappi? Where is the Scappi?" *Où est le Scappi?*

In fact, there was a pertinent book in the exhibit—in a room that Quellier appeared not yet to have visited—elegantly bound in white leather, a unique, handmade presentation copy. It was dedicated to

Catherine de' Medici. It came from her private library. The title was *Il cuoco segreto di Papa Pio V*, and the author was Bartolomeo Scappi.

Even I had been stunned to find it, having come to believe (incorrectly) that Catherine de' Medici was, in effect, a metaphor of the Italian Renaissance, and that the lessons of the Italian kitchen had been spread to France in the way that any culinary movement crosses borders, not in translation, but by the word-of-mouth of cooks, and by the dishes they learn, bit by bit, in the conversation among people who make food. But then to see the very volume: Wow. It seemed like some kind of message.

To be fair to Quellier, it is curious that Scappi wasn't translated into French, whereas so many other, lesser texts had been. But Scappi was also scarcely translated into other languages. It now appears that, in 1570, his famous book was published as an era was nearing its end: as was the Italian Renaissance. The end of the Italian culinary Renaissance is often marked by historians with the publication, a hundred years later, of Antonio Latini (he who persuaded his readers that the tomato wasn't poisonous), but there were few texts of note published in the seventeenth century. When Scappi sat down to write his book, he was describing a kitchen that no longer existed. The book was a work of retrospection.

In fact, the Italian dominance of the kitchen was in decline just as the French kitchen was being born.

VIII

France (Finally)

Young people today no longer have gout, but mope around on diets: noodles without butter, butter without bread, bread without sauce, sauce without meat, meat without truffles, truffles without scent, scent without bouquet, bouquet without wine, wine without drunkenness, drunkenness without gaiety. . . . Saints of Paradise! I would rather have gout than deprive myself of all of life's charms.

ÉDOUARD DE POMIANE, *VINGT PLATS QUI DONNENT LA GOUTTE*
(*TWENTY DISHES THAT GIVE YOU GOUT*), 1938,
TRANSLATED BY JESSICA GREEN

I bought a facsimile edition of La Varenne and sat down to read it—an early-seventeenth-century script, an obscure diction—and didn't get past the second page. I could read French—and found an early-nineteenth-century text (like Carême) to be as accessible as a book printed today—but the seventeenth-century page was too obscure. There were also so many words that aren't words anymore, like the ten terms that describe "duck"—not the same kind of duck, evidently, but ten different ducks. A modern English translation by Terence Scully was valuable for its research and its notes, but seemed oddly flat, as if the rough original had suffered by being distorted into intelligibility. (What I should have read, I now know, was the translation that appeared in London two years after *Le Cuisinier françois* was published in France, a heroic piece of labor that captures the struggle and ingenuity of the original.)

I came upon a reference to a La Varenne text that I hadn't known about, *L'École des ragoûts* (*The School of Ragùs*), published in Lyon in 1668. I needed a copy. The title alone seemed to mesh into one word the two cultures of my study, Italy and France. In Italian, the word is written *ragù,* and there are few words that convey more resoundingly *la cucina italiana*. The Bolognese on your spaghetti: a ragù. Any meat slow-braised until it's a sauce to dress your pasta: a ragù. The founder of French cooking promoting a school of ragù? Even if the title had nothing to do with the text inside, it was at least a cultural testament: It was what the printer believed would sell.

But I couldn't find it. Even Gallica, the digital collection of the Bibliothèque Nationale, didn't have a copy. (It now does.)

Then I came upon it on eBay.fr, not prohibitively expensive, and bought it. I was thrilled by my copy when it arrived, a miracle in an ordinary envelope, delivered in the normal manner into our apartment mailbox. It was small, three inches by five, but thick, 425 pages, bound in a patterned, cracking cowhide leather, frayed along the edges, with some tunnels left by bookworms. It was the fourteenth edition. Was that possible? Or just a title-page sales pitch?

On the inside flap, one of the book's owners had written, in that flawlessly flowing fountain-pen hand that my children had been taught to do in school, an account of a day's food shopping, spending 6 francs and 60 centimes for sultanas, cod, a chicken, green beans, sausage, lard, and salad. The cod was 1.20 francs, the chicken 2.78 francs, about what people were paying in Paris around 1890 (which I knew because I had a decade's worth of the fortnightly publication *Pot au Feu,* a very seasonal how-to of French cooking for the French housewife, which included price updates on what could be found in the market).

The first recipe I opened to was three pages long and perfectly easy to read: a pâté in the Italian style encased in puff pastry, filled with veal, three partridges, and ingredients of the Italian Renaissance (raisins, chestnuts, pine nuts, cinnamon, sugar, and a piece of cured lemon). I held the book in my hand, this early specimen of the early printing press, a treasure then, a treasure now, produced more than five decades before the American Declaration of Independence, and closed my eyes and just imagined—well, everything.

Only later did I discover that it was a fraud. The text inside wasn't even by La Varenne. No one knows who wrote it. (A good writer, however.)

I was now fully intrigued. I could feel the beginnings of what was probably going to become an obsession. Who was La Varenne, and why don't we know more about him? He was the French kitchen's equivalent of Shakespeare. It all started with him.

He was the chef for a grand figure, a military man, a marquis, Louis Chalon du Blé.

Du Blé was governor of Châlon, on the Saône, roughly midway

between Lyon and Mâcon, and resided in a grand château, Cormatin. It had been in the family since it was built by his grandfather who was patronized (coincidentally, of course) by Maria de' Medici. Du Blé had been born at Cormatin, as had his father, and as was du Blé's first son, whose birth is recorded in the local church records, in the winter of 1652, the year after *Le Cuisinier françois* was published. Terence Scully points out that it seems likely that La Varenne cooked at the château, although, unfortunately, his kitchen has since burned down and been rebuilt. The château, which was open to the public, was less than an hour away from our home, on our very river. It seemed fitting that the godfather of French cooking would be, in effect, Lyonnais. On a summer Saturday, I took the family on a day trip to see what we might find—a letter, an artifact, some unexpected buried treasure.

In addition to *Le Cuisinier françois,* La Varenne was the author of two other books, *The French Pastry Chef* and *The French Confectioner* (jam making again), although, as with *The School of Ragùs,* it is possible that the name La Varenne was less a name than a brand. Most of what we know about him is in the first book: in its internal references (the chapter on the battlefield kitchen, fascinating for its blunt practicality—e.g., take five sheep . . .), and its preface, which includes allusions to cooking colleagues and expressions of gratitude to his employer, du Blé.

The château was now owned by three families. In exchange for saving a historic building from ruin, they were rewarded with what was, in effect, a high-luxury, high-status time-share. They held costume balls, and masquerades, and dinners, and at the end of the day pulled their vehicles into the grounds, closed the gates, and enjoyed the premises as if they were their own.

There was a moat and a garden maze, where our boys disappeared behind head-high shrubs for an uncomfortable-making long time. I found myself studying the kitchen that had a service door, where traders would have appeared (their visits implicit in La Varenne's ingredients): gamekeepers, gardeners, river fishermen, trappers, poachers, bearing freshwater eels and mussels, black birds, woodcock, swan, wild boar, and the many different kinds of ducks, like the *allebran,* not just a wild variety but the *young* wild variety.

One owner was in the courtyard, mending a long piece of white linen. It seemed inconceivable that nothing from La Varenne's kitchen had been preserved. Something must have been retrieved from the fire—an invoice or an inventory, a cache of letters, a journal. He was too important.

I introduced myself and mentioned my interest.

"La Varenne," he said. "Yes. I've heard of him."

"He was the chef under the marquis du Blé," I continued. "Many regard La Varenne as the founder of French cooking."

The owner stared at me. He was Spanish: Monsieur Olvidaros. Maybe French cooking wasn't his strength.

"He is believed to have cooked here, but the kitchen he worked in burned down in the eighteenth century."

"Yes, a fire destroyed the south wing."

I described what I was hoping to find, any record, any scrap, an archive.

"When was this?"

"From 1630 to 1650."

"No."

"No?"

"They weren't here then. They were in Paris."

"In Paris? For twenty years?"

"No one was here."

This wasn't making sense. "That can't be possible."

"The château had been effectively abandoned."

"What about Nicolas du Blé, the firstborn son?"

"I don't know about him."

"He is said to have been born here, in January 1652. According to church records. In Chalon-sur-Saône."

"We don't know." *On ne sait pas.*

"And his father," I pressed on, perplexed, "he was a military man, always in battle. . . ."

"Yes."

"How could he raise an army in Paris?"

"On ne sait pas." He stared at me. "In any case, there is nothing."

"Nothing?"

"Nothing."

I didn't believe him. I didn't think he was lying. I just didn't think he knew. But what I did or didn't believe was immaterial. The kitchen was gone, and the records were gone. Even the house in Paris: gone. My search for a buried treasure? Zip.

The three-and-a-half-page preface to *Le Cuisinier françois* contains everything we know about La Varenne.

I would be back.

Meanwhile, I had a distraction. The MOF: the hardest competition in French cooking. No, I wasn't a contender. And yet, in a way, I was.

DUCK PIE

I hadn't signed up for the MOF because I didn't regard myself as one of the most trained and disciplined cooks in all of France and didn't see the virtue, or the comedy, in failing (yet again) spectacularly.

The MOF is designated by that badass French-flag collar worn by Viannay and Bocuse and Le Cossec and Michel Guérard and just about every grand chef in the country. It was conceived in 1913 to honor the good work being done by the many hitherto unrecognized artisans and laborers, *les meilleurs ouvriers de France,* the best French workers, and then, having been held every four years, like the Olympics, had, for kitchen people, gradually acquired an unanticipated stature that only France, with the mystical value it places on food, could ever have facilitated and then socially rewarded. You get named an MOF and you're set for life, and everyone—Christophe, young Mathieu, Frédéric, Ansel, two chefs from Boulud's kitchen in New York, even Florian— had thrown their names into the proverbial hat, because, after all, what have you got to lose?

But not me.

When the dishes were announced, they didn't seem impossible. There was a fish to start with, and a duck to follow, and both looked eminently doable (I flattered myself into believing), especially the duck, which was prepared two ways: the breast sliced into thin *aiguillettes* and dressed with a cider-based sauce, and the thighs rendered in a puff-pastry "pie." And *that* is exactly what it was called: a "pie."

I thought: I know how to do the breast. You remove it, you slow-sauté it, you flip it over, you're done. Removing it is a little tricky, and the slow-sautéing has to be really slow, fat side down, fifteen to twenty-five minutes or longer, until the skin is crisp and the creamy white layer underneath is rendered.

The breast: the easy part. The challenge: the "pie."

But I thought: I can make pie. Not only did I think I could make it, but I also wanted that pie in my repertoire. (Viannay called it a *tourte,* not a pie, from the same Italian root that gives us *torta* and hence *tortelli* and *tortellacci.* A *tourte* figures as a centerpiece in a sixteenth-century tapestry of a royal meal on display at that exhibit at Blois; I've come to regard it as a handoff dish between Italy and France.)

The Saturday after the dishes were announced, we ran into Christophe and Viannay at our Potager bistro, and joined their table. Christophe was in training; Viannay, his coach. Christophe was temporarily relieved of his kitchen duties in order to practice his technique, his speed, his puff pastry, his sauce making. His test center was in Marseille. All the contestants, so they would not be known by the judges (who were local chefs), were dispatched far from home.

Christophe had become my friend. *Tu nous manques,* he said again, softly but unmistakably. It was, I would learn, not an unusual transformation, the unexpected feelings of mutual respect between boss and novice, and though I can't condone the French apprentice system—the unregulated bullying and humiliation—I had to concede that I had never learned so much. It made me into a cook. And the lessons seemed to have imprinted themselves into my psyche, permanently, in a way that I am not sure would have been the case had the instruction been more gently humane. (To this day, I hear Christophe's bark when I am cleaning up: *"Pas propre!" "Sale!" "Pas propre!"*)

The Potager meal—Viannay, in honor of my being at the table, ordered a magnum of fine Burgundy—was unexpectedly inspiring. I looked at the MOF instructions. They weren't a recipe as such, but a set of conditions: ingredients you were allowed to use, others that were forbidden, the size of your serving dish, the weight of your duck. For the pie, you couldn't make the puff pastry in advance. But you could arrive with a *pâton,* that wet pastry that you wrap your butter into. Stock: You were forbidden from using veal, but allowed to show up with chicken broth. The number of mushrooms was specified (twelve basic ones, called *champignons de Paris,* caps only), as was the number of prunes (six, pitted, from Agen), but not of turnips. And as for the duck itself: The breast was to be removed, cooked by itself, and served in thin slices dressed by a cider-based sauce; the meat from the legs was for the pie and to be cooked in whatever way you chose (*"cuisson libre"*). It was a test, but also a puzzle.

I had continued practicing puff pastry and had frozen my efforts. In the freezer, I also had quantities of chicken stock. *I thought:* I really can do this. I set out to locate the requisite serving dish, but there was none in town. Every single one had been bought up by the contestants. (There had also been a run on the fish—*carrelet,* plaice—which wasn't really in season. The local news ran a story on how it had increased from MOF demand: from 1 to 5 euros a kilo to 113 euros: the cost, obviously, of living in a city of aspirational gastro-cheffy types.)

I searched for recipes in Escoffier, then everyone else. The specific MOF dishes were nowhere but everywhere . . . maybe. I found plenty of dishes that used cider. There must have been two hundred duck-and-turnip recipes. I settled on cooking the legs for a pie filling as a *ragoût,* although I had invariably thought of it as a *ragù,* the Italian spelling.

My first effort wasn't a disaster. I began by boning the duck. As with a chicken, you remove the legs first. For the breasts, you remove the wishbone and the wings and carve out the "steaks"—or at least I've come to think of them as steaks. They are separated by a long breast-bone, and you start from there, slicing down on one side and loosening the meat from the breast plate, scraping, scraping. A duck's breast cavity is different from a chicken's, flatter, less oval, and the meat is more like the shape of a sirloin.

I put the breasts aside. They would be for later.

I chopped up the carcass, roasted it, put it in a stockpot, added a splash of reduced cider, and covered it with chicken stock. This would be my basic *jus.*

The pie's filling would come principally from the legs, plus what-ever scraps I could get from elsewhere, including the "oyster," what the French call *sot-l'y-laisse* (what only a fool leaves behind). The boning of the legs yielded up a disappointingly modest pile of morsels. (How would these fill a pie?) I browned and then gently simmered them in a small quantity of duck *jus*. I was reminded that there is a point when meat, even after it has been cooked for a long time, will hold its shape and texture. Then there is the point, *just* after, when it goes smoosh. Mine went smoosh. It was more ragù than ragoût, and would have been more appropriate atop a plate of freshly made pappardelle.

I reviewed my instructions, including the press release, and noticed something that I had missed before: On the day of the test, journalists could visit a *centre d'épreuves* (a test center), provided that they showed up after the cooking had started and didn't disturb the candidates. I looked at a list of centers. The nearest one was in Dardilly, just outside of Lyon. Why not?

It was at a *Lycée,* a high school—teenagers with books, lounging on grass, looking so relaxed that the sight of them, their youthful leisure, was both disconcerting to come upon and nostalgia-making. The test kitchen was elsewhere in every possible sense. You followed a long dark hall to its end, climbed a darker staircase, and opened a door, and the atmosphere hit you: body odor, and cooking fumes, and a strong feeling that things were going badly wrong.

The administrators were a married couple, late sixties, with the fussy rapport of two people who had uneasily spent most of their lives together. They were busy with a clipboard. Some candidates had submitted their dishes under the wrong number, and they couldn't figure out what the numbers should have been. They had been administrating since five in the morning, were groggy, looked at me blankly, and asked what I wanted.

I had a letter of accreditation. "I am a journalist. I am here to observe."

The woman, two hands on the counter, dropped her head. *"Merde,"* she whispered. "Find Pierre," she said, and the husband went off to look for him.

The kitchen was in the back, with a judging alcove off to the side, behind a "pass" where a candidate had just shown up with a tray of six plates, a plate for each judge—thin slices of duck arranged in a fan, a bright red-brown sauce, and a slice of "pie." It was the first time that I had seen the finished dish. It looked like what you would be very happy to be served in a restaurant. It didn't look particularly ambitious or difficult. It just looked right. The candidate—his apron flopped around him like a kite; there was also a stain on his jacket—had evidently failed. He was twelve minutes late. A candidate advances to the final with a near-perfect or perfect score—nineteen or twenty out of a possible twenty. By his tardiness, no matter how elegantly rendered his duck might have been, he was disqualified.

Pierre then appeared, an elderly, elfin figure in a crisp white jacket and the bright collar flag. I knew him! It was Pierre Orsi! Lovely Pierre! Everyone knows Pierre. By now I'd seen him several times, with Boulud and in the dining room—Jessica and I ate there to celebrate an anniversary and were happily overwhelmed by his attentiveness. In me, he recognized a friend, and ushered me into the judges' alcove as though offering me the best table in the house (which, in fact, it was).

The faces of the judges said: This cannot possibly be protocol.

But Pierre was the MOF in charge, and had, by his habits of civility, unreflectingly made an executive decision. What's more, I already knew three of the six judges: William Jacquier (one of my first teachers at L'Institut Bocuse), Christian Têtedoie (a hotspur of ambition, who, over the course of months, had opened up four different restaurants in impressive succession, not counting the *bouchon* that he scooped up from Boulud), and none other than Jean-Paul Lacombe, the proprietor chef of Léon de Lyon, which, in one rendering of my adventure, might have been the place where I started. Michel Richard came to mind, a memory of our last day together, when he had told me that, in Lyon, I would meet all the city's chefs, and I had dismissed the prospect; I then couldn't even speak French. But he turned out to be right.

Lacombe and I had since become friends, after a return visit to Léon de Lyon, when I told him how I knew Michel Richard. Lacombe, like others who had met Richard, regarded him as among the elite of the elites, and I was once again burnished by the brightness of his glory. Lacombe was the only chef without an MOF collar, and looked strikingly underdressed.

Roger Jaloux was another judge, one of the city's elders. I didn't know him but knew his reputation, ex-Bocuse (the executive chef for four decades) and patron of two of the historic bistros in the city. I missed the names of the other judges and didn't ask them to repeat themselves. I kept my notebook under the table. It seemed to burn in my hand.

The judges were finishing up candidate number fourteen. They had been talking about his sauce. Jean-Paul Lacombe, who had seated himself directly across from Têtedoie, liked it. He gave it five points. Each submission was assessed on four criteria, each worth a maximum of five points.

"How can you possibly believe that number fourteen was 'good'?" Têtedoie asked. "The sauce was insipid."

"It was not insipid."

"It was."

"No, it wasn't. I liked it. It tasted of apples." It seemed that "apples" was a reference to an earlier exchange and something that the judges expected to find in a sauce made with cider. Lacombe looked impish.

"Apples! It tasted of nothing. It was banal."

Lacombe knew that the remark would provoke Têtedoie. He persisted. "Five."

"No. Four."

"Five."

"Four."

A long pause. "Okay," Lacombe conceded, "four."

The difference between four and five was enough, probably, to keep a candidate from advancing.

"The pie?"

"Five," Lacombe said.

"Absolutely not," said Têtedoie. "Did you taste the mushrooms?"

"Of course I tasted the mushrooms."

"I ate one that was hard." *C'était dur.* "It had not been cooked on one side." The mushrooms were sliced and sautéed. Someone—whoever number fourteen turned out to be—must have been in a rush and inadvertently left the side of one mushroom incompletely cooked.

"Four," Têtedoie said.

"Okay, okay. Four."

The anonymous number fourteen would never know how one mushroom had tripped up his or her advancement to the final.

The group moved on to number fifteen. I inched my chair back quietly from the table, opened my notebook, and began writing in it on my knee.

"*Le visual de la pie?*" asked Roger Jaloux. The pie's presentation, the look of it?

"*C'est bon. Une belle présentation,*" Jacquier said. It was good. Pretty. Five points. Four judges agreed. They gave it five.

Têtedoie was last and furious, and his fury—his focus, an almost spitting rage—was directed at Lacombe. "*Non. Non, et non.*" It was immaterial that everyone else had liked the pie so much that they had unanimously given it five points.

"Oh, Christian," Lacombe sighed, in a tone that said, Ease up, please.

"Four!" Têtedoie insisted.

A judge I didn't know dropped his head in resignation. The group had been judging for many hours.

"Okay, four," Jaloux said. "But, Christian, please behave yourself, *s'il ta plaît*? There is a journalist present. He is taking notes."

They continued. With the pie, the concern was either the filling (it needed *fondant*—a thick meltingness, a buoyancy—and most efforts were missing that) or the puff pastry, referred to during the judging as *le feuilletage,* which was often not cooked through ("*Pas cuit*"). You could never be an MOF if you couldn't cook a puff pastry properly.

"*Le feuilletage* of number twenty-one had *un soufflé très beau,*" Lacombe said—a beautiful puffiness—and he stretched out the vowels in *beau* like a poem.

"No," said Têtedoie, "it was too big."

"And the sauce," Lacombe continued, with provocative obliviousness, "was *ravissante*"—ravishing.

"*Ravissante?* Really, Jean-Pierre? It completely lacked personality." (And there was that—how do you give your sauce personality?)

The longer the judging went on the more obvious that the argument between Lacombe and Têtedoie was about something other than the dishes. Was it because Lacombe wasn't an MOF? He was soft to the touch, rather frumpy to look at, almost cuddly. (Was he just a little vain? His hair appeared to be dyed blond.) He could also seem like a sack in his chair. He was a sloucher.

Têtedoie, twelve years younger, was trim, with indefatigable posture, closely cropped silver hair, and fine features. He was the human equivalent of a perfectly pressed shirt. The look wasn't military. It was steel. His executive chef had just won the honor of representing France at the next Bocuse d'Or, and the honor was as much Têtedoie's as the candidate's. Têtedoie seemed to be grooming himself to be the future of Lyonnais cooking, and the future was one of discipline and rigueur. It was exacting. No contestants got a perfect score, although a few would have had Têtedoie not been there, holding up a standard that his colleagues found uncomfortably high. No MOF candidate from Dardilly would advance to the final. And what do I know? Maybe that was correct.

"Number twenty-two?" Jaloux asked.

"Absenté." Absenté wasn't a no-show. It was an effective no-show: late.

"Number twenty-three?"

"Absenté."

"Number twenty-four?"

"Absenté."

"Number twenty-five?"

"Catastrophic," Têtedoie said.

The session wrapped up. I put my notebook away, thanked the judges (Jaloux looking sheepish and embarrassed), and made my way to the exit. The administrators saw me and realized that I had been there all along—in their agitation they had forgotten me—*and* that I had just come from the judging alcove. I had been sitting in on the judging! *"Mon Dieu!"* the wife declared. "But at least you weren't taking notes."

The next morning, I contacted Têtedoie and asked if I could see him.

We met at the bar of the Restaurant Christian Têtedoie, midway up the steep hill of Fourvière, on a windy, idiosyncratic ancient road—stone walls, monasteries, and Renaissance buildings. The restaurant was a modern structure, rather appealingly at odds with everything around it, with glass and right angles, a twelve-foot-long banner congratulating Têtedoie's executive chef, and a panoramic, limitless-seeming view of the city below.

The MOF had intrigued me, I explained, by its insistence that French food had to be made perfectly. "The dishes are not in themselves neces-sarily so difficult?"

"No, they're not. But they are very difficult to make perfectly."

"They are also very French."

"Very."

I asked why, during the judging session, he insisted on lowering the scores of his colleagues.

He seemed pleased that I'd noticed. "My colleagues were too generous."

What was going on between him and Jean-Paul Lacombe?

Têtedoie again seemed pleased. "It was nothing personal. Jean-Paul is a very good bistro chef. But an MOF is cooking at the highest possible level. It can never be merely 'good.'"

I described how I had been practicing the duck with turnips, and the pie. "Could I cook it for you? Would you judge my dish with all the intensity of judgment that you brought to the judging session?"

And he agreed.

I left, exhilarated and frightened. The dish was like an act of gradua-tion. I then learned that every one of my friends had failed: Christophe, and Frédéric, and the two chefs from Boulud's kitchen—everyone. None would advance to the finals.

My challenge was that *fondant* quality.

I looked at Escoffier again and found two recipes that seemed helpful. One was a *civet de lièvre à la française*. *Lièvre* is hare. *Civet* is a way of cooking it: by marinating it in wine, braising the meat in the marinade, and then mixing the marinade with the animal's blood to make a sauce. It is rich and profoundly French. The preparation wasn't so different from what I had already been doing (minus the blood): I was cooking a tough meat in a lovely sauce until it was tender and highly flavored; i.e., as a ragoût (or ragù).

The second recipe was rabbit (hare's smaller, leaner cousin). It also called for Calvados, the brandy made in Normandy from apples (an appleness intensified), and was treated like a ragù— *"traités en ragoût"* (slow braising, rich liquid, sauce, etc.).

I thought: I was right! Ragoût! Or ragù. They were basically the same process.

I also thought: Calvados! Of course! No mention of it in the MOF instructions, which gave me pause. Then again, there was no mention of *not* using it. But, if you're prepared to accept it, why stop there? Cider → Calvados → apple-cider vinegar (why not?) → quince, the medieval apple-pear fruit = appleness very, very intensified (and damn it, my sauce was going to have an absolutely outsized personality).

I got to work: boning the thighs, making a Calvados-and-apple-cider-vinegar marinade, browning, then adding my *jus,* another splash of Calvados (*pourquoi pas?*), not enough to submerge the meat, more a puddle than a pond, and then spooning the liquid on top, not long, about thirty minutes, enough to render it soft. And the result?

Much better than last time. It was less mush and more identifiably meat (you would never put it atop a plate of spaghetti). But, surprisingly, it was disappointingly dry. It was actually very dry. In fact, it was like cardboard.

It was an example of what I now think of as the Boeuf Bourguignon Paradox: how, when you braise a meat (in liquid) it comes out being the opposite of wet. It tastes dehydrated. It can be an issue with *coq au vin* (braised in a bottle of red wine). The fix is fat (which is to say that what is missing after a long braise is fat, and its absence creates the sensation of dryness). Julia Child understood: She famously proposed cooking *boeuf bourguignon* with *lardons*—small rectangles of *poitrine,* the French equivalent of pancetta—i.e., bacon.

But in Lyon, they don't use *poitrine,* usually sold as an industrialized pre-cubed product in a stiff plastic container. They use a very animal, sweaty, and slightly smelly flap of *couenne.* Even for *boeuf bourguignon,* our local butcher told me, you use *couenne.* "It's the real thing." (He also recommended not using stewing beef—shoulder, leg, butt—but the animal's cheeks, heavily worked muscles, needing more time to melt the collagen, and more expensive, but much higher *and* longer in flavor. And he was right! It is now the only way I make it.)

Couenne (pronounced "coo-en") is a layer of fine fat just under the outer lining of a pig's skin. You clean it by dropping it briefly in boiling water, then add it to the bottom of your casserole pot, and let it melt into your meat as you cook it. *Couenne* replaces what the wine is boiling away. It creates a meat that glistens. The recipes in my 1894 edition of *Le*

Pot au feu call so often for *couenne* that, like salt and pepper, it is rarely listed among the ingredients: It's assumed that you have some. In Lyon, you can get *couenne* at every butcher shop, at the Sunday farmers' market, and at Monoprix, the chain supermarket. It makes braised dishes work. A "pub" behind our home, just up the hill from the boys' school, was called La Couenne. It was such an insider foodie reference that, on seeing the sign, I fell in love with Lyon all over again. (Can you imagine a midtown bar called The Stomach Lining?)

I tried other tricks. There was so much liquid that I risked making a roux to thicken it. (Equal parts flour and butter—just a little, twenty-five grams of each, whisked aggressively over a low flame until it turns blond-brown.) Most nineteenth-century recipes call for roux. Most late-twentieth-century recipes banish it. The *Gault & Millau Nouvelle Cuisine* editors condemned it: Why use flour to thicken a sauce when you can reduce it instead and intensify the flavor? If you mention roux to chefs today, they imitate the sounds of sticky mastication, imagining a gooey, dry dough adhering to the roof of the mouth. But I was making a pie filling, not a sauce, and I had a lot of liquid that just was calling out for some bouncy *fondant*-like thickening.

The turnips also added a fluffy *fondant* feel, because I cooked them dusted with flour and finished with a ladle of my duck-stock-cider *jus*. It was *another* Escoffier preparation (who knew that old geezer had so many good tips?) and, on tasting a bite straight from the pan, I was surprised by its radical sweetness. I had cooked new spring turnips at La Mère Brazier, but they were always what I expected them to be, fibrous, watery, little flavor. They tasted healthy more than fun. But here the sauté pan had converted the starches. And the result wasn't just sweet: It was the tuber equivalent of a fruit. Even today, when duck is prepared in many exotically competitive variations—topped by the bright tart Griotte cherries you get only in August, or by wild mountain blueberries marinated in a Savoyard syrup of *génépi* flowers—you will, in France, still find it served up with turnips. The combination, as old as the farm, has a rustic harmony, fat and sweet, bird and earth, that works.

One weekend in Mâcon, Jessica had shared a photo with her WSET candidate friends that featured yours truly at the end of a *bouchon* meal being embraced by three visiting American-based chefs—Daniel Bou-

lud, Thomas Keller, and Jérôme Bocuse, the son of Monsieur Paul. Olivier, Swiss French but living in London, was astonished.

"Damn," he said, "look who your husband is surrounded by. When are
we coming for dinner?" When they all then had passed their final exams
and she earned her diploma, it was settled: I would cook my MOF dish
for them to celebrate; they would represent my first trial.

And then there was Bob. Duck pie didn't sound like an example of
grand cuisine, but if it was what the MOF organizers had deemed to be
worthy of preparing, then it was likely to be grand enough for Bob. He
would be next.

Meanwhile, I prepared three rehearsal pieces in anticipation of my
first trial. Each time, I couldn't stop myself from admiring the simple
fact of what I'd done: a pie that was crispy and golden and smelled of
butter and braised duck and autumnal apple cider. It was a preposter-
ously beautiful piece of work. Damn, I made that. Hot diggity dog.

I would like to believe that my determination to identify the engine,
the heart, the starting point of the French kitchen—that moment that
engendered a powerful culinary culture—would have kept me returning
to La Varenne and made me a student of his book, looking for the meals
that changed everything. In fact, what made me pick up his books were
the words *ragoût* and *ragù*. My understanding of ragù hadn't been quite
the same as what a French cook meant by ragoût. When I cooked my
duck as a ragù, it was delicious mush. When I cooked it gently, spooning
my duck stock over it, heating from below and above, aiming not for an
Italian sauce (a *sugo*), but for something like a sauced tenderness, then I
could see that I was doing something different, which I *believed,* possibly, was a ragoût. The uncertainty is because the word "ragoût" has been
peculiarly elusive. It is not much used today, but for nearly three centuries, from 1651 to around the 1930s, it was so common as to be rarely if
ever defined. After a fairly comprehensive search of nearly three centuries of cookbooks and culinary dictionaries, I couldn't find an author or
a chef who defined what "ragoût" meant. It was always assumed that the
reader knew. (Finally, I did find a definition, a contemporary one, in my
Institut Bocuse textbook, which does indeed describe a ragoût as being
cooked from above and below and by spooning the sauce over. The

idea is that the sauce flavors the meat, and the meat flavors the sauce, or what my textbook describes, dubiously, as "the phenomenon of osmosis.")

It also seems likely that the word's first appearance in print, as it applied to food, was in La Varenne. I needed, urgently, to return to the Château Cormatin. I had been looking for the wrong treasure.

It was La Varenne's boss who was important, the employer, du Blé. Without him, there would have been no cookbook. (After all, La Varenne was in du Blé's employment; he didn't call his agent in Paris and ask him to fix up a book deal.)

There was a painting of du Blé on a mantelpiece in a room somewhere. A library? A study? I hadn't paid it much attention. It was a guy in armor. Now I realized he was the clue.

We returned and were directed to what today would be called a living room, a sprawling theatrical space for receiving guests, and the painting was so prominent that I was surprised I hadn't noticed it before: a straightforward simple oval, with a depiction of its subject from the waist up, a young man in black armor, with a red sash across his chest, a knight's helmet in his left hand, and the crenellated neckwear that I associate with Elizabethan England. ("Completely out of date," observed the scholar Jessica. "The French were so far behind the rest of Europe.")

I had got the marquis wrong.

On paper, and in the long salutation that La Varenne addresses to him in his introduction ("The High and Mighty Lord, My Lord Louis Chalon du Blé, Counselor of the King in his Privy State Councils, Knight of his Orders," etc.), he had assumed a vague form in my mind, a type, something like a country squire as depicted by Henry Fielding: entitled, pompous, a grandee, much older-seeming than his age, whatever it might be. But du Blé had been a man-child when the portrait was painted. He is young, with fair skin, shoulder-length red hair, soft pink lips—"dashing" in the clichéd use of the word—not more than twenty-five years old, and probably younger, possibly a teenager, because (I finally appreciated) he was *really* very young. He was clearly La Varenne's junior.

Du Blé was born on Christmas Day, 1619. He entered battle, having just been made commander of his first regiment, at the age of nineteen. From the internal references in the introduction, he was around twenty when he hired La Varenne. He was thirty when La Varenne finished *Le Cuisinier françois*. Du Blé, I would discover, very close to power, was the youthful future of France at a time when France was thinking constantly about what it meant to be French. And food interested him—we know this because La Varenne tells us that it did. Du Blé taught him a technique that would become the centerpiece of La Varenne's cooking. It is the first thing he mentions in the introduction, once he gets through the routine throat-clearing "your humble servant" gratitude-speak:

In the ten full years that I was in your employment, I discovered in your home the secret of preparing meats finely.

I'ay trouué dans vostre Maison par un employ de dix ans entiers le Secret d'aprefter delicatement les Viandes.

Until that moment, before La Varenne, meat, broadly speaking, was cooked in one of two ways: as a braise or by direct heat (grilled or by rotisserie), which contracts the tissue and makes for toughness. It is the same in Italy—*brasato* or *alla griglia*. One is stewed; the other, various stages of being torched.

What La Varenne appears to be referring to is cooking meat as a ragoût. (Seventeenth-century French is different from the modern language, and *Viandes* did not necessarily mean "meat," and *delicatement* was more like "finely" or "carefully." But *Viandes* in *Le Cuisinier françois* very clearly has the sense it does today, and even *delicatement* seems to be pretty close to our "delicately.")

A ragoût, I was discovering in my own ad-hoc implementation of it, is a mode in between *brasato* and *alla griglia;* the meat is cooked gently, carefully, from below and above.

Ragoût is an early-seventeenth-century word. It first appears in print to describe an exuberant play or an exciting painting or a flamboyant piece of text—with some extra quality that wakes up the audience member or art appreciator or reader. *Ragoût* is *goût* exaggerated (the prefix *ra-* is an intensifier), and *goût* is an essential word in both the French language and the French kitchen. It means "taste" or "pleasure" or "flavor." La Varenne is the first to apply the word *ragoût* to food—in print, and with a specific sense. My suspicion is that he wasn't, however, the first to use it. Why? Because he never tells you what it means.

Ragoûts abound throughout *Le Cuisinier françois*. There are, by my casual count, considerably more than two hundred. If you read the chapter about what to cook on the battlefield (sixty-three ragoûts), you will learn, if you have been lucky enough to secure a cow while otherwise engaged in armed combat, the different ways to prepare each cut. Like the shoulder, which you can roast. Or prepare as a ragoût. Or the breast, which you can stuff, roll, and cook as a roast. Or chop up and cook as a fricassee. Or do as a ragoût. The tongue: You can marinate it. Or do it as a ragoût. The head: *Many* possibilities. Or as a ragoût.

Where would La Varenne have first heard the word? From other cooks, his professional colleagues, the very ones he addresses as his readers. And, thanks to du Blé: It was *"le secret"* to cooking meat tenderly. He had picked up what was going on in the French kitchen because he had been uniquely positioned to be eating the best of it. Du Blé, in Paris, between battles, lived in a rarefied circle. In his introduction, La Varenne mentions cooking for members of it, and dares to say (*"J'ose dire,"* in the Middle French type) that he carried out his job with enough flair to win high praise (*"grande approbation"*) from the guests who gathered round his employer's table: princesses, grand marshals of France, and an "infinity of people" of noble standing. It was a formidable crowd. France was in a sustained period of reforming itself: politics, warfare, culture, the language, the arts, and the kitchen. In its way, the period was akin to what northern Italy had been undergoing in the early days of its Renaissance. And in La Varenne's text we have this new happy word, *ragoût,* a glimpse, perhaps of what was going on during this undocumented period before French cooking became so uniquely itself.

The word originated in Italy, I assumed, like most other early items of French culinary diction.

Italian dictionaries tend to be vague on its origins but emphasize its importance: that a ragù is one of the most famous Italian dishes in the world (*"sicuramente uno dei piatti italiani più famosi sia in Italia che nel mondo"*), that it is as old as antiquity but didn't appear in print until the end of the eighteenth century (*"nascita alla fine del 1700"*). In fact, it is possible to date the word's origins exactly: 1682, the year when *Le Cuisinier françois* was published in Italian in the city of Bologna as *Il cuoco francese.*

Ragoût doesn't come from *ragù*. *Ragoût* is a word that the Italians borrowed from the French. It is the turning point.

In the culture of the kitchen, the moment marks a monumental shift, like a river reversing. Until then, culinary words (*zabaglione* → *sabayon, becamele* → *béchamel, pasta* → *pâte*), ingredients (artichokes, shallots, melons, citrus, green beans, asparagus), preparations (mortadella → rosette), service (*forchetta* → *fourchette*), and the profoundly Renaissance sense of *convivium* (*festa* → *fête*) entered France from Italy. With La Varenne—and in particular via the word *ragoût*—the culinary discoveries began emanating from France.

The test duck preparation for Jessica and her wine colleagues: once again, not a disaster but not quite as planned, if only because it was not quite planned. I was, in effect, still revising. (I also cheated, I admit, and added a couple extra legs to the ragoût—it was otherwise so ungenerous.)

I rehydrated the prunes with Calvados. Then, finding the pie's filling too sweet, I added salty olives to compensate: olives and duck, almost as old as duck and turnip—why not?

I set out to cook the mushrooms, but decided to sauté them in *poitrine* fat instead of butter, because I was also now adding *lardons,* in addition to the *couenne,* to my ragoût (for the fat, for the salt, because it seemed to be needed), and then, feeling liberated, decided to toss in a little cinnamon (because of its apple associations) and vanilla (ditto), and then more apple vinegar to compensate for the sweetness associations.

Then, running late, wanting to get the food to the table, because the longer the meal took arriving, the more everyone drank of the bottles they had brought with them to celebrate earning their diplomas, I swung from the stovetop with my sauce in its saucier just as one of the guests (the already impressively very drunk Olivier) popped into the kitchen to see if he could help, and the carefully curated sweet-sour-salty-umami-heady liquid flew out of its container and splattered on Olivier en route to landing glisteningly on the kitchen floor.

I stared at it, crushed.

Olivier wiped himself off, picked up the saucier, and cheerfully said, "There's still some sauce left!" (And there was, just.)

How drunken was dinner? In itself, not excessively, except that no one lasted until dessert, because, by then, no one was at the table. They were in the living room, where the sofa, two armchairs, and a footrest were each draped, like a bulky, heavy blanket, by a comatose guest.

I needed one more test run—with Bob—and then I would cook for Têtedoie.

EARLIER, IN THE SUMMER, WE HAD TAKEN BOB OUT. The invitation had been too long in coming. I now understand that he would have preferred the community of a meal in our home, that it was a Lyonnais rite of friendship, but he was happy to be asked. He picked the day: a Tuesday—i.e., not a school night (Bob closed on Wednesdays, like the schools, so he could be with his daughter, and had both bathed and shaved, a radical sight). He also determined the itinerary, which began with his friends at L'Harmonie des Vins, because he knew they had just taken delivery of *the* new Saint-Péray, a small-production white wine made by Alain Voge. Bob taught us that, where we lived, a wine sometimes has a release date, like a theatre's opening night, and excitement surrounds your being among the first to taste it.

Bob talked and talked and talked. About his father, still alive, a farmer's son ("My grandfather, my great-grandfather, my great-great-grandfather, all of them, for generations, were *paysans*"), who became a renowned town baker, a patriarch whom his many children sought advice from before making major decisions, and who, for no reason that anyone understood, no longer spoke to Bob's mother. He hadn't uttered a word to her in five years. ("It was strange. He spoke to the rest of us.")

About his mother, eighty-five, who pretended not to be distressed that her husband of fifty-nine years and the father of her seven children no longer spoke to her.

About his wife, Jacqueline, a single mother with one child when he met her on a holiday he took to Cuba on his own, with whom he fell in love, and to whom he eventually proposed marriage, which she accepted but only if blessed by her priest, a disciple of Santería, the Caribbean slave-era religion.

About the effort to bless the marriage, returning to Cuba to attend a ceremony, people dancing and chanting, many falling into a trance, until the priest stopped the proceedings: "He held my face between his hands, and looked into my eyes, and declared: 'Your family traded in the flesh of our ancestors. You cannot marry Jacqueline. Leave my sight.'"

About his return to France, heartbroken, but his then being told by his mother that there had been merit in the priest's declaration, strange as it might sound, and that there had been a terrible rupture in the family, because one branch traded in slaves from West Africa and the other found the practice unacceptable, and there was an acrimonious split, and the two sides never spoke again.

About how Bob returned to Havana and explained his history to the priest, who then blessed his marriage, and Bob and Jacqueline (along with a child from Jacqueline's first marriage) made their way to Lyon.

About his six siblings—by then we were at Les Oliviers, another restaurant, another friend—Bob talking faster and faster, with even more urgency, there being so much that he wanted to say: Marc, the lawyer in Paris who got Bob a job in the law library (which he loved); Jacques, who lived in Geneva, doing this and that; a couple sisters, I didn't get their names, because of Bob's hurry; another brother, and *then* Philippe, dear Philippe, the second youngest in the family, a year older than Bob, and the one he talked to the least because he thought about him the most. Every member of the family worked in their father's boulangerie at Christmas and Easter. Only Philippe became a baker, a great one, who had opened half a dozen bakeries, worked the ski resorts in the winter, the Caribbean during the spring, cruise liners if the pay was good enough. Bob said: "Philippe is my greatest friend. He is half of my soul."

Bob knew plenty about us. He now wanted us to know about him.

It was late when we drove slowly back to the Quai Saint-Vincent. The heart of the evening, I reflected, was the story of Bob's cleaved family and the message implied by it—that, in Bob's view, his branch had an imperative in its moral DNA to be on the side of the just and good. It was his origin myth and how he explained himself, the youngest member of the family, the seventh child, "the baby," with a mission: There are not many people with a deeper sense of selfless justice. He made bread. It was just bread. And it wasn't.

Bob told us to drop him off at the boulangerie—he had something to pick up—but in the rearview mirror I saw that he went straight into the Potager bistro for another drink and—who knows?—maybe another dinner. There was poignancy in the sight, caught in reverse, of Bob's needing to fill every possible minute of a nonworking evening, his only time off. There seemed to be loneliness.

Two weeks later, Bob's father died.

"It wasn't unexpected," he said, and left to attend the funeral in Rennes.

"He told us to buy the boulangerie," Bob reminisced when he returned. His brother Jacques had been in Lyon and came upon the property for sale, situated in front of the footbridge across the Saône, and on the ground floor of the very building where the history of the city was painted, *La Fresque des Lyonnais*. It was where three roads met, the *quai,* the rue de la Martinière, and the Roman Rhine road. It had been inhabited for millennia, at least since the Allobroges, the indigenous Gallic tribes.

Jacques summoned the father, Bob (who was living in Paris), and Philippe. They came immediately by train.

"My father looked at the property from the outside and said, 'Yes, this is a good boulangerie.'" There were two floors, old stone walls, a worn stone staircase. "He said, 'Bread has been made here for a long time.'" There was a wood-burning oven. Philippe wiped off the soot. It said 1805.

Roberto Bonomo, the chef-owner of the quartier's Italian restaurant, describes the space as "spiritual." "You walk into it. You feel you are connecting to something bigger than yourself."

The family bought the boulangerie for 60,000 francs, about $11,000 at the time.

Philippe said, "Bob, come help me open it." Bob served notice at the law library, and the two brothers got the place ready. It was probably—I couldn't keep myself from thinking—the last time the floors were cleaned. (I have since learned that my suggestion is defamatory. The floors were cleaned—once a year, when the boulangerie closed—although there were at least three years during our stay when it never closed.)

At Bob's insistence, a sign went up—PHILIPPE RICHARD ARTISAN BOULANGER. It seems unlikely that Philippe intended to remain. He had a family and a business in Rennes, eight hours away. He was experienced at start-ups. The occasion, this time, was different. He was training his little brother: *"une formation."* He was helping him to find his calling.

Philippe stayed. How long? Bob can't remember—"Six months? A year?" Eventually, Philippe announced that he needed to return to Rennes; his wife insisted. But he'd be back, he said.

So far, Philippe hasn't returned, not yet. It has been fifteen years. On paper, the brothers are partners. In fact, the boulangerie is Bob's. But the sign hasn't changed. "I will never take it down."

One bright morning in the early summer, with a mountain breeze coming off the Saône, the windows open, I stood out on our balcony, taking in the smells of the boulangerie, only a hundred feet away. When you live here, you have no choice: Bob's bread enters your living space and then your lungs and then your heart. There were many reasons for our liking where we found ourselves, but Bob was high among them. The boulangerie was the village equivalent of a campfire. It held the restaurants together. It united chefs and diners. It made the quartier a gastronomic destination.

I wondered: Is there any chance that we can buy our apartment?

Then, without warning, Bob's beloved brother Philippe died.

I was the first person Bob told.

I had popped into the boulangerie in the late morning. Bob was in the back. No one else was there. I waited several minutes before he walked out to the front.

"I was on the phone with my mother. My brother Philippe. He had an aneurysm this morning. He is dead."

Il est mort.

Bob was pale, flat eyes, no affect, and able to relay the news of his phone call, repeating a construct in language, but seeming unable to understand what he was saying. "He is forty-seven. He *was* forty-seven. An aneurysm. This morning. I spoke to him last week. Philippe is dead."

Bob left to attend the funeral. He returned four days later. He was changed. He was ponderous, in manner and movement, in everything. One morning, he didn't show up at the boulangerie. Another time, I watched him standing by a streetlight at the end of the rue de la Martinière, seeming to stare at nothing. The light changed. He didn't cross. It changed to red. It changed to green. He didn't cross. Once, he was headed directly to the front of our apartment. He often parked his car on a street behind us. I waited for him. He didn't see me. "Bob," I said, and he walked past. "Bob," I repeated, and he stopped, and turned, and looked at me as if he had just been slapped awake.

"*Bonjour,* Bill," he said softly and walked away.

His thoughts were like a black tide moving back and forth inside his head. He didn't seem to be mourning; he seemed to be in a depression. I feared for him.

"Without Philippe," Bob said, "I would be nothing."

He shared his distress with Jessica. "I am working too much. I have to change my life. I must make Lucas a partner." Lucas was the first baker Bob had employed whom he trusted, who "got it" and had the Bob-like lightness of touch. "I have to share the workload."

On another occasion: "I will take vacations."

He seemed to have instantly gained weight. It wasn't alarming—he had always been heavy—but it was evident. He wasn't sleeping, which, since he scarcely slept anyway, meant he had to be suffering physically, minute by minute. The nights, Bob said, were the hardest. "That's when I think of him. I have never been closer to a human being, those nights, making bread."

One morning, Bob told me, "I talk to him at night."

Our Liverpool friend, Martin, walking by the boulangerie late, on his way home, heard Bob sobbing.

One Saturday night, a kid threw a rock at the window in the back room, shattering it. On Saturday nights, everyone comes into Lyon—it is the only city in the Rhône Valley—and the traffic on the *quai* always backs up and remains backed up until dawn. It is noisy, and drunken, and stuff happens. And on this particular Saturday, Bob was in the back, thinking of his brother. The broken window was an affront. Bob gave chase down the Quai Saint-Vincent.

Did Bob really think he could chase down the vandal? By what impulsive leap of the imagination did Bob regard himself as a sprinter?

The fact that he tried seemed a symptom of his desperation and his aloneness. The *quai* there was badly lit, the curb stacked with long irregular boards left over from a construction project never completed. Bob ran a hundred feet and tripped and fell and badly broke his leg, a complete break, in two places. He had to pull himself back onto the narrow sidewalk to get out of the way of the traffic. Bob, whose work means standing on his feet, had to give up the boulangerie for an inconceivably long ten weeks.

He needed some love and affection. He would, I was sure, really like a piece of duck pie.

Roberto was in touch with Bob and provided updates. He was still mainly supine, Roberto told us, although the breaks seemed, finally, to be healing. Bob had attempted walking with crutches.

The boulangerie continued with impressive consistency—Lucas's bread was flawless—with one persistent problem: The flour kept running out. Lucas didn't know how often Bob ordered it. In most bakeries, flour is an inventory staple. You buy it in bulk, you get the best price, it is always there, you don't think about it. But Bob got his flour from that small farmer who valued its freshness. Bob might get some at the beginning of the week. On Friday, he would ask for more. Or on Wednesday. The deliveries would be stacked by the staircase, or, when there was no threat of rain, just outside the back entrance. Not a lot. Forty big dusty sacks, fifty. Lucas, suddenly without flour, had to close.

Roberto, meanwhile, was moving his restaurant out of the quartier to the other side of the Rhône. We would now have to drive there and find a place to park and remember not to drink too much, because then we would have to drive back and find another place to park. Also, he was the first in the quartier to leave, which seemed philosophically incorrect.

"You'll come," he said. "The food will be just as good."

On Sunday, when he was normally closed, Roberto was hosting a farewell party, only his regulars, his best food, the best wine. "Bob promised to be there. He'll still be on crutches, but he'll come."

It was time to begin my prep for the Bob duck dinner.

I wasn't going to do the duck as if it were an MOF submission, the ticking clock, everything made on the spot. This was for Bob; I'd do my Têtedoie time-trials against a stopwatch later. I resolved, like any restaurant chef, to do as much as possible in advance, beginning with the puff pastry. I took my duck stock (I had plenty in the freezer), mixed it with a liter of cider, and reduced it to what I regarded as my "all-purpose *jus*" (it would be added to the ragoût, the sauce, and the turnips). I also made the ragoût ahead of time and froze it. But I put off the garniture— the Calvados-soaked prunes, the mushrooms, the Escoffier turnips— until the day of, when I would prepare each separately and add them at the end.

We arranged a sitter, even though we were only crossing the street to Roberto's. We also wore winter coats, even though we were only crossing the street. It was the first of the season's Alpine gales, and the restaurant was warm to step into. Roberto had removed the tables and lined up chairs along the wall like on New Year's Eve. He gave us a bruschetta with tomatoes and fresh garlic and a glass of good wine.

"Bob *probably* won't be coming," he said. "He couldn't find a sitter."

I regretted that we hadn't been in the loop. Suzanne, Bob, and Jacqueline's lovely child could have stayed with our boys and our sitter.

"But I saw him!" Roberto said. "Yesterday, at Potager. It was his first time out. On crutches, but mobile. He will be back soon."

Owing to Lucas, we didn't miss Bob's bread. We missed Bob. His joy, his wholly present-tense presence, his bighearted affection. We also missed learning what we had missed out on: his giving chase in the night, his injuries, the brother, the father, the details of his plight.

Roberto's food offerings continued, helpings of headcheese and lardo, small plates of pastas—*cacio e pepe,* homemade tagliatelle with white truffles. He was in high hospitality mode.

Where do you get your ingredients? I managed to ask in Italian. Roberto insisted on speaking to us in Italian. Jessica's was as fluent as ever. Mine was almost entirely eradicated. Jessica's brain could hold several languages in it at once. Mine had only one foreign-language compartment, the equivalent of a narrow broom closet. There wasn't enough room for Italian if I was going to stick French in there as well. (There was also the fact that Jessica was a lot smarter.)

A plate of grilled octopus appeared, a platter of meat braised in red wine. The room, by now cheerfully crowded, every chair taken, people having to stand, felt surprisingly Lyonnais. The food was not, obviously, but the people eating it were, definitively. I surveyed the guests, every one of them French and seeming to enjoy the exotic truancy of a cuisine from the other side of the mountains. They respected handmade food, whatever its origins might be, and understood the wonderful thing that happened when you brought people together to eat it, even if you knew no one else there. And most people didn't. Roberto's had been each guest's little secret. We were only now discovering how many people shared it.

I was at ease with these strangers—there was a philosophy of food that we shared, one that I had first understood from the *filles*—and they had come to seem, somehow, like my people. When I then fell into a conversation with a man next to me and mentioned that I was American, another person, a woman, having overheard the exchange from across the room, said loudly that it wasn't possible. "You are Lyonnais. Your face. Your eyes. Everything about you. You have to be Lyonnais." She turned to the man next to her. "Look at him. He's Lyonnais, isn't he?" And he agreed, and the foreignness I had felt since we arrived in the city, like an unnecessarily heavy coat that I put on every morning before going out, seemed instantly to fall away.

I pondered her observation. It was my look. Jessica—fair skin, red hair, a defined profile—didn't have it. People didn't stop her and ask for directions. But I was stopped regularly. Drivers, lost, would stop in mid-traffic when they spotted me. *"Pardon, monsieur, je cherche . . ."*

Once, on a bus, I randomly studied the physiognomies of my fellow passengers. The women, all of them, all ages, were consciously self-presented—they had attended to their appearance. They were as attractive as every cliché about Frenchwomen would lead you to expect. But the men? I can't be blunt enough. They were ugly fuckers. Even the ones who appeared to be partners of beautiful women: The disparity between the sexes was unequivocal. Every man was bald or balding, stocky (with big shoulders, a forthright torso, or just outright fat), and *very* hairy. And not just very hairy, but bald *and* very hairy, as if the body were a plant that had been pruned back just a little too savagely on top and had compensated with random but vigorously thrusting black outpourings below.

Augustus Caesar, two thousand years ago, had observed that the locals, "these Allobroges," were not so different to look at from Romans, except in one regard: They had abundant amounts of curly, very dark body hair everywhere, on their chests, their arms, their backs, their necks, their ears. They were like a species not quite evolved from the animal—they were people with fur.

These blokes on the bus, these *mecs,* these Neanderthal cousins: I looked like them. We understood each other. I recognized the type on the first day, when Jessica and I arrived at the airport. In fact, if I had come across any of them at any time in history—fifty thousand years ago, say, all of us cautiously emerging out of our caves on the first warm spring morning—I am sure I would have recognized the affinity, and we would have instantly dropped our clubs and grunted in that understated, mumbled way that men of this kind regard as a sign of affection and solidarity.

Jessica and I returned home late, light-headed and happy from Roberto's red wine, feeling absolutely good about absolutely everything. I wouldn't be cooking a meal for Bob this week. But I would cook it for him soon; my prep was frozen. The beginnings of the dish now seemed remote—getting the pastry wrong, the mushy filling, learning what I wanted the sauce to express, learning that the sauce should be expressing anything in the first place. The dish, and my relationship to it, put me in mind of Alain Chapel—and how cooking is much more than recipes. A dish is arrived at not by following a set of instructions but by discovering everything about it: the behavior of its ingredients, its history, and a quality that some chefs think of as its soul. (The Swedish chef Magnus Nilsson once described something similar to me—we were talking about the cooking of Michel Bras—as an essence that seems to radiate, almost spiritually, from a plate of certain foods.) My duck pie was now mine. Têtedoie might reject it for deviating too far from what had been prescribed. But it was what I wanted the dish to be. It was what I would serve Bob.

Jessica mentioned that she had a coffee date planned the next day with our American friend Jenny Gilbert. She wanted to talk about her new venture, a restaurant that she and fellow musician Tamiko wanted to open: a noodle shop, the kind that you don't see around Lyon, but one that both of them, frequent visitors to Tokyo, felt they understood. She had found a property on the Place Sathonay, in the heart of our quartier.

In the morning—windy and now viciously cold—Jessica went off. I settled down at my desk. Twenty minutes later, she phoned.

"I have bad news. Jenny just told me. Please sit down." She paused. "Bob is dead."

He died while we were waiting for him. While we were drinking our wine and eating our bruschette, Bob was in trouble. He had been supine too long. A clot developed in the leg. In his being newly mobile, it came loose, rushed up an artery, and lodged in his lungs. He knew it was happening, Roberto told us later. Bob knew at once that he was in fatal trouble. Jacqueline called an ambulance. He was unconscious before it arrived.

I rushed down to the boulangerie. I didn't know what else to do. I opened the door, and the bell jingled, and Ailene, one of Bob's helpers, came out from the back, because it was the routine to come out on the sound of the bell. She saw me and stopped, lower lip trembling, holding herself still. I stopped, too. I thought: Very few people know. I thought: If she carries on as though nothing has changed, if Lucas carries on as though nothing has changed, if he makes the bread at 4:00 a.m., as he did today, and she sells it, can we all pretend, for just a little bit longer, that Bob is still at home recuperating?

The bell jingled, and one of the quartier's restaurant people appeared, a waiter from the Restaurant Albert. He had always kept to himself. He was bald, quiet, thin, one of the five people (including the owner, chef, and dishwasher) who ran a purple-painted place decorated with chicken images, serving handmade food, never radical, utterly honest. The waiter was bearing a large empty bread sack that needed filling. He handed it over to Ailene, and said he'd pick it up later.

"*Bisous à Bob.*"

"Bob is dead." *Bob est mort.*

The waiter stopped. He stood, unmoving, taking in the simple declarative piece of news, which seemed to echo in the quiet, still bakery, not as a sound but as an idea. *Bob est mort.* I watched him. Ailene watched him. He continued standing and saying nothing, although it seemed that at any moment he would say something. He was silent so long that our watching him started to seem too intimate and invasive, except that the issue was death, and intimacy and privacy didn't seem to matter in death. The longer the silence continued, the more I found myself admiring him. He didn't ask Ailene to repeat herself. He didn't ask "how" or "when" or "where," and there was an unexpected heroism in his not asking. The questions, any questions, would have been an evasion, an effort to fill this sudden void with noise.

Bob est mort.

"*Putain de merde,*" he said finally.

Putain de merde. A nonsense phrase. Two bad words in one, as though it were the worst thing you could say. Or it was just what you say when you don't have the words.

Putain de merde.

I hadn't known that, when you live on a river, you are never not thinking about it. You see it on waking, hear it in nighttime barges that sluice through it, feel it in the dampness of the air. It's never the same, rising, rushing, sinking, slow when foggy, thick in the summer, and is also always the same. It is so easily a metaphor that I find myself insisting that I will not allow it to be one. It's a river. Bob used to throw his unsold baguettes into it. The sight wasn't a metaphor. It was just melancholic, plain and simple. Only now does it occur to me that, with bread that he had single-handedly made, he couldn't do the obvious and throw it away in a sack. He seemed to need to replicate the making of it in its unmaking, tossing each baguette, one by one, end over end, as if returning each one to nature for the birds and the fish. I will never see the sight again, and such a prospect is even more melancholic.

Lyon, grayly falling into winter, has a slightly putrid, cloying smoke that comes from somewhere upriver and hangs in the air. Burning leaves, a faraway fireplace, damp wood, coal, pungent and sticky. In the late autumn, the city smells of mortality. The river is about to become dangerous, fast, Alpine cold. Bodies will be recovered from it—after New Year's Eve (just about always), after the weekend (more often than I would have thought possible).

I was standing on our balcony, in the cold.

I wondered what you might have heard, standing here or on whatever had been here before, a chapel, a monk's chamber, a potter's storehouse. I have never lived so close to so many historic events. Would you have heard the report of a sniper's rifle during the Nazi occupation? Our quartier bears plaques to fallen members of the Resistance. In 1943, students were removed from the boys' school, L'École Robert Doisneau, including thirteen-year-old Rita Calef and her younger brother Léon, because they were Jewish. Would I have heard the wails of the mother when she turned up to take them home for lunch?

The Place des Terreaux, the administrative open square of the city, is a three-minute walk. Would I have heard the jeering crowd that gathered there on warm summer nights in 1553? Their jeering would have echoed off buildings that are still standing. Protestants had been appearing in Lyon, proselytizing, and were seized and burned on a bonfire erected on the square. (Would I have smelled the flesh's melting? It would have depended on the river and the wind.) When Protestants later returned, it was to take over the city, ransack churches, and drive out the Italians who had made Lyon home for three centuries. The cries of a riot: It happened just here.

Lyon has historic reasons for treating outsiders with suspicion.

In 177 A.D., Roman officials arrested a young Christian named Blandine for her refusal to renounce her faith, whipped her, and tied her to a post in the Amphitheatre of the Trois Gaules to be fed upon by animals. They didn't touch her. There were other efforts—a chair of red-hot coals, a bull—but they were unsuccessful, too, so an official slit her throat. I wouldn't have heard her, in her stoical silence, only the crowd's baying voices, amplified in the round.

A river, sometimes, is just a river.

I never cooked my dish for Christian Têtedoie. I completely forgot.

QUAI SAINT-VINCENT, LYON. The boulangerie was reopened by Bob's wife, Jacqueline, an act of bravery and will and need. Her young daughter, Suzanne, sat on a stool in a corner, nibbling on a croissant, shy beyond talking.

Jacqueline was going to make it work, she said. She had put in the hours, been behind the counter every Sunday, and had long lived by Bob's clock, the ineluctable cycles of fermentation. Lucas agreed to help—by now he was working at another boulangerie but wasn't the first Lyonnais to hold two jobs. Jacqueline's first weekend was a success. It seemed to continue Bob's legacy. It seemed to continue Bob. Once again, we had good bread.

The weekdays were harder, with the burden of restaurant orders and delivering them, the day-in-day-out-ness of it all. One Friday, the boulangerie didn't open. It was incomprehensible: A boulangerie never just doesn't open. All day long, an endlessly replenishing queue of customers showed up and read the sign pasted to the locked door ("for reasons beyond our control . . ."), and shook their heads and were confused.

Jacqueline brought in help. One weekend, she had three boulangers in the back, a talented crew, each member new to me. I didn't know where or how she had found them, but their competence was manifest.

"We're going to make this work!" Jacqueline roared. The shop had its former busyness, it was loud again with Bob's salsa soundtrack, she was excited and confident—I hadn't seen such confidence before—and there were handfuls of cash.

But she had made a miscalculation. The cash she brought in didn't match the cash she had to pay out. It seems extremely unlikely that Bob had ever talked to Jacqueline about cash flow and how tight his margins must have been, and how much work he had to put in to keep the price of a baguette under a euro. The boulangers in the back went unpaid and never returned.

In all this, what Bob had done was evident as though in silhouette. In the hours, in the grit, in his determination to do all the work himself. If you deviated from Bob's do-it-by-yourself business model, then the business didn't work. In fact, Bob had no business model. Bob's boulangerie was Bob.

"I hate Jacqueline," Roberto said. "She ruined that space." Roberto was being unfair. He missed Bob. We all did.

Once again, the boulangerie closed. And then, toward the end of the month, it reopened again, but for only a few days. Maybe Jacqueline's rent was due. Then it closed again—forever, I assumed—until, unexpectedly, it had something to celebrate: The city was going to put an image of Bob upon its famous wall.

The city of Lyon had commissioned a painting and was going to find a space for it among the *fresque* of historic Lyonnais, the same *fresque* that included Emperor Claudius, Paul Bocuse, the Lumière brothers, Verrazzano, Antoine de Saint-Exupéry, two saints, and twenty-three other figures essential to how the Lyonnais regard themselves. It was such a magnificent gesture, and the recognition that Bob deserved, and proof, yet again, that his bread was more than just bread.

A poster went up announcing the "inauguration" at 7:00 p.m. on a Thursday, March 29, of "Yves 'Bob' Richard sur la Fresque des Lyonnais."

On the day, more than two hundred appeared. It was spring, it was warm, and Jacqueline set outdoor speakers and played very loud salsa music—Bob's music, her music, and now our music, everyone dancing, everyone bumping into each other.

"He hears us," Jacqueline told me. "He is dancing, too." She was passing out small pizzas, toasted slices of bread dressed with tomato sauce, and bottles of beer.

The site on the *fresque,* however, was small, and around the corner from the main display, and the space was right there at the bottom, almost level with the pavement. You could kick it. A curtain (tiny, like a stage set for a kitten) was lifted. It was—what? I had to bend over and twist my head to take it in. The space, about eight by ten inches, had been rendered as a hardback book on a shelf of other books. Bob was the subject of the cover. Why put him among minor Lyonnais authors? He read, but not much—he didn't have the time. In fact, what he mainly read was the local paper. The likeness was good, jowly, eyes with an impish twinkle, and a muted droll smile. The boys touched his painted cheeks. And we were all much happier that it was there than not there. But it felt nevertheless that we—and Bob—had been just a little bit too much cheated.

It was the last time I saw Jacqueline and Suzanne.

IX

The Gastronomic Capital of the World

In this connection, we had dinner the other night with Curnonsky, who is 80, and at the party was a dogmatic meatball who considers himself a gourmet but is just a big bag of wind. They were talking about Beurre Blanc, and how it was a mystery, and only a few people could do it, and how it could only be made with white shallots from Lorraine and over a *wood fire*. Phoo. But that is so damned typical, making a damned mystery out of perfectly simple things just to puff themselves up. I didn't say anything as, being a foreigner, I don't know anything anyway. This dogmatism in France is enraging (that is really about my only criticism, otherwise I adore them).

JULIA CHILD, *AS ALWAYS, JULIA:*
THE LETTERS OF JULIA CHILD AND AVIS DEVOTO

Bron, rhône-alpes. Daniel Boulud phoned me early. He was in Brussels, with Jérôme Bocuse, having attended a fund-raiser for the Bocuse d'Or, and a wealthy patron had loaned him a jet to fly them to Lyon to see their families. Could I pick them up at the small airfield in Bron?

It was an exotic request, the airfield was where Saint-Exupéry used to take off from, and of course I agreed. For a brief flicker of a thought, I wondered: Why doesn't he take a taxi? But I dismissed the question—who knows why?—and, besides, I was flattered.

I first dropped off Jérôme, who was staying in the Croix-Rousse with his mother, Raymone Carlut, his father's mistress and travel companion.

"Paul's love life is complicated," Boulud said as if by explanation.

We proceeded down the other side of the hill, a windy, steep road that I hadn't known, Boulud directing me. And then, as if on cue, he pulled out his phone and called the great man himself, right then and there, and said he'd be seeing him in five minutes.

"Do you mind?" he asked me. "Every time I come to Lyon, I have to see Paul, first thing."

It is only now, in retrospect, that I realize that this was another instance of Boulud's silent enhancement of my life in Lyon. He knew all along that he would be seeing Bocuse. He didn't need a ride from the airport.

I may have been driving slowly—or maybe there was a shortcut I didn't know—because, by the time we reached L'Auberge, Jérôme was already there, having a cup of coffee with his father. Evidently, Jérôme, too, needed to see "Paul, first thing."

A breakfast was produced—cakes, mainly, and toast—and it seemed evident that the three of them—dad, son, and Daniel (who could have been called the "surrogate other son")—met often, talked more, and were extremely at ease with each other.

Monsieur Paul touched his chest, a modest cough, which both of his sons noticed, and he explained that he had been having trouble breathing.

Daniel and Jérôme were instantly solicitous. ("Have you seen your doctor?" "Have you tried steam?")

Bocuse was frail, and everyone panicked when he was ill. "But no," he said, "it is not a medical issue." He insisted: "Really, it's not."

"It's the pollution," I said, maybe a little loudly, emboldened by having suffered the same trouble and by being able to contribute, however modestly, to a conversation among the representatives of three generations of great Lyonnais chefs at one table.

Bocuse turned to me. "That's it." *C'est ça.* "You're right. He's right," he said. "It's the pollution."

"The two of you don't live in Lyon," I said. "You don't know."

"That's right," Bocuse said again, and I liked that we agreed, both of us emissaries of the city in our different ways, and that we both were prepared to say the thing that is never said: that Lyon, this uniquely soulful, historically evocative, and seldom visited beautiful gem of a city, a sand castle between great rivers, neglected and in need of defending, has pollution. The city is not to blame, unless it can be faulted for the accidents of geography. The pollutants are from factories along the east of France, and from vehicle emissions from the north-south traffic on the Autoroute du Soleil. They funnel into the Rhône Valley and, on hot, still days, seem to gather heavily as a brown pestilence, float above the summer-languid Saône, and not move.

As the breakfast proceeded, which no one was eating except yours truly, who was not about to pass up a chance of eating anything chez Bocuse, it seemed that Jérôme and I were joining a continuing tutorial between Monsieur Paul and Monsieur Daniel. Boulud and I had completed our project, the two dozen "iconic dishes," and, without my knowing, he had been regularly in touch with Monsieur Paul to ensure that he was getting the dishes right.

"The *poulet en vessie,*" Bocuse asked. "You sorted out the knot?"

Boulud's kitchen team had run into a problem keeping the bladders from deflating.

Boulud confirmed that he had.

"The *volaille à Noelle?*" he asked, alluding to the miraculous performance piece of the completely boned chicken then reinflated with various mousselike fillings.

"It looked good," Boulud said. It was really very flashy.

"You remembered the asparagus?" Bocuse asked.

"Yes, thank you, Paul." One mousse was made with asparagus.

"White or green?"

"Green."

"Johannès used white," Bocuse said, alluding to the elder Nandron.

"White?" Boulud asked.

"Always."

"Oh," Daniel said. (He turned to me and whispered, *"Merde!"*)

"And the *jambon au foin?*"

"Yes, thank you, Paul," Daniel confirmed. "The *jambon au foin* was very successful."

"And the herbs?" *Les aromatiques?*

"The herbs?" Daniel asked.

"Yes, because hay isn't fragrant enough."

Daniel looked at me again in a panic. This, too, we had made together, with a tractor's worth of alfalfa, but the barnyard aromas had dissipated in the cooking. We had both noticed it, but didn't make a big deal about it, because it was what it was—hay. It smelled sweet, maybe, if you stuck your nose right into it, but more like a muddy football field in midwinter than the poetry of cut grass on a summer day, and nothing like the animal's feeding trough that we expected.

"I always add rosemary," Bocuse said.

"Rosemary?"

"Yes." *Beaucoup.* "Lots and lots of rosemary."

"Merde, merde, merde," Boulud whispered.

Daniel and I walked back to the car. "How could I forget that it was white asparagus?" He looked stricken. "I knew it was white. I'd seen it."

Bocuse knew Gérard Nandron, Daniel's first boss. He knew Nandron's father, Johannès. He knew Jean-Paul Lacombe when he started at Léon de Lyon, because he knew his father, Paul Lacombe. He knew Anne-Sophie Pic when she started in Valence, because he knew both her father, Jacques, and her grandfather André. He knew not only the great Alain Chapel, but the great man's father, Roger. Bocuse had been there. He knew exactly how food had been made in Lyon for the last hundred years—and much longer—because he knew the people, generations ago, who had learned how to cook from the generation before them. I don't know anyone else who has this kind of firsthand, eyewitness know-how. Bocuse, himself the son and grandson of chefs who had made food on the very spot where we now found ourselves, was a steward of the region's historical culinary record.

In an instant, I understood a Bocuse dish—not the preparation, which was chicken cooked in a bladder, but the name, poulet à la Mère Fillioux. Bocuse hadn't worked for Mère Fillioux. She died in 1925, the year before he was born. He had worked in the kitchens of Eugénie Brazier and Fernand Point. At La Mère Brazier, he was in charge of poultry operations. I liked the connection: that I had been in the same places, both of them, and had learned the dish just as Bocuse had done (i.e., Mère Brazier → Fernand Point → Paul Bocuse → me!!!). But I was missing the point.

In Lyon, Fillioux remains a culinary icon, even though no person living has eaten her food. She continues to appear, in murals and photographs, in the same costume, overdressed in her prudishly puffy clothes, hair bundled up, bearing her miraculously tender chicken. And of course Eugénie Brazier, before she became *Mère* Brazier, worked in Fillioux's kitchen. That's where Brazier learned the dish. And then, at the hands of Brazier, Bocuse learned it.

Bocuse was the handoff guy.

Bocuse is known as the leader of nouvelle cuisine, the most prominent member of the pack of innovative chefs who, inheriting a cuisine that had been codified and largely unchanged for 150 years, had been united by a battle cry to make it new. In fact, Bocuse was not a nouvelle-cuisine guy. He never called himself a "nouvelle-cuisine chef." He was instead merely the most prominent member of a generation of chefs when French cooking, in many forms, nouvelle and not-so-nouvelle, had a wonderful postwar flourishing, a renaissance that had been two or three generations in the making. He was, in effect, just the most charismatic guy.

What he was, more than anything else, was a Lyonnais chef. His food: It is what people have been eating in Lyon for a very long time (made new, sometimes, and sometimes just made well).

Michel Richard was a nouvelle-cuisine chef: not of the first generation but powerfully liberated by it. His influences: Fernand Point (for his philosophy), Michel Guérard (for his inventiveness), and Gaston Lenôtre (for his creed: "as long as you make it better"). Bocuse opened a restaurant with Lenôtre. He was Guérard's good friend. He enjoyed their company but wasn't the same kind of chef. Bocuse's worldview was local. Every item on his menu has an archaeology: Mère Fillioux's *poulet en vessie;* Mère Brazier's sea bass *en croûte;* Fernand Point's Dover sole on fresh, handmade tagliatelle. Then the local dishes: the chicken from Bresse, the chicken *au vinaigre,* the quenelle from the local river fish, the lake fish, the local crawfish.

What makes Lyonnais food exceptional is—just as Bocuse had told me when I first met him—a chef's access to the nearby ingredients. Lyon is a geographical accident of good food and food practices. The Dombes, with its birds and its freshwater eels and monkfish; the rivers, with their *brochet;* the mountain lakes (Lac du Bourget, Lac d'Annecy) with their unique fish varieties, found there and nowhere else; the farmyard cooking of Vienne and Condrieu and Ampuis, with their pigs and goats; the Alps with their cheeses; and everywhere, in each place, a local wine. All the ingredients are "cartable," the distance, between fifty and seventy-five kilometers, that food was conveyed before the era of motorized vehicles, by foot or animal or boat, basically the route to a market city since the invention of the wheel and the domestication of animals and the discovery that wood floats.

Lyonnais food is quite simple. The simplicity is what gives the region its reputation. It is not necessarily elaborate cooking. It is local dishes, which are good, served with local wines, which are good, and the meals are always very good value.

X

The Greatest Adventure in the Lives of Our Family

Their thoughts, for the most part, were solely of hunger, and their conversation, about food. I first witnessed this collective hysteria at the immensely large camp of Petrisberg—all prisoners knew or experienced it—which consisted of manic reminiscing about past feasts. They would gather in small, feverish groups with the sole purpose of talking about eating. A peasant would recite the menu of his wedding dinner and the specialties of his terroir, and the gourmands would describe in detail the menus of La Mère Poulard, Le Restaurant Larue, and Le Chapon Fin. Amateur cooks would exchange recipes with a precision that would intimidate a Cordon Bleu graduate, while others would take notes. . . .

FRANCIS AMBRIÈRE, *LES GRANDES VACANCES,* 1946,
TRANSLATED FROM THE FRENCH BY FREDERICK BUFORD

A

T THE FOOT OF THE GRANDE MONTAGNE DE VIRIEU, BELLEY.
Six years after reading Brillat-Savarin's famous book in my
urban cubicle in the offices of *The New Yorker* and vowing
that, one day, I would replicate his walk into the high mountains to visit
a monastery, I was doing it: Finally! I was off! I was on the trail! I was
making my ascent! Then, I got lost.

I wasn't lost as in I'm-in-a-forest-and-can't-find-my-way-home lost. I
wasn't even lost in the sense of I-now-don't-know-which-way-to-turn
lost. There was basically only one direction—up. But there had been
several up-trending possibilities to choose from, when the trail just disappeared: smooshed into nonexistence by what seemed to have been a
large herd of elephants suddenly deciding to take a group nap.

Also—and this seemed peculiar to me—there was no one around.
Since I'd started: not a soul. I found the situation, well—creepy, actually. It was a Saturday, the morning beautiful, the sky October blue, the
weather fair, the breezes gentle. Where was everybody? Was I really the
only one visiting this ruin? To be so unequivocally alone, *and* lost, even
if I knew the likely direction to be heading in, wasn't entirely comfortable. Guns were being fired—bird hunters, I assumed, which seemed
seasonally apposite even if less than reassuring.

Jessica had bought me a topographical hiker's trail map in which
every dinky forest, partial meadow, and dried-up brook was precisely
represented—the document, published by the French National Geo-

graphic Institute, was, in my judgment, among the greatest navigational events since the invention of feet—and, after consulting it, I saw that I had mistaken the flattened grass for the trail (cows, rather than elephants, having been the likely culprits). I retraced my steps, located my route, and resumed my journey.

There was a paved road, the D-53, which Brillat-Savarin obviously hadn't followed since it hadn't yet been created, so I tried to avoid it. The one I settled on had a chance of being the very trail that he had followed if only because there didn't seem to be a better one. It started in the town of Virieu-le-Grand, at the base of the mountain. Brillat-Savarin describes it as a steep five-thousand-foot climb. I looked up—a sheer, flat, white rocky face (the kind you would take a ski lift to reach the top of or wear a parachute to jump from)—and thought: Oh, shit.

Brillat-Savarin, I should clarify, hadn't done the walk on his own. He was a member of a group of musicians in his hometown of Belley, about seven miles due south, and they had been invited by the abbot to celebrate the day of Saint Bernard, the monastery saint. No fine music had ever penetrated its elevated isolation, the abbot had said, and a musical performance would delight not just the monks but also the neighbors (*"nos voisins"*).

In my own effort, I wasn't trying to follow in Brillat-Savarin's footsteps, as such—because, after more than two centuries, what would I expect to find? My hike was more like an act of reflective homage. Brillat-Savarin had undertaken his monastery visit at a time when its traditions were still intact: namely, a place where, for about a thousand years, really good food and drink got made. He wrote about it thirty years later, and he is clear about why. In the intervening period, the French Revolution happened, and the monasteries were ransacked, and the monks driven off. Many of the current generation, he says, have never seen a monastery or met a monk, and have no idea what they have contributed to the national cuisine.

I had planned to go up and down the mountain on the same day, early start, late-ish return, and was staying at a hotel not in Virieu-le-Grand but the next village in the valley, Artemare, owing to a report of the good food there: an auberge in a former village schoolhouse, a venerable oak tree in the front—jumbly, cluttered (at the end of my hall were a vacuum cleaner and a priest's confessional), and unselfconsciously old-fashioned. The night before, I ate *féra,* among the most prized of the lake fish, with an unusually firm meatlike texture (from Lac Léman— you rarely see it in Lyon), that had been cooked *à la meunière,* served with *épinards au gratin,* and topped with four identically turned vegetables, a carrot, a potato, a zucchini, and a turnip. The meal confirmed an enduring French expectation that, when you stay at a village hotel, you won't get Michelin flash, but you can count on eating well.

Like the hotel, the area—referred to as the massif of Bugey—was also delightfully anachronistic. Brillat-Savarin came here every autumn to shoot birds, a practice that was obviously still observed today. The villages still had communal water troughs and ovens to bake bread in, which were very much in use, blackened, a stack of wood nearby, a peel alongside it (the flat trowel that you slide under a loaf to remove it when it's done). The sight of them revived in me a connection to Bob and what he had tried to re-create in his ovens on the Quai Saint-Vincent, some preindustrial, earth-produced taste that he had grown up with and I hadn't. Jacques Pépin once told me that the greatest food of his life was the bread of his Lyonnais childhood, just out of the oven, with butter, and I regretted that no one was making any in the village ovens today.

After my dinner, I approached the hotel's husband-and-wife owners— they were eating dinner on television trays, drinking a local mountain wine, and watching the news—and asked if I could trouble them to make me a sandwich for my hike.

"Chicken?" the wife confirmed, and the next morning I was handed most of the meat from a roasted *poulet de Bresse* crushed between two rustic slices and wrapped in foil. I put it in my backpack. It smelled like a Sunday lunch. My other items were a very large bottle of water, sunblock, a map of the site made after a nineteenth-century archaeological dig, and two books—my volume of Brillat-Savarin and a small handmade collection of recipes. I had bought it on eBay.fr. The author, who is never identified (although there are clues), was a French prisoner of war held in a camp in Nazi Germany. The recipes were compiled as Europe appeared to be falling to the Nazis and seemed, like the Brillat-Savarin, to be written in the hope of being able to hold on to something that was very threatened—French food and everything that it had come to represent.

In all this—the monastery, the handmade recipe book, even my chicken sandwich—there was, for me, a simple assumption that I feel compelled to make explicit: namely, that we are born needing to eat but not knowing how to make food.

Among the functions essential to our survival (e.g., drinking, breathing, evacuating, sleeping, reproducing, etc.), eating, at least since the invention of fire, is different. Cooking—the how-to, the what—is taught: a set of skills handed over by those who know to those who don't, and from one generation to the next (what a grandmother hands over to a grandchild, a parent, aunt, uncle to children, what Julien Boulud learned from his uncles eighty years ago and passed on to his son Daniel). Before the modern era, that knowledge was diurnal; it was the behavior of your local patch on the Earth, the modulations of the seasons. *This* is what will feed you in the winter. *This* is how to cure meat so that you have some when you have nothing else. *This* is how you make cheese, or wine, or bread. This is what food tastes like. And this is the knowledge that monasteries, like the one I was hiking to, the abbey of Saint Sulpice (founded in 1033), were great repositories of. If the knowledge isn't handed down—if for reasons of war or famine or industry or revolution or a massive volcano that buries your civilization in ash—then the chain is broken, and there is the possibility that the knowledge will be lost.

Saint Sulpice had only been granted protective status as a national treasure in 1994. But it was now officially a *monument,* in the fullest sense of the word: It marked a place where something happened which now was gone.

During the walk, I came upon other reminders, monuments that I hadn't expected, including a yellow trail sign for a *stèle*—a marker, in the high altitude of nowhere. I followed it and came upon a French flag, a high white rock, and a stone inscription revealing that, on June 15, 1944, fifteen Resistance fighters were ambushed here by German soldiers and killed. I paused and read each name. They would have been local lads— quite possibly descendants of the *voisins* around the monastery—and would have known these woods, the ins and outs of them, better than any foreigner.

I came across another war memory, a mile or two further along, a sign with a simple text: On June 15, one Émile Clayet had been tortured and then shot.

I contemplated what he had been subjected to and what information the German soldiers were hoping Monsieur Clayet would reveal. I hoped it didn't relate to the ambush.

I made other discoveries of a more pedestrian nature: that, for instance, you should never, ever, hike in a pair of boots without first breaking them in. I also learned that you can never have enough water. I had finished my bottle long ago. At the outset there had been waterfalls and a rushing stream, even if a little precarious-making to reach from the trail, and I didn't try. I was confident I'd find more later; the map told me so. And I did, but here, where the massif flattened, there were pastures, and the water wasn't moving much, and cows were standing in it, and I decided that, nah, I wasn't really that thirsty.

I also learned this about the monastery: It wasn't there.

What a curious thing.

There was a chapel, so I knew I had come to the right place. (It would be Jessica's first question when I told her: Are you sure you didn't get lost again?) It may have marked the original entrance to the monastery property—it was dedicated to a Saint Vital—and was unearthed only recently, in the 1970s (and escaped therefore at least a century or two of pillaging). An effort to reconstruct it—a wheelbarrow, a wood plank to push it across, a pile of stones—was very much on display. Yes, I appeared to be in the right place. But where was the monastery hiding?

There was a dead-end road sign—the only indication of a civil authority—which led up a hill. On my left: a discarded ceramic bathtub, a sink, blue plastic bags. On my right: an electric fence. I then saw it, on the other side of the gate, which not only told you to keep out but promised to electrocute you if you disobeyed.

Or at least I believe I was seeing it. *It* (i.e., an oddly raised piece of earth, like a long hill with a dirt roof) was not so much a ruin as a ruin that had been buried. *It* was a shape, high on what was the highest hill, with jaggedy bits, looking not unlike funeral mounds, and about two hundred feet in length, around fifty across. Historical archaeological digs had also confirmed the structure. But whatever had been uncovered at the time had been covered up since.

The electric fence was disconcerting. So, too, were the property's inhabitants: four young bulls. They were in the shade at the top of the hill. They appeared to be guarding the monastery. I really hadn't expected to find four young bulls.

They arranged themselves in a row and stared at me. I wasn't going to be thwarted by the fence or the animals, and I refused to regard the impediment as a big deal. But actually it was a big deal.

I checked my phone. I had battery but no reception.

I continued up the dead-end road to the outer perimeter of the property, following the electric fence. I was looking for a place where I might slide under.

The bulls turned, still in a row, and continued to stare.

I cut into the woods, still running alongside the fence, where it was steeper and bumpier, and I found a spot. I lay facedown, scooted under, and rolled. I was in the property.

The bulls, meanwhile, had turned a full 180 degrees, to keep me in view. They were remarkably attentive.

I was now in the sun, and I was hot. The bulls were on the higher ground, in the shade, standing amid the ruins of the monastery. They were where I wanted to be.

They were still in a line, but had pressed themselves together more tightly. One bull was now in advance of the others. He fixed on me.

He stared. I stared back.

This is ridiculous, I thought. I clapped, loud, and then made a noise, a shout. The bull inched forward. His stare was impressively intense.

He snorted. No question: That was a snort. He then seemed to paw the ground. He pawed it a second time. He pawed it a third time. He was preparing to charge.

I thought: This could be a good ending for my book.

I thought: This could be a rather bad ending for me.

I changed my plan and slowly, my gaze averted, made my way down the other side of the hill in the direction of the chapel. I made a very big circle, and didn't look back. On reflection, I decided, those bulls—they can have their monastery.

Eventually, I reapproached from the other side, where the bulls weren't facing. By then (it had been a long walk) they were eating grass and had wandered down the hill, ceding their position to me.

I found the spot where I thought that the church's altar might have been buried and sat down against a trunk of a tree and, feeling that I'd been holding my breath for a long time, exhaled deeply. When Brillat-Savarin got up here, he had unusually refined thoughts—he describes an evening stroll, between the second and third feast of the day, and breathing "the pure air of those high meadows"—and discovered that it refreshed "a man's soul and disposed his imagination to quiet thought and to romanticism." Then again, he probably didn't have to deal with a bull.

I calmed down, opened my backpack, and addressed the prospect of my long-overdue lunch. In the circumstances—and possibly owing to the pure air of these high meadows—that chicken sandwich was the best chicken sandwich I have eaten in my life.

I consulted the map from a nineteenth-century dig and concluded that, yes, I was directly over the altar. I was also near a graveyard housing eight centuries of monks. I thought: That's a lot of dead monks. I opened my Brillat-Savarin.

He got a few things wrong. The altitude, for instance, wasn't five thousand feet but, according to my trail map, more like half that height. (Then again, after my own effort to climb it, I can attest that it felt like five thousand.) Otherwise the basic surroundings haven't changed much. Brillat-Savarin describes pine trees to the west—the very forest that I'd hiked through to find my way under the electric fence—and how the monastery itself was on a plateau between two mountainlike ridges, with a pasture in between. And it was beautiful—on this crisp autumnal afternoon, it seemed like a natural-world paradise—this wide-open valley, the bright green grass, the forest, the utter isolation. The monastery began with twelve monks. By the time of the Revolution, there were more—two dozen? three?—overseeing ten thousand acres, including vineyards and a man-made lake. Everything they ate, they made—or freshly harvested with their own hands.

According to Brillat-Savarin, there was a bountiful variety. He describes his first meal ("a truly classic *déjeuner*"), a banquet of such generous proportions as to resemble the monastery itself: a pâté rising out of the middle of the table like a church, flanked on the north by veal, on the south by pork, on the west by artichokes, and on the east by a monumental ball of butter. (The monks, who were fasting for their saint, had prepared the feast in advance, wholly committed to the high principle of hospitality, even if they couldn't join.) After the mass—the musicians performing throughout—a dinner was prepared inspired by the taste (*le goût*) of the 1500s, including various meats done as simple ragoûts (*"une bonne cuisine"*), local mountain vegetables with more flavor than town-dwellers had tasted before, followed by fourteen platters of roast ("abundance was the rule"). At nine, there was a light supper. The neighbors showed up for a long night of drinking and singing and games that culminated in the last food of the night, hot bread and butter with a tub of sweetened eau-de-vie that arrived alight.

The neighbors, from the local villages, returned seven years later. Thézillieu, which I could view from my seat against the tree trunk, was the closest, and I imagined seeing their coming, *les foules,* the throngs, on a warm night in August 1789, crossing the wide-open pasture, bearing torches and crude weapons. They would have chased the sandaled inhabitants out of the abbey and down the mountain. They then began to take the buildings apart—the demolition appears to have taken many, many years—and carted away the bricks to build their homes and barns with. And they set everything on fire, archives, manuscripts, books, eight centuries of history.

Brillat-Savarin doesn't mention that night, nothing to mar the sharp cold clarity of the hike he made to reach a monastery, intact and wholly functioning. Even so, the visit doesn't seem to be the point that Brillat-Savarin wanted to make. It was that no such visit will recur. That world is gone. In all my imagining of my own visit, I had never thought there would be nothing left.

I put down my volume of Brillat-Savarin and pulled out my handwritten book of recipes. On the cover the author had written *Recettes* at an angle and underlined it. I'm not sure if it was a title or simply a declaration of purpose.

I came by it owing to an interest I had developed in old secondhand cookbooks, especially those of the "Mère" variety. It started when Michel

Richard told me that one had inspired him to start cooking. When he was ten, while his mother was at work, he read her copy of *La Véritable Cuisine de famille* by "Tante Marie," and decided, then and there, that he would hereafter make dinner for the family, then six people. (Or seven? Or maybe nine? It was never clear, not least because at least two of them were "unofficial.") I found a copy published in 1948, the year of Richard's birth, and quite possibly the very edition he cooked from, the spine suitably obliterated, with a back cover attached by a strip of brittle yellow tape, for the price of 5 euros. The title translates as "True family cooking," and the book could be seen as akin, in its idiosyncratic French way, to what *Joy of Cooking* would become in the United States, a go-to guide for making dinners and holiday meals that many families had to have. But "Tante Marie" was much more casual than her American counterpart and, faced with the challenge of rendering French cuisine for home cooks, rose to it by going light rather than heavy, in short punchy paragraphs, three or four recipes a page, no ingredients list, and not much fuss about measuring them: a glass of this, a coffee cup of that. Her approach was evident on every page: "You can do this!"

I acquired lots of Mère books. I coveted stained, used, filthy ones, and found an almost addictive pleasure in flipping through pages that had been studied, in some cases, more than a century before. They were a household's most used volume and seemed to reveal their histories, of people gathered around tables, of celebrations, of children growing up, and the intimacy that food seems to effect. They also had a quality that I want to describe as an "aura." French cooking, as I knew perfectly well, has to be learned, and it is certainly not hereditary even if it is an important element in one's French heritage. These books were purposeful. There was urgency between the teachers and the readers, most evident in what was published from around 1890 or so to the 1920s, when French families seemed to believe that their veritable "Frenchness" rested on their being able to make a French meal. There was also a flourishing of how-to magazines, "gazettes," broadsheets, public lectures. It was a historically unique moment, when cooking, *French* cooking, was no longer a conversation held among chefs, but also among families.

The first handwritten family cookbook that I came upon was started during World War I. I was startled to discover that such things existed and that you could actually buy them—again for little money; nobody was interested. The little book—it measured three inches by four—conveyed both mystery and sadness: the mystery of someone, invariably a woman, trying to make a household function *and* be French, an artifact that was itself stuffed with artifacts, how-to dishes written up on paper scraps from friends, a postcard from a general on the front, a shopping list, the scarcity of butter, of meat, of sugar, a menu plan for Christmas Day. Jessica and I sat at our own kitchen table and examined the pages, and everything else that we found between them, and felt ourselves voyaging via an unexpected vehicle of time-travel into someone else's cooking space, which wouldn't have had refrigeration and where a gas-burning oven was a novelty.

And the sadness? The fact that it was now in my hands. It had been a kitchen tool for at least three generations, beginning around 1915, a seventy-year conversation between a grandmother, a mother, and a daughter, until finally it was swept out in an estate-clearing auction of whatnots and ended up on eBay.

I collected these home recipe collections—I must have three dozen by now—in the hope that, one day, I would find an unexpected piece of text that might teach me something new about the French kitchen, an insight, a surprise. I may have found it in the handwritten recipe book that I had brought with me.

The book is inescapably handmade. A thick piece of cardboard was bent in half. Sheets of another era's very thin paper have been folded and slipped inside, and number sixty-eight pages. Each sheet is lined, perfectly, lightly, on both sides, in pencil. Nothing is revised, no corrections, except for a few words that have been crossed out. I counted five. There isn't a misspelling or a stray accent. Only one page has fingerprints, from three fingers, that interrupt a densely written account of the Burgundy recipe for poaching eggs in red wine (*oeufs en meurette,* one of my favorite lunchtime wintry dishes). The effort is meticulous. It is bound by candy-cane-striped string looped through the spine. I brought it with me because it seemed to resonate with Brillat-Savarin's memoir.

There are clues as to the book's origins, all of them frustratingly incomplete, like initials on the front cover, compressed as though the author was experimenting with a logo. They are also smudged, as if he had tried to rub them out, and are hard to read. They might be "MR." The other side of the cardboard reveals that it was cut from a Red Cross relief box. ("From: American Red Cross—USA. To: International Red Cross Committ"—the last letters sliced off to fashion the cover.) There is an address, "Stalag IX, Ziegenhain," and an addressee, only the first five letters: "M O I S O."

Might this be the name of the author? Possibly so, possibly not. Ziegenhain was a POW camp that filled up mainly with French soldiers captured when Germany entered France in 1940. Inmates who agreed to tend the Nazi vegetable garden were rewarded with a relief box. Was our author among the gardeners? Or just the recipient of the cardboard afterward?

We can't know. I didn't know. I knew nothing, really, except that this handmade book in my own hands seemed to be among the most unique cookbooks I have ever held. I spent nights examining it, smelling it, reading it, feeling the pages for the impressions made by the pencil that wrote the recipes, imagining the circumstances, the concentration, the hunger of its author, his exhaustion, and a fantasy life that consisted of recollecting French dishes in impeccably precise detail.

I have since discovered there was a context. I read it in a memoir written by a French officer who, captured near the border after Germany invaded France, spent the rest of the war in several camps of this kind, including a six-month stint, mainly in solitary confinement, at Ziegenhain. The book, *Les grandes vacances* (*The Long Vacation*), by Francis Ambrière, was published in 1946, won the Goncourt (even though it wasn't fiction and never purported to be), and became an instant best seller, satisfying the curiosity of a nation that longed to know, and mourned on learning, what happened to their captured fathers and sons and brothers (estimated to be about 1.8 million).

Ambrière showed me that my anonymous author wasn't alone. In the first year of captivity, he writes, Frenchmen, starving, were obsessed by memories of their national cuisine. "In the first days of captivity, hundreds of cookbooks were written in vengeful hope of our returning soon to France." Ambrière had long appreciated French cuisine. But in Germany, in a prison camp at Petrisberg, he discovered its poetry, spoken in the haunted tones of nostalgia and tenderness: "It expressed not just hunger but something deeper: defiance, the revolt of reason, a joy in life."

Was my handmade book one of the hundreds? How many have survived? So far, I've found no others. And why this one? (I contacted the seller. He didn't know where the book came from. It was in a box of war memorabilia.)

There *are* similarities between Brillat-Savarin's recollection and the *"recettes"* of my anonymous author: At the very least, both works might be described as accounts of culinary mourning at a time of terrible upheaval. More profoundly, both books seem to be struggling to articulate how food in France has come to be so much more than food: It has become, on many levels, who you are.

The differences are as important, including the most basic: Brillat-Savarin wrote on a full stomach; the anonymous chef wrote on the verge of starvation. A hypothesis that I dreamed up—that he may have been made a chef for German officers, and that this volume had been his recipe book—was dashed on my learning the actual eating arrangements, thanks to the documentary efforts of the camp's last and most robust prisoners, the Americans. No one ate well, including the prison officers, although they did eat. Their leftovers, when there *were* leftovers, were made into a once-a-day soup that, by the last year of the war, "fed" approximately twenty thousand inmates. The majority of the inmates at Ziegenhain died of starvation.

Who was the anonymous chef?

I read and reread looking for more clues. The early pages are devoted to classic dishes—two ways of preparing hare, for instance, one a roast with a chestnut purée, and the other *à la royale* (a *civet de lièvre,* the animal cooked slowly in its blood). Many of the preparations are quite discursive. In an unusually long account of how to make puff pastry, the author remarks at the end that, as with all pastries, you should dust your worktop with flour to keep your dough from sticking. (I read this and thought: Really? This is what occurs to you when you are starving in a German camp?) Likewise for a *pâté-en-croûte,* he reminds us not to forget to make a chimney in your crust, to let the steam escape.

A chef or just an obsessive?

Where is he from? There are chicken recipes but no duck—or none that he was able to get around to writing. There is fish sauce—a "Normande," the very one that was made for the boys at their school canteen, with fish stock, oyster juice, and double cream—but no fish preparation. (So maybe not from the sea?) There is a cassoulet from the southwest, and a *cervelas de Strasbourg* from Alsace, in the northeast. But there are enough recipes from Brittany to make me think: Maybe from there?

The last pages are uncomfortably compelling.

They are different in look. The ornate script of the beginning (the author has a knack for starting each paragraph with an orthographic flourish) has disappeared. The writing doesn't get sloppy, but it gets small, compressed. There is so much he wants to say but he has only sixty-eight pages, and he wants to get all of French cooking into them, to make a record, get it written down. It is who he is. It is Frenchness. But he doesn't finish: three empty pages in the "Sauce" section, six in a section called "Cuisine," twelve in "Fruit," probably representing a whole food group to be addressed later. Twenty-three pages are blank.

Recettes is urgent. French food is on the verge of being erased. It can't be. It is too important. Food—*la cuisine*—is no longer the obsession of an aristocratic butterfly, but everyone, peasant and gourmand. It needs to be preserved, like civility, like dignity, like the table, like a shelter that protects us from the ugliness just outside our front door—the crudeness, cruelty, selfishness, the incomprehensible injustice. Cuisine, the author of *Recettes* recognizes, protects us in our humanity.

What a thing French food has become since La Varenne. And how radiant and sad and beautiful.

L'ÉCOLE DE ROBERT DOISNEAU. George and Frederick had entered what we called "the big boys' school," a different building, no longer "pre-K." Their first day was like a parade, everyone aware of the rite of passage the school represented, the students and parents arriving at pretty much the same time, exuberantly festive. The children all had new school backpacks, so outsized that the bottom of the frame bounced again their calves. They were little people about to become a little less little. Jessica knew what the "big boys' school" represented. I was unprepared for the pathos of it. The boys were no longer toddlers. The morning was magic to witness, all the more so because—well, it was France.

The boys had learned to read and write. They were taught to connect the letters in their words, each character crafted and uniform, and to adhere to a ruler's straight line. They had homework. They were learning their numbers, French numbers.

For our part, we carried on, with the difference that the time we had once regarded as "research" was now our lives: our lives in Lyon. Jessica, accredited now with a WSET diploma, set out to become a Master of Wine, a many-year undertaking, widely regarded as among the most difficult credentials in a world of I'm-tougher-than-you credentials. I carried on doing stints in kitchens, to learn a dish or a preparation. I studied the archives. I wrote.

One day, the boys were at the sink, in front of a mirror, with a comb, a brush, a running faucet, and hair gel. George, in bossy mode, had taken charge, telling Frederick what to do, how to wet his hair, smooth it out, and apply massive quantities of goop with a comb. Frederick, in resister mode, ignored the comb and picked up a brush. Jessica joined the audience. I began videoing.

They are speaking to each other in French, completely self-absorbed with their images in the mirror. Jessica puts a question to them, in English. They switch languages, but their first thoughts come out wrong and have to be corrected. *"La prochaine . . ."* George says, and stops. "Next time . . ." But then he forgets what he was going to say or can't translate the thought. Their English is word by word.

The boys have been away from New York longer than the time they lived there. I urge them to write to their grandmothers in the wonderful script, and they try, but they don't know how to write in English. I try to teach them words, but they find it too difficult.

"We need to return to the United States," Jessica says. "We don't want to, but we do."

I ponder the proposition.

I suggest the local bilingual schools.

They are not properly bilingual, Jessica says. With English classes taught by a French person? They are also private. And even if we could afford them, which we can't, there will be no Muslims, no Gypsies, blacks, Moroccans, Algerians, Croatians, all the rough and tumble that make the boys' school like life, a real Lyonnais life.

But they are too young to give up their French. They are seven. The magic age is said to be nine: If children can keep up two languages until then, they are likely to remain bilingual until adulthood. I don't want them to lose what our adventure has given them.

In Manhattan, there is a famous *"lycée."* Jessica sends an application to the headmistress; Daniel Boulud, whose daughter attended it, writes a letter in support of the boys. We never get a reply.

I mention beginning an application for French citizenship.

"Really?"

Without my knowing, Jessica has already approached an admissions officer at a bilingual school that has opened in our absence, L'École Internationale de New York (EINY for short), which, astonishingly, is only a block from our New York City apartment. Again without my knowing, Jessica (not exactly "clandestinely," but not necessarily *not* "clandestinely") submits the boys' academic records, and learns that, with their French education, they could be admitted—if *only* there were room. They are put on a waiting list.

"They can't attend a public school," she says suddenly. "They can't read or write in English."

By mid-August, three weeks before the Lyon school semester resumes, the admissions officer contacts Jessica, whereupon she informs me (defiantly, definitively) that we are returning to America. ("We are? How did that happen?")

And so, like that, we prepare to go back. It is so fast that we don't have time to say goodbye to anyone. It is so fast that we don't have time to move our belongings. It is so fast that we are suddenly leaving for the airport, on the last Tuesday in August, for a first day of school two days later (owing to the perversity of a school that observed the French calendar—*it was* la rentrée!—and not the American one, which began after Labor Day).

I take a last picture of the boys in our apartment at five in the morning, our long hallway with its brightly waxed wood floors, the heavy front door, Frederick's arm thrown over his brother's shoulders, both of them in shorts and sweatshirts, the weather fair but brisk. The boys look as hopeful as Christmas Eve. When we arrive at JFK, it is muggy, filthy, brown-sky August hot, which feels completely right.

The return occurs so impetuously and so lightly that it has an airy inconsequence.

On the boys' first morning, before their first day of their new school, they pause in front of our New York building, under the prototype Manhattan awning, their hair newly trimmed and washed, their ties bulkily knotted by their father, the beginning of a new morning ritual, gray slacks, the navy-blue blazers each with a single gold button, and a new generation of massively oversized book bags. They are little French guys, skinny, with elfin waists, delicate shoulders, thin arms, good posture, and an ability to look directly into the eyes of the adults who speak to them. On the first day of their new American life, they are neither apprehensive nor hopeful: They are confident. At L'École Robert Doisneau, the boys were the celebrated *New-Yorkais*. Now they are New Yorkers in New York.

I pick them up. They say little. Once home, and in view of their mother, they drop their book bags, as if on cue, and—their ties undone, their shirts untucked—collapse into heaps, and wail.

Their school should have been a soft re-entry. It was French, small classes, good teachers, near our home. But now I wonder if it was *too* similar to where they had been before. A normal American public school, in all its radical differences, would have been easier because the boys would have shown up there with no expectation of its being like anything else they had known.

They had issues with the food. At the school, the "chefs" didn't wear toques, George complained at dinner. Also, they didn't cook, he said.

"They use a microwave," Frederick explained. The expressions of both boys conveyed utter astonishment that a microwaver would ever have the audacity to call him- or herself a chef.

Was the food French? American?

They didn't know. They knew only that it was nothing like what they ate in Lyon. (They also didn't know that what they ate in Lyon was among the unique culinary experiences on the planet.)

In New York, they discovered pizza by the slice, Shake Shack cheeseburgers, and chocolate-chip cookies, but were perplexed by how they were eaten.

On their first Friday night back, George and Frederick met up with twin boys their own age for a night of watching movies together, a cinematic playdate with new friends. Their parents had once stopped in

Lyon to see us on their way back from a Provençal holiday. But when our boys showed up at their West Village home, the twin hosts, under the supervision of an indifferent nanny, had already eaten. A leftover pizza was on a counter, grease showing through the cardboard. George and Frederick looked baffled, climbed awkwardly onto kitchen stools, and ate by themselves.

"That's not dinner!" Frederick told me when I picked them up.

I perversely enjoyed the clear-eyed purity of his initial shock and felt that I was lucky to have witnessed it, for all the evening's distress.

Their New York classmates were mainly Parisians. George and Frederick had never met Parisians before. They didn't like them. Their pronunciation was different, their words were slangy. "They're all white," George said. They were rich, or seemed to be. One was driven to school in an Uber; one came from a family with airplanes. Lyon—its motley, improvised population, the pervasive smell of meals being cooked at home, the open-window sounds of families finishing dinner—seemed exotic and far away.

A senior teacher assessed the boys' command of English. I was invited to join. Each was asked to read a page aloud, the teacher confident that the talkative verbal children of verbal literary American parents wouldn't have a problem. The boys looked up blankly. They understood nothing. The look was painful to witness. It was a rebuke in the making: By insisting they go as native as possible, and keeping their French intact long enough to retain it for what I had hoped would be the rest of their lives, had I handicapped their education?

They were assigned to an English-as-a-second-language class and every day called out of their 10:00 a.m. English "Humanities" to attend it. George took to English quickly and after ten weeks returned to English "Humanities." Frederick had gone deep into French. One late-spring Saturday, well into Frederick's second semester, I sat with him in a park, helping him with his homework, a simple English-language children's book that he was meant to read aloud. The effort made him cry. After two paragraphs, he was exhausted.

I had a new fear: not that Frederick would need a long time to learn English, but that he would never learn it properly. He beat his head with his book.

Recently, he told us—at a family dinner—that he'd had so much instruction outside of his normal English "Humanities" that he missed learning crucial bits of knowledge and was still lacking them, like certain multiplication tables or even the basic calendar. He didn't know what came after August. (George, skeptical, asked him in French, *"Donc, qu'est-ce que c'est que le mois après août?"* *"Septembre,"* Frederick answered reflexively.)

Once, George, sitting by himself, pulled out a school photograph of his class at the Robert Doisneau. He had brought it back in his backpack. He stared at it intensely and touched the picture of each one of his classmates with a finger. The rims of his eyes welled up; I couldn't resist trying to get a snapshot, a first experience of loss and longing, and slyly took a shot from what felt like an inconspicuous distance.

George spotted me. He was embarrassed. He asked why I would do that, take a picture of him like that, when he was sad. He was cross, and was justified in being cross. I couldn't justify taking the photo.

But he didn't put the picture away, and when he glanced at it again, it immediately seized all of his attention, and he carried on staring at it, openly, without inhibition, oblivious of me, and I did, I admit, get a few more pictures.

LAC DU BOURGET. I returned to France on my own for a week. I hadn't done fish. I hadn't done the lake. I wanted to spend some days on Lac du Bourget, the largest lake in France, and the place where most of the fish that we eat in Lyon come from.

I had a contact, a fisherman, and a chef who promised to introduce me. Jessica arranged a place for me to stay. It was called La Source, a farmhouse made into a restaurant with rooms run by a husband-and-wife team, atop a wooded river valley that fed into the lake. The husband was a member of "the Maîtres Restaurateurs"—a chefs' collective that adheres to a code of self-sufficiency and making as much food "in-house" as possible. We discovered it by chance, on a road trip in the Loire Valley, with boys who had got hungry after an extended vineyard visit. We had stopped at the first eatery we saw, a restaurant on the Île Brochard, where the butter was churned by hand, the bread baked in-house, and the ice cream made from scratch daily. The Maîtres de

Cuisine are masters of the foods that most kitchens buy already made. For us, they were much more than restaurants. They were "old-school" culinary schoolhouses, and we sought them out.

When I sat down to dinner at La Source, where I was the only diner, the evening was crisp and autumnal. By the time I retired to my room, I was also the hotel's only guest. I opened my windows and saw nothing. Between the end of my meal and my walk upstairs, a fog from the lake had rolled up the valley and had encircled the hotel and was so thick that I couldn't see the ground below. The isolation—the hotel situated at the end of a three-mile road, with no neighbors, no nothing—was exhilarating.

I got up at six. The husband, Éric Jacquet, was already in the kitchen, making my breakfast. He seemed a not unfamiliar type: fifty, a military haircut, studiously unsmiling, wary. He wasn't unwelcoming—after all, he had been up before dawn to look after me—but he wasn't an obvious ambassador of the evidently overrated practice of French hospitality.

He put items out on the table, retreated to the other side of the room, and, leaning against a doorframe, told me what he had prepared: bread (which he had made), butter (which he had churned), jam (*"groseille et framboise sauvage"*—red currant and wild raspberry—"which I canned in August"), a pear drink ("I juiced it this morning"), and an egg.

I asked (I couldn't help myself), "Did you make the egg?"

He crossed his arms against his chest. "No," he said.

"No. Of course not." I began eating. He watched. (In the quiet breakfast room, just Monsieur Jacquet and me, the sounds of my mastication seemed to echo loudly in the cavern of my cranium.)

"Where are you from?" Jacquet asked.

I swallowed. "The United States."

"Yes, I know that. But your French—?"

"Oh. Lyon. We lived in Lyon for the last five years."

"I thought so. It's your accent."

"Thank you."

"I hate the Lyonnais."

Lyon is the administrative head of a region to whom the Savoyards pay taxes. The Savoyards are famously proud. "Why should I pay taxes to Lyon?" he asked. "What does Lyon know about Savoie?"

"I couldn't agree more," I said. I had, I admit, never once thought why the Savoyards should pay taxes to Lyon.

Savoy, an Alpine kingdom since the early eleventh century, was annexed to France in 1860—which, in relative historical terms, could seem like yesterday—and the good Savoyards are still very grumpy about the situation. You see signs demanding independence, and trees and stones are painted with the Savoyard flag, a white cross on a red background. I liked the sight of the flags, their ideological belligerence, and, it was true, Savoy didn't seem like France. It also didn't seem like Italy. It had a charismatic premodernity.

"My wife thinks I'm Savoyard," I said, upbeat, positive.

Jacquet said nothing.

"And, according to my grandfather, there is a one-in-five-billion chance that our family comes from Savoie."

Jacquet, arms still crossed, still leaning against the door, had, I now recognized, the polemic manner of someone on a mission. That is what I was recognizing. A quality of purposefulness, the uncompromising kind.

"Why are you here?" he asked.

I explained that I had long been intrigued by the lake and especially its fish, which no one outside this part of Europe ever has a chance to taste and which are among the fundamental elements in the Lyonnais menu.

He stared at me.

"And," I continued, "I'd really like to go out with a fisherman. I have a name."

"Who?"

Olivier Parpillon, a friend of a friend.

"I know Olivier. Everyone knows him. He won't take you."

"Oh."

"You are wasting your time."

"No chance?"

"None," he said.

I took a sip of the juice. I was surprised. It was the liquid expression of a perfect pear. I finished the glass.

"It is from our trees," Jacquet said.

"I thought so!"

I scooped up butter on the tip of my knife and tasted it. It was fatty and beautifully bovine. The bread was curious. It had been sliced from a rectangular loaf and, to my prejudiced eye, looked store-bought and industrial. I had a bite. It wasn't store-bought. Wow, I thought. This is good bread.

"Americans don't like sliced bread," Jacquet said. There had been complaints on Yelp. "They think I haven't actually made it if it's sliced. They think it's not fresh if it wasn't baked on the day. *Some* breads are good for a day. *Some* last longer. This bread is good for a week."

"Americans can be so ignorant," I said, while thinking: What? Week-old bread? I didn't come all this way to eat week-old bread.

I tasted some of the jam. Intense, fruity, not too sweet.

"I hate the Lyonnais," Jacquet said.

"I understand," I said.

"I hate Lyon."

"Perfectly reasonable," I said.

I finished my bread. "I was wondering if I might have another slice?"

After breakfast, and before I set out to waste more time, I phoned Olivier Parpillon. I had been calling him every day for a while. He hadn't picked up. I had left a message every time. He didn't pick up today, and I left another message. So I thought I would venture out and hope to find him and his boat.

Parpillon's operation was at the end of an affluent cul-de-sac, on the lake's west side. He wasn't there, which seemed completely appropriate, and I introduced myself to the members of his team. They were the fisherman equivalent of butchers, three men, two women, in white rain-gear overalls, talking among themselves in a local patois, less Italian or French than some mountain Savoyard-speak, cleaning the day's catch (scale, poke, slice, gut), a haul of *lavaret*, found here and nowhere else: fifteen inches long, with a white subtle flesh, cited in texts as early as the fifteenth century and with a delicacy favored by the voracious Rabelais.

"No *féra*?" I asked. I was making conversation. *Féra* was a fish that

I had become particularly fond of. It, too, you can't find in any other part of the world. I had eaten it at the hotel in Artemare, on my Brillat-Savarin walk.

Féra, they told me, is not found in this lake. It is in Lac Léman (Lake Geneva is called Lac Léman in France), and they didn't like it. "*Féra* eats other fish, grows fast, and is bigger than *lavaret,* with a different taste." *Goût.* "Stronger, meatier."

"*Lavaret* is here, and I prefer it," a member of the team said. "*Lavaret* don't eat other fish. They live on the health of the lake. The *goût* is very delicate."

I nodded, although I feel compelled to observe that these Lake People, with their patois and their highly local prejudices, were obviously culinary chauvinists whose palates had been ruined by an excessive diet of delicate (i.e., less flavorful) ecofish, and that, even though I wanted to be their friend and have them take me out onto the lake with them, their views about the flavor of *féra* were boneheaded and wrong, and, furthermore, even though it comes from a lake often seen as Swiss (i.e., Lac de Genève), and is therefore possibly outside the scope of this book, the fish has a *goût* or whatever you want to call it, a good-tasting-ness, that probably comes from all the other creatures it gobbles up, and is outstanding and unlike that of any other freshwater fish I can recall, and if you *ever* have a chance to eat it, do not hesitate: *Pounce.* But this was just my opinion.

I carried on watching.

They did a fish in ten seconds. They did it without thinking. They did it without looking at their hands. While I stood there, they did five hundred *lavarets.* The atmosphere seemed like the seaside—a lake as big as an ocean, the white rain gear, the volume of the haul—but the fish were not for long keeping. You smell their fragility. (Sea fish seem to keep, lake fish don't, because sea fish are preserved in their salinity; lake fish are best eaten at the lake.)

Parpillon appeared and got out of his vehicle, warily. What was I doing, fraternizing among his people?

I did my shtick, how the rest of the world will never be able to eat the fish that one finds here, and how I wanted to describe it, and that he was my last stop. I would be flying to New York in two days.

"What do you want?" he asked.

Parpillon was a robust thirty-something, with dark hair, seal-like fit, more swimmer than rugby player, a goatee, closely cropped hair, and had a no-nonsense manner.

"I want to go out with you in your boat," I said.

"I can't take you." He was matter-of-fact. "Look at the size of our haul. I need three others working with me. There isn't the room. We'll capsize."

I did as he instructed, and took in the size of his catch. "Of course," I said.

I asked if I could watch, and I was tolerated. At lunchtime, everyone went home to their families, and I got a crêpe in town. I returned in the afternoon, and continued watching.

Parpillon appeared later and seemed, I'm not sure why, a little friendlier.

"I've been thinking about your idea," he said. "Maybe we could do a smaller fish, like perch. Why don't you come back tomorrow evening? We'll go out together."

I woke early at La Source and went downstairs. Éric Jacquet was waiting for me, no one else in the breakfast room, no one else in the kitchen, no one else in the hotel, arms crossed, leaning against the doorframe, having put out his usual offering.

I thanked him and sat down, my place set so that I would, as before, sit directly in front of him.

"What now?" Jacquet asked.

"Today?"

He nodded his invisible (Did I actually see it?) nod.

I wanted to tell him about my visit with the fishermen, but I was hungry, and the display of local urgencies was particularly appealing, especially the jam, which today was quince and pear and apple, all the orchard flavors of the season in one jar. I spread it, with Jacquet's home-churned butter, on a piece of bread, took a bite, and then found myself studying the color of my slice: light but not white, but more white than brown, and it didn't seem like whole wheat or whole grain. Even so, it was perfectly satisfying, and lean on the palate, and was also fruity. I ate my egg but hadn't needed to. The bread was a meal in itself.

I thought: When was the last time that I described bread as a meal in itself? I have had this bread before.

"Where does your flour come from?" I asked Jacquet, who had assumed his position, arms folded, leaning against the doorframe. I half-expected him to say, "The Auvergne." I wanted him to say it, an eccentric confirmation: "Actually, my wheat comes from the Auvergne, just like your friend Bob's."

But Jacquet didn't understand the question. It is possible that I was the first American ever to ask it. It is possible that I was the first person ever to ask it. I repeated the question.

"Nearby."

"Where exactly?"

"Le Bourget-du-Lac."

I knew the town. It was on the other side of the lake, not far from the motorway to Geneva.

"The wheat is actually milled here?"

"Of course. Everything on your plate is from here."

He told me the name of the miller, Philippe Degrange. I wrote it down. It didn't seem right. "Grange" is the place where you store your grains. Degrange? Really?

"And the wheat?" I pressed. "What is it?"

"Sixty-five grams."

He was referring to the protein content. "No, I didn't mean the flour. Where does the wheat itself come from? Before it's milled?" *Le blé.*

He looked at me suspiciously. What was I asking? "It's local," he said.

"Really?"

I hadn't meant to sound skeptical. I was just trying to remember if I had ever seen a wheat field nearby.

"The wheat is grown *here.*" *Ici!* "The wheat is milled here. The flour is from here. It is local. Everything is local. Everything is from here." *Ici!* "It is Savoyard."

My breakfast done, I got up, and then remembered that, in the bread excitement, I had forgotten to share my news.

"Oh, and Parpillon agreed to take me out."

"I know," Jacquet said.

"You do?" I stared at Jacquet, and was sure that I saw the edge of his upper lip shudder slightly. It was almost the beginning of the intention to smile. "You called him, didn't you?"

The almost imperceptible nod.

"Thank you."

"I told him to take you out."

These Savoyards: They're a little tricky.

I had to pick something up at the pharmacy. I remembered one on the other side of the lake. I completed my errand and stopped at a café on the square.

Jacquet said that the miller was here, in Le Bourget-du-Lac. Were modern grain mills now so compact and computerized that they could coexist with affluent neighbors? Le Bourget-du-Lac has modern homes, pretty squares, mowed lawns, and a bike path. It is leafy.

I thought: Degrange? Really? It would be akin to a milkman's having the first name Dairy. If Degrange was here, I should be able to google him. And there he was. Minoterie Degrange. What was *minoterie*? I looked it up. A "flour mill." A flour mill right here on the very road where I was having my coffee? It appeared to be within walking distance.

I set off.

Recently milled flour was one of the reasons that Bob's bread was different. The *paysan* farmer's thinking (and almost all of Bob's thinking was a *paysan* farmer's) was to mill as needed. You could taste the freshness of the flour.

After half an hour of walking, my doubts returned. The addresses were erratic, and the street—flower beds, trimmed hedges, garages for parking the family car—was as suburban as ever. Was there really an operation here, milling only local grains? But then, just when I decided to turn back, *voilà*! In the dark shade of tall trees, half obscured by thick foliage, was a small letter-slot mailbox, no street number, but a name, Minoterie Degrange, and a limited company called Le Moulin du Prieuré. The Mill of the Priory. I paused, taking in the name.

The trees and a high metal gate, which was covered with graffiti, hid whatever was behind. Next to the mail slot was a speaker box. I pressed a button.

"*Oui?*" the speaker box said, a woman's voice.

"*Bonjour,*" I told the speaker box. "I have eaten a bread made from your flour, and I would like to meet the owner, Monsieur Degrange?"

Nothing.

"But it's lunchtime," the speaker box said finally.

"Of course. I'm sorry. I'll wait."

Another protracted silence. Then the gate opened and revealed an industrial yard, completely out of keeping with its neighbors. There were several cab-pulled diesel trucks, two with container tanks, and one with a high-sided trailer, which had been hydraulically raised to empty its contents onto a loading dock. The image was like finding an automobile factory in your closet. It was startling. There was an assortment of buildings, including the mill, which, even though three or four stories high, would have been out of view from the street because of the trees in front. A man emerged from behind a screen door, bald and round and robust, with a factory foreman's forthrightness, emanating a What-do-you-want? authority, wiping his mouth with a napkin. He looked at me hard. The look said, "You are interrupting the supreme moment of my day."

"Monsieur Degrange?" I confirmed. "Please excuse me. I ate a slice of bread that was made, I believe, with your flour, and it reminds me of the bread that my friend Bob used to make."

He pointed to a vehicle. "Get into the car."

I got in.

"It's all about the flour," he said. "I'll take you to Boulangerie Vincent. You've heard of it, yes?"

"No," I said.

"That's not possible. Have you been here before?"

"Yes."

"And you don't know about Boulangerie Vincent? People come from Paris just to eat at Boulangerie Vincent."

It was a few miles down the road I had been walking, just before the on-ramp to the motorway to Geneva. The boulangerie was more than a boulangerie. It was also a bar and a pub and a restaurant with tablecloths.

The door opened directly onto the *four,* the boulangerie's oven, and a cooling rack built against a wall. The top two rows were for *boules* ("balls," the ancient way of bread baking), 1.5 kilos, resting on their sides, about thirty of them. On the bottom were *couronnes,* 2.5 kilos, massive, each fashioned into a ring like a crown. A woman, carefully dressed, affluent in manner, was negotiating with the bread guy.

"*Mais, Pierre, s'il vous plaît.* Just one *boule,* please. I have guests tonight."

"I am very sorry, madame, but every loaf has a name attached to it. You know that. If you haven't reserved, I can't give you one."

"Please!" She made as if she was about to kneel on the floor.

Degrange whispered, "The bread is what people come for."

Pierre looked at his order book. "Someone canceled. I have one *couronne.*"

"But, Pierre, I can't serve a *couronne.* It's too big!" *Trop gros!* But she accepted the *couronne,* and left looking both frustrated and lucky. Pierre returned with his paddle to the oven, brightly radiating the red and black of embers burning. A price list was posted on a brick wall; everything was 3.20 euros a kilo. There was an apology written out at the bottom, that the boulanger never knows how big or heavy his bread will be, and that there will be variations in prices.

"He does two ferments," Degrange said, "and starts at seven in the evening. The bread needs ten hours. Or twelve. Sometimes fourteen."

Inside, the café bar was like an English pub, the "saloon," and mainly men—repairmen, electricians, cable people, metalworkers, painters, *mecs.* The room roared with conviviality. It also had the accidental arrogance of a place that knew that it was always busy, and you had to push forward to get yourself noticed—even Degrange, who was obviously well known. (Everyone, I got the sense, was a regular, and so no one, therefore, was special.) Degrange ordered us *diots* and a glass of wine, a local Mondeuse. A *diot* is a Savoyard sausage. Through the door to a small kitchen, I saw hundreds of *diots,* drying in the air, end to end, looped by a string. They are made with pork, fat, and salt, and are no different from sausages I once made at a butcher shop in Italy (except for the garlic—since at least Shakespeare's time, the French have been known as "garlic eaters," but no one eats garlic like Italians). The *diots* were cooked in a large, deep sauté pan with onions, red wine, and two bay leaves, and served folded into a bread roll made with Degrange's flour.

This was what I had tasted at breakfast. I asked for another roll and broke open the *croûte* and stuck my nose into *la mie,* the crumb, Frederick's routine. It smelled of yeast and oven-caramelized aromas, and something else, that fruitiness that I had once thought was unique to Bob's bread. Here it was. I had identified it this morning, without putting a name to it. I closed my eyes. Bob.

"You recognize it," Degrange said. "It comes from wheat that is a living plant and not an industrial starch."

"Where do you get it?"

"Small farms. Nothing more than forty hectares."

I must have made a face. Degrange took it for skepticism.

"Ridiculous, no? There are only a few of us." His son was in Israel, he said, and had just phoned, having tasted a bread like the kind he had grown up eating. "I told him to find out where the wheat came from. But he'd already asked. 'Very small farms,' he said."

Forty hectares. A hundred acres. I recalled my drive through the French breadbasket, the "Panier de France," where the "farms" were measured in thousand-hectare units.

"Where are the farms?"

"Here in Savoie. And the Rhône Valley. They grow an old wheat, a quality wheat. And the Auvergne. I love the wheat from the Auvergne. Everyone does. The volcanic soil, the iron-rich dirt. You can taste it in the bread."

We drank another glass of Mondeuse, and Degrange proposed that we go back. "I want to show you the factory."

On the way out, I stopped to order a *boule* for the morning, when I would be flying back via Geneva. I contemplated the prospect of arriving in New York bearing a *boule* for my children that had been made here, near Le Lac-du-Bourget, earlier that very day.

A Degrange has been milling flour here, or on a site closer to the river, since 1704, an operation that, until modern times, had once been powered by water and wind. For more than three centuries, it was the veritable mill of the priory. On a wall was a grainy black-and-white photo of Degrange's father and grandfather, seated before an enormous mill-paddle wheel, three times their height. There are no mill paddles today. The process now is inaccessible to the novice—whirringly hidden in pipes and generators and computer screens—except for the source material, freshly picked wheat that was being tipped out from the hydraulically raised trailer. I followed Degrange up steep ladderlike stairs to a third floor, where he opened the cap of a pipe and retrieved a cupful of a bright-golden grain.

"Taste."

It seemed to dissolve in my mouth, creamy and sweet and long in flavor. "What is it?"

"Wheat germ."

I wanted to take some home. "You'll have to refrigerate it. It is like flour but more extreme. It has fat, which spoils rapidly."

"You rarely get a good baguette in France," he said. We were in his office. He'd asked his assistant to get him an example. He wanted to show me the air pockets, small and uniform, that you get in a good crumb. "The best French baguettes are now made in Algiers or Morocco, using fresh flour from the wheat of small farms where it has been grown in the same way for millennia."

What do small farms have? I asked.

Here, in France, they are often the only farms with a soil that hasn't been ruined.

He described conventional flour production, like the massive farms in the French breadbasket or the American Midwest. Some use a plant called "dwarf wheat," short roots, voracious thirst, fast-growing, planted in soils that are so manipulated they could have been created in a chemistry lab. It is then milled in quantities so vast that the wheat—which is a plant, after all—goes to starch. It is not refrigerated. Its sell-by date is completely wrong. It has no food value.

"The bread that you make from it has the texture and the smell of bread. But it doesn't have the taste, the *goût*." He tore off another piece of the baguette and looked at it approvingly.

"In the country, we don't change as fast as people in the city," Degrange said. "For us, the meal is still very important. We don't 'snack,'" he said, using the English word. "What I learned from my father and grand-father is what they learned from their fathers and grandfathers before them. There is a handing off between generations." The word he used was *transmettre. Le goût et les valeurs sont transmis.* Flavor and value: Those are the qualities that are transmitted. Only in France would "fla-vor" and "value" have the same moral weight.

In a very simple respect, Degrange completed my French education. I had come here to learn many things—to cook, Frenchness, history, the role of the Italians—but I knew that my education began with taste. I had come here to discover what food should taste like. And I had. What I hadn't realized until now was that I had discovered it very early on, in Bob's bread.

Degrange gave me a ten-kilo bag of his flour. A gift. I would add it to my carry-on along with my 1.5-kilo *boule.* But what would I do once I used it up? Return here for more? Or give up bread?

I said goodbye, an affectionate embrace, feeling an unexpected close-ness to this man I had reached by pressing a button on an intercom only a few hours ago, who instantly knew what I was talking about and who recognized that very few people would, and who then succeeded in put-ting a word to something that I had been learning since I arrived. *Goût.*

At dawn, on my way to the airport, I stopped at the Boulangerie Vin-cent. There were no lights on inside, just the red glow from the oven. I picked up the *boule* I had reserved. It was hot to the touch and irresist-ibly fragrant.

In New York City, I cut a few thick slices and put out some butter.

"I think you will like this," I said.

Frederick picked up a slice and sniffed it and sniffed it again and then slammed it into his face, inhaling deeply. "It's like Bob's."

George ate a slice and asked for another, and added butter.

When the loaf was done, I made more from the ten-kilo bag. It was good—not as good as the *boule* from the Boulangerie Vincent—but still good. It had flavor and fruit and complexity and a feeling of nutri-tiousness. A month later, it was gone, and I stopped making bread.

"I'll pick some up the next time we're over."

There is a Curnonsky quote. *"La cuisine, c'est quand les choses ont le goût de ce qu'elles sont."* Cooking is when things taste like what they are. I wonder if a modern version might be: Cooking is when things have a flavor that few of us know anymore?

Among the many things we learned in France is a simple one, an appreciation of the taste of food that hasn't been ruined by industrial tricks, chemicals, manufactured aromas, pesticides, sugar, the conveyor belt of manipulated protein or starch or sweet goops that are hardened or toasted or coated and wrapped and distributed, the panoply of efficiencies that characterize the making of mass-marketed alimentary products just about everywhere, but nowhere more pervasively and menacingly than in the United States.

We learned the taste of good food. That comes from a place, as it has for thousands of years, from a soil that is a testament to its ancient history. Good food tastes of itself.

I had gone to France to learn basics. The basics of its kitchen. The basics of place, and what grows here and what doesn't grow there. I wanted to get as close to my sources as possible, where the words come from, how we arrive at flavor. I wanted to re-examine my assumptions about the kitchen, to restart my education, to get as elemental and as primary as possible. Heat. Water. Labor. Place. And its dirt.

Just About
Everybody Dies

Augusto, my Institut Bocuse Brazilian friend (the "assembler" of the witheringly reconstructed prosciutto-and-zucchini starter), now has a restaurant called, suitably enough, Augusto! It is in the heart of Lyon, occupying the premises of a former *mère bouchon* (the kitchen in the back, near the toilet, as per normal), where he makes Italian food. It was on the cover of a Lyonnais magazine. Every table was taken, with people waiting out front, when I discovered him in the back, sleep-deprived, buzzing with adrenaline, a single Institut Bocuse *stagiaire* as a deputy. "Augusto!" I declared. "This was your dream! How many people realize their dreams?" (Then, in 2019, he realized his dream two-fold and opened a second, Brazilian restaurant, Doppio Augusto.)

Mathieu Kergourlay ("Young Mathieu") now has a sprawling piece of paradise called, suitably enough, the Restaurant et Hôtel Mathieu Kergourlay—a château with rooms and a flashy haute-cuisine dining room, amid one thousand acres, most of it a protected forest, near the coast of Brittany. Once he completed his training in Lyon, he returned to his birthplace, got married, had children, earned a Michelin star, and was now an officially recognized kickass *grand chef* in the making—*and* had a trophy to prove it, awarded by Gault & Millau as a "Grand de Demain."

Hwei Gan Chern (aka Jackie Chan) moved to Burgundy and opened a restaurant. He called his, curiously, Le Parapluie (The Umbrella).

He didn't know what the word meant when he first heard it, but liked its sound ("I thought it was beautiful"), and promised himself that it would be the name of his first restaurant. In Burgundy, he had a following for his style. It was an inverted East-West approach: not Indonesian dishes with French techniques, but French dishes with Asian assumptions—less salt, less fat, more vegetables, and an absolute, no-compromise commitment to seasonality. Le Parapluie is witty and anarchically understated, like its owner.

Even unsmiling *Christophe Hubert* has a successful restaurant—or did, at least, for a while. He persuaded two people from La Mère Brazier to join him (the restaurant's best cook and best waiter), gave Viannay no notice ("I have never," Viannay said, "in all my years in the kitchen, been treated with such disrespect"), and, with 10,000 euros, opened a big-windowed establishment with an unencumbered view of a massive concrete parking garage. It was redeemed by the joyful, enthusiastic greeter, table seater, wine pourer, and omnipresent front-of-house person (Ewa, the dark-haired smiling woman I had once seen outside the Scottish pub in Christophe's company—i.e., now his wife). He called the restaurant L'Effervescence, a perfectly good name for anyone except the chef running it. The food was superb—easily on the level of La Mère Brazier—but the restaurant wasn't getting diners, and, after a hard year, was about to close (his staff agreed to miss a paycheck; Christophe prepared for bankruptcy), when Gault & Millau awarded it eighteen out of a possible twenty points, honored him with a "Jeune Talent" trophy (Young Talent), and welcomed him into the pantheon of Lyonnais greats. The Michelin Guide followed and gave Christophe a star. I was rapturous in my pride. "Christophe! You did it, and you are now very, very busy!" I cried out when I visited him during his prep, and then photographed and videoed him, and, making fun of his earnestness, almost provoked a smile, until, finally, he cried out, "Billou, stop. I don't do photos."

The couple had a child, a joyful expression of their success, and Ewa remained at the front of the house. She had a second child, also joyful but more challenging, and, although Ewa tried to carry on, it was too much, two infants at once, and she left. And in her absence . . .

I ate there on my own one evening. The food was as good as ever. The atmosphere? Maybe not so effervescent. The waiters were men, and dour, like walking echo chambers of their boss, like-minded missionaries of solemnity. Their manner had a message: "Here, your plate, it's art." There was no one to distract me from the massive concrete parking lot. And, like that, the restaurant was over. Gone. And Christophe?

"He has disappeared," Viannay told me when I asked about his former executive chef, and then smiled.

The others? I couldn't keep up with all of them. *Frédéric* did a stint in Japan, and was now the chef of a bistro on the Place Carnot in Lyon.

I asked Chern. Was *Florian* still in a kitchen? Or *Michael,* the *garde-manger* cook who disappeared after crashing a car with his girlfriend? Or *Ansel the asshole*?

"I have no idea," Chern said, "but you're right about Ansel. He is an asshole."

Sylvain Jacquenod, such a compelling study in focus and discipline and frustration, had landed in a happy place. He had been invited to quit Bocuse's Brasserie du Nord and be the chef of L'Argot, a new enterprise in Lyon—part eatery, part butcher shop. On an outstandingly busy Saturday night, we ate steaks that Sylvain selected and cooked for us. He was a chef at last, and every time someone addressed him as such ("Chef! Chef!"), his chest seemed to swell perceptibly with pride. His picture was published in *Le Progrès,* and his achievements were written up in local food guides. His gigantic smile was once again wholly and radiantly intact. (Viannay, characteristically Viannay, offered his characteristic summary: "Sylvain has found his level. He is at last content.")

Hortense? She completed her education at L'Institut Bocuse, graduated, and left cooking. She is now a fashion executive, married, and lives in Paris. Should she have been a cook? Was she, like Chern, developing her own style? She was intelligent, brave, shy, and ambitious, and her cooking spirit had been crushed. She had been the only woman in an enterprise made famous by one of the most flamboyant women chefs in the history of France. She had been there just as the French kitchen was only beginning to change.

Lyon was also changing.

Our local bistro, Potager, was bought by a couple of restaurateurs from Panama for 1 million euros. Owners *Franck and Mai Delhoum* then opened two new restaurants around the city. In Lyon, their success was celebrated with uninhibited joy.

Our friend *Yves Rivoiron* (the partner of Isabelle of Bouchon des Filles) sold his historic restaurant, Café des Fédérations. He bought a boat and was last sighted at a harbor somewhere on the Mediterranean. His son, whom we had only recently met at one of our annual fêtes, was now the chef of a popular anti-establishment restaurant in the anti-establishment city of Barcelona.

Jean-Paul Lacombe sold Léon de Lyon—in his family since before he was born—to a television comedian, the sum not disclosed, but said to be a lot of money. Lacombe and his wife appear to be committed to traveling around the world many times.

One of our first Lyonnais friends, the American musician *Jenny Gilbert,* sold her noodle restaurant.

Lyon had always been a city where anyone could open an eatery. You needed a space, gas, and (usually) electricity. Rent was almost a negligible item on the bottom line, and small, idiosyncratically creative places proliferated. It hadn't been a city where restaurants were bought and sold for speculation or profit. We couldn't deny it: The word had got out. Lyon had felt like our secret—a historic gastronomic epicenter that, since World War II, seemed to have been neglected by the commercial rest-of-the-world, but it was no longer so private or so secret.

In New York City, *Michel Richard* became a neighbor! After more than fifteen years in Washington, he was now, suddenly, at the age of sixty-five, in Manhattan! He accepted a grand, high-paying position as the chef overseeing the restaurant, bistro, and pâtisserie at the Palace Hotel, perhaps the grandest address in New York.

Manhattan was where his American life had begun, in 1974, as the head of Gaston Lenôtre's first foreign venture, the Château France, on Fifty-Ninth Street. When, one year later, Lenôtre was forced to close, Richard accepted the first job that he was offered (in faraway Santa Fe) and left New York with a vow that he would one day return. But he didn't. And now: *Voilà!* He was back. It was a tremendous moment in Richard's career.

I was thrilled to witness it. Richard had given me my beginning. And now: maybe my ending?

I joined him, his assistant Mel, and his wife, Laurence, on day one. Laurence's enthusiasm was innocent and guileless. "Today," she said, "I'm going shopping downtown. By subway!"

Mel would be interviewing PR firms "in my suite!"

The kitchens would close for renovations—"according to my specifications," Richard said; he paused, seeming to think about what those renovations might entail, and laughed. His affect was delicious.

I then followed Richard into the *"labo," le laboratoire,* the temperature-controlled pâtisserie-confection space, where, for two weeks, I watched his teaching his new American pastry chef all the basics—puff pastry, éclairs, *pain au chocolat, pâte sable,* croissants—each one tweaked, if not outright improvised on.

Midway through the first day, I stepped back, enjoying the historical perspective—that every one of the recipes Richard was teaching had been unchanged for at least two hundred years until now improved by Richard—and declared, "Michel, these are brilliant innovations." A thought occurred to me that now seems blaringly obvious. "You can't make a food unless you change it, can you?"

"No."

"As in 'not at all,'" I continued. "If you can't improve a recipe, you don't touch it. It is boring. It is not your mission. . . ."

"I have to feel that I'm making it better."

"Even a basic butter pastry. A fundamental unit of the French kitchen. Unless you can make it better . . ."

"I can't make it."

I had never understood him so well. By going to Lyon and being trained there, by learning how *it* was done, whatever *it* happened to be, I was now able to recognize that Richard didn't do *it.* He did *his.*

We stepped out of the serene *labo* and got an ominous welcome to the rest of the kitchen. Loud music, different jumbly tunes at the same time; someone singing; someone whistling. A guy was pushing a trolley fast, and hadn't seen Richard, or did and expected him to step aside, or didn't care—he was just another chef (there had been many, many chefs)—and hit him from behind and swore at him afterward.

"Hey, *puto,* get the fuck out of the way."

The restaurant was in a hotel, with a hotel union that had outlasted everyone who had worked there. The chef wasn't in charge. Everyone knew he would end up being a visitor. And most important, he was not allowed to touch the food.

Chef Alain Ducasse told me that he had tried to dissuade Richard: "'Michel,' I said, 'you cannot take this job. You will have no control. You won't be able to taste the food. Do not open in a New York hotel. You will live to regret it. Turn it down.'"

"'But I can't,'" Ducasse said Richard replied. "'I need the money.'"

I attended a dress-rehearsal dinner, "friends and family," a week before the restaurant opened, in the most ornate room in Manhattan. I knew the dishes. I had made them—some, like the breadcrumbed fried chicken, I'd done at home. There were six courses. They were good. But—and there was no escaping the realization—they were merely "good." Michel Richard's dishes don't work if they are good. They need to be perfect. They aspire to nothing less than spectacular.

The New York Times rates restaurants with one to four stars. Richard got zero. The food, wrote the critic Pete Wells, was awful. "Was Mr. Richard not the chef I had thought? Were the ecstatic reviews, the five awards from the James Beard Foundation, the induction into the Maîtres Cuisiniers de France, all a mass delusion?" Wells ventured down to Washington to try the dishes at Central, Richard's French-American bistro, where David was now in charge. There they were "terrific." Was this "a symptom of the deal-making culture that afflicts the restaurant business"?

Four months later, the restaurant closed. Richard returned to Washington.

He was changed. The force that drove the man was gone. There were health issues; he had never taken care of himself. A doctor diagnosed diabetes (evident to everyone), obesity (ditto), heart disease (his two strokes), and dementia, which wasn't evident, and those who know Richard believe that the idiosyncratic, unpredictable, highly distracted way that his brain routinely worked was mistaken for a disability. At a doctor's suggestion, Laurence put Richard in an assisted-living facility. Then she filed for divorce. They argued over the value of the estate, most of it having been spent. They were still arguing when he was felled three years later by a stroke, his third, on a Saturday morning in August. He was sixty-eight.

He is remembered for making Washington a "capital of dining," for teaching Americans how to play with their food, for being among the rare great chefs (like Carême, Point, Lenôtre, and Michel Guérard) who brought the high technical skills of pastry to the whole kitchen. What do his friends miss? Richard's inventiveness, his uncanny confidence that he could make every dish better (and did), his Frenchness (because, finally, just about everything was provoked by something in the classic repertoire), and mainly his joy in the kitchen. And his company at the table: In my life, there has been no one more fun to have a meal with.

Four weeks later, *Dorothy Hamilton* died.

The head of the French Culinary Institute (now renamed the International Culinary Center), once my modest antagonist, had become a robust good friend. I was now a Hamilton devotee. She doted on George and Frederick, who called her Aunt Dorothy. She regaled us with stories of Julia Child and made us feel connected to her with a vividness that surprised and moved me. Hamilton had a sage's confidence about the influence Jessica would wield over a new generation of women wine drinkers. She and Jessica set up a dinner to plan a joint venture of some kind and scheduled it for the week after she returned from Nova Scotia. She had grown up in a fishing village, Fourchu, and was now campaigning to promote a local celebrity crustacean, the Fourchu lobster. It was a characteristic Dorothy endeavor: a financially selfless act to benefit a small community (the fishermen had no idea of their worth) that was ultimately about the natural purity of a simple North Atlantic Ocean flavor. En route to a meeting with the Fourchu City Council, she collided with a pickup truck and trailer. The driver had been speeding with such abandon, passing on curves, that witnesses later stepped forward to testify to his recklessness. Hamilton had been coming around one of those curves when she was hit head-on. These things happen, we die, but the circumstances—the selfishness of the driver, the selflessness of the victim (with so many good acts in her future), the fact that the driver and his bud were pulled from their burning cab and lived while Hamilton, trapped in her vehicle, was dead—were brutal in their capricious indifference.

After the memorial service, one of monumental sadness, a New

Orleans Dixie funeral band, with loud percussion and unrestrained Dixieland brass, marched mourners down cobbled Crosby Street to the International Culinary Center. There followed a feast held on every floor of Hamilton's five-floor school, each one given over to the cooking of a different region of France. Dorothy's memorial and Michel's were a week apart.

We were in Lyon in the summer of 2017, the boys eleven, and there were two restaurants I wanted them to try. One was La Mère Brazier, where they had the lunch that Viannay had told me, on our first meeting, they deserved to eat.

It featured, finally, both Viannay's quenelle (the airy lake-fish soufflé looked like a slice of exotic French toast, with a brownly caramelized crust) and his *poulet en vessie,* cooked in its rustic sack, as per tradition, but coated with a green version of a *sauce suprême,* which was not the tradition. The sauce was intensely vivid to look at and to inhale and seemed like a tribute to a lush summer garden. It was served with bright, perfectly popped-out-of-their-skins peas. I enjoyed the peas especially. I ate them slowly, one by one, my pleasure enhanced by knowing just how long someone in the back had spent squeezing out each one just for *me.*

"She is here, you know. Mère Brazier. We all feel her presence in the kitchen, her spirit, whatever it is. She will always be here. She was here before me. She'll be here after."

"Of course," I said.

A waiter gave us menus. They used to be silver and gray, and conveyed urban (and a rather masculine) sophistication. Now they were firecracker red. They were brash. A history of the restaurant was told on the back (also red—or rather *RED!!!!*) and included a short essay by the granddaughter Jacotte and a photograph of Viannay kissing an almost life-sized Brazier doll on the cheek. Her image—in photos and cartoons—seemed to be everywhere. The feeling was loud, maybe a little crude, and verging on caricature. It was as if Viannay had connected to a spirit that, yes, we had in fact all felt in the building, and the building had rewarded him with resounding success.

And the food: It was no longer his. It was his take on hers.

Viannay was joyful, self-deprecating, forthcoming, and easy to be with. In the evening, he was flying to Dubai to sign a contract to open a restaurant there, and he had, on top of everything else, the manner of a man who was about to take a luxurious vacation *and* be paid loads of money. Even the boys' drumming on their Limoges plates with their spoons didn't disturb him or, to be strictly accurate, only *eventually* disturbed him when, suddenly, he stopped talking and looked pointedly at them.

"*C'est bien, garçons?*" he asked. (George, in a moment of spontaneous cheekiness, replied: "*Très bien, et vous?*")

"I will be taking them later in the month to eat their first meal at Paul Bocuse," I said, and Viannay nodded. "I've always wondered—how did you meet him?"

"Here. Once I got to Lyon, I drove out to L'Auberge and asked if Bocuse would see me."

"When you were making sandwiches?"

"Yes, when I was making sandwiches. I explained to him that I regarded Lyon as my culinary and spiritual home." Viannay's uncle, his father's brother, was from here, and had a house in the watery Dombes, and Mathieu had spent summers there with his cousins.

Bocuse liked Viannay. "You will always be welcome at L'Auberge," he said. "You will always be able to reach me on my cell."

When Viannay opened his first restaurant, Les Oliviers, he had a well-known diner on his first day—Paul Bocuse. When he opened M, Bocuse was again in the dining room. As Viannay was preparing to open La Mère Brazier, Bocuse asked if he could eat lunch there before everyone else. For Bocuse, La Mère Brazier was at the heart of what Lyon represented.

He ate there with Jacotte Brazier, the granddaughter.

"There were workmen downstairs," Viannay said. "On his way out, Bocuse had to step over wood planks, but he was already on his cell phone. He was calling François Simon."

Simon, who then wrote for *Le Figaro,* was France's most feared and influential restaurant critic. Simon phoned Viannay the next day, the day before the restaurant's opening. He would be there at 6:00 p.m., he said and needed to be on a train to Paris by 8:00 p.m. He wrote the review in transit. It was the headline in the weekend edition: LA MÈRE

BRAZIER IS BACK! (in English for no reason except for its headline punch). It was exhilarating. It was somehow a bugle call to Frenchness. *Le Monde* followed, and *L'Express, Libération,* the local news, the national evening news, the national afternoon news, and the French news in English. La Mère Brazier was not just back. It was relaunched.

"This was all Paul Bocuse," I said.

"It was all Paul Bocuse."

We had made a 7:00 p.m. reservation at L'Auberge on the last day of our Lyon visit. The boys were electric in their anticipation. It was akin to going to the North Pole.

Bocuse had been appearing rarely. The preceding winter, he had missed the Bocuse d'Or, even when it seemed possible that an American team might win the trophy, his dream, because he was in the hospital with a lung infection. (In the event, the Americans *did* win the trophy, an incomprehensible feat, and all summer long our Lyonnais friends grumbled: "It was rigged. They did it for Monsieur Paul.")

Afterward, Bocuse resumed his appearances, but not reliably.

I called Boulud in New York. "The boys haven't met Bocuse. Could you help?"

"I will phone him," he said. In fact, he ended up phoning a lot of people before he called me back. "Paul is tired. But he will try to come down. I changed your reservation to six p.m. Be early."

I reflected on my hitherto unexamined reasons for wanting to see Bocuse. I wasn't a complete stranger to him. He recognized me at events and made small gestures to indicate acknowledgment. But I was scarcely a longtime friend. I wasn't even a short-time friend. The truth, which I was not entirely comfortable admitting, was that I wanted to see him before he was no longer there to be seen. I wasn't the only one. The restaurant's manager and headwaiters were busy, with people coming to pay respects before respects were actually called for. What did we want? To touch the hand of the handoff guy? To feel we were among the chosen to carry on the mission?

I arrived with my family and was positioned at a table facing the corner he would come from. We ordered. The boys, now fully trained in matters French culinary, were at ease, and hungry. Once again, I fell into utter admiration of what made the food here unusual: its meticulousness. You could eat just about every dish on his menu somewhere in Lyon, or nearby, or in the Rhône Valley. But no one made the dishes with the same precision. Of all the many qualities that Bocuse is meant to have embodied, the one rarely mentioned was the most obvious: He made perfect Lyonnais food. I kept looking up from my plate. He wasn't coming. I imagined him upstairs, in his bedroom, sleeping.

It was a mournful autumn, when Lyon is lonely like no place I've ever known, and damp, and decaying, and winter comes in intermittent warnings, those cold blasts. The city seemed to be waiting for a father who was ill, and uncomfortable, and wouldn't die, and you didn't want him to die, and you didn't ever want to imagine a life without him, but he would die, and so, despite yourself, you imagined it, briefly, reluctantly, and then he was dead. Paul Bocuse died on January 20, 2018.

In an instant, you find yourself thinking not of the end of the life but of the whole life, the kid in the picture at his vast father's feet, the mustache he sported in his thirties, the Michelin tires always on his vehicle, the success during France's wild "golden era"—the late 1960s and '70s (Brigitte Bardot and Club Med and Serge Gainsbourg and filterless Gauloises and *la libération*). There was a photo that I kept looking at, over and over again, of the young Bocuse giving chase to a young woman shaded by a parasol on a hot day—Raymonde, who would become his wife. Another showed him giving Mère Brazier a tour of the cellars at L'Auberge (and the look on her face of utter horror at the grime and filth of the place). Other photographs, a bunch of them, never published, and only just discovered by Mathieu Viannay in a drawer of the home that, in his new prosperity, he had bought in Beaujolais. They depicted a party that the house's previous owner, a female vigneron, had hosted for Bocuse at her château—plus Georges Blanc, Michel Guérard, the Troisgros brothers, others, everyone in various states of undress. I flicked through them quickly, everyone kissing, being kissed, the food and drink, the idea probably at the core of Bocuse's life that raucous good things happen at the table.

Daniel Boulud was among the friends who gathered at L'Auberge the night before the funeral—no speeches, a solemn repast, Bocuse still upstairs in his bedroom, dressed in his whites, in a coffin. In the morning, in a cold, beating wintry rain, a cortège of three hundred police led the hearse along the now gray Saône, down to the Cathédrale Saint-Jean-Baptiste, where Henri II and Catherine de' Medici had been received, and where Henri IV and Marie de' Medici were married, and where the hypocrite scumbag Charles-Maurice de Talleyrand was ordained bishop, and where Napoleon and Josephine were honored, and where a child Mozart performed, and where Paul Bocuse would make his final appearance, fifteen hundred inside and a modest crowd outside, under umbrellas.

The funeral was military in manner, as though a great general had passed, with a strict hierarchy: the central pews occupied by French-collared MOFs, the undecorated chefs whitely in the wings, the Bocuse family in the front, the civilians in the back, but there weren't many. The kitchen was saying goodbye to their chef. The best speech, the most felt, might have been that of Gérard Collomb, the city's mayor, with a righteous politician's gift for rhetoric, honoring the passing of the man who understood the city and how both it and the man himself had been shaped by its history, by the generations before him, just as he had shaped everyone who was there to honor his death. Paul Bocuse was Lyonnais. (Two years later, on January 18, 2020, the Michelin Guide removed one of Bocuse's stars and, for the first time since 1965, his restaurant, the Auberge, had only two. Although it is the Michelin practice when a chef dies to remove a star, it was still a shock.)

More fitting, and true to the spirit of the city, was the achievement of Andrea Petrini, an Italian transplanted to Lyon (like so many Italians before him), and now a local culinary entrepreneur and the mad captain behind the World's 50 Best Restaurants, who put together a food festival in the city two months after Bocuse's death. There were kitchen "performances" in twelve new restaurants, a "Night Canteen" featuring a new dish every hour from 10:00 p.m. to 4:00 a.m., a goat fête, displays by visiting chefs (high achievers all), and, appositely enough, a Bocuse tribute involving a dozen masters, Têtedoie among them, reinterpreting Monsieur Paul's greatest hits. The fête was a week in duration with just about every kitchen called into service. It was an answer to Bocuse's death. The city's restaurants had never been more vibrantly gastronomic. Lyon creates chefs. And, yes, the achievement arises from where Lyon happens to find itself, among vineyards and rivers and mountain lakes, among birds and pigs and fish, but mainly because of the belief, shared by everyone here, that what happens at the table is among the most important activities in civilization. It is about intimacy, *convivium,* creativity, appetites, desire, euphoria, culture, and the joys of being alive.

The Pope of Lyon has died. But what a culture he has left behind. What a privilege it has been to be a member of it.

ACKNOWLEDGMENTS

The quote at the beginning of "No Food Road More Important" is from *Mémoires de chefs* (2012), compiled and edited by Nicolas Chatenier. The early history of cheese ("Small Brown Cows on High Green Hills") draws from conversations with Michel Bouvier, historian of the wine and foods of antiquity, and from his *Le fromage, c'est toute une histoire* (2008).

The text for La Varenne's *Le Cuisinier françois* is the 1651 edition, introduced by Mary and Philip Hyman (2001). The text of Nostradamus's 1555 treatise on jam-making, *Traité des confitures,* is edited by Jean-François Kosta-Théfane (2010). The facsimile edition of *Ouverture de Cuisine* (1585) by Lancelot de Casteau is edited by Léo Moulin (1983). The text of the 1555 *Livre fort excellent de Cuysine,* published in Lyon, is a bilingual edition translated and edited by Timothy J. Tomasik and Ken Albala (2014). Most of the other primary sources are online at Gallica, the digital holdings of *la Bibliothèque nationale de France.*

Among secondary sources, the following are noteworthy: Ali-Bab, *Gastronomique pratique* (1928); Dan Barber, *The Third Plate* (2015); Joseph Favre, *Dictionnaire universel de cuisine pratique* (1905); Henry Heller, *Anti-Italianism in Sixteenth-Century France* (2003); R. J. Knecht, *Renaissance Warrior and Patron, The Reign of Francis I* (1994); Giles MacDonogh, *Brillat-Savarin, the Judge and his Stomach* (1993); Marjorie Meiss, "L'Italie à la table des Guise (1526-81)," *in Table de la Renaissance—Le mythe Italien,* edited by Florent Quellier and Pascal

Brioist (2018); Marie-Josèph Moncourgé, *Lyon 1555, capital de la culture gourmande au XVIe siècle* (2008); Prosper Montagné, *Larousse Gastronomique* (1938); William W. Weaver, *Beautiful Swimmers—Watermen, Crabs, and the Chesapeake Bay* (1994); Edward White, "Cooking for the Pope," in the *Paris Review* (March 3, 2017); and Ann Willan, *The Cookbook Library* (2012).

I am privileged to have been able to consult Dan Barber, Alain Ducasse, Allen Grieco of la Villa i Tatti in Florence (the Harvard Center for Renaissance Studies), Thomas Hauck; Jean-Pierre Jacob (chef of the now-closed *Le Bateaux Ivre* on Lac du Bourget), Steven Laurence Kaplan, Harold McGee, Magnus Nilsson, Alain Vigneron, and Jean-Georges Vongerichten. I am especially privileged to have had Michel Richard, Daniel Boulud, and Mathieu Viannay as my teachers in the kitchen.

In fundamental ways, this adventure would have been impossible without the help of our Lyonnais friends, and expressions of gratitude are in order to the following: our downstairs neighbors *la famille* Azouley; Julien ("Papi") and Marie ("Mami") Boulud; Roberto Buonomo; Martine and Marc Broyer at Lavis Trafford; the principal of l'Ecole Robert Doisneau (whom I still know only as "Brigitte") plus students Ambre, Marcel, Ben Omar, Salomé, Tristan, and Victor; Isabel Comerro and Yves Rivoiron (Le Bouchon des Filles); Franck and Mai Delhoum (Le Potager); writer and cook Sonia Ezgulian; Georgette Farkas; Jenny Gilbert; Jean-Charles Margotten; l'Institut Paul Bocuse, including alumni Edouard Bernier, Hwei Gan Chern, and Willy Johnson; Jonathan Nossiter; Martin Porter; Christophe and Marie-Laure Reymond; Emmanuelle Sysoyev of Only Lyon; Laura Vidi and Gerald Berthet; and Victor and Sylvie Vitelli.

Early readers of the manuscript include Leslie Levine and Lexy Bloom (who read every draft and is my unofficial and heroic coeditor) at Alfred A. Knopf; John Bennet, David Remnick, and Nick Trautwein of *The New Yorker;* my literary agent, Andrew Wylie; and my gifted in-house line editor, Jessica Green. The fact-checkers were Gillian Brassil, Clio Doyle, and Michael Lo Piano. Lydia Buechler was the copy chief.

Fat Man in a White Hat, a two-part documentary made for the

BBC, based on my arrival in Lyon, was commissioned by Emma Willis, produced by Roy Ackerman and directed by James Runcie. Annie Arnold was the assistant producer and Christophe Foulon the sound recordist.

The book was commissioned and overseen by Sonny Mehta—a privilege to have one of the world's greatest publishers, and a friend for nearly four decades, as my editor. He was available to me just about always and often with no notice—for impromptu meetings, a phone call, lunch, a drink, or just to hang out in his office—and he directed me in ways that were subtle and profound. He lived to see the book completed, and I am grateful that he did, but died on December 30, 2019, before it appeared in print. I am among many, many people who mourn and miss him dearly.

A NOTE ABOUT THE AUTHOR

Bill Buford is the author of *Heat* and *Among the Thugs*. He has received a Marshall Scholarship, a James Beard Award, and the Comune di Roma's Premio Sandro Onofri for narrative reportage. For eighteen years, Buford lived in England, where he was the founding editor of the literary magazine *Granta* and the founding publisher of Granta Books. He moved to the United States in 1995 to join *The New Yorker,* where he has been the fiction editor, a staff writer, and a regular contributor. In 2008, he moved with his family to Lyon, France, and lived there for five years. He was born in Baton Rouge, Louisiana, educated at UC Berkeley and Kings College, Cambridge, and now lives in New York City with his wife, the wine educator and writer Jessica Green, and their twin sons.

A NOTE ON THE TYPE

This book was set in Adobe Garamond. Designed for the Adobe Corporation by Robert Slimbach, the fonts are based on types first cut by Claude Garamond (ca. 1480–1561). Garamond was a pupil of Geoffroy Tory and is believed to have followed the Venetian models, although he introduced a number of important differences, and it is to him that we owe the letter we now know as "old style." He gave to his letters a certain elegance and feeling of movement that won their creator an immediate reputation and the patronage of Francis I of France.

Typeset by Scribe,
Philadelphia, Pennsylvania

Printed and bound by Berryville Graphics,
Berryville, Virginia

Designed by Pei Loi Koay

DATE DUE JUL 2 3 2020

PRINTED IN U.S.A.